Bach and Mozart

Bach and Mozart

Essays on the Engima of Genius

Robert L. Marshall

R UNIVERSITY OF ROCHESTER PRESS

First published 2019

University of Rochester Press
668 Mt. Hope Avenue, Rochester, NY 14620, USA
www.urpress.com
and Boydell & Brewer Limited
PO Box 9, Woodbridge, Suffolk IP12 3DF, UK
www.boydellandbrewer.com

ISBN-13: 978-1-58046-962-3
ISSN: 1071-9989

Library of Congress Cataloging-in-Publication Data

Names: Marshall, Robert Lewis, author.
Title: Bach and Mozart : essays on the enigma of genius / Robert L. Marshall.
Other titles: Eastman studies in music ; v. 161.
Description: Rochester : University of Rochester Press, 2019. | Series: Eastman studies in music, 1071-9989 ; vol. 161 | Includes bibliographical references and index. |
Identifiers: LCCN 2019026475 | ISBN 9781580469623 (hardcover) | ISBN 9781571138231 (pdf)
Subjects: LCSH: Bach, Johann Sebastian, 1685–1750—Criticism and interpretation. | Mozart, Wolfgang Amadeus, 1756–1791—Criticism and interpretation. | Music—18th century—History and criticism.
Classification: LCC ML410.B13 M2718 2019 | DDC 780.92/2—dc23 LC record available at https://lccn.loc.gov/2019026475

Portions of this book were previously published and are reprinted here with permission:

Prologue: "The Eighteenth Century as a Music-Historical Epoch: A Different Argument for the Proposition," *College Music Symposium* 27 (1987): 198–205.
Chapter 1: "Toward a Twenty-First-Century Bach Biography," *Musical Quarterly*, 84 (2000): 497–525.

Copyright page continued on page 331.

For Traute
Wie immer
Für immer

My final goal: to produce a regular church music to the Glory of God.

—J. S. Bach, 1708

To express my thoughts and feelings . . . by means of tones: I am a musician.

—W. A. Mozart, 1777

For the use and profit of the musical youth desiring to learn.

—J. S. Bach, *The Well-Tempered Clavier*, 1722

Music . . . must please the listener, or in other words must never cease to be music.

—W. A. Mozart, 1781

For music lovers, to refresh their spirits.

—J. S. Bach, *Klavierübung*, 1726–1741

Contents

Figures

Preface

The original versions of the essays brought together in this volume were written over a period of some thirty years. They draw on a diverse arsenal of interpretive approaches ranging from text criticism to style criticism, from Freudian analysis to Schenkerian analysis, from Harold Bloom, Theodor Adorno, and Edward Said to Maynard Solomon, Charles Rosen, and Peter Shaffer. All these approaches, or strategies, are deployed in the service of a single objective: the desire to gain a deeper understanding of two of the greatest composers in history—a deeper understanding of them not only as supremely gifted creators but also as fellow human beings.

Since there was no hard separation between life and work in the lives of these towering figures, there is none in these essays. Those primarily concerned with biographical matters usually address musical matters as well. In others the primary emphasis is on the music, while biography plays a supporting role.

Before introducing the protagonists directly the volume begins with a Prologue. The essay, admittedly, is an academic exercise of sorts. It questions the long-held, traditional, view that the music of the eighteenth century naturally falls into two contrasting halves—a "late Baroque" followed by a "Classical" period—and suggests rather that the hundred-year span from 1700 to 1800 (i.e., the eighteenth century in its most literal sense) can be plausibly and more helpfully understood as forming a single stylistic whole: one unified, bounded, "music-historical epoch." The proposition is not altogether original: it has been argued elsewhere on different grounds. But it remains unorthodox—and controversial.

After that preliminary "throat-clearing" historiographical contemplation of the "Century of Bach and Mozart," fifteen numbered chapters devoted to the two masters follow in roughly chronological succession. Chapter 1, originally written on the occasion of the 250th anniversary of Bach's death, begins with a summary review of Bach research in the second half of the twentieth century before turning to the topic of Bach biography. It calls for a less hagiographical, more "humanizing" approach to its subject both in the portrayal of his character and in the critical assessment of some of his early works. To illustrate how this desideratum could be satisfied, it drafts a provisional biographical account of "Young Man Bach."

Three biographical chapters follow. They address, in turn, rather narrowly defined questions raised by the life and career of J. S. Bach. It asks, specifically: (a) what do the "little keyboard books" (*Klavierbüchlein*) that the composer prepared for his wife and his oldest son reveal about his domestic life and his own conception of the family constellation (chapter 2); (b) what more, if anything, is still to be learned about the significance of Martin Luther in the career and self-understanding of J. S. Bach (chapter 3); (c) what, in the final analysis, does the St. John Passion tell us about Bach's personal attitude toward Jews (chapter 4).

Bach's music is the main focus of the next five chapters. Chapter 5, the longest of the volume, offers an extensive discussion of the keyboard compositions. After considering the question of the instrument(s) Bach had in mind with the designation "clavier," the remainder of the chapter proposes a new periodization of Bach's artistic development: one not determined (as in the traditional approach) by his places of employment—Arnstadt (1703–7), Mühlhausen (1707–8), Weimar (1708–17), Köthen (1717–23), Leipzig (1723–50)—but rather by the stages in his stylistic evolution and his changing compositional concerns. These are designated in turn: "First Decade, ca. 1703–1713: Apprenticeship and Early Mastery," "First Synthesis: 1713–1723," "Second Synthesis: Leipzig, 1726–1741," and "The Final Decade."

Chapter 6 belongs to the musicological discipline of "performance practice," a perennial playground of Bach research, one subcategory of which (namely, the choice and identification of instruments) was already broached in the discussion of the keyboard music in the preceding chapter. Indeed, the gigantic topic encompasses an enormous number of subcategories. The inquiry in chapter 6 is limited to the still highly contentious matter of the size of Bach's chorus. It suggests that the proper, and intended, size of Bach's chorus was not fixed—as advocated in their opposing ways by what I designate as both the "traditionalist" and "minimalist" camps. On the contrary: it was a function of both chronology and genre. Bach's choral resources in Mühlhausen and Weimar were normally smaller than those at his disposal in Leipzig; fully scored compositions with trumpets and drums and elaborate writing for a four-part vocal ensemble demanded a larger chorus than did a solo cantata or music for a private funeral service.

The following three chapters trace Bach's artistic and stylistic development as it unfolded in the vocal works of his Leipzig years. "Truth and Beauty" (chapter 7) describes how Bach's liturgical compositions give voice to theological Truths or demonstrate "truths" about the nature of music itself, while his secular works, in contrast, frequently give expression to more "personal" sentiments and apparently embrace the increasingly ascendant aesthetic of Beauty for its own sake. (The chapter in effect concludes a "trilogy" of studies on related themes, the first two of which were published in my previous essay collection, *The Music of Johann Sebastian Bach: The Sources, the Style, the Significance*—"Bach the Progressive" and "On Bach's Universality.") Chapter 8 documents the culmination of the composer's flirtation in the *Christmas Oratorio*, written at the turn of the year 1734/35, with the "progressive," or *galant*, style associated with the generation of his sons. It then notes, and attempts to account for, his sudden abrupt turn immediately thereafter—at the threshold of his late works—to the severe stylistic traditions associated with the gen-erations of his ancestors. Chapter 9, building on the previous chapter, contemplates the paradigm of the "late style" phenomenon as it is described by Theodor Adorno, Edward Said, and others. The discussion eventually centers on one of Bach's last compositions, the Mass in B Minor—specifically, the Confiteor movement (perhaps the very last music the composer ever wrote)—a work extraordinary even for J. S. Bach, with its astonishing turn toward archaicism, on the one hand, and (even more spectacularly) a breathtaking, "visionary," futurism on the other.

Before introducing the second leading protagonist of the volume, the spotlight settles on Bach's musical sons. Chapter 10 inquires into the filial and fraternal rela-tionships among them—in particular, how they came to terms personally and artis-tically with the daunting example of their unsurpassable father. It reports on the strategies each son developed to cope with that towering figure (some of them disas-trous). Chapter 11 pursues clues left by contemporary observers, along with implicit insinuations by later scholars, bearing on the personal life—more specifically (and, admittedly, provocatively), the erotic life—of Johann Christian Bach.

Chapter 12 finally introduces Wolfgang Amadeus Mozart. But his introduction takes the form of a transition. That is, the chapter continues to consider Bach while broaching the topic of Mozart. It is a study in comparative biography that attempts to account for the contrasting "styles" of genius rooted in the personal histories and psychological dispositions that drove and shaped the creative efforts of the two musi-cal giants. Chapter 13, adopting a substantially different literary tone from that pre-vailing up to this point, ponders Mozart's enigmatic character yet further—this time through the lens of the theatrical and cinematic sensation, *Amadeus*. Acknowledging the work's dramatic success as a work of drama and applauding its deep apprecia-tion of Mozart's musical achievement, the chapter mostly confronts its challenge as a work of biography by measuring its depiction of the protagonist (or antagonist) against the known facts. Musical issues return to center stage in chapter 14, whose agenda is to describe the several stages of Mozart's evolving artistic indebtedness to Bach. After pointing out that Mozart's first serious encounter with Bach's music took place some ten years earlier than traditionally assumed, the essay suggests that Bach's influence on Mozart's style unfolded in distinct, ever more sophisticated, phases: designated, respectively, "transcription," "imitation," "assimilation/synthesis," and "transcendence."

Chapter 15, the last numbered chapter, addresses the body of works left unfin-ished at Mozart's death. The mere existence of such musical fragments is a reflection and a fitting symbol, perhaps, of the fact that Mozart's brief life itself can be regarded as a "fragment." After surveying the corpus of fragments as a whole and noting cer-tain patterns in their distribution, the inquiry examines the manuscripts of a handful of concertos for less common solo instruments or combinations of soloists dating from the Salzburg through the late Viennese period. The differing states of incomple-tion preserved in them suggest a change in Mozart's compositional procedures—at least in this genre—from what is described as a "block" or "sectional" approach to a more holistic "horizontal" method. The final example discussed is the draft for an unfinished concerto in G major for basset horn. Mozart began the composition sometime in the year 1787 but then, for unknown reasons, set it aside. He took it up again, however, during the final weeks of his life, reworking it into the form of his last finished masterpiece: the Clarinet Concerto in A Major, K. 622, completed sometime between September 28 and November 15, 1791, weeks before his death on December 5.

Apropos of final things: the volume concludes with a literal postmortem. In an affront to sober, scholarly method, the "Epilogue" indulges in a fictional fancy: namely, a speculation—grounded, however, in the known facts—about what Mozart is likely to have done and to have composed, had he lived on for another decade or more.

❧ ❧ ❧

With but one exception the items included in this volume have been published before. They have all been revised here—to a greater or lesser extent (depending on the age of the essay)—to reflect and incorporate recent research developments. They have also been edited with a view, on the one hand, to removing occasional duplications of substance and, on the other, to strengthening the thematic inter-connections between them. Essays existing in more than one previous version have been combined into a single consolidated, "final" version. The author has also taken this occasion to include not only additional musical examples and images but also the original German texts of the letters of Bach and Mozart, along with other con-temporary documents. Their inclusion (in addition to the standard English transla-tions) should enable a reader with a reasonable reading knowledge of German to gain a more vivid sense of the two masters' personal, colorful, linguistic idiosyn-crasies—along with a firsthand experience of the wit and the emotional force of the originals—revealing qualities inevitably and regrettably "lost in translation." To this end the transcriptions of the eighteenth-century texts throughout this volume retain in addition the idiosyncratic orthography and punctuation of the original documents as published in the standard critical editions: above all, the volumes of the *Bach-Dokumente* (BDOK), and *Mozart Briefe und Aufzeichnungen* (MBA). (The distinction between Latin script and German script—a distinction observed by J. S. Bach—is rendered by printing the former in italics, the latter in roman type.)

❧ ❧ ❧

It remains only to express my gratitude to the following individuals for their valuable suggestions regarding one or the other of these essays: Lynn Edwards Butler, Don Franklin, Ellen T. Harris, Allan Keiler, Mark Kroll, Robin A. Leaver, Joel Lester,

Michael Marissen, Mary Oleskiewicz, Martin Rumscheidt, Anne Schnoebelen, Maynard Solomon, Jeffrey S. Sposato, Eberhard Spree, George Stauffer, and Andrew Talle. An anonymous reader was immensely helpful. Matthew Cron prepared the musical examples and figures with his peerless, expert skill. Sonia Kane, editorial director of the University of Rochester Press, and her staff were invariably resourceful in shepherding the volume into print. The author is particularly indebted to Ralph P. Locke, senior editor of the Eastman Studies in Music, for his encouragement of this project from its most embryonic stages, and for his unfailingly cogent advice and wise suggestions over the course of its gestation.

Traute M. Marshall, as always, has been for this enterprise, as she has for all my endeavors over the past fifty-plus years, a proofreader and copy editor *nonpareil*, a treasure trove of information and insight, my most sympathetic reader, my sternest critic, my cherished companion.

Abbreviations

BDOK I   *Bach-Dokumente, Band I: Schriftstücke von der Hand Johann Sebastian Bachs.* Edited by Werner Neumann and Hans-Joachim Schulze. Kassel: Bärenreiter; Leipzig: VEB Deutscher Verlag für Musik, 1963.

BDOK II   *Bach-Dokumente, Band II: Fremdschriftliche und gedruckte Dokumente zur Lebensgeschichte Johann Sebastian Bachs, 1685–1750.* Edited by Werner Neumann and Hans-Joachim Schulze. Kassel: Bärenreiter; Leipzig: VEB Deutscher Verlag für Musik, 1969.

BDOK III   *Bach-Dokumente, Band III: Dokumente zum Nachwirken Johann Sebastian Bachs 1750–1800.* Edited with commentary by Hans-Joachim Schulze. Kassel: Bärenreiter; Leipzig: VEB Deutscher Verlag für Musik, 1972.

BDOK VI   *Bach-Dokumente, Band VI: Ausgewählte Dokumente zum Nachwirken Johann Sebastian Bachs 1801–1850.* Edited with commentary by Andreas Glöckner, Anselm Hartinger, Karen Lehmann. Kassel: Bärenreiter, 2007.

BG   *Johann Sebastian Bach's Werke.* Complete edition of the Bach-Gesellschaft. 46 volumes. Leipzig: Breitkopf & Härtel, 1851–1900. Reprint edition. Ann Arbor, MI: Edwards, 1947.

BJ   *Bach-Jahrbuch.*

BP   *Bach Perspectives*

BR   *The Bach Reader: A Life of Johann Sebastian Bach in Letters and Documents.* Edited by Hans T. David and Arthur Mendel. Revised edition. New York: W. W. Norton, 1966.

BWV   *Thematisch-systematisches Verzeichnis der musikalischen Werke von Johann Sebastian Bach (Bach-Werke-Verzeichnis).* Revised edition. Edited by Wolfgang Schmieder. Wiesbaden: Breitkopf & Härtel, 1990.

Helm | *Thematic Catalogue of the Works of Carl Philipp Emanuel Bach.* Edited by E. Eugene Helm. New Haven, CT: Yale University Press, 1989.

JAMS | *Journal of the American Musicological Society.*

JRBI | *Bach: Journal of the Riemenschneider Bach Institute.* Berea, OH: Baldwin Wallace University.

Köchel 6 | *Chronologisch-thematisches Verzeichnis sämtlicher Tonwerke Wolfgang Amadé Mozarts.* Edited by Ludwig Ritter von Köchel. 6th edition. Edited by Franz Giegling, Alexander Weinmann, Gerd Sievers. Wiesbaden: Breitkopf & Härtel, 1964.

Letters | *The Letters of Mozart and His Family.* Chronologically arranged, translated and edited with an Introduction, Notes and Indexes by Emily Anderson. Originally published 1938. 3rd edition. London: Macmillan, 1985.

MBA | *Mozart Briefe und Aufzeichnungen. Gesamtausgabe.* Edited by the Internationale Stiftung Mozarteum Salzburg. Collected and with commentary by Wilhelm A. Bauer and Otto Erich Deutsch. 7 vols. Kassel: Bärenreiter, 1962–75.

MDB | *Mozart: A Documentary Biography.* Edited by Otto Erich Deutsch. Stanford, CA: Stanford University Press, 1966.

MDL | Mozart: *Die Dokumente seines Lebens.* Collected with a commentary by Otto Erich Deutsch. *Neue Ausgabe sämtlicher Werke.* Serie X, 34. Kassel: Bärenreiter, 1961.

MJb | *Mozart-Jahrbuch*

MQ | *The Musical Quarterly*

NBA | *[Neue Bach-Ausgabe.] Johann Sebastian Bach: Neue Ausgabe sämtlicher Werke.* Edited by the Johann-Sebastian-Bach-Institut, Göttingen, and the Bach-Archiv, Leipzig. Kassel: Bärenreiter; Leipzig: Deutscher Verlag für Musik, 1954–2010.

NBA . . . KB | *Neue Bach-Ausgabe . . . Kritische Berichte.*

NBR | *The New Bach Reader: A Life of Johann Sebastian Bach in Letters and Documents.* Edited by Hans T. David and Arthur Mendel. Revised and enlarged by Christoph Wolff. New York: W. W. Norton, 1998.

NGD | *The New Grove Dictionary of Music and Musicians.* Edited by Stanley Sadie. London: Macmillan, 1980.

NGD2   *The New Grove Dictionary of Music and Musicians*. 2nd edition.
            Edited by Stanley Sadie. London: Macmillan, 2001.

NMA   [*Neue Mozart Ausgabe*.] *Wolfgang Amadeus Mozart: Neue Ausgabe
            sämtlicher Werke*. Edited by the Internationale Stiftung Mozarteum
            in Collaboration with the Mozart Cities Augsburg, Salzburg, and
            Vienna. Kassel: Bärenreiter-Verlag. 1956–2007.

Warb   *The Collected Works of Johann Christian Bach, 1735–1782*. Vol.
            48/1: *Thematic Catalogue*. Edited by Ernest Warburton. New York:
            Garland, 1999.

Wq   *Thematisches Verzeichnis der Werke von Carl Philipp Emanuel Bach*.
            Edited by Alfred Wotquenne. Leipzig: Breitkopf & Härtel, 1905.

WTC   *The Well-Tempered Clavier*

Prologue

The Century of Bach and Mozart as a Music-Historical Epoch: A Different Argument for the Proposition

In the autumn of 1966, my first term as a teacher, it fell to me to offer a gradu-ate course called "Music in the Eighteenth Century." It was part of a two-year-plus sequence of courses at the University of Chicago, conceived as a comprehensive, if basically conventional, history survey. The first year, covering the thousand-odd years from the birth of Christian chant to 1600, was divided into three parts in accordance with traditional historical and compositional categories: medieval monophony, medieval polyphony, and music of the Renaissance. The remainder of musical history, though, was not similarly divided according to the well-established stylistic categories into courses on Baroque, Classical, Romantic, and Modern music, but rather—largely as a matter of scheduling convenience—into more or less even slices of time as suggested by the calendar: with ten-week courses devoted in turn to the music of the seventeenth, eighteenth, nineteenth, and twentieth centuries. While this may not have made much difference in the case of the other style periods, the division into calendrical centuries certainly seemed arbitrary, even unnatural, in the case of the eighteenth century. For the central musical fact about the eighteenth century—as every music student knows (even before entering graduate school)—is that it was split almost precisely in half into two distinct, and virtually antithetical, "music-historical epochs."

It was possible, of course, to ignore the fundamental historiographical problem and simply treat the musical events that occurred between circa 1700 and circa 1800 as a chronicle, taking up, one after the other, the topics and issues associated with the music of the Late Baroque, Pre-Classical, and Classical periods. The sylla-bus attempted to trace the general stylistic history of the eighteenth century as well as could be done in ten weeks (i.e., twenty ninety-minute class sessions)—which inevitably was not well at all. To begin with, the repertoire was enormous: more composers (both amateur and professional) no doubt having written more music during the eighteenth century than in any other. Moreover, the century obviously bore witness to a disproportionate number of great composers and great compositions—arguably the most impressive such concentration in the history of music. This fact in turn made it necessary to consider two fairly distinct, parallel, repertoires: the "great works" that every informed musician simply has to know, as well as the historically important and "typical" works.

In outline the course was organized into categories and sessions as follows:

I. THE LATE BAROQUE
    1   Opera and Secular Vocal Music
    2   The Concerto
    3   Chamber and Keyboard Music
    4   Church Music

II. BACH AND HANDEL
    5   Bach—Church Music
    6   Bach—Instrumental Music
    7   Handel—Opera and Secular Vocal Music
    8   Handel—Oratorio and Church Music

III. OPERA
    9   Opera Seria before Gluck
    10   Gluck and Reform Opera
    11   Comic Opera—Excluding Mozart

IV. THE STYLE SHIFT
    12   Empfindsamer Stil
    13   Development of the Pre-Classical Sonata and Chamber Music
    14   Development of the Symphony and Concerto

V. THE HIGH CLASSIC
    15   Haydn—Sonata and Chamber Music
    16   Haydn—Symphony and Church Music
    17   Mozart—Opera and Church Music
    18   Mozart—Instrumental Music

VI. THE LATE CLASSIC
    19   Early Beethoven and Clementi

The twentieth session was actually the first: the introduction to the course. Besides explaining the nature of the assignments and apologizing for the breakneck pace at which we would be constrained to try to "cover" such a vast amount of material, I decided to take the opportunity provided by that initial session and "inspired" by the bizarre chronological limits of the course I was stuck with—to entertain the following proposition:

That the time span 1700 to 1800 was not an altogether artificial and arbitrary division of musical history: beginning before the end of one epoch and breaking off before the end of another; that despite the apparently undeniable fact of a fundamental shift at some point during the course of the century (ca. 1720? ca. 1730? ca. 1750?) from a well-established and long-standing "Baroque" style to something evidently quite different, an intellectually defensible case could be made nonetheless for regarding the period from 1700 to 1800 as a historical unit, or, as Carl Dahlhaus would put it some twenty years later: "a music-historical epoch."

I was therefore rather gratified as well as bemused, and of course greatly interested, to read the provocative introductory chapter by Carl Dahlhaus to the fifth volume of *Das neue Handbuch der Musikwissenschaft: Die Musik des 18. Jahrhunderts*, first published in 1985, and, in an English translation by Ernest Harriss, in the 1986 issue of *College Music Symposium*.[1] It was gratifying to learn that no less a figure than Carl Dahlhaus was seriously pursuing—in his words, "daring to attempt"—a line of inquiry characterized as "contrary to the current historical consensus" that had more or less been thrust in my way by an accident of academic scheduling. But I was bemused (if that is the correct word) to read that, until the publication of the Dahlhaus chapter, "no one has dared to become involved with a radically different conception," from "the prevailing model for the music history of the eighteenth century" as it "was developed in its essentials by German musicologists of the late nineteenth and early twentieth centuries" (p. 1). As I had never "dared" to publish my lecture notes of autumn 1966, that claim would have to go unchallenged. Finally, I was naturally interested to compare the substance of Dahlhaus's case with my own.

The main elements in Dahlhaus's thesis are these: (1) The eighteenth century is defined as the period between 1720 and 1814, based on the assumption that there was indeed a "break in continuity" and that it "took place between 1720 and 1730" (p. 3). (2) To be properly understood, the music of the period has to be approached not so much in compositional, technical, or stylistic terms but rather from the perspective of social and cultural history. In Dahlhaus's words: "The history of composition will not emerge from a mere bundling up of technical traits" (p. 3). (3) In adopting this point of view and eschewing the distorted bias inherent in the "history of heroes" cultivated by the bourgeois and nationalistic German musicologists of earlier generations, one realizes that "the essential musical institution of the eighteenth century was the system of Italian court operas that extended from Naples and Madrid to St. Petersburg and from London to Vienna." The eighteenth century was "neither the 'Epoch of Bach' during its first half nor an 'Age of Haydn and Mozart' during its second half." "If one were to speak of the music in the aesthetic of the age, then what is meant is . . . opera, and indeed mainly opera seria" (pp. 3–4).

For Dahlhaus "the prescriptive-historical fact that the works of Bach and Handel, Gluck, Haydn, Mozart, and Beethoven were the ones that survived in the concert and opera repertoire while Metastasian opera fell victim to the 'fury of oblivion'

(Hegel) is *thoroughly inappropriate* and misleading as a point of departure for a music history that sets claim to historical truth or adequacy" (p. 6; emphasis added). Indeed, from his point of view, Dahlhaus is prepared to dismiss J. S. Bach altogether as a historically irrelevant "outsider," an "esoteric who knowingly withdrew from the world and drew the compositional consequences from that" (p. 2). Handel's name is barely mentioned in the essay.

While Dahlhaus's position could have served as a healthy corrective to the distortions inherent in the traditional "history of heroes," its formulation here is too extreme in its emphasis on a purely social and cultural reading of musical history. If the historical significance of the great figures is characteristically exaggerated in conventional accounts, it is unduly minimized here; if the cultural domination of the court and the aristocracy, epitomized by the opera seria, is often glossed over elsewhere, there is too little recognition here of the formidable cultural achievements of the rising bourgeoisie in the course of the eighteenth century. As for the opera seria: even if it was the major social fact of eighteenth-century music, it was by no means the century's principal artistic legacy. That distinction belongs to the creation and perfection of compelling, large-scale, instrumental musical forms.

Dahlhaus's account, however, not only underestimates the *historic role* of the "heroes" (quite aside from their *aesthetic achievement*): it does not really do justice to the cultural or social facts of the time. Even if one were to grant, for the sake of argument, that "the system of Italian court operas" was the "essential musical institution of the eighteenth century," it was by no means the only significant institution of the time. The theorists and commentators of the period certainly did not focus so exclusively on opera; they emphasized, rather, that art music was cultivated in three domains: the church, the chamber, and the theater, each with its own appropriate conventions, styles, and genres. Moreover, during the first part of the century they discussed music in terms of several national styles. Important music did not emanate from Italy alone. Contemporaries perceived, first of all, a bipolar hegemony shared by Italy and France. As for other nations: it was their mission—quite explicit in the case of the Germans—to effect some sort of reconciliation, or union, of the principal national styles with their own tradition.

The early fruits of this effort to create the *vermischter Geschmack* propagated by Quantz and others are evident in J. S. Bach's "fusion" and Handel's "coordination of national styles" (to borrow the apt descriptions of Manfred Bukofzer).[2] By the second half of the century, the notion of a union or synthesis of national styles had matured into the idea of a universal musical style—of music as a universal language. The ultimate form of this universal musical language was rooted, admittedly, in formal conventions and procedures developed first in Italy—those manifested in the basically Italian sonata—but colored by folk music idioms imported from many national and ethnic traditions and enriched, finally, with sophisticated harmonic and contrapuntal techniques inherited from the Germans. I am describing, of course, the music of the Viennese Classical masters.

The telling point, however, is that these "heroes" were consciously aware of their historic and cultural mission. Gluck spoke in 1773 of his wish to write music that "would appeal to all peoples" and "wipe out the ridiculous differences in national music." And he would have been gratified to read, a dozen years later, that his music represented "the universal language of our continent." And, as is well-known, Joseph Haydn once remarked, "My language is understood in the whole world."[3] It is simply a fatal distortion of the historical facts of the eighteenth century to drive the major figures to the periphery.

Equally pertinent is the fact that the crystallization of discrete and powerful national musical styles was complete by and recognized by the turn of the eighteenth century. One need only recall François Raguenet's *Paralele des Italiens et des François*, published in 1702, and the response by Le Cerf de La Viéville, *Comparaison de la musique italienne et de la musique françoise*, published in 1705.[4] Consolidating the phenomenon of national styles of music, and then confronting the challenge posed by their existence, in fact constitutes one of the hallmarks (and basically a "stylistic-compositional" hallmark, at that!) of the eighteenth century as a "music-historical epoch." The entire century would be occupied first with the definition and description; then with attempts at their combination, coordination, and fusion; and ultimately with their transcendence and transformation into something perceived as ideologically and aesthetically far more desirable: a universal musical style. The duration of this process, incidentally, was approximately coterminous with the actual calendrical century.

One final word on heroes: It is symptomatic that the eighteenth century did not just produce an inordinate number of musical geniuses, it created the very idea of the musical genius—defined, that is, as a human personality rather than as a gift or talent one possessed. The conceit was evidently the inspiration of Diderot who, in offering Jean-Philippe Rameau as the symbol of this "genius" in his novel *Rameau's Nephew*, even introduced the necessary linguistic adjustment, replacing the hitherto normal usage *avoir du génie* with the new formulation *être un génie*.[5]

The major hallmark of eighteenth-century music, however, is again one of a distinctly technical character. The generation of composers who came to maturity circa 1700 was the first one born into the mature system of functional tonality—to inherit it, so to speak, as a native language—after it was first consolidated in the music of the Italian concerto composers of the preceding generation. Tonality, of course, was to prevail as the supreme system of musical syntax in Western civilization for the next two hundred years. But its gradual dissolution had begun, significantly, by the beginning of the nineteenth century. The first seeds of this epochal development were sown, perhaps, by Joseph Haydn—in the "Representation of Chaos" that serves as an introduction to his oratorio *The Creation*, a work composed circa 1798.[6] And by the end of Beethoven's life almost all the "self-evident" principles of organization and coherence that underlay the tonal system had suffered at the least their first significant challenge.[7]

The first and the principal benefits of the tonal system were to be derived not in the realm of opera, or in vocal music at all, but in instrumental music—until the last two decades of the seventeenth century a distinctly limited channel for the cultivation of ambitious musical invention. The establishment of the tonal system enabled the construction of autonomous, closed, instrumental compositions on a large scale for the first time in the history of Western music. The consequence was the rapid evolution and perfection of two impressive instrumental forms: the concerto and, soon thereafter, the sonata—the latter engendering in turn (still in the early decades of the new century) the early prototypes of the symphony and the string quartet.

It is hardly coincidental that the emergence and standardization of the solo concerto—as a three-movement work based on the principles of ritornello structure and solo-tutti thematic differentiation—took place in the compositions of Torelli and Albinoni dating from the 1690s and early 1700s. There was, as well, a notable shift of emphasis at just this time (signaled by Corelli's sonatas, Op. 5, published in 1700) from the trio to the solo sonata. It may or may not have more than nominal significance that the first use of the term "sonata" with reference to works for solo keyboard seems to appear in Johann Kuhnau's *Biblische Historien*, published in 1700; but it is certainly significant that in this collection Kuhnau not only transferred the Italian church sonata to the solo harpsichord but combined it with the largely French idea of programmatic instrumental music. The program, however, was something typically German and Lutheran owing to its religious theme. At just the same time— the 1690s—the Frenchman François Couperin began to adopt the Italian sonata, as well, composing trios that he would later publish under the title *Les nations*. That is, both the coming of age of instrumental music and the interest in exploring and exploiting the distinctions between the national styles of music, mentioned earlier— what Couperin himself in another collection would call *Les goûts-réunis*—had begun in earnest just about the year 1700.

As for the social context of these developments: the courts, despite their passion—and even their preference, above all other things—for Italian opera were by no means oblivious to the importance and attractions of the new instrumental music. Frederick the Great, after all, engaged not only Hasse and the brothers Graun to write operas for his theater but also Quantz and C. P. E. Bach to write concertos and other instrumental works for his chamber. Domenico Scarlatti certainly composed and performed his harpsichord sonatas for the delectation of a monarch; and Mozart's "Prussian" quartets, no less than Haydn's "Russian" quartets, were dedicated to, and no doubt commissioned by, European royalty.

It would be hard, though, to determine the relative importance of the courts and the bourgeoisie in cultivating the development of instrumental music in the eighteenth century. Commercial concert life was just beginning at this time; but middle-class subscription concerts such as Mozart's "academies" in Vienna were nonetheless increasingly important in stimulating and molding creative activity. Music publishing, in any event, was an emphatically middle-class business whose growth in importance during the course of the century had an overwhelming impact not only on the circulation of particular works and the making of individual reputations but also in transmitting and disseminating new styles and genres. One need only recall the impact and influence of the symphonies of the Mannheim composers owing to their publication in Paris in the 1750s and 1760s.

Nor was the bourgeois influence by any means as negligible even in the realm of opera as Dahlhaus suggests. As early as 1728, after all, aristocratic opera seria was practically annihilated in London by that quintessentially middle-class phenomenon, *The Beggar's Opera*. The demise of the Royal Opera gave rise, however, not only to such arguably trivial entertainments as the ballad operas and their counterparts in France, Germany, and elsewhere. One of the most noble accomplishments of the age—the Handelian oratorio—was an immediate consequence of that event. It too, then, was a creature—a most popular one, at that—of middle class artistic will.

We must finally address the fundamental question about eighteenth-century music. Did, in fact, a "style shift" ever take place at all? Or was it more apparent than real, the figment of a historian's imagination? And if such a thing did take place, when did it occur? Traditional music history, as Dahlhaus reminds us, posits a style shift around mid-century: the end of the "Baroque" era marked by the deaths of Bach and Handel, to be followed by around thirty years of a preparatory "Pre-Classic" style until the mature masterpieces of Mozart and Haydn in the early 1780s heralded the advent of the "High Classic" or "Viennese" Classical style. Dahlhaus himself asserts that "the stylistic break . . . falls between 1720 and 1730" and maintains that "the traits of the new style (homophonic texture, short-phrased melody, rhythmic squareness, and slow harmonic rhythm) are too striking to ignore or to dismiss as irrelevant" (pp. 2–3). In fact, they can be traced back even further: Edward Downes claims to have observed such basic features of the new style as additive structure and the repetition of sections and particles in Antonio Bononcini's opera *Il trionfo di Camilla*, first performed in Naples in 1696, that is, when J. S. Bach was still a child.[8] And such elements of the new style as mixed rhythms, homophonic textures, and periodic phrasing were a hallmark of instrumental music—specifically, dance music—throughout the seventeenth century and earlier. For these reasons, then, as well as those adduced earlier (the establishment of tonality, the emergence of expansive forms and genres of instrumental music, the crystallization of national styles), it is tempting to argue not only that the eighteenth century was quite decidedly a music-historical epoch but that it in fact began at just about the turn of the century—and not some twenty years later.

As for the position of J. S. Bach in the larger context of eighteenth-century developments—clearly the most troublesome historiographical issue facing the musicologist: I would like to direct the reader to my own previously published thoughts on this issue.[9] But the most thoughtful and compelling treatment of this question is to be found in an essay, "On Bach's Historical Position," by Hans Heinrich Eggebrecht.[10] Eggebrecht formulates the question this way: "How could Mozart be possible so soon after Bach?" (p. 247). His answer, in brief, is that the historical process did not go "from Bach to Mozart" at all. Rather, both masters belonged to, and indeed represented in each instance, the historical culmination of two separate lines of development: in the case of Bach the Protestant tradition of central and northern Germany, for Mozart the secular tradition that had its roots in the south, that is, in Italy.[11]

There is still one last question remaining. Granted that the eighteenth century, as a music-historical epoch, began around 1700: when did it end? This is more difficult to say. Dahlhaus suggests 1814 but offers no justification for this year. To me the most plausible suggestions would be 1798, the year of Haydn's *Creation*, or 1803, the year of the "Eroica": both landmark works that confirm the arrival not only of new harmonic, tonal, and formal procedures but of a new musical aesthetic—indeed of a new musical ethos—as well.[12]

Chapter One

Young Man Bach

Toward a Twenty-First-Century Bach Biography

For admirers of Johann Sebastian Bach, the year 2000 did not just mark the 250th anniversary of the composer's death. It was also the fiftieth anniversary of the modern era of Bach research—a period that produced some of the most impressive achievements ever recorded in the annals of musical scholarship. This "golden age" of Bach scholarship—if we, the participants in it, may so smugly refer to it thus—began in 1950, the two-hundredth anniversary of Bach's death, with the publication of Wolfgang Schmieder's *Bach-Werke-Verzeichnis* (BWV) and the decision to prepare a new complete critical edition of Bach's works, the *Neue Bach-Ausgabe* (NBA).[1] Work on the NBA led in turn to the development of new empirical methods—methods such as paper, ink, and handwriting analysis (previously more typical of disciplines like criminology than musicology)—in order to organize the materials and lift from the realm of largely subjective impression the indispensable tasks of establishing authenticity and dating sources. They have since become indispensable for all "basic" musicological research.

An unexpected and, as it turned out, epochal consequence of this sorting activity was logged before the end of the 1950s when Alfred Dürr and Georg von Dadelsen (the Crick and Watson of Bach research), working in friendly rivalry, succeeded in constructing a chronology of virtually the entire corpus of Bach's vocal music precise enough to date the majority of Bach's vocal compositions to within a week.[2] In demonstrating that the vast majority of Bach's surviving Leipzig church music, consisting of some 150 compositions, had been written between 1723 and 1727, Dürr and Dadelsen had completely overturned the conventional view of how a major stretch of Bach's career had unfolded. It seemed almost as if Bach had been in a hurry to get the job of composing cantatas over with. And if he had not been spending a substantial portion of his twenty-seven years as Thomaskantor composing church music, then what had he been doing? The prevailing understanding of Bach's life and outlook and artistic development clearly had to be reconsidered.

It was not long before the gauntlet was thrown down by Friedrich Blume, arguably the preeminent German musicologist of the postwar period. In his widely circulated essay "Outlines of a New Picture of Bach," Blume argued that the conventional view of Bach as primarily a religious composer was mistaken. According to Blume, Bach had seen himself, and had to be seen by posterity, above all as a secular composer, a Kapellmeister by nature and inclination who only reluctantly spent most of his creative life in the service of the church: in his early years as an organist, later as a church music director.[3]

Sharp responses to Blume's deliberately provocative article followed shortly; but for the most part Bach scholarship hunkered down for the next twenty years systematically examining the musical sources, preparing the complete edition, or scouring the archives in a (surprisingly fruitful) search for ever more original sources and documents.[4] By the time of the tercentenary celebrations of Bach's birth in 1985 these efforts had posted major achievements, although none quite so spectacular as the Dürr-Dadelsen chronology.[5] In addition to the discovery of several dozen small Bach compositions,[6] and Bach's own annotated copy of a Lutheran Bible commentary,[7] work with the original sources (whether in connection with the publication of the new critical edition or not) led to more precise knowledge about Bach's working methods.[8] The history of many works—their origins, revisions, and versions—was clarified, and a number of authenticity issues were resolved. (Others were raised for the first time.)[9] Making use of the new empirical and evidentiary methods, extensive work was carried out on the study of Bach's performance practice: instruments of the period were reconstructed, and players learned to play them; and clues were sought bearing on the proper size of Bach's ensemble, the nature of his tuning system, the proper execution of ornaments, and the proper rendition of rhythms, tempos, slurs, and dots.[10]

While the volume of new information was being amassed and digested, the task of producing a comprehensive reinterpretation of Bach's life and work was postponed. In reality, Bach scholars were avoiding this challenge, and we knew it. The discovery and ordering of new facts—"hard" evidence—was by no means easy work; but it held out the seductive promise of objective certainty and reassuringly added to the pile of accumulated knowledge.

Inevitably, of course, the need to come to terms anew with the larger meaning—to risk interpretation—of the phenomenon of Johann Sebastian Bach proved irresistible. Apart from the premature attempt by Blume in the immediate wake of the Dürr–Dadelsen discoveries, efforts to understand how all the new discoveries had affected our fundamental conception of Bach's achievement began to appear in the mid-1970s and have been gathering momentum since. Some of the most significant work has addressed, on the one hand, the question of Bach's historical position and significance—the nature and degree of his indebtedness to his forerunners, contemporaries, and younger contemporaries. On the other hand, efforts have been undertaken to ascertain the very meaning, the message, of his music. Following upon Albert Schweitzer's description of Bach as a "terminal point: nothing comes from him; everything merely leads up to him," he has been portrayed as the "culmination of an era." He has also been depicted variously (again, mostly on the testimony of his music) as a "progressive," a radical revolutionary with a political agenda, an anti-Enlightenment social critic, a profound—and profoundly orthodox—Lutheran theologian, and a trans- or supra-historical unicum.[11]

With the exception of the ongoing accumulation and editing of documents, however—an effort that has added substantially to our knowledge of Bach's whereabouts, his activities, and routines[12]—little serious effort has been made toward a comprehensive reconsideration of the composer's life.[13] From one point of view, of course, the fact that recent Bach research has emphasized the music rather than the man is as it should be. The scope, complexity, and depth of expression of the towering, even staggering, musical achievement are manifest enough for all to hear, sing, play, admire, and contemplate (typically with a sense of awe approaching disbelief). The music obviously calls for explication. Just as obviously, Bach's music, like all artistic achievement, is surely a product not only of the traditions that feed it but of the talent, temperament, and experience of its maker. It follows that in order even to begin to understand the work satisfactorily (nobly suppressing, if we can, our often less than noble natural curiosity about the private lives of extraordinary people)—to understand, for example, why some genres were cultivated rather than others, or how and why a personal style evolved the way it did at the pace it did—we need to know and understand as much as we can about the artist's life, personality, and circumstances.

Johann Sebastian Bach's life, however, was notoriously and frustratingly uneventful. He was a family man who resided in small, often provincial, towns all his life. He was never abroad. He led a fundamentally private existence devoted to cultivating and perfecting his talent for music, an activity and occupation that he considered a divine calling. Beyond his immediate environment he apparently had little to do with the intellectual, cultural, or social elite of his time. He had no truly famous friends or enemies. The surviving documents bearing on his life, whether written by others or by Bach himself, are almost invariably official in character: bills, receipts, letters of recommendation, and complaints or reprimands from employers and other authorities.[14] There are no diaries, no memoirs. Not a single letter from Bach to any of his children, to his first wife, Maria Barbara, or to his second wife, Anna Magdalena, has survived; we may assume that not many were ever written.[15]

Nonetheless, genius is inherently mystifying and provocative. We crave some sort of illumination, some understanding of how the achievement came about and why it took the particular form it did.

❧   ❧   ❧

In coming to terms with Bach's personality and character, all studies known to me—until the appearance of John Eliot Gardiner's 2013 account—have stood squarely in the nineteenth-century tradition of inspirational, indeed hagiographical, composer biographies. The great man was portrayed as a sympathetic hero endowed not only with almost superhuman abilities but with a virtuous and largely unblemished character. He is typically depicted as a man repeatedly misunderstood, mistreated, and unappreciated.[16] Little cognizance was taken of modern developments in biographical writing about creative genius—the psychologically probing approaches pioneered by Sigmund Freud (on Michelangelo, da Vinci, and Dostoyevsky) and Erik Erikson (on Luther and Gandhi) and applied to musical figures by Maynard Solomon (on Mozart, Beethoven, and Schubert), Stuart Feder (on Ives), and others.[17] Perhaps, in light of the relative dearth of primary personal documents, such an endeavor was considered futile. Perhaps it was considered blasphemous. Bach, after all, intimidates us like no other composer: his supreme, iconic stature renders us unwilling or unable to assess him or his music critically. Precisely the fact that we know so little about the man encourages us to approach the work as something not even manmade but rather as an awesome natural phenomenon: something that is (and, we find ourselves believing, always has been) simply there.

In consequence, most of the ocean of literature ultimately failed to humanize Johann Sebastian Bach. As Gardiner's biography demonstrated, we are surely ready by now to make the attempt. At all events, the following remarks, originally written in 2000, would seem to have constituted an early effort toward that end and continues to propose interpretive avenues to coming to terms with the phenomenon Johann Sebastian Bach that have not yet been further pursued. They will be largely, but not entirely, limited to Bach's youth and early maturity. In the spirit of Erik Erikson's classic study of Martin Luther, the essay has now been dubbed "Young Man Bach" (its former title now serving as the subtitle).

With sufficient effort the known symptomatic actions of Bach's life, along with the surviving documents, as recalcitrant as they are, can surely be cajoled to shed more light on Bach the man than would at first appear. To begin with, however, we must not sanitize the sources. For example, in 1705 Bach was brought before the church consistory in Arnstadt, where he served as organist of the New Church from 1703 to 1707, to answer a complaint that he had drawn his sword against a student named Geyersbach and called him a *Zippelfagottist*. This term was translated by Hans David and Arthur Mendel in the old *Bach Reader* as "nanny goat bassoonist." In NBR it is rendered as "greenhorn bassoonist."[18] Both terms fail to capture the pungency and vulgarity of the original. According to the *Deutsches Wörterbuch* of the Brothers Grimm (the *OED* of the German language), *Zippel*, in Thuringian dialect and elsewhere, was a designation for the male member.[19] Bach was calling Geyersbach, to his face, "a prick of a bassoon player."

Bach's capacity for coarse language and even sexual innuendo makes itself evident musically as well at about the same time in the fragmentary wedding "Quodlibet," BWV 524, a product of one of those rowdy gatherings of the Bach family described by Johann Nikolaus Forkel (1749–1818) in his classic biography of the composer:

> As it was impossible for them all to live in one place, they resolved at least to see each other once a year. . . . Their amusements . . . were entirely musical. . . . The first thing they did, when they were assembled, was to sing a chorale. From this pious commence-ment they proceeded to drolleries [*Scherzen*], which often made a very great contrast with it. For now they sang popular songs, the contents of which were partly comic [*possierlich*] and partly naughty [*schlüpfrig*], all together and extempore, but in such a manner that the several parts thus extemporized made a kind of harmony together. . . . They called this kind of extemporary harmony a *Quodlibet*, and not only laughed heartily at it themselves, but excited an equally hearty and irresistible laughter in everybody that heard them.[20]

In the present instance the occasion for the reunion was a family wedding that took place—as the reference to two solar eclipses in the same year allows us to con-clude—in the year 1707. The very first word that survives in the manuscript torso of this boisterous composition, from which both the beginning and ending are miss-ing, is *Steiß*, meaning backside or rump (and omitted, incidentally, from the English translation included in the facsimile edition), which sets the tone at once and gives an idea of its literary *niveau*.[21] At one point in the depiction, or recollection, of various silly games and antics evidently engaged in by the members of the clan (and altogether evocative of a peasant scene by Brueghel), a series of parallelisms paired into rhymed couplets provides the occasion for a flurry of sexual *double entendres* inspired by the initial proposition: *Große Hochzeit, große Freude / Große Degen, große Scheide* (i.e., Great big wedding, great joy / Large sword, large scabbard—*Scheide* being also the standard German term for vagina). Some other couplets: *Große Pfeile, große Köcher / Große Nasen, große Löcher* (Large arrows, large quivers / large noses, large holes [i.e., nostrils]); *Große Jungfern, große Kränze / Große Esel, große Schwänze* (Large maidens, large wreaths / Large donkeys [i.e., fools], large tails [i.e., penises]). Further suggestive pairings include *Große Fässer, große Zappen* (big barrels, big plugs); *Große Köpfe, große Hörner* (big heads, big horns); *Große Kugeln, große Kegel* (large [bowling] balls, large pins); *Große Klöppel, große Trummel* (large drumsticks, large drums). The Rabelaisian spirit informing the revels is made explicit: *Pantagruel war ein sehr lustiger Mann / Und mancher Hofbediente trägt blaue Strümpfe an* (Pantagruel was a very merry man / and many a courtier wears blue stockings).

The taste for such humor was shared by at least one other member of Johann Sebastian's immediate family: his second wife, Anna Magdalena (1701–60), who entered into her famous musical album of 1725 a curious wedding poem, *Ihr Diener, werthe Jungfer Braut*.[22] The second verse of this exercise in doggerel reads:

Cupido, der vertraute Schalk,
Lässt keinen ungeschoren.
Zum Bauen braucht man Stein und Kalk
Die Löcher muss man bohren,
Und baut man nur ein Hennen-Haus,
Gebraucht man Holz und Nägel,
Der Bauer drischt den Weizen aus
Mit gross und kleinem Flegel.

(Cupid, that trusted rogue,
Lets no one go unshorn.
To build one needs both stone and lime,
The holes must be bored.
And even for a henhouse
You need both wood and nails.
The farmer threshes the wheat
With large and tiny flails.)

It is noteworthy—and quite understandable—that the English edition of Spitta tacitly omits this stanza altogether. In fact, no complete English translation of it was published until 1990.[23]

The Geyersbach incident attests to more than Bach's use of sexual vulgarity: it makes clear that there was an unmistakably harsh edge to his personality. Famously confrontational and insubordinate all his life, the documents, including his own letters, reveal from the beginning a pervasive sense of persecution and an attitude of spiteful defiance toward authority. While still in Arnstadt he was reprimanded for overstaying a four-week leave by twelve weeks.[24] In requesting his dismissal from his next (rather good) post, in Mühlhausen, in 1708, after only a year, Bach complains (in his first extant letter) about inadequate pay (another constant theme in the Bach correspondence, although, as we know, he usually was far better paid than his predecessors or colleagues in the same position) and working amid "hindrance" and "vexation."[25]

In Leipzig Bach was clearly the servant of too many masters: the church, the school, and the municipal government. One by one he confronted and antagonized them all. The first dozen years or so of his tenure as Thomaskantor seem to have been a succession of bureaucratic battles over turf. In 1725 he was at odds with the university, in 1728 with the church authorities, in 1736 with the school administration.[26] More than once Bach was willing not only to confront his superiors but to carry his complaints to the Saxon king, Frederick Augustus (I or II, as the case may have been) in Dresden, who might have wondered whether the Thomaskantor was mad, bothering his majesty and imperial elector with (from the royal perspective) parochial grievances about payments for university performances or the choice of hymns for the service. In the crisis of 1730 Bach was formally criticized by the city council for neglecting his teaching duties. One burgomaster reported that he had "spoken with the cantor, Bach, but he shows little inclination to work."[27] Like Achilles, Bach was sulking in his tent. In October of that year he writes to a child-hood friend, "I must live amid almost continual vexation, envy, and persecution."[28] Nor can he restrain himself from mentioning, three years later, in the letter accom-panying his dedication of the B-Minor Mass to Frederick Augustus II, that he has "innocently had to suffer one injury or another."[29]

We must resist the inclination to act as apologists for the Kantor and, taking Bach's cue, invariably cast him in the role of the unjustly wronged, embattled pro-tagonist. We must be willing to acknowledge the repeated pattern of belligerence, distrust, and defiance. But that is not enough: having acknowledged the uncomfort-able fact, we have to make an effort to account for it. Ascribing it to the prerogatives and idiosyncrasies of genius will not do: Joseph Haydn's life, like Bach's, unfolded in a tenured security postulated on unquestioned deference to powerful authority. Yet Haydn remained genial enough. How, then, do we account for this powerful, and less than attractive, strain in Bach's character?

ᴣᴠ ᴣᴠ ᴣᴠ

We all know that character formation is the work of childhood. The decisive fact about Bach's formative years is that he was an orphan. He lost both parents by the time he was ten: they died within one year of each other. Shortly after the death of his father the family broke up, and the ten-year-old Sebastian, along with his thir-teen-year-old brother, were taken in by the oldest of the surviving siblings, Johann Christoph. Being thus catastrophically deprived of his parents—which was no doubt experienced by the child on some level as abandonment and betrayal—understand-ably put the boy on his guard, evidently engendering in him a lifelong "basic dis-trust" (to use Erik Erikson's phrase) of an unreliable, even treacherous, world and predisposing him to religion, especially (and conveniently) to the Lutheran religion of his fathers, with its message of personal faith and salvation, combined with a determined rejection and distrust of the world, with its pleasures, promises, cov-enants, rules, and rulers.[30]

The first ten years of Bach's childhood, then, the formative crucible of his life, bequeathed to him a remarkable, if contradictory, legacy. On the one hand, he was heir to the Bach family musical inheritance, a positive and empowering genetic and social privilege. The negative legacy was the defining existential and religious expe-rience represented by the early loss of both parents in short succession—a double blow—and the breakup of the family.

There is more to be said about Bach's orphanhood. If we are willing to lend any credence at all to the findings of the past hundred years of psychological observa-tion (and to acknowledge common experience), and if we are willing to indulge a degree of plausible speculation in the absence of documented evidence bearing on a child's early affective life, then we may assume that Sebastian, like any child, harbored ambivalent feelings about his parents. As the youngest of eight children, four of whom died young, he may—as is often the case with youngest children—have been more pampered and protected than some of the older ones; but as a child of the seventeenth century he surely was punished severely when he misbehaved. At all events, there must inevitably have been moments when he entertained, at the least, hostile and resentful thoughts toward his parents. A parent's death must be experienced by any child, then, both as the catastrophic loss of a loved one and, to some degree, as an evil, sinful wish fulfilled. Moreover, in Bach's case he not only must have resented his mother's having "abandoned" him by her death; one can imagine that, like many children, he must have resented his widowed father's remarriage after the mother's death, just months before he was carried off himself.[31] The child's grief at his parents' death, in short, must have been complicated by ambivalent feelings—sadness, vulnerability, resentment, anger—and this ambivalence in turn may well have called forth a sense of guilt.

Equally complicated, we can be certain, was Bach's attitude toward his elder brother, who was called upon to take in his two younger brothers, Sebastian and Johann Jacob, after the father's death. There must have been a subconscious blending for Sebastian of his father, Ambrosius, with his father-like brother, Johann Christoph. Johann Christoph (1671–1721), thirteen years older than Sebastian, had moved to Ohrdruf in 1690, married in October 1694 and, in July 1695—presumably shortly after the arrival of his brothers from Eisenach—had become a father in his own right. The twenty-four-year-old organist and freshly minted *pater familias* was now entrusted as well with his brothers' care and upbringing. How Sebastian dealt with the usual, but now unusually complicated and fused, fraternal/filial tensions and rivalries is surely hinted at in the famous story about the forbidden music scroll, locked away behind a latticed cabinet door and copied surreptitiously by Sebastian at night by candlelight.[32] If the story is true, it is significant enough. If it is untrue—a legend created no doubt by Bach himself—and constituting a major element in what we may consider his oral autobiography, intended to be (as it was) passed down to his children and on to posterity—then the legend is, if anything, even more significant. Nor does it matter whether or not Bach was on good terms with his brother in later years. For the upshot of the anecdote, or legend, is that Bach wanted it known or believed that he had heroically overcome obstacles set in his path and, in acquiring a major portion of his musical training, had been willing to defy authority.

In doing all this, he would have us know, he had to the same degree created himself as a musician. (C. P. E. Bach had reported to Forkel in this connection that his father, "through his own study and reflection alone . . . became a pure and strong fugue writer in his youth." [33] It is worth noting that Bach describes this childhood conflict (or rivalry) wholly in reference to his older brother—cast here, it seems, for the purpose of the legend, in the traditional fairy-tale role of the wicked stepfather.

Conversely, we learn next to nothing in the obituary or Forkel's biography about Bach's actual father, beyond the fact that he was a town musician in Eisenach and had an identical twin brother—another Johann Christoph—and that these brothers, in Forkel's words, "tenderly loved each other!"[34] One is left to speculate whether Sebastian would have characterized his childhood feelings toward his brother Johann Christoph thus. At all events, in 1700, at the age of fifteen, Bach was "orphaned" once again when he was obliged to leave his brother's overcrowded and financially overextended house—no room at the inn (a second child was born in 1697)—and set out for Lüneburg. Few of his ancestors, by the way, had ventured so far from Thuringia.

Another likely consequence of Bach's orphanhood—one seemingly in conflict with his understanding of himself as a self-created musician—was his fascination with the family history. Bach's interest in genealogy was his hobby. We know of no other hobby of his—nothing like Mozart's numerous amusements, from cards to billiards to horseback riding. Why genealogy? The "Origin of the Musical Bach Family" (henceforth: Genealogy) was compiled by Bach around 1735.[35] The impetus for doing so at just this time—the same time, incidentally, that he seems to have begun to compile the *Alt-Bachisches Archiv* (a collection of music composed by his ancestors)[36]—may well have been his having reached the age of fifty in that year, an age after which the past often assumes an ever-greater role in one's consciousness as the future ever more rapidly shrinks. The significance of this birthday—indeed, its ominous import—must have been considerably intensified in Bach's case by virtue of the fact that his father, Johann Ambrosius (1645–95), his mother, Elisabeth (1644–94), and his brother Johann Christoph (1671–1721), all died at age fifty.

The Genealogy has a mythic quality to it, evoking as it does a biblical list of the generations. It attests to Bach's need to establish his roots and to identify the *Urvater*, the *Ur*-Bach, the Bach-*Quelle*.[37] Johann Sebastian may have had no parents, but he certainly could demonstrate that he belonged to a great family, a clan whose roots he could trace back almost two hundred years—the *musicalisch-Bachische Familie*. Just as it was something special (if unenviable) to be an orphan, to be a Bach in Thuringia was to be part of a privileged elite: a musical aristocracy and dynasty. It was clearly a source of tribal, almost nationalistic pride from which he derived his birthright and principal identity: that of a musician. (Bach the musician had no need to fabricate a "family romance," a fantasy in which a child imagines that his parents are great or famous personages.) At the same time the clan, the family network, was a source of security and protection. In the secular sphere, then, it was manifestly to the family, and not to any prince or town, not to mention a larger entity like Saxony or Thuringia, much less an abstraction like the "German nation," that the Bachs pledged their allegiance.

By tracing the family back to the Hungarian miller, Vitus (or Veit) Bach (ca. 1555–1619), however, Sebastian had found a way to connect himself and his family to the early years of his people in a larger sense—his people being not the German nation per se but those of the Lutheran faith. Indeed, Vitus, the *Ur*-Bach, is portrayed by Sebastian as a hero of sorts who, in the words of the Genealogy, "had to flee Hungary in the sixteenth century, on account of his Lutheran religion."[38] This can only have reinforced Bach's identity as a Lutheran and built upon his sense of personal identification with Martin Luther himself deriving from their common Thuringian heritage. This sense of an almost familial bond with Luther no doubt developed early on in Eisenach, where Bach had spent his early childhood literally in the shadow of the Wartburg, where Luther, after taking his famous defiant stand at the Diet of Worms, had found refuge and set about translating the New Testament, and where, like the reformer, Bach had attended the St. George Latin School. The fact that Bach's father was a native of Erfurt, another significant Luther town, cemented the connection all the more.[39] The Genealogy, then, exposes and fuses into one the principal strands of Bach's identity: a Bach, a Lutheran, a musician.

It is worth noting that Bach does not include all the musical members of the family in his genealogy of the "musikalisch-Bachische Familie"—Hanns the Jester (1555–1615), for one, does not appear.[40] In compensation, perhaps, there are a few non-musicians: a surgeon (Johann Nicolaus Bach, no. 20), a shopkeeper (Johann Christoph, no. 26), and a music-loving Johann Christoph (no. 28), son of the Eisenach organist, who "has never taken on a regular position, seeking his greatest *plaisir*, rather, in traveling."[41] Those musicians who are accepted into the list are all town or court musicians, organists, or Kantors. There are no church music directors. Nor do we find, for that matter, any theologians or clergymen among the relatives and ancestors Bach bothers to inventory.

The ancestor on whom Bach bestows his highest praise—the highest praise he ever bestowed on any musician—is his father's first cousin, Johann Christoph Bach (1642–1703; no. 13), who served for thirty-eight years as the court and town organist of Eisenach. Bach describes him as *ein profunder Componist*. Such a characterization—one manifestly applicable to Johann Sebastian Bach himself—attests not only to Sebastian's admiration but to his strong sense of identification with this Johann Christoph. For Bach's parents, however, the Eisenach organist thoroughly fulfilled the criteria of what psychologists call a "negative identity," namely, "an identity a family wishes to live down . . . and . . . tries to suppress in its children."[42] Consider the case of Johann Christoph Bach. Throughout his tenure at Eisenach, he had had a notoriously hard time with the Eisenach town council. Although his knowledge about organs, his organ playing, and his music were recognized and respected, his frequent insistent appeals and strongly worded complaints about his inadequate salary, his frustration with trying to collect the various incidental fees owed to him, and his precarious living accommodations were repeatedly rejected or ignored.[43] Nor does it seem that Johann Christoph got on well with his cousin Ambrosius. At all events, the fact that Johann Christoph was asked to play essentially no godfather role in Ambrosius's family, except one time by default (when Pachelbel could not make it), has been taken as a clue that relations between the cousins may have been less than cordial. Johann Christoph, in short, may well have been represented to Sebastian, even as a child, as the relative not to be emulated: a gifted, brilliant musician, but a man who could not get along with his superiors, living on the edge of poverty, heroically pleading his cause on behalf of his art. No wonder Sebastian admired him!

In April of 1702, at Easter time, Bach graduated from St. Michael's Gymnasium in Lüneburg and eventually returned to Thuringia—but not, so far as we know, to Eisenach. When Johann Christoph Bach died in March of 1703 the post of court and town organist became available. It does not seem that Sebastian, who was in the service of Duke Johann Ernst at Weimar at the time, ever applied for it. In August, however, he accepted the position of organist at the New Church at Arnstadt. The Eisenach post, for which Sebastian was surely more than qualified, would have been more prestigious, and, not surprisingly, it went to a Bach: Johann Bernhard Bach (1676–1749) of Erfurt. Could the eighteen-year-old Sebastian have admired the great Johann Christoph too much to consider stepping into his shoes by succeeding him as the most important organist in the city of his birth?

The lesson of the Genealogy and of this early history is that Bach, despite his orphanhood, had a profound sense of rootedness. Coming from a musical family, Bach (unlike Handel) never felt the need to stray far from home, nor did he have to travel a great physical (or psychological) distance to find or confirm his calling. For Bach the matter of his "identity" as a musician was never in doubt. But there was a crisis—indeed several—as to what kind of musician he was, and what it meant to be a musician.

Shaping, or finding, one's identity is the work of the young adult—work in which an assertion of freedom and independence often goes hand in hand with the voluntary submission to strict, rigorous discipline, and in which one seeks to balance the search for adventure on the one hand and the simultaneous exploration and affirmation of tradition on the other. There are obvious musical analogues to this in the forms chosen by the young Bach. Consider the improvisational passagework or harmonic experimentation alternating section for section with strict imitative, fugal counter-point in the early toccatas, or the combination of ever changing variations over the simultaneously sounding, stubbornly repeated ostinato in the passacaglia. The auda-cious "strange variations" in the Arnstadt chorales, for which Bach was famously called to task by the church consistory,[44] are a particularly vivid example of youthful probing of the boundary between adventure and tradition—as well, of course, as a show of defiance and youthful, adolescent rebellion that brought down the expected (and perhaps desired) reprimand. Desired, obviously, because it would furnish the internal justification and pretext for pursuing his artistic objectives elsewhere should that prove necessary—as of course it did.

Unfortunately, none of Bach's surviving organ chorales can be unambiguously identified in connection with the reprimand. But an early, if undatable, composition such as *Allein Gott in der Höh sei Ehr*, BWV 715, gives an idea of what would surely have confused any congregation. Ostensibly a straightforward four-part harmonization with free passagework interludes between the chorales lines, not only are the harmonies quite bold ("strange") and chromatic, and the interludes unpredictable in length and tonal direction, but several melody tones of the chorale itself are (arbitrarily) chromatically altered. This last liberty represents precisely what the reprimand describes as having "mingled many strange tones" and "introducing a tonus peregrinus" into the chorales (exx. 1.1a and 1.1b).[45]

In this connection, it is worth remembering that for all his difficulties with his superiors at later posts, Bach was never again formally reprimanded for transgressions of a musical kind. In Leipzig it was Bach himself, not the town council or the rector, who characterized his music as "incomparably more difficult and more intricate" than that of other composers[46]—intricacy or complexity, one may add, that was a consequence of the mature composer's commitment to pursuing the implications of his materials, an attitude altogether unrelated to the young musician's typical impulse to be daring, to shock and provoke for its own sake.

Crossing the threshold of adulthood, we all know, is difficult. The search for a mature identity, after all, entails the shedding of one's childhood self, a process that can resemble mourning: mourning for one's idealized, innocent past and a nostalgic yearning for its recovery. That Bach passed through such an episode at just this time in his life, sometime before the age of twenty, and chose to bear musical witness to it, is attested by the *Capriccio sopra la lontananza de il fratro dilettissimo* (*Capriccio on the Absence of the Most Beloved Brother*), BWV 992, that curious, surprisingly sentimental tone poem, with its depictions of grieving friends imploring the unidentified "fratro" not to journey forth, worrying about what may befall him, poignantly lamenting the departure, taking leave, and finally, to the sound of the posthorn, accepting the inevitable.[47] Sentimentality is a typical attribute of youth, but not of Bach. It is as if the young Bach had consulted Elisabeth Kübler-Ross's famous text, *On Death and Dying*, with its precise descriptions of the psychological stages of the death process—denial, anger, bargaining, depression, and acceptance—and decided to set them to music.[48]

Bach, of course, did not have to wait until adolescence to experience death or to discover the affects associated with mourning and grief. But coming to terms with the experience of death—musically, emotionally, and theologically—was destined to be a lifelong preoccupation. It is no coincidence that Bach's breakthrough to artistic maturity in the realm of vocal composition (the counterpart, in this respect, to the Passacaglia and Fugue, BWV 582)—works, that is, that can unhesitatingly be acknowledged as masterpieces of the highest order—are concerned with death: the Easter cantata, *Christ lag in Todesbanden*, BWV 4, and, even more, the funeral cantata, the *Actus tragicus: Gottes Zeit ist die allerbeste Zeit*, BWV 106, both written—like the passacaglia, presumably—when the composer was in his early twenties.

Example 1.1a. *Allein Gott in der Höh sei Ehr*, plainsong melody; text: Nikolaus Decius (1539)

Al - lein Gott in der Höh sei Ehr und Dank für __ sei -
dar - um, daß nun und nim - mer - mehr uns rüh - ren __ kann __

ne Gna - de. Ein Wohl - ge - falln Gott an uns hat; nun ist groß Fried
kein Scha - de.

ohn Un - ter - laß, all Fehd hat nun ein En - de.

In exploring the nature and meaning of death, the *Actus tragicus* inexorably confronts the nature and meaning of the Law, God's law (or covenant) according to the Old and New Testaments. As a symbol for the Old Law—the superseded law of the Old Testament and its harsh verdict, namely, "Es ist der alte Bund: Mensch, du mußt sterben!" (It is the old covenant: Man, thou must die!)—Bach uses the fugue. Fugue, of course, happens to be the musical procedure Bach, from the beginning, felt most comfortable with and is most identified with—fugue, and, later on, musical law of an even more rigorous kind: canon. Can we say that, in doing so, Bach was determined to master the "law," as manifested in music, to conquer it and make it his servant? We know from the Calov Bible commentary that Bach annotated the book of Leviticus, the third book of Moses.[49] It is interesting that he bothered to read Leviticus at all (with its innumerable rules and prohibitions pertaining to sacrificial rites, permitted and forbidden foods, sexual crimes, slavery, property rights, and so on), that he knew it so well, and that he cared about these arcane and, for a Christian, irrelevant laws. In general, we have hardly begun to learn the lessons that the Calov Bible has to teach us about Bach's theological and even existential outlook. (For example, Bach seems to find his sense of persecution, or at least his distrust of authority, confirmed in Abraham Calov's gloss on Deuteronomy 23:4, for he underlines the passage reading (in translation): "If you want to make a prince . . . from one who you know seeks your ruin out of innate hatred, that is not only disgraceful and inept but also foolish and wicked, even tempting God.")[50]

But to return to the main discussion: establishing an identity in early adulthood means, among other things, setting a life's agenda. In the private sphere the traditional outward symbol of the assumption of independence and the willingness and ability to take on the long-term responsibilities and commitments of adult life is marriage and the formation of a family in one's own name. In the second half of 1707, at the age of twenty-two, Bach, in rather rapid succession, accepted a new position as organist at Mühlhausen, resigned from his Arnstadt post, and, in

Example 1.1b. *Allein Gott in der Höh sei Ehr*, BWV 715, mm. 1–17

Example 1.1b.—*(concluded)*

October, married his cousin Maria Barbara, née Bach (1684–1720). Sebastian was apparently the only member of the family to marry a namesake.

What is the significance of Bach, parentless since the age of ten, having married a close relative, one bearing his own family name? One hesitates to state the obvious: it is as if, in marrying a female Bach, Sebastian was managing symbolically to replace both his father and his mother and restoring family integrity. (Incidentally, just as Bach's mother was a year older than his father, his new wife was a year older than he.) Moreover, in marrying Maria Barbara he was forming a sacred union (that is the phrase) with the most creative branch of the family tree, for she was the daughter of his father's first cousin, Johann Michael (1648–94). Unlike Bach's own father, Ambrosius, Johann Michael—whom Sebastian would have addressed, had he been alive, as "father"—was a composer, and, in the words of the genealogy, an "able" composer (*ein habiler Componist*). Michael's brother, moreover, was none other than the Eisenach organist, Johann Christoph (1642–1703), the *profunder Componist*. As with Johann Christoph, Sebastian's high regard for Johann Michael, too, is clear from his choice of adjective.[51]

For the more gifted and ambitious, of course, setting a life's agenda at the commencement of adult life means more than settling down, marrying, starting a family, and embarking on a new job. The gifted often proclaim marvelously grandiose and idealistic goals. Bach did just that in the earliest letter to survive from his hand. Dated June 25, 1708, the document contains the twenty-three-year-old organist's request to be allowed to leave his Mühlhausen post.[52] In explaining his desire to change jobs (for the second time in as many years), Bach described his ultimate (life's?) goal—his *Endzweck*, as he put it (employing a rather lofty term derived from the Latin *consiliorum finis* and a concept later explored by Kant and Goethe), "namely, a regular [i.e., professional] church music to the Glory of God" (nemlich eine *regulirte* kirchen *music* zu Gottes Ehren).[53] The same document, as indicated earlier, introduces us from the beginning to a number of leitmotifs of Bach's character: his complaints about "hindrance" and "vexation," his obsession with money and the high cost of living, his envy of better conditions elsewhere, and his initiative and energy—in having put together "not without cost, a good store of the choicest church compositions" (*nicht sonder kosten, einen guthen apparat der auserleßensten kirchen Stücken*). Regarding the evident intensity of the young man's ambition: one of the Mühlhausen church authorities considering Bach's request observed that "since there is no stopping him, his dismissal obviously has to be granted" (*Weil er nicht aufzuhalten, müste mann wohl in seine demission consentiren*).[54] And how does Bach propose to fulfill his *Endzweck*? By taking a position at the Weimar Court Chapel and Chamber Music (*Hoffcapell und Cammer music*), a position that involved playing the organ and composing secular chamber music—that is, *not* performing church cantatas to the Glory of God. That opportunity would only come six years hence with his promotion to Konzertmeister, a circumstance that Bach, in 1708, could hardly have foreseen, much less taken for granted.

With Bach's marriage in 1707 and his move in 1708 to the small but culturally ambitious court of Weimar (where he would remain for nine years, until he was thirty-two years old), both his personal life and his career settled into the stability, and took on the responsibilities associated with the status, of a fully mature adult. Having arrived at this plateau in Bach's life, we can turn our attention from the man to the music.

❧ ❧ ❧

As in the case of Bach biography, what is missing from virtually all writing on Bach's music is a critical stance, an issue that can only be touched upon here. In brief, not all of Bach's music is equally perfect, and we need to dare to contemplate Bach's shortcomings as a composer. Of course, we all know (or prefer to believe) that great composers never write bad music: they write great music and pieces that are—shall we say—"problematic."

Example 1.2. Minuet from Ouverture in F, BWV 820

Undeniably well short of perfect, for example, is the minuet from the Ouverture in F, BWV 820, an undated keyboard composition but assumed, on the basis of its source transmission and primitive style, to have been composed around 1705 (ex. 1.2).[55] (There is really no way, however, of ascertaining how early it may have been written.)

The number of infelicities the composer has managed to incorporate into this brief—and admittedly early—work (even allowing for occasional scribal errors) is quite stunning. Most striking: the second three-measure phrase is virtually identical to the first, so that, with the repetition of the first part of the movement, the same phrase, with its constricted range and stiff rhythmic pattern (**3** ♩ | ♩| ♫♩. | ♪ ♪.) is presented four times in immediate succession. Moreover, the rhythm continues, appearing for its fifth time in succession immediately after the double bar, and will return once again (in mm. 13–15). In addition, the number of voices of the movement wavers inconsistently between two and three; the harmonic direction of the second phrase of the second part (mm. 10–12) veers unstably from D minor to F major and back to D minor; and the momentary shift to C major in the following phrase (mm. 14–15) is both too sudden and too brief, while its cadence (m. 15) is both rhythmically dead and harmonically empty. Only the final phrase of the movement, an expansive and expressive descent through the

Example 1.3. Mozart, Minuet in G, K. 1 (1e)

octave (with flatted seventh), using a modestly varied form of the prevailing rhythmic pattern, offers any redeeming interest.

Whether this composition is the effort of a twenty- or even fifteen-year-old Johann Sebastian Bach, its level of basic craftsmanship does not compare favorably with the compositional skill, much less the sophistication and elegance, displayed in the eight-year-old Mozart's well-known Minuet in G, K. 1 (ex. 1.3).[56]

One delights here in the frank euphony and admires the unity created by the pervasive sounding of melodic and harmonic thirds, sixths, and tenths, a compositional program announced in the first two measures and maintained throughout with remarkable consistency. (One is reminded of Nannerl Mozart's comment about her brother as a three-year-old, recorded in her reminiscences: "He often spent much time at the clavier, picking out thirds, which he was always striking, and his pleasure showed that it sounded good.")[57] The characteristic upbeat pattern and the use of sequential repetition as the primary means of continuation further enhance the composition's unity, while the expressive, poignant, already altogether Mozartean chromatic inflections that steer the brief turn to the minor at the beginning of the second part, along with the clever metrical shifts between triple and duple that propel the approach to the cadence in both parts of this miniature gem (and that avoid the rhythmic monotony of Bach's minuet), provide the necessary variety and contrast.

But there is no need to belabor this invidious comparison. No one has ever claimed, after all, that Bach was a child (or even adolescent) prodigy. Moreover, one could more than counter Mozart's advantage in the sphere of the youthful keyboard minuet by comparing his attempt (as an adult) at a keyboard fugue in the style of J. S. Bach (the Fugue in C Major, K. 394/383a) with its model (the C-Major Fugue from *The Well-Tempered Clavier* I, BWV 846/2).[58]

Substantially more significant than the primitive quality of an obscure work by the adolescent composer is the occasionally problematic nature of much of Bach's writing for solo voice—specifically, many of the Italianate arias in operatic style such as predominate in the cantatas of the early Leipzig period. There is no disputing that Bach composed the greatest Lutheran church cantatas in history. Nonetheless, they still form, all in all (and despite the undeniable presence of numerous outstanding masterpieces among them), perhaps the least "inspired" corner of his oeuvre. Part of the explanation for their uneven quality is really an obvious and valid excuse: they were written under the unimaginable time pressures of the weekly rate of composition—a severe strain, we can be sure, on the inspiration and imaginative powers of even a Johann Sebastian Bach. But there is more to it. Bach's early training was as a choirboy, brought up on motets and hymns. And this fact partly accounts for why, generally speaking, his vocal writing is at its best in choruses and chorale settings and less effective in solo arias. In his choral music Bach was not only working within traditions he thoroughly understood and revered, they were traditions particularly congenial to his skills and imagination as a contrapuntist, premised as they largely were on the techniques of imitative polyphony and cantus firmus setting.

In writing music—at least "modern" music—for solo voice, Bach was at a disadvantage. Unlike Handel, he never went to Italy in his youth nor was he otherwise extensively exposed early on to the operatic conventions that were about to be imported into German church music. That is, he lacked early firsthand experience of the kind that would have enabled him to develop an intuitive grasp of the differences between, say, instrumental and vocal coloratura, or instrumental and vocal bel canto. It is notable that Bach's most memorable, "singable" melodies were instrumentally conceived: the thrice-familiar Air from the Orchestral Suite, BWV 1068, and the slow movement of the F-Minor Harpsichord Concerto, BWV 1056. Even in pieces such as "Schafe können sicher weiden" (Sheep may safely graze) from the "Hunt Cantata," *Was mir behagt, ist nur die muntre Jagd*, BWV 208, the memorable melody is the instrumental obbligato, while the lovely, unpretentious, vocal line, for its part, resembles nothing so much as a chorale cantus firmus (ex. 1.4).[59]

Finally, because Bach was by predisposition an instrumental composer, like Haydn and Beethoven (as opposed to Handel and Mozart), his natural inclination (to oversimplify) was to generate compositions out of a single governing idea: a motif or a ritornello theme. In an aria, as in an instrumental composition, the motif or theme itself normally is not repeated literally very much: its constituent elements are disconnected and recombined, and it is altered harmonically, intervallically, or texturally according to the processes of sequential and motivic development. In an aria, however, the governing idea is connected to words or phrases that cannot be

Example 1.4. "Schafe können sicher weiden," from *Was mir behagt, ist nur die muntre Jagd*, BWV 208/9, mm. 1–15a similarly modified or transformed but only repeated verbatim numerous times. Such a procedure can become—problematic.

From the purely aesthetic point of view—discounting for the moment its theological dimension—we must also consider the ramifications of the fact that Bach's religious music is "monothematic." The theme, of course, is the Christian theme: theologically rich, powerful, maybe even inexhaustible, but in the end, perhaps, too limited in its range of affective situations, and offering a similarly limited number of compositional situations. At all events, Bach evidently thought he had exhausted them after fewer than six years in Leipzig, and, with more than twenty years of his life remaining, he largely abandoned the composition of German church music by the spring of 1729. Instrumental music, in contrast, offered him a stylistic and affective range for exploration limited only by his imagination, that is, really not at all.

The astute reader will have long since realized that the subtitle of this chapter is meant provocatively. The central lesson, after all, is that the time has finally come to bring Bach biography and Bach criticism into the twentieth century—not to mention the twenty-first.[60] The interpretive and critical approach to biography advocated and tested here is neither bold nor new; in fact, as reported early on, it has been applied for some fifty years now, with varying success, to several major composers and creative artists. The reasons that, until quite recently, it had never been attempted on an extensive scale in the case of Johann Sebastian Bach were also suggested earlier: they are mainly to be found, again, in the paucity of personally revealing primary documents and in the composer's iconic stature. There may even be a reluctance to appear to be attempting to topple the great man from his pedestal by investigating ("exposing") his temper, his taste in humor, his obsessions, his resentments, his human frailties—in brief, his humanity. Needless to say, there is no need to fear such a thing. Bach's exalted position upon that metaphorical pedestal, thanks to the unchallenged, almost incomprehensible magnitude of his achievement, is unassailable. The hope here, rather, is that the figure atop the pedestal be formed out of something less like marble and more like flesh and blood.

Chapter Two

The Notebooks for Wilhelm Friedemann and Anna Magdalena Bach

Some Biographical Lessons

With the exception of William Shakespeare we probably know less about the private life of Johann Sebastian Bach than we do about that of any of the other supreme artistic figures of modern history. As reported in chapter 1, the extant documents bearing on his life are almost invariably "official" in character. But, although no letters from Bach to any members of his immediate family have survived, one letter addressed to his childhood friend, Georg Erdmann, does touch, if ever so briefly, on his private situation. It is dated October 28, 1730. It is, typically, essentially a business letter in which Bach expresses his interest in leaving Leipzig and asks his friend to see what he could do. Quite untypically, Bach appends a concluding paragraph, much in the manner of a postscript, or at least a reluctant afterthought, in which he notes:

> Now I must [*Nunmehro muß doch*] add a little about my domestic situation [*meinem häußlichen Zustande*]. I am married for the second time, my first wife having died in Cöthen. From the first marriage I have three sons and one daughter living. . . . From the second marriage I have one son and two daughters living. . . . The children of my second marriage are still small. . . . But they are all born musicians, and I can assure you that I can already form an ensemble both *vocaliter* and *instrumentaliter* within my family, particularly since my present wife sings a good, clear soprano [*zumahln da meine itzige Frau gar einen sauberen Soprano singet*], and my eldest daughter, too, joins in not badly. I shall almost transgress the bounds of courtesy if I burden Your Honor

any further, and I therefore hasten to close remaining . . . Your Honor's most obedient and devoted servant Joh. Seb. Bach.[1]

Ten years before Bach wrote this letter, his first wife (and cousin), Maria Barbara, had died suddenly in July 1720, after less than thirteen years of marriage, at the age of thirty-five. Less than a year and a half later, on December 3, 1721, Bach, the widowed father of four young children, married Anna Magdalena Wilcke, then twenty years old. We should not be surprised to notice that while Bach may have failed to mention to Erdmann the names of any of the members of his family, he did not fail to mention that his second wife was musical and even to offer a brief, if modest, assessment of the nature of her talent. Anna Magdalena Bach, however, was not merely musical; she was herself a professional musician. She was, in fact, Bach's colleague at Köthen, where she was employed as "Singer to His Highness the Prince" and as a "Chamber Musician" (i.e., an instrumentalist) as well. And, like Bach, she came from a family of musicians. Her uncle was an organist; her father, Johann Caspar Wilcke (or Wülcken), was "Court and Field Trumpeter of Music of His Highness the Prince of Saxe-Weissenfels." Anna Magdalena Wilcke was born in the small Thuringian city of Zeitz on September 22, 1701, but moved with her family around 1718 to Weissenfels, a court famous for the vitality of its musical life. From 1716 on it supported, among other institutions, a vocal ensemble for young girls (probably the first of its kind in Germany), and it is likely that Anna Magdalena received her musical training there as well as from her father.[2]

Bach had close ties with Weissenfels. His earliest surviving secular cantata, *Was mir behagt*, the "Hunt Cantata," BWV 208, was composed for the birthday of the duke of Weissenfels in 1713. Later Bach bore the title of "Honorary Kapellmeister" (*Kapellmeister von Haus aus*) to the court of Saxe-Weissenfels. He almost certainly made the acquaintance of the Wilcke family there; and it is likely that Bach himself, in his capacity as Kapellmeister at Köthen—a post he held from 1717—was instrumental in recruiting Anna Magdalena for the Köthen musical establishment.[3]

Anna Magdalena Bach, then, was a musician; and it is perhaps not insignificant that she is accorded an entry of her own in Ernst Ludwig Gerber's *Historisch-Biographisches Lexicon der Tonkünstler*. She is described there (in terms considerably more enthusiastic than Bach's) as an "outstanding soprano" (*eine vortrefliche* [*sic*] *Sopranistin*), who, however, "never made use of her excellent talent in public" (*ohne jemals öffentlich von diesem ihrem vortreflichem Talente Gebrauch gemacht zu haben*).[4] The last remark is obviously incorrect, since Anna Magdalena had been professionally employed. It may be, though, that she did not appear in public after her marriage. In any event, we have it on the authority of Bach himself, as we have just seen, that Anna Magdalena made use of her musical talent in the privacy of their home. Indeed, it is clear from the letter to Erdmann—from Bach's having mentioned just about nothing else in connection with his "domestic situation"—that the identity of his family as an intimate community of musicians held the greatest significance in the consciousness of the composer. In other words, music and music-making occupied a central position in Bach's private life and was at the core of his relationship with his wife and children.

Owing to the absence of any pertinent documents, we know nearly nothing for certain about the affective relationships among the members of Bach's immediate family.[5] We are fairly well informed, however, about the character of its domestic musical situation; for a few musical documents survive from the Bach household that shed light on this sphere of the composer's private life. These curious documents are the notebook that Bach prepared for his oldest son, Wilhelm Friedemann, and the two similar volumes belonging to his second wife, Anna Magdalena.

The three albums differ in their content, origin, and purpose; and, accordingly, each illuminates the musical private life of the Bach family rather differently. Bach began the *Clavier-Büchlein vor Wilhelm Friedemann Bach* on January 22, 1720, for his nine-year-old son. It was clearly conceived as a systematic, pedagogical keyboard method, beginning with an explanation of the clefs, the names of the notes, and the principles of keyboard fingering. We find here the famous *Explication* of the baroque ornaments; the volume goes on to offer a "gradus ad parnassum" of keyboard instruction. It includes the first versions of the Two- and Three-Part Inventions and Sinfonias, as well as eleven of the preludes of what was to be *The Well-Tempered Clavier* I, and it leads the pupil over the threshold of independent composition.[6] In short, Johann Sebastian Bach appears to us in the *Clavier-Büchlein* for Wilhelm Friedemann in the dual role of father and teacher.[7]

Sometime during the first year of his second marriage, Johann Sebastian Bach began to put together another *Clavier-Büchlein*, for Anna Magdalena. The title page, written in a highly ornate and stylized script (but presumably by Anna Magdalena), reads: *Clavier-Büchlein / vor / Anna Magdalena Bachin / ANNO 1722*. The volume, as it has survived, is a torso: two-thirds of it have apparently been lost or cut out. In its present state it contains only fifty pages, although the binding reveals that, like the *Clavier-Büchlein* for Wilhelm Friedemann and the later notebook for Magdalena, it originally contained about 150 pages.[8]

From the contents of the 1722 notebook we can observe that Anna Magdalena was not a beginner at the keyboard at the time of her marriage, but rather a quite competent player. And it is apparent that Sebastian intended the volume to serve not so much for his wife's instruction as for her pleasure. Moreover, it seems safe to conclude that the album reflects Anna Magdalena's particular, rather French, musical taste. Instead of Inventions and Sinfonias in imitative polyphony, the larger part of the 1722 notebook is taken up by the earliest draft of the first five French Suites, BWV 812–16. (As to the lost portions of the manuscript, it is clear that sixteen to twenty pages contained sections of the first three French Suites, which appear in the notebook in a fragmentary state. The remaining eighty-odd missing pages apparently were located between the *Air*, BWV 991, and the chorale prelude, BWV 728. Since they did not follow directly after the fifth French Suite, there is no compelling reason to assume the notebook contained the sixth French Suite, BWV 817, or any of the other suites often transmitted with the French Suites in early manuscript sources.)[9]

Anna Magdalena's second notebook is different yet again. In contrast to the earlier volume, it seems to be not so much for her as by her; it was presumably Anna Magdalena herself who, for the most part, decided on the contents and character of the volume.[10] The absence of a title page from the album can be taken as a hint to this effect. An inscription on the front cover of the original binding reads simply: *A. M. B. 1725*. It is true that this volume begins, as did the first one, with entries by Johann Sebastian. Again they are familiar compositions in suite form: the earliest versions of the keyboard partitas in A Minor and E Minor, BWV 827 and 830, later published as numbers 3 and 5 of "Part 1" of the *Klavierübung*. But thereafter the volume becomes a remarkable mélange. It is no longer exclusively a "little clavier book" but includes a number of vocal pieces: sacred and secular arias, chorales, even cantata movements. Furthermore, unlike the 1722 notebook, it is not devoted exclusively to the music of Johann Sebastian Bach. There are works by other composers, including the simple and popular keyboard miniatures: the *galant* minuets, polonaises, and marches that were the fashion in Germany in the 1720s and 1730s, which one no doubt thinks of first today in connection with the notebooks of Anna Magdalena Bach. Most of these pieces were entered into the notebook by Anna Magdalena herself, who surely not only wrote them down but also selected them.[11]

The large representation specifically of minuets and polonaises in Anna Magdalena's anthology is worthy of comment. She seems to be paying tribute to the two principal cultural poles exerting their attraction throughout Germany at this time: Paris and Dresden. In a real sense, the French minuet, with its historical associations with the Parisian court of Louis XIV, had its counterpart in the Polish polonaise, a favorite dance at the Dresden court of August the Strong.[12] The technical simplicity of these trifles (especially when contrasted with the suites and partitas entered into the notebooks by Johann Sebastian for Magdalena) suggests that, like the keyboard pieces in the notebook for Wilhelm Friedemann, they, too, were meant to serve an instructional purpose. But it is hard to believe that the pupil was Anna Magdalena. It seems more plausible that she was the teacher this time and that she used the pieces in giving keyboard lessons—perhaps dance lessons, too, as has been suggested[13]—to her children.

We may be reasonably certain, however, that the songs were included for Anna Magdalena's own pleasure. With one exception the melody line in all the vocal numbers is notated in the soprano clef;[14] but there is no reason that they should not be performed today by other voices. The text of a song such as the "Erbauliche Gedanken eines Tobacksrauchers" (Edifying Thoughts of a Tobacco Smoker), BWV 515, certainly suggests a male singer. The text of the first strophe reads:

So oft ich meine Tobacks-Pfeife,
Mit gutem Knaster angefüllt,

Zur Lust und Zeitvertreib ergreife,
So gibt sie mir ein Trauerbild—
Und füget diese Lehre bei,
Daß ich derselben ähnlich sei.

(Whene'er I take my pipe and stuff it
And smoke to pass the time away,
My thoughts, as I sit there and puff it,
Dwell on a picture sad and gray:
It teaches me that very like
Am I myself unto my pipe.)[15]

Moreover, Bach himself had no reservations about transposing arias from one vocal range to another. For example, the recitative "Ich habe genug" and aria "Schlummert ein" from Cantata no. 82, *lch habe genug*, originally a solo cantata for bass, appear in the 1725 notebook arranged for soprano and continuo.[16]

The first vocal piece in the notebook is the chorale Lied "Gib dich zufrieden," composed, and copied into the volume, by J. S. Bach. Bach notated the composition twice in succession: the first time, with text, in the key of G minor (BWV 511); the second time, without text and transposed to E minor (BWV 512). The transposition seems to have been made in order to avoid an exposed high b-flat^2 in the third measure before the end—a clue perhaps to the limits of Anna Magdalena's range. (All the other songs in the notebook keep within the range of c^1 to a-flat^2.) The "tobacco song," for its part, was copied into the notebook twice in succession as well. The first version was once surmised to be in the hand of Gottfried Heinrich Bach (1724–63), the first son (and second child) of Sebastian and Anna Magdalena. In fact, the copyist was Bach's one-time pupil, Bernhard Dietrich Ludewig (1707–40) and dates from circa 1735.[17] It is notated in the key of D minor (range a–c^2) and lacks the text. The second version, presumably entered shortly after the first version, includes the text of the first strophe under the soprano line and has been transposed up a fourth to G minor (range d^1–f^2)—this time, presumably, to avoid a low a. The copyists were Anna Magdalena and Johann Sebastian Bach working in collaboration: Anna Magdalena entered most of the soprano line; Sebastian composed a new version of the bass.[18]

It is tempting at this point to speculate whether any of Bach's eight surviving soprano cantatas—BWV 51, 52, 84, 199, 202, 204, 209, and 210/210a—could have been intended for Anna Magdalena, using the c^1-a-flat^2 (b-flat^2) vocal range of the notebook as a provisional indicator. Although BWV 52 (range: d-flat^1–a^2), 84 (d^1–a^2), and BWV 199 (c^1–a-flat^2) all keep within this range, it is altogether unlikely that Anna Magdalena, as a woman, would have participated in performances of regular *de tempore* church cantatas. BWV 51 can be similarly discounted—especially in view of the vocal range extending to c^3. The occasion for which BWV 204, *Ich bin in mir vergnügt*, was composed (ca. 1726/27) is unknown. Its range—c^1-b-flat^2—could perhaps have been negotiated by Anna Magdalena. She presumably would have had no great difficulty with the d^1–a^2 range of BWV 209, *Non sa che sia dolore*, a work traditionally thought to have been composed (if by Bach at all) about 1729 but likely considerably later.[19] Of the two wedding cantatas, BWV 202 and 210/210a, the $c\#^1$–$c\#^3$ range of the latter clearly exceeds Anna Magdalena's limits as implied by the notebook. It is easy to imagine, though, that *Weichet nur, betrübte Schatten*, BWV 202, was written for her. The range (d^1–a^2), the occasion (a wedding, i.e., a domestic function), and its presumed origin in the Köthen period during Anna Magdalena's years of professional activity, all argue for her.[20]

Although none of the miniatures copied into the notebook by Anna Magdalena carries an attribution, several have been positively identified. Most notably, the Minuets in G Major and G Minor, BWV Anh. 114 and 115, among the most popular and well-known pieces in the collection, are now known to be from a *Suite de Clavecin* in G by Christian Pezold (1677–1733), court organist at Dresden (ex. 2.1).[21] (Similarly, the Polonaise in G, BWV Anh. 130, is part of a keyboard sonata by the leading exponent of the *galant* style in Germany, Johann Adolf Hasse.)[22]

Among the unattributed items copied into the notebook by Anna Magdalena is the theme of the Goldberg Variations, the "Aria."[23] Frederick Neumann has argued that this theme could not have been composed by Johann Sebastian Bach. He cites the theme's "un-Bachian flavor, the flimsiness of its substance, the shallowness of its melodic content," its "certainly un-Bachian" ornamentation treatment, and, finally, the fact that it was entered by Anna Magdalena into the 1725 notebook "untitled and unattributed . . . and in the company of several single works by other composers."[24] In Neumann's view, the original author must have been an as yet unidentified Frenchman. As we have just seen, though, Anna Magdalena was frustratingly casual about attributions. It is therefore no surprise that she failed to provide either title or attribution for the "Goldberg" aria any more than she did for the vast majority of pieces in the notebook, including pieces by her husband, such as the indisputably authentic C-Major Prelude from *The Well-Tempered Clavier* I and the recitative and aria from Cantata 82.

There is in fact a strong indication that the melody was composed—in the latest French style (why not!)—by Bach. Bach himself rarely failed to supply attributions when copying works by other composers or, indeed, even when borrowing themes for variation and elaboration. The "Menuet fait par Mons. Böhm," for example, is the only work by another composer copied into the Anna Magdalena notebooks by J. S. Bach. Unlike his wife, Sebastian named the composer.[25] And the best surviving sources of Bach's fugues, variations, sonatas, and concertos based on themes and compositions by Albinoni, Corelli, Legrenzi, Reinken, and "Vivaldi" as a rule prominently mention the composer (or presumed composer) of the borrowed material in the heading or on the title page.[26] In light of this, is it at all credible that Bach would have failed to provide the name of the composer of the "Goldberg" aria when he submitted his colossal set of variations for publication, if it had been anyone other than himself?

Example 2.1a, Christian Pezold, *Suite de Clavecin* in G, Minuet, BWV Anh. 114

Example 2.1b. Christian Pezold, *Suite de Clavecin* in G Minor, Minuet, BWV Anh. 115

The 1725 notebook is not only a personal compilation of Anna Magdalena's (favorite?) pieces by her husband and his modish contemporaries. As is well-known, it served also as a "family album," containing pieces copied and sometimes composed by three of the Bach sons over a period of about ten to fifteen years, extending from the early 1730s—with entries by C. P. E. Bach—to the early and mid-1740s—with entries by Johann Christoph Friedrich and Johann Christian Bach, the two youngest sons of Sebastian and Magdalena. By the time Philipp Emanuel makes his appearance in the notebook (between 1730 and 1734) with his first known compositions—two pairs of marches and polonaises in alternation, BWV Anh. 122–25 (= Helm 1), including the popular *Marche* in D Major, BWV Anh. 122—he had already achieved a respectable level of competence as a budding *galant* composer. Another composition of his (entered into the notebook ca. 1733/34 by Anna Magdalena)—a *Solo per il Cembalo*, BWV Anh. 129—later served, in a revised version, as the opening Allegro of a three-movement Sonata in E-flat, Wq 65/7 (H 16).

As for the contributions of the two youngest Bach sons: Johann Christian's entry, BWV Anh. 131—dating from around 1745 at the earliest (Christian having been born in 1735)—is nothing more than a heavily corrected exercise consisting of the outer voices of a song in binary form, while Johann Christoph Friedrich's is a fragmentary set of thorough-bass rules copied sometime during the early 1740s.[27] Christoph Friedrich's entry appears on the overleaf of a curious item entered by Anna Magdalena herself, circa 1733/34. It is a wedding poem—of rather dubious taste—beginning "Ihr Diener, werte Jungfer Braut" (Your servant, worthy maiden bride), and adorned with *double entendres*.[28] The poem itself is a most peculiar postscript following directly on Anna Magdalena's last musical entry in the notebook—one that she had decided would occupy this position early on in the history of the volume[29]—a melody/bass setting of the traditional Death and Resurrection chorale, *O Ewigkeit, du Donnerwort*, BWV 513.

The historical value of the notebooks for Wilhelm Friedemann and Anna Magdalena Bach can hardly be exaggerated. They bear witness, first of all, to the origins and later compositional histories of works as significant as the French Suites, the Partitas, and *The Well-Tempered Clavier*. Moreover, as family albums, indeed, these miniature volumes come as close as anything to providing a family chronicle documenting over a quarter century, from 1720 on, the earliest musical training and the compositional debuts of the most talented of the Bach sons and tracing the development of their musical handwriting (along with that of their mother) as central members of the Bach circle of copyists. Finally, they constitute a remarkable family "portrait" of sorts—even a mirror, particularly of Anna Magdalena (and in this respect compensating in part perhaps for the loss of the oil painting once in Philipp Emanuel's possession)—revealing her abilities as a singer and a keyboard player, and reflecting her own eminently personal musical (and literary?) predilections.

Chapter Three

Bach and Luther

I

In the year 1708, that is, at the age of twenty-three, young Johann Sebastian Bach resigned his respected post as organist of the Blasiuskirche in the imperial free city of Mühlhausen. He announced, among other things—as we have seen—that his "ultimate goal" was to perform what he described as "a well-regulated church music" (*ich stets den Endzweck, nemlich eine regulirte kirchen music . . . gerne aufführen mögen*).[1] But it is not altogether clear exactly what the composer had in mind. The translation in NBR (p. 57) reads: "I should always have liked to work toward the goal, namely, a well-regulated church music to the Glory of God." It thus avoids translating the operative German verb "aufführen." Usually rendered in English as "to perform," it also can mean "to present" or "produce." One would like to think that for the formidably gifted Johann Sebastian Bach it also implied "to create"—that is, to compose, and not just to perform. Regarding the term "regulirt": Ulrich Siegele argues that by "regular church music" (*regulirte kirchen music*), Bach was not thinking of regular—that is, weekly (or monthly)—performances of church cantatas (as easily assumed), but rather of performances delivered by "regular," essentially professional, musicians—hence his use of a term commonly associated with a "regular" (i.e., professional) army.[2] Bach's letter continues, "and therefore [I] have acquired . . . not without cost, a good store of the choicest church compositions" (*und darümb . . . nicht sonder kosten, einen guthen* apparat *der auserleßensten kirchen Stücken mir angeschaffet*). The reference to having "therefore" (*darümb*) "purchased" ("acquired") (*angeschaffet*) "the choicest church compositions" (no doubt works composed by others) strongly suggests that his *Endzweck* at this early point in his career may, after all, have primarily entailed providing first-rate performances of first-rate music with a professional-level ensemble of church musicians.[3]

As it turned out, his first ambitious contribution to church music (broadly defined) upon leaving his Mühlhausen post was the composition of what he called an *Orgelbüchlein*—a little organ book—actually an extensive series of miniature, but highly sophisticated and expressive organ chorales, whose contents were to include chorale preludes for the principal feasts of the church year, a series of chorales on the articles of the catechism, and, finally, a collection of miscellaneous hymns for a large variety of occasions and circumstances.

It is now thought that work on the *Orgelbüchlein* had commenced much earlier than had hitherto been assumed—virtually as soon as Bach had taken up his new duties as court organist at Weimar.[4] But even though Bach continued to work on it over the course of the next two decades, the project was left unfinished. Of the 164 chorales originally planned only 46 were ever completed. But it is worth noting that of these 46 no fewer than 28—well over half—are Reformation-era chorales, 12 of them by Martin Luther himself. Had the *Orgelbüchlein* been completed, it would have contained 30 of the 36 chorales ascribed to the Reformer.

Indeed, it is hardly possible to overstate the importance of the Lutheran congregational chorale in the music of J. S. Bach. Of the approximately 1,130 compositions attributed to Bach, 450 (or more than one in three) are chorale settings, ranging from simple four-part harmonizations to chorale preludes, variations, partitas, and fantasias for the organ to chorale motets and cantatas for voices and instrumental ensemble. Moreover, a disproportionately large number of these compositions are not only based on Lutheran chorales but literally on the chorales of Martin Luther himself and other poets of his generation. The dominant position occupied by the chorales of Martin Luther and his contemporaries—in comparison to those composed later in the sixteenth century, or those from the Baroque and Pietist periods— is dramatically evident in every category of Bach's oeuvre.

While the chorale preludes of the *Orgelbüchlein* were to be miniature in scale— each one only a page or two in length—in Bach's other collections of organ chorales the individual compositions frequently assumed breathtaking dimensions. The Eighteen "Great" (i.e., large-scale) Organ Chorales (BWV 651–68) were also begun in Weimar, perhaps at about the same time as the *Orgelbüchlein*, but these were revised (though again never quite completed) late in Bach's life.[5] They may well have been deliberately conceived as providing a contrasting counterpart to the miniature format of the *Orgelbüchlein* chorales, representing, as it were, the epic as opposed to the lyric modes of chorale composition—or perhaps they were regarded as an analogue to the smaller and larger catechisms of Martin Luther.

Although the rationale of the design of the collection of the "great" chorales, taken as a whole, is not altogether clear, it is clear that the chorales of Martin Luther quite literally occupy pride of place.[6] Disregarding the problematic eighteenth chorale, the group is framed by Luther's *Komm, Heiliger Geist, Herre Gott* (Come, Holy Spirit, Lord God), BWV 651, at the beginning and, at the end, by his *Komm Gott Schöpfer, Heiliger Geist* (Come, God, Creator, Holy Spirit), BWV 667. The midpoint is marked by an elaborate setting of yet another of Luther's invitatory chorales, addressed this time to the second person of the Trinity: *Nun komm, der Heiden Heiland* (Now come, Savior of the heathens), BWV 659. The opening measures of the opening composition, *Komm, Heiliger Geist* evoke at once the sense of monumentality and grandeur that Bach was striving for in this collection (ex. 3.1).

Example 3.1. *Komm, Heiliger Geist, Herre Gott*, BWV 651, mm. 1–14a

Example 3.1.—(concluded)

Monumentality is also the hallmark of Bach's mammoth collection of keyboard music, the *Klavierübung* (Keyboard practice), the four volumes (or "Parts") of which were published over a period of fifteen years during Bach's Leipzig period. Only the third "Part" of the *Klavierübung*, BWV 669–89, is devoted to sacred keyboard music. It consists of twenty-one organ chorales: nine chorales constituting the Lutheran *Missa brevis* (Kyrie and Gloria), and twelve settings of catechism chorales. This time, the reference to Luther's large and small catechisms is overt: there are two settings, one large and one small, for each of the six catechism chorales. It may be more than mere coincidence that "Part 3" of the *Klavierübung*, with its collection of liturgical chorales for the organ, was published in the year 1739, the year of the bicentennial celebration of the adoption of the Augsburg Confession in Leipzig.

Bach's last great contribution to the literature of the organ chorale, the *Canonic Variations on Vom Himmel hoch da komm ich her* (From heaven on high I come here), BWV 769, published in 1747 or 1748, has as its substance what the author of the text, Martin Luther, described as a "children's song for Christmas Eve" (fig. 3.1).

Bach's treatment of the venerable and beloved children's song, however, is not child's play. As its title suggests, the *Canonic Variations* are a compositional *tour de force*, a display of the most rigorous techniques of strict canon. It is known that they were composed, and published, as part of Bach's initiation into Lorenz Christoph Mizler's honorary Society of Musical Sciences (ex. 3.2).

Nonetheless, the work could have been conceived as a companion work to the other *magnum opus* of contrapuntal craft with which the composer was occupied at just this time in the final years of his life: the *Art of Fugue* (*Kunst der Fuge*), BWV 1080. The two publications, taken together, not only reflect the two general spheres, into one or the other of which all music necessarily belongs—either the sacred or secular—they also represent the two fundamental principles of musical invention as they were inherited and described by musical theorists and commentators from time

Figure 3.1. Martin Luther, *Vom Himmel hoch*, chorale (with heading as it appears in *Das Babstsche Gesangbuch* 1545)

immemorial: the *Art of Fugue* manifesting the principle, or the genre, of "free" composition, that is, works making use of original, freely invented thematic material; the *Canonic Variations on Vom Himmel hoch*, on the other hand, belonging to the age-old tradition of the "bound" composition: works based on a pre-existent melody.

ȋ ȋ ȋ

In turning to Bach's vocal music we encounter, once again, the dominating presence of the Great Reformer. First of all, two of Martin Luther's most revered chorale texts serve—once again—as a frame: this time for Bach's life work as a church composer. Bach's earliest known chorale-based cantata is the Easter composition, *Christ lag in Todesbanden* (Christ Lay in the Bonds of Death), BWV 4, presumably composed

Example 3.2. Canonic Variations on *Vom Himmel hoch*, Variation 1, BWV 769/1, mm. 1–6

during Bach's year at Mühlhausen, 1707/8. At the other end of the composer's life, the cantata on *Ein feste Burg ist unser Gott* (A Mighty Fortress Is Our God), BWV 80, was put into its final form (after numerous revisions) sometime between 1744 and 1747, and was very possibly Bach's last German church cantata altogether.

But the period of Bach's most concentrated involvement with the chorale in the context of cantata composition falls almost exactly in the middle of his career. The beginning of that involvement, in fact, can be dated precisely: to the first Sunday after Trinity, June 11, 1724, when the composer began his second full year as Kantor of the Thomaskirche and "Director of Church Music for the City of Leipzig." On that day Bach launched a series of weekly cantatas with *O Ewigkeit, du Donnerwort*, BWV 20, a setting of a hymn by Johann Rist (1607–67). All of the cantatas for the remainder of the church year were to be based on the congregational chorale appropriate for the particular Sunday or feast day. It is tempting to think that the decision to inaugurate such an ambitious cycle of chorale cantatas specifically during

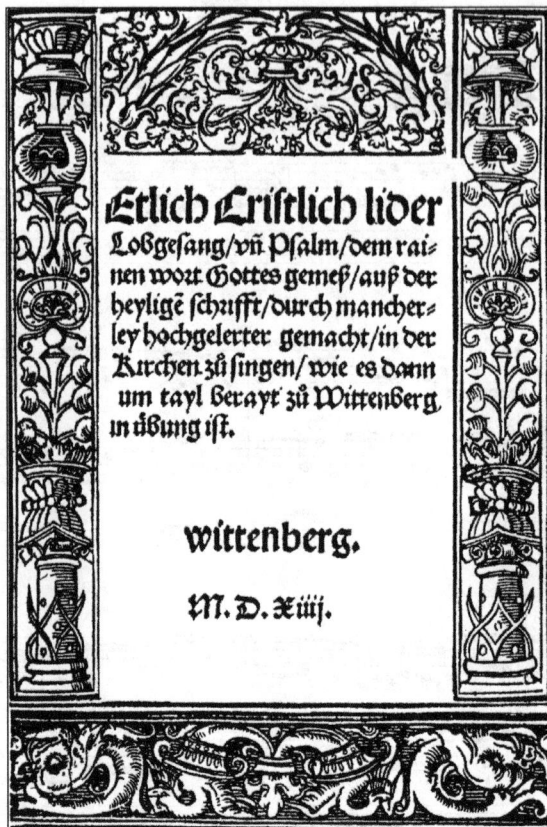

Figure 3.2a. Title page of *Etlich Cristlich lider* ("Achtliederbuch"), "Wittenberg" (recte: Nuremberg), 1524

the year 1724–25 may have been informed by a desire to commemorate the two-hundredth anniversary of the first Lutheran hymnbook publications: the so-called *Achtliederbuch* (Book of Eight Hymns—the very first Lutheran hymnbook); the two Erfurt *Enchiridia*; and the *Geistliches Gesangk Buchleyn* (Little Spiritual Songbook), all of which appeared in the year 1524 (fig. 3.2a–b).

Over the course of the next nine months Bach composed or performed at least forty-four such "chorale" (or "chorale-paraphrase") cantatas, concluding the series on Easter Sunday, 1725, with a performance of a revised version of his early masterpiece, *Christ lag in Todesbanden*. Virtually all the cantatas, however, were newly composed—and composed at the astonishing rate of at least one per week. Not surprisingly, in this repertoire, too, the hymns of the Reformation generation occupy the same pre-eminent position as they do in Bach's organ works. Over a third of the cantatas of the 1724/25 cycle are set to texts of Luther and his contemporaries.

ʃＥyn Ｅnchiridion oder Ｈandbüchlein. cynem ytz
lichen Christen faʃt nutzlich bey ʃich
zuhaben/zur ʃtetter vbung vnd
trachtung geyʃtlicher geʃenge
vnd Pʃalmen/Recht
ʃchaffen vnd kunʃt
lich verteutʃcht.

Ｍ. ＣＣＣＣＣ. xxiiij

ＣＡm ende diʃes Büchleins wirʃt
du fynden eyn Regiʃter/yn wil
chem klerlich angezeigt iʃt/ was
vnd wie vill Geʃenge hieryn be
gryffen ʃynd.

Ｍit dyʃen vnd der gleichen Geʃenge ʃoltt man bil
byllich die yungen yugendt aufferzihen.

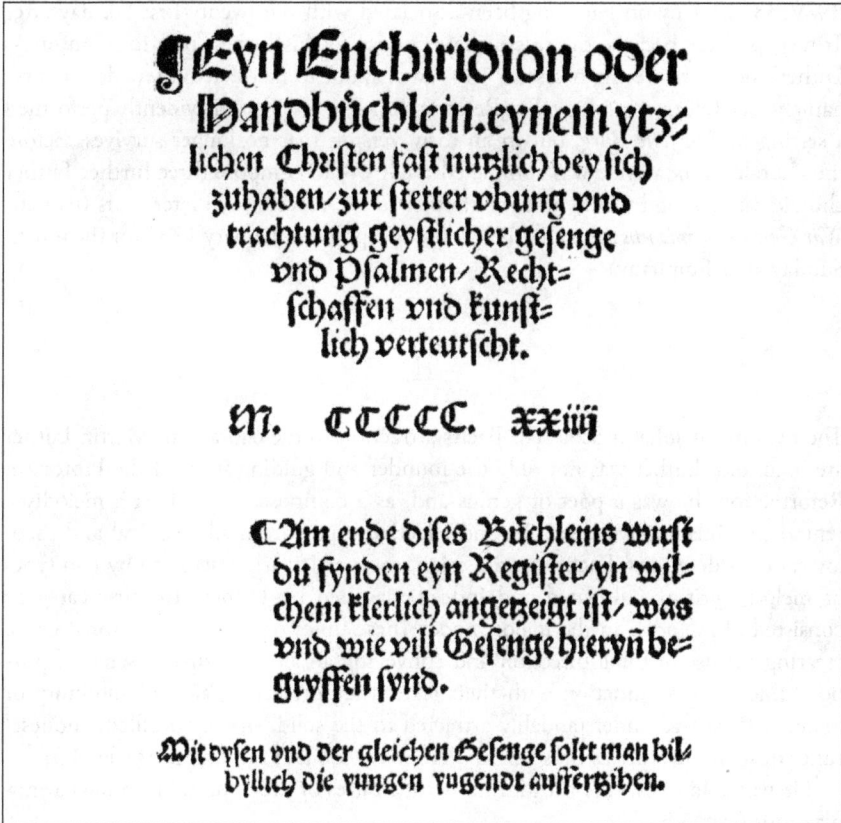

Figure 3.2b. Title page of *Eyn Enchiridion oder Handbüchlein* ("Ferberfaß Enchiridion"), Erfurt, 1524

And, once again, Martin Luther's own hymns stand out not only numerically but also by virtue of their placement in the cantata cycle. Although the series began with a setting of a hymn by a seventeenth-century poet, almost all the auspicious and high feasts of Bach's chorale cantata cycle were celebrated with compositions based on the hymns of Martin Luther. For the first Sunday of Advent, the official beginning of the church year, Bach composed a new cantata on Luther's *Nun komm, der Heiden Heiland*, BWV 62, traditionally the principal hymn for that day. (Bach had already composed a cantata on *Nun komm*, BWV 61, ten years earlier, during his Weimar period.) Luther's chorales were also chosen for the first two days of Christmas.

Bach turned to Luther again for the cantata intended for performance on the twenty-first Sunday after Trinity. In the year 1724 that Sunday fell on October 29, thus making it the last Sunday before Reformation Day. The chorale Bach chose to set on this occasion was *Aus tiefer Not schrei ich zu dir* (In deep need I cry to Thee),

BWV 38. That hymn had long been associated with the twenty-first Sunday after Trinity, perhaps because the reassuring response to this earnest plea for comfort—Luther's poetic rendering of Psalm 130—was about to be offered a few days hence, namely, on Reformation Day. For Reformation Day itself Bach evidently performed a setting of *Ein feste Burg*, but in an early version that no longer survives. Before the chorale cantata cycle was completed Bach would compose three further Luther chorale cantatas and would add yet another to the repertoire in later years (namely, *Wär Gott nicht mit uns diese Zeit*, BWV 14, composed in January 1735 for the fourth Sunday after Epiphany).

II

The reasons for Johann Sebastian Bach's attraction to the chorales of Martin Luther are manifold. Luther was not only the founder and guiding spirit of the Protestant Reformation, he was a poet of genius and, as a composer (or at least a melodist), remarkably imaginative, versatile, and effective. Apart from all liturgical and theological considerations, Bach, as a musician, was particularly fascinated by two types of melody writing cultivated and indeed mastered by Luther. The first category consisted of melodies in the major mode. These tunes proceed to clear tonal goals, creating a sense of tonal direction and conveying an almost palpable sense of purposefulness. In conjunction with their texts, they project an aura of sublimity or majesty. Bach was understandably attracted to the solid, sharply profiled, "honest" tunes of such melodies as those of *Vom Himmel hoch* and *Ein feste Burg* (fig. 3.3).

He was able to capture the affirmative attributes of these tunes in simple harmonizations (exx. 3.3a, b).]

But they also inspired him to displays of contrapuntal artifice that clothe the folk-like tunes in something resembling the musical equivalent of the mantle of royalty, while they also represent a devoted and devout musician's labor of homage. Perhaps, too, such grandiose designs were conceived as a reflection, or symbol, of the miraculous intricacy and order of God's universe.

Consider the opening of Bach's last church cantata, the final version of *Ein feste Burg*. Dating from the last decade of his life—the same period during which the composer produced a series of increasingly elaborate explorations of the complexities of canon and counterpoint, the Goldberg Variations, the *Musical Offering*, the *Art of Fugue*, the *Canonic Variations* on *Vom Himmel hoch*—the opening chorus of Bach's Reformation cantata is, technically considered, his most complex chorale chorus but also his most exhilarating. Without any instrumental introduction, the voices of the chorus enter at once singing the chorale text to melodic lines obviously derived from Luther's tune in busy fugal imitation until the unembellished chorale melody itself, the *cantus firmus*, sounds from on high, in long notes, by the instrumental forces

Figure 3.3. Martin Luther, original melody for *Ein feste Burg* (with heading as it appears in *Das Babstsche Gesangbuch* 1545)

Example 3.3a. *Ein feste Burg*, BWV 80/8 (final movement)

Example 3.3b. *Ein feste Burg*, BWV 303

(three oboes in unison),[7] and is then thunderously answered, in strict canon, three octaves lower, by the instrumental basses and organ. The sense of heaven and earth opening wide and resounding with the glory of God has never been more vividly evoked (ex. 3.4).

But Martin Luther was also gifted at creating melodies that occupied the opposite end of the stylistic and expressive spectrum from that represented by *Ein feste Burg* and *Vom Himmel hoch*—and Bach was just as attracted to them. Consider such

Example 3.4a. *Ein feste Burg*, BWV 80/1, mm. 1–6a

melodies as *Aus tiefer Not schrei ich zu dir* or *Ach Gott vom Himmel sieh darein* (fig. 3.4a, b).

Quite unlike the modern-sounding, major-mode melodies described above, those of *Aus tiefer Not* and *Ach Gott vom Himmel* sound archaic, indeed exotic, even alien. They belong to the medieval church modes (obsolete even in Bach's time): in particular the Phrygian mode, in which the second scale degree is only a half step above the tonic pitch. When such melodies, like Luther's, are well crafted—with sharply delineated contours and sensitive placement of the characteristic steps and intervals of the mode—they can be both memorable and deeply expressive.

The archaic idiom of hymn melodies of this sort frequently inspired Bach to adopt a self-consciously archaic compositional style when setting them as cantata movements or even as organ chorales. A case in point is the opening chorus of *Aus tiefer Not schrei ich zu dir*, BWV 38, which dispenses almost entirely with the

Example 3.4b. *Ein feste Burg*, BWV 80/1, mm. 11–14

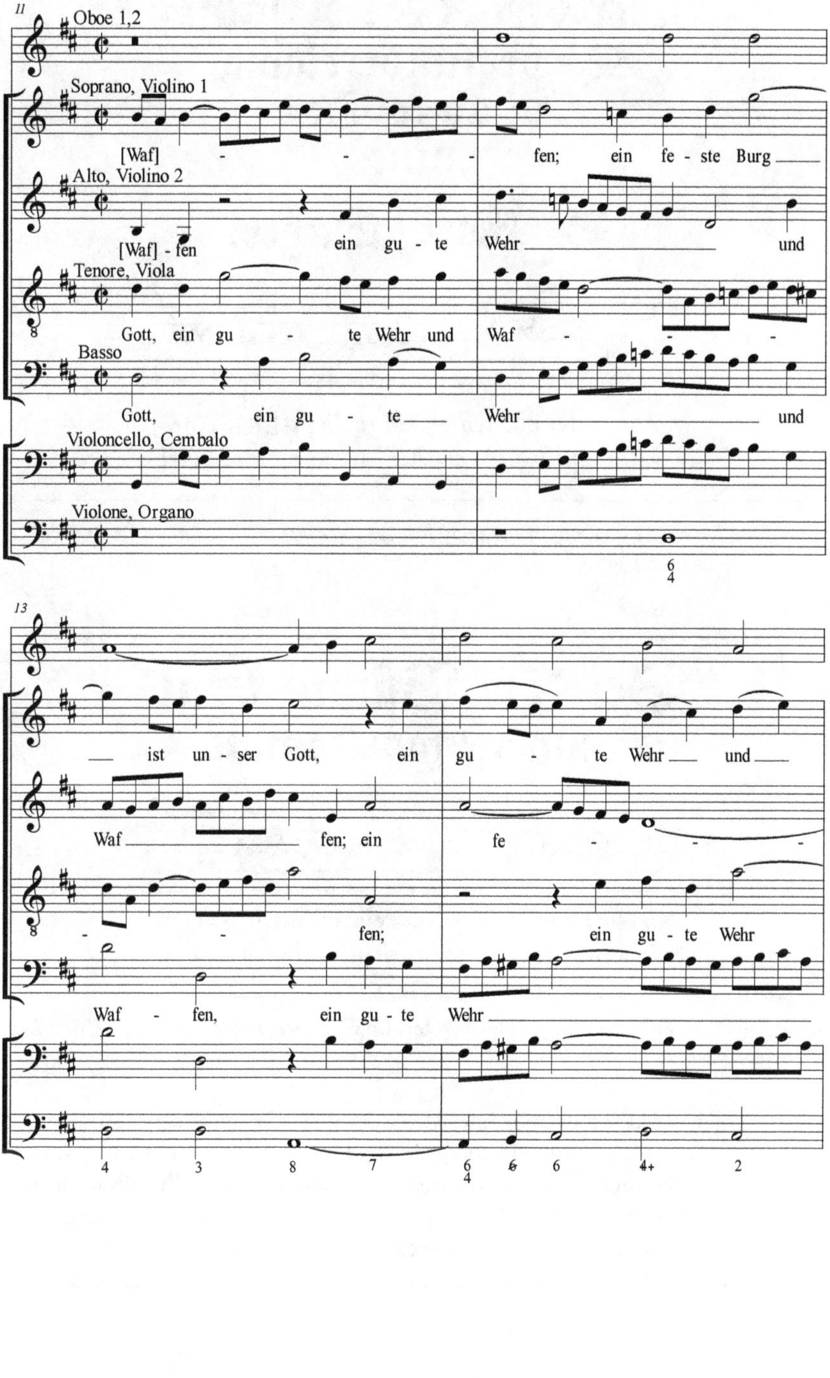

Figure 3.4a. Martin Luther, original melody for *Aus tiefer Not schrei ich zu dir* (from *Das Babstsche Gesangbuch* 1545)

Figure 3.4b. Martin Luther, original melody for *Ach Gott vom Himmel sieh darein* (from *Das Babstsche Gesangbuch* 1545)

brilliant color palette and lively motivic activity of the independent instrumental ensemble, as well as with the energetic rhythms and clarity of form—elements imported from the contemporaneous Italian concerto—that typically inform the style of Bach's cantata choruses (ex. 3.5). The result is a compositional idiom reminiscent of Renaissance polyphony, specifically associated with the sixteenth-century motet—a style of composition that would have been thoroughly familiar to Martin Luther.[8]

Example 3.5. *Aus tiefer Not*, BWV 38/1, mm. 1–19

III

Bach's stature as the greatest composer of the Lutheran church has long since been beyond debate. Indeed, it is not infrequently suggested that, next to Luther himself, Bach may well be the most important Lutheran in history. Even so, it is quite possible that we might, if anything, actually be underestimating the importance of Martin Luther in the life and artistic development of Johann Sebastian Bach.

Some years ago the literary critic Harold Bloom developed a provocative theory of poetic influence, which he published under the title *The Anxiety of Influence*. Bloom's central thesis, enunciated at the outset of his book, is this: "Strong poets make history by misreading one another, so as to clear imaginative space for themselves." He continues: "[Strong poets] . . . wrestle with their strong precursors, even to the death. Weaker talents idealize; figures of capable imagination appropriate for themselves."[9]

Although Bloom speaks only of lyric poets, his thesis clearly applies to great (or, in Bloom's preferred term, "strong") creative artists of any medium. For example, in the sphere of music, we are all aware of the giant shadow, and the attendant Anxiety of Influence, that Beethoven cast on virtually all the composers of the nineteenth century that followed him, and the similar, often suffocating, influence that Richard Wagner exerted on his contemporaries and followers. Beethoven himself admitted to having had to struggle with the overwhelming influence of both Mozart and Haydn. As for Mozart: he demonstrably did not reach full artistic maturity until he had seriously studied and absorbed the music of J. S. Bach.[10]

Bloom calls attention to a notable exception to his theory of influence. He writes: "The greatest poet in our language is excluded from the argument. . . . Shakespeare belongs to the giant age before the flood, before the anxiety of influence became central to poetic consciousness."[11] In an important sense J. S. Bach, like Shakespeare, belonged to "the giant age before the flood" in the history of music. In the same sense that one could assert, admittedly with some hyperbole, that there were "no great poets" before Shakespeare, it is possible to argue that there were "no great composers" before Bach. It is true that Bach has the reputation of being the "culmination of an era."[12] In the famous words of Albert Schweitzer: "Bach is a . . . terminal point. Nothing comes from him, everything merely leads up to him."[13] In a far more profound sense, however, Bach was in fact the *beginning* of an era. He was, upon reflection, the *first great composer*—at least in modern times: that is, the era that continues still—and is, in fact, ours. In the beginning was Bach, the ultimate source of all modern Anxiety of Influence in the art of music. This means that, unlike all his great and famous successors, Bach had "no" great musical precursor with whom to wrestle. Whoever was there—Buxtehude, Vivaldi—he merely "swallowed up."

In this connection Harold Bloom cites an example of what he calls "Goethe's appalling self-confidence."[14] The immortal poet once observed: "Do not all the achievements of a poet's predecessors and contemporaries rightfully belong to him?

Why should he shrink from picking flowers where he finds them? Only by making the riches of the others our own do we bring anything great into being."[15] Bach, it seems, did not suffer from the Anxiety of Influence any more than did Goethe. He, too, felt free to "pick the flowers where he [found] them." In the list of composers whom Bach (as reported by his son Carl Philipp Emanuel) had "heard and studied" in his youth, we find the names of Froberger, Kerll, Pachelbel, Fischer, Strungk, "some old and good Frenchmen," Buxtehude, Reinken, Bruhns, and Böhm.[16] A respectable list; but there are clearly no giants among them: no Beethovens, Mozarts, Wagners—or J. S. Bachs—again, because, for all intents and purposes, at least in Bach's world, none had existed. Of course, there were brilliant musicians, even musicians of genius, before Bach: Josquin des Prez, Claudio Monteverdi, to mention just two. But it is doubtful that Bach knew their music, or perhaps even their names. He was, however, almost certainly aware of the music of his greatest German predecessor, Heinrich Schütz.[17] What is most striking is that neither Schütz's name nor the name of the composer who surely had the greatest influence of all on the formation of Bach's mature style, the one to whom he was clearly most indebted, is missing entirely from his son's list of acknowledgments: Antonio Vivaldi.[18]

As far as his art was concerned, Bach did not so much have formidable individual precursors to confront as prevailing idioms, conventions, and traditions to study, assimilate, and transcend. But any serious artist, especially an artist of genius, must have a worthy model against whom he can measure, and challenge, himself. Surely the only mortal who could be described as having served, in the deepest sense, as a model and inspiration for Johann Sebastian Bach—someone worthy of his emulation, stimulating his creative imagination, and serving indeed as an inspiration (exciting both admiration and awe)—was Martin Luther.

There can be little doubt that Bach revered Martin Luther, strongly identified with him, recognized him as a supremely towering figure, as a truly "great man," and venerated him almost to the point of obsession. One telling symptom of this reverence is to be found in Bach's personal library. Dominating this library were writings of Luther, which Bach possessed several times over, including at least two extensive, and expensive, collected editions. Robin A. Leaver reports: "There were twenty-one fat folio volumes devoted to the writings of Martin Luther in Bach's library. If one also adds the quarto volume of Luther's *Hauß Postilla* and the octavo volume of Johannes Müller's *Lutherus Defensus*, which were also in his library, then something of the high regard Bach had for the great German Reformer and his writings can be clearly seen."[19]

Particularly intriguing is the seven-volume edition of Luther's *Schriften*, which Bach purchased from a dealer at a book auction in 1742. Bach seems to have paid the considerable price of 10 thalers for the deluxe edition of Luther's works. (Bach claimed that his annual income at Leipzig was around 700 thalers, or some 60 thalers per month.)[20] But Bach actually paid more than 10 thalers. The price on the receipt has been changed, apparently from something considerably higher: perhaps double or even triple the putative price. One can only agree with Leaver's surmise that the alteration of the price of the volumes hints that Bach may have been "reluctant to reveal to his wife how much he paid for them."[21] The document reads: "These German and magnificent Writings of the late D.[octor] M.[artin] Luther (that came from the library of the great Wittenberg theologian D.[octor] Abrah:[am] Calovius, which he probably used to compile his great *Teütsche Bibel*; and also, after his death, passed into the hands of the equally great theologian D.[octor] J.[ohann] F.[riedrich] Mayer) [I] have acquired for 10 thl. Anno 1742. Mense Septembris. Joh. Sebast. Bach."[22]

IV

Bach's profound veneration for Luther is not difficult to understand. First of all, it obviously built upon the respect and reverence naturally flowing to the founder of the composer's religious confession. But there were other sources nurturing Bach's personal identification with the Reformer; for example, the almost familial bond deriving from their common national—indeed, regional—heritage. As mentioned in chapter 1, Bach, like Luther, was a native Thuringian. Moreover, he was born and spent the first ten years of his life in Eisenach, that is, in the town where Luther had translated the New Testament into German and therewith had determined the precise form in which the Holy Word that was at the core of the new dispensation would be proclaimed to the German-speaking world.

There is another element as well coloring the nature of Bach's personal relationship with Luther, one having to do, once again, with the extraordinarily gifted creative individual's need for a credible model, a "great man" worthy of, and capable of inspiring, emulation. In his classic essay, *Moses and Monotheism*, Sigmund Freud allows himself a lengthy digression in order to speculate on what, exactly, is a "great man."[23] After discounting such attributes as beauty, physical strength, military heroism, and worldly success in general, he adds:

> We should certainly not apply the term to a master of chess or to a virtuoso on a musical instrument, and not necessarily to a distinguished artist or a man of science. In such a case we should be content to say he is a great writer, painter, mathematician, or physicist, a pioneer in this field or that, but we should pause before pronouncing him a great man. When we declare, for instance, Goethe, Leonardo da Vinci, and Beethoven to be great men, then something else must move us to do so beyond the admiration of their grandiose creations.[24]

After further such teasing, Freud finally concludes:

> It is the *longing for the father* that lives in each of us from his child-hood days, for the same father whom the hero of legend boasts of having overcome. And now it begins

to dawn on us that all the features with which we furnish the great man are the traits of the father. . . . The decisiveness of thought, the strength of will, the forcefulness of his deeds, belong to the picture of the father; above all other things, however, the self-reliance and independence of the great man, his divine conviction of doing the right thing, which may pass into ruthlessness. He must be admired, he may be trusted, but one cannot help also being afraid of him.[25]

One need not be a doctrinaire Freudian to find that this insight rings true. And it is hardly necessary to argue that these attributes of the great man, which Freud, of course, proceeds to apply to Moses, apply just as well to Martin Luther. As far as the present discussion is concerned, it is important to remember that Bach had no father. Indeed he was an orphan before the age of ten. As suggested in chapter 1, the devastating deprivation of his parents may well have predisposed him to an attitude of "basic distrust" toward an unpredictable and often hostile world. Such an outlook alone would have strongly drawn him to the Lutheran religion, which, along with its repudiation of worldly things and its message of personal faith and salvation, would have provided him, in the person of its founder, with the ideal image of an inspiring, indeed awe-inspiring, longed-for father.

There was yet a further, perhaps decisive, reason that Bach would have been drawn to the person and doctrine of Martin Luther, and that is the uniquely important place Luther accorded to music. Luther put it most succinctly in his posthumously published *Tischreden* (*Table Talks*—a copy of which Bach owned) when he declared: "Music is an outstanding gift of God and next to theology. I would not want to give up my slight knowledge of music for a great consideration. And youth should be taught this art; for it makes fine skillful people."[26]

Luther's enthusiasm for music embraced both its least pretentious and most sophisticated manifestations: from the simple folk-like tunes to be sung by the congregation to the most elaborate polyphonic settings. Nowhere, perhaps, is Luther's admiration for the highest musical art expressed more eloquently and lyrically than in this passage from his preface to Georg Rhau's *Symphoniae iucundae* (1538): "It is most remarkable that one single voice continues to sing the tenor, while at the same time many other voices play around it exulting and adorning it in exuberant strains and, as it were, leading it forth in a divine roundelay so that those who are the least bit moved know nothing more amazing in this world."[27] For all its enthusiasm and poetic exuberance this passage could serve as a technically precise description of a typical polyphonic chorale setting such as one encounters in a church cantata by J. S. Bach—for example, in the opening chorus of *Aus tiefer Not schrei ich zu dir*, or even, if one adds the instruments, *Ein feste Burg is unser Gott*.

The implications of such statements for Bach's self understanding—and Bach almost certainly knew them—are abundantly clear: Martin Luther, quite literally, has done nothing less than justify (even glorify) Bach's existence as a musician and indeed defined his earthly mission.

Chapter Four

Redeeming the St. John Passion—and J. S. Bach

I

The St. John Passion is Johann Sebastian Bach's most controversial work. The sticking point is the fact that the Gospel according to St. John specifically and repeatedly identifies those hysterically crying out for the death of Christ as "the Jews" (*die Juden*). And Bach has set those moments all too effectively. The Gospel according to St. Matthew, in contrast, like the other two synoptic gospels, does not use the "J" word in this context at all: it consistently refers to the crowd simply as "the people" (*das Volk*). Some professional Jewish musicians have refused to participate in performances of the St John Passion at all; the musicologist Richard Taruskin has severely condemned what he characterizes as the work's anti-Semitism.[1] In recent decades, performances of the St. John Passion more often than not are accompanied by a "hazmat" warning label of sorts in the form of a scholarly symposium or pre-concert lecture designed to come to terms with the unquestionably troubling problem the work poses for contemporary sensibilities. One scholar alone, Michael Marissen, the author of *Lutheranism, Anti-Judaism, and Bach's St. John Passion*, has, by his own reckoning, taken part in literally hundreds of such public events.[2]

I heard the St. John Passion for the first time in 1960—just fifteen years after the end of the Second World War when the psychic wounds were still raw. To say that the experience was deeply disturbing would be an understatement. It was nothing less than devastating. The music, as expected, was powerfully expressive and beautiful, and breathtakingly complex in that inevitable, inexorable way that is Bach's alone. But, owing to the words set to that music, it was altogether painful for me to hear.

Bach was back then—as he has always been—the principal god in my personal pantheon. Like most American musicians of my generation, Jewish or not, my acquaintance with Bach was largely through his instrumental music: in my case the keyboard music. My familiarity with his church music was extremely limited. So

I had not expected to encounter anything like the relentless denunciation of the Jews—my own eternally suffering people—that one is exposed to in that composition. Indeed, there is nothing like it anywhere else in Bach's work—secular or sacred. And this was all being expressed in the German language, the sound of which to English speakers in those years was inextricably linked with ranting tyrants and demagogues and marauding SS troops. One could readily imagine Goebbels hollering "Die Juden aber schrieen . . . 'Weg, weg mit dem, kreuzige ihn!'" (But the Jews screamed . . . "Away, away with him. Crucify him!"). English speakers of my generation effectively never heard the German word "Juden" except when it was spoken—that is, shouted—by a Nazi.

Thank God (and one can take that figuratively or literally), the roughest edges have by now, almost sixty years hence, been smoothed to a great extent, if certainly not completely, and we have learned to put Bach's St. John Passion into historical, cultural, and theological perspective. Moreover, musical scholars and theologians are still working on that project.

Nonetheless, the St. John remains Bach's most controversial work. In fact, it is really his only controversial work. Virtually all other controversies surrounding his music are concerned with the relatively trivial matters of authenticity and chronology: "Did Bach really write a particular work and, if so, when?" One can add to them the perennial issues of proper performance style. Not many people outside the scholarly community care very passionately about such arguably provincial things. Just about everyone cares, though, whether a towering work of art by one of the world's most venerated creative geniuses is conveying a doctrine of murderous hatred, or depicting dehumanizing stereotypes.

One could try to excuse or relativize the Passion's "Jewish problem" by noting that anti-Semitic, or at least anti-Jewish, stereotypes are part of the Western cultural tradition. The St. John Passion is arguably the musical counterpart of *The Merchant of Venice*. The caricatures and utterances of Jews in the works of Shakespeare, Dostoyevsky, Dickens, T. S. Eliot, Ezra Pound (just to name a few Western giants) are familiar to us all. The arguments for the prosecution and for the defense have been presented for them all. Our contemporaries—as individuals—have rendered their several verdicts.

Let us linger for a moment on *The Merchant of Venice*. The play, if anything, seems to have become ever more popular in recent years, with ever more stage and even film productions. Clever directors have succeeded in finding layers of nuance and complexity in what at first encounter seems to be, in the figure of Shylock, a mercilessly anti-Semitic caricature. (In fact, it is becoming difficult to recall a time when Shylock was routinely depicted as the villain rather than as the victim of the piece.) In contrast, performances of Bach's St. John Passion over the same period are undertaken with, at the least, considerable trepidation.

The different attitudes on the part of modern audiences toward the two challenging masterpieces are readily accounted for. *The Merchant of Venice* is a work of the imagination: Shylock a single, grotesque, fictional individual. The Gospel according to St. John, in starkest contrast, purports to be factual, to convey historical—indeed Revealed—truth. And the Jews in it—whether they are taken to represent only the "authorities" or the entire Jewish people—are more than a single repellent individual invented for a play or poem or book. They stand accused and convicted of the blackest of all crimes: deicide.

The supreme irony in the strikingly dissimilar reception of both works in contemporary cultural life is this: unlike Shakespeare, Dickens, Dostoyevsky, and those other troubling geniuses who willingly contributed to the West's anti-Semitic cultural tradition, Bach was not the author of the text of the St. John Gospel. As director of music for the Orthodox Lutheran church of Leipzig, and in accordance with the guidelines established by the clerical authorities there, Bach was obliged to set his music to the holy biblical text of the Passion story—the word of God as expressed in the Gospel according to St. John and translated by Martin Luther, the founder of his Protestant faith—verbatim. The performance took place on the most somber day of the Christian liturgical calendar, Good Friday.

II

Bach's great Passion settings, like virtually every part of his artistic legacy, are a synthesis of musical styles and traditions. They are descended, on the one hand, from a long medieval liturgical tradition, in which the Gospel readings of the Passion story during Holy Week were presented as sung dramatizations. The narrator, that is, the Evangelist, was joined by solo singers taking on the roles of Jesus, Pilate, and other personae, while a chorus took the role of the various crowds: soldiers, priests, the mob. After the Reformation these "responsorial Passions" were sung in the vernacular, the language of the people: German, not Latin. By the seventeenth century appropriate congregational hymns (chorales) were added to the pure biblical text. Their purpose was to meditate on the larger meaning of biblical events for the contemporary believer.

Bach built his Passion settings on a considerably more recent, and secular, innovation as well: the Passion oratorio. These nonliturgical compositions, developed only twenty or so years before Bach composed the St. John Passion in 1724, were settings of rhymed paraphrases (rather than the literal biblical text itself) in the style of the recitatives and arias of the contemporary Italian opera. The North German city of Hamburg was at the center of this development. The libretto for the first true Passion oratorio of this kind, *Der blutige und sterbende Jesus* ("The Bloody and Dying Jesus"), dating to 1704, was by Christian Friedrich Hunold (1681–1721, pen name: Menantes). The most significant and influential Passion oratorio text, however, was by Barthold Heinrich Brockes (1680–1747). His libretto, *Der für die Sünden der Welt gemarterte und sterbende Jesus* ("Jesus, Martyred for the Sins of the World"), published in 1712, became enormously popular and influential: eventually set to music by almost a dozen composers, among them Georg Philipp Telemann and George Frideric Handel.

The development of the Passion oratorio in the progressive city of Hamburg was an early symptom of Enlightenment thinking and religious tolerance.[3] The clergy, not surprisingly, objected to replacing the Gospel verses with a modern paraphrase; but the secular establishment, the Hamburg Senate, sought to ensure that the new text would not incite religious animosity. In a remarkable, and hitherto largely neglected, document dated April 14, 1710—that is, two years before the publication of Brockes's oratorio text and unquestionably known to him—the Senate, explicitly invoking the name and authority of Martin Luther (and paraphrasing the Reformer's own "Meditation on Christ's Passion" of 1519), issued this stern injunction: "Our blessed Luther . . . emphatically indicates that the right and proper goal of the reflection on the Passion must be aimed at the awakening of true penitence . . . and of a life pleasing to God. The other things, such as violent invectives and exclamations against Pilate, Judas, the Jews (especially when entire sections are filled with them) can by no means be tolerated."[4]

Some have argued that the Brockes text is virulently anti-Semitic. And yet, for all its graphic, bloody, Baroque imagery, the Jews are never mentioned explicitly except in the phrase "King of the Jews" or as part of the caption "Chorus of Jews" found only in the libretto, that is, not sung aloud. Christ's tormenters are characterized, rather, as sinners, murderers, henchmen, devils, as "a furious brood of vipers" (*Sünder, Mörder, Schergen, Teufel, ergrimmte Natterbrut*), but also, innocuously, as "they" (*sie*).

In 1717, a successful performance of Telemann's setting of the Brockes Passion in Leipzig persuaded the local conservative church authorities to permit such "theatrical" treatments of the story in the city's main churches—so long as they retained the biblical texts rather than adopt the newly minted rhymed versions of them. By 1721 Bach's predecessor as Thomaskantor, Johann Kuhnau, inaugurated an annual Good Friday tradition in Leipzig with a performance of his own St. Mark Passion. (Henceforth, Passion performances were to alternate regularly from year to year between the Thomas and Nicholas churches and also, presumably, to present settings of the four Gospels in some sort of rotation.)

Following the Leipzig prescription, the exact words of chapters 18 and 19 of Luther's German translation of the Gospel according to St. John (not a paraphrase) provide the narrative framework for Bach's composition, presented in dramatized form. Following the long-standing tradition mentioned above, a tenor, in the role of the Evangelist, relates the events while a bass takes on the role of Jesus. Other solo voices represent Peter, Pilate, and some of the lesser characters. In the crowd scenes the chorus variously takes on the roles of the high priests, the mob, or the soldiers. Bach's settings of these scenes draw on the full spectrum of choral techniques, from incisive chordal outbursts to free polyphony to formal fugal expositions. It is precisely these powerful crowd choruses that have become the locus of distress for the modern listener.

III

Some modern theologians have argued that the rhetoric of the St. John Gospel, the last of the four to be set down, reflects conflicts among traditional and early Christianized Jewish communities in the period following the destruction of the Temple and that St. John, himself a Jew (like all the disciples and, of course, Jesus), was directing his resentment toward the religious establishment: in short, "the Jews." Others maintain that John's target encompassed all those who rejected Jesus and refused to follow him (that is, not only those who had official status): in short, once again, "the Jews." The implication, then, is that the problem is with John's choice of words, specifically the Greek noun "hoi Ioudaioi" and, following it, in Luther's translation: "die Juden." Could the Greek expression have been translated as "the Judeans," that is, the residents of the province of Judea? In Luke's narrative of the Nativity (2:4), Luther's version states that Joseph left Nazareth and entered "in das jüdische Land zur Stadt Davids—Bethlehem." The German "das jüdische Land" would most readily be translated into modern English as "the Jewish territory" or "the land of the Jews." In the King James Version, however, the passage reads, "Joseph went into Judaea, unto the city of David." But there is no gainsaying the fact that all other standard English translations, and, I suspect, the standard translations in just about all the modern languages, render John's Greek in the Passion narrative as the equivalent of "the Jews."[5]

The biblical, theological, and linguistic problems, then, along with the modern moral problem, persist; and theologians continue to grapple with them. A new German translation of the Bible published in 2006, *Die Bibel in gerechter Sprache* (The Bible in fair language), for example, prepared by a consortium of scriptural scholars, aims to rectify these troubling passages by rendering Luther's "die Juden" most usually as "die jüdische Obrigkeit" (the Jewish authorities).[6] The theologian Martin Rumscheidt has suggested:

> What the [compilers of the new text] are after is to make it completely clear that the writer of John does not accuse the entire Jewish population present in Jerusalem at the Passover time of having [wanted] Jesus killed but only the Obrigkeit—that is, the religious authorities—who were in fact the real "government" in the Roman province of Judea (rather than King Herod)—[and] who wanted Jesus out of the way for fear that he could upset the delicate arrangements between Rome and themselves. All of the scholars involved in the . . . translation maintain that the "writer" of John was a Jew and not a Gentile and had, like the whole Jesus movement at the time, little use for the "Obrigkeit."

Rumscheidt adds: "I would claim therefore that the so-called anti-Semitism or anti-Judaism of the Gospel of John is a later interpolation on the Gospel by people who were anti-Semitic and anti-Judastic like John Chrysostom of Constantinople."[7] Michael Marissen, among others, would disagree.[8]

Others perhaps can judge better than can the present writer whether the new German translation (and recent theological explanations like those of Martin Rumscheidt) "redeems" and makes palatable—if not the whole can of worms—at least some of the most disturbing passages in the St. John Gospel.

Bach, in any event, was able to redeem the St. John Passion without the help of modern theological revisionism. He did so by means of the texts of the remaining two-thirds of the work and their extraordinary settings. As is well-known, the text for the St. John Passion, like that for the St. Matthew and Bach's other large-scale oratorios, draws on biblical verses, but also the repertory of traditional congregational hymns and contemporary poetic verse. While the Gospel narrative relates the historical events, the poetic verses, set mostly as elaborate arias, express the emotional responses of the individual believer. The congregational chorales assume a more reflective, timeless perspective, that of the Christian community as a whole: in a word, the Church.

All these roles and points of view were entrusted, in Bach's time, to the same performers. The *dramatis personae* of the biblical story, the participants in the meditative chorales, and the soloists in the arias were all members of Bach's chorus. This means that each singer was called upon to empathize with, to portray, and to enact a number of roles in the course of the performance. The same bass, who sang the role of Jesus in one recitative, was part of the crowd calling for Christ's blood in another. In short, the singers were all, in turn, believers, disciples, Romans, Jews—victims, tormenters, the damned, the blessed.

Bach could do nothing about the words themselves of the Gospel according to John, but he almost certainly played the decisive role in the selection of the other texts that were included in the Passion. They express compassion, empathy, and gratitude for Christ's suffering and a resolve to follow him and at least to try to emulate his mercy—to weep and mourn his sacrifice, and to rejoice in it, as it is that act that brings everlasting life. They go on to counsel awareness of Christ's innocence and the corresponding awareness of one's own sins. The sermon these texts impart teaches that it is one's own sins—and, by clear implication, not only those of some Jewish zealots who lived in the Middle East two millennia ago—that are responsible for Christ's suffering. Paul Gerhardt's chorale (movement 11 of the Passion) asks: "Wer hat dich so geschlagen?" (Who has struck you thus?) and answers: "Ich, ich und meine Sünden, . . . Die haben dir erreget das Elend / Das dich schlägt." (I, I and my sins . . . These have brought you / This misery that assails you.)

IV

Below the surface of all the modern controversy and hand-wringing about the "Jewish problem" of the St. John Passion is one particularly fraught and disquieting question: What, if anything, does the mere existence of such a work reveal of Bach's personal attitude toward Jews? The short answer is—nothing, because literally nothing definitive is known about Bach's personal relations with Jews. But the point is worth pursuing.

A case can readily be made that the devout Lutheran Bach was, if anything, unusually tolerant of other religions for someone of his time and place and situation. His relationship with his favorite patron, Prince Leopold of Köthen, a Calvinist, was exceptionally warm, almost brotherly. Bach later described his years at the Calvinist court of Köthen as the happiest of his life. Later still Bach repeatedly made an effort to ingratiate himself with the Catholic court at Dresden. He famously offered to provide music for the church service there by sending to King Frederick Augustus II of Saxony, as a modest display of his earnestness (and his ability), a handsome dedication copy of the B-Minor Mass—a work that the Bach family later referred to as "the great Catholic Mass."[9] It is striking, in fact, that Bach's relations with both the Calvinist prince during his Köthen years and the Catholic court in nearby Dresden during his Leipzig years were considerably better than those with any of his Lutheran employers (the "Obrigkeit," we might say)—co-religionists all—whether in Arnstadt, Mühlhausen, Weimar, or Leipzig.

Returning to the matter of Bach and the Jews: it is not known whether Bach had ever had any personal contact with Jews, because—with few exceptions—they were generally banned from living in Leipzig and the regions of Thuringia and Saxony, where Bach spent almost the entirety of his life. They could and did, however, visit the Leipzig trade fairs, and Bach may have met Jews on those occasions.[10] (Earlier speculation that Bach's friend, Johann Abraham Birnbaum [1702–48]—the university professor of rhetoric who published a famous defense of the composer's music in the 1730s—may, owing to his name, have been a Jewish convert, has been put to rest. The baptismal records for Birnbaum's family have been traced back to the sixteenth century.)[11]

Far more suggestive is the evidence provided by the underlinings and marginalia in Bach's personal copy of a massive annotated edition of the Bible known, after the name of the editor, as the "Calov Bible." It is striking that the composer completely ignored passages that can be read as hostile to the Jews. On the contrary: apparently the only remark in the volume specifically concerning the Jews that Bach was inclined to mark at all was a fairly favorable one—in the book of Ecclesiastes. The annotator observes: "The writings of the Jews differ from those of the Gentiles in that the Jews have received God's word and commandments and that they teach us through their writings that everything proceeds according to God's will and order, and for that reason these writings are all the more useful to read."[12]

It is easy to conclude, moreover, from Bach's marginalia that the biblical figure whom the composer most revered (after Christ, of course), and the one with whom he most identified, was King David, the legendary author of the Psalms. Bach annotated three passages in 1 and 2 Chronicles, which narrate the life of David. At 1 Chronicles 25, which describes the musical forces provided by David for the divine service, Bach writes, "NB: This chapter is the true foundation of all God-pleasing church music" (*NB. Dieses Capitel ist das wahre Fundament aller Gottgefälliger Kirchen Music*). At 1 Chronicles 28:21, commenting on David's injunction to Solomon "to use every willing man who has skill for any kind of service," Bach observes, "NB: Marvelous proof that, along with other parts of the divine service, music, too (and especially), was ordained by God's spirit through David" (*NB. Ein herrlicher Beweiß, daß neben anderen Anstalten des Gottesdienstes, besonders auch die Musica vom Gottes Geist durch David mit angeordnet worden*). Finally, Bach entered the following remark at 2 Chronicles 5:13–14, which describes the use of musical instruments to praise the Lord, "NB: Wherever there is devotional music, God, with His grace, is ever present" (*NB. Bey einer andächtigen Musig ist allezeit Gott mit seiner Gnaden-Gegenwart*).[13] These three observations make up fully half of the grand total of six comments—as opposed to the numerous underlinings and strokes in the margins—that Bach entered into his Calov Bible.

Note, too, that Bach launches his monumental setting of the St. John Passion not with some newly invented modern poetic verses penned by his librettist (as he does the St. Matthew Passion) or some appropriate chorale text or a passage from the New Testament. He instead chooses to open with lines taken almost verbatim from the psalms, specifically Psalm 8. The text of Bach's chorus runs, "Herr, unser Herrscher, dessen Ruhm in allen Landen herrlich ist!" (Lord, our ruler, whose fame is glorious in all the earth.) Luther's rendering of the corresponding lines of Psalm 8 reads, "Herr, unser Herrscher, wie herrlich ist dein Name in allen Landen." (King James Version "O Lord, our Lord, how excellent is thy name in all the earth.")

Besides fulfilling theological purposes such as stressing Jesus's divine nature from the outset, the citation can serve as an implicit homage to King David, whom Bach viewed not only as a biblical hero but also as a fellow musician whose conviction that music was an indispensable adornment to the divine service enriched and justified his own calling.

Moreover, with this prominent reference to the Book of Psalms on the most somber day and, certainly, in Leipzig, the musical climax of the church year—Bach's first year as Thomaskantor—the composer was perhaps revealing his interest in shaping the sacred music he had produced so far during that inaugural year into a coherent cycle of sorts. For he had introduced himself to the Leipzig congregations of the St. Thomas and St. Nicholas churches just ten months earlier, on successive Sundays in the two churches, with a pair of ambitious cantatas (Cantatas 75 and 76) that, like the St. John Passion, open with elaborate choral settings of texts from the Book of Psalms.[14]

❧ ❧ ❧

The St. John Passion gives voice to some of the loftiest sentiments of the human spirit. It does so through the medium of some of the most profound, beautiful, and moving music ever conceived by the mind of man. Neither that supreme masterpiece nor its incomparable maker needs any apology.

Postscript

A version of the foregoing text was delivered on March 10, 2012, in Sanders Theater, Harvard University, Cambridge, Massachusetts, preceding a performance of J. S. Bach's St. John Passion by the Back Bay Chorale, Scott Allen Jarrett conducting. It turned out, much to my surprise, that the Jewish and Gentile members of the audience who cared to express their views after this talk had completely different responses to it.

For the most part, Christians reported that they barely registered the negative depiction of the Jews in the St. John narrative. Many apparently were not even aware that there was a "problem." They seemed to regard it, along with the depiction of the Romans, Pilate, the High Priests, and so on almost as a background story. That is, they did not seem much (if at all) inclined to connect this historical account of events that happened centuries ago with present-day Jews. The Christians' focus, they assured me, when they hear or perform the Passion, is on the message that Jesus was crucified for the salvation of all mankind: that we are all guilty of it, that we all should be thankful for it and rejoice in it.

In starkest contrast, the Jewish members of the audience who were moved to voice their opinion confessed that they have difficulty noticing anything in the St. John Passion other than the harsh portrayal of the Jews. They were grateful, they said, that I owned up to having had a similar experience. Needless to say, others lecturing on the St. John Passion may have observed different reactions.

Chapter Five

Bach's Keyboard Music

Johann Sebastian Bach's reputation as one of the supreme figures of Western musical history rests primarily on the legacy of his keyboard music. Whereas the composer's church music and ensemble compositions, including such masterpieces as the Mass in B Minor, the Passions, and the Brandenburg Concertos, fell virtually into oblivion after his death, the Inventions and Sinfonias, the harpsichord suites, the Goldberg Variations, the chorale settings, and the preludes and fugues of *The Well-Tempered Clavier* have been the objects of unbroken study, veneration, and emulation by generations of musicians—amateur and professional—from Bach's day to the present.

During his lifetime Bach had already been celebrated as the greatest living keyboard player. But it is essential to recognize that for Bach and his contemporaries, harpsichordists and organists were, more often than not, the same people. In the early eighteenth century, as throughout the seventeenth, the term "clavier" was generic and embraced all keyboard instruments, whether they were attached to strings or pipes. And it followed that a "clavier" player was equally at home on all the available keyboard instruments.

Defining the Repertoire

Naturally enough, during the Baroque era the various keyboard instruments, including the organ, shared a common repertoire to a significant extent. This is true not only for the earlier masters but also—far more than has generally been acknowledged—for much of the "clavier" music of Bach. This means specifically that we must abandon the deeply entrenched "binary" categorization that is literally centuries old but nonetheless an anachronistic one.[1] We must recognize, rather, that with regard to performance medium, Bach's keyboard compositions do not fall into two strictly separated categories—consisting of works either for the organ or for the stringed keyboard instruments—but rather into three: works exclusively or primarily for organ, works exclusively or primarily for harpsichord, and works for "clavier," that is, for any keyboard instrument. Only such a three-part division of Bach's keyboard repertory does full justice to the explicit designations contained in the sources and to the historical circumstances of keyboard performance in the Baroque era.

Compositions making use of preexistent sacred material (typically chorale settings) or calling for an obbligato pedal—and hence often designated *pedaliter*—were no doubt expected to be played primarily on the organ. Conversely, dance suites and variations on secular tunes were no doubt expected to be played primarily on the harpsichord. Not surprisingly, such works never have obbligato pedal parts. Finally, free keyboard compositions for manual(s) alone generally belonged to the common "clavier" repertory. The early sources for many of these compositions often carry the designation *manualiter* to indicate the absence of an obbligato pedal part—although in practice *manualiter* compositions occasionally contain isolated pedal points.[2] Since no other instrument but the organ was normally equipped with a pedal board, the appearance of a *manualiter* indication in a work (by J. S. Bach or anyone else) would be redundant if applied to any other keyboard instrument, and implies, at the very least, the acceptability of—if not a preference for—an organ rendition. The rationale for the existence of a *manualiter* (organ) repertoire is not hard to find: the organs in many small Thuringian churches often lacked pedals; moreover, many provincial organists often lacked the pedal technique for any real obbligato part, even if they could produce an isolated pedal point.

Most of J. S. Bach's "generic" clavier music dates from the first decade of his career and typically belongs to the genres of prelude (or toccata, or fantasia) and fugue, but it also includes keyboard transcriptions of ensemble compositions and presumably embraces not only the Inventions and Sinfonias but perhaps even *The Well-Tempered Clavier* as well.

This chapter will be limited to a discussion of Bach's keyboard works in the modern, more narrow, sense of compositions specifically for harpsichord and those more generally for "clavier" without pedals, that is, for harpsichord, clavichord, organ *manualiter*, or, indeed, fortepiano.

Bach's Instruments

The estate catalog for Bach, drawn up by his surviving kin and their trustees shortly after his death on July 28, 1750, informs us that Bach owned no fewer than eight stringed keyboard instruments, five of them (at least nominally) harpsichords. They are listed, along with their assessed values, as follows: "1 veneered *Clavecin*, which is to remain in the family if at all possible" (valued at 80 thalers); 3 *Clavesins* (each valued at 50 thalers); 1 *ditto*, smaller (value: 20 thalers); 2 *Lauten Wercke* (each valued at 30 thalers); 1 *Spinettgen* (value 3 thalers).[3]

The monetary values most likely reflected the values of used instruments. A new, single-manual harpsichord in Saxony at the time fetched between 60 and 100 thalers, a double-manual instrument between 100 and 200 thalers. The four used harpsichords valued at 80 or 50 thalers, therefore, were probably all two-manual instruments.[4] (As a point of reference: Bach indicated in a 1730 letter to a friend that his annual income in Leipzig at the time from all sources amounted to 700 thalers.)[5]

Clavecin/Clavesin, of course, normally designated a harpsichord. Whether the term in this instance was meant literally to specify a keyboard instrument with plucked strings or more broadly, perhaps to include the fortepiano, as well, is not clear. What is known is that Bach in his later years was a sales agent for the organ builder Gottfried Silbermann (1683–1753), and had sold—no doubt on commission—at least one (in Bach's words) "instrument called Piano et Forte" for the handsome sum of 115 thalers.[6] The *Lautenwerck*, or lute harpsichord, owed its name to the use of gut strings that gave it its characteristic sound. J. S. Bach's onetime pupil, Johann Friedrich Agricola (1720–74), reported that he "remembers, about the year 1740, in Leipzig, having seen and heard a lute-harpsichord [*Lautenclavicymbel*] designed by Mr. Johann Sebastian Bach and executed by Mr. Zacharias Hildebrandt, which was of smaller size than the ordinary harpsichord, but in all other respects was like any other harpsichord. It had two [8-foot] choirs of gut strings, and a so-called little octave [*Octävchen*, i.e., 4-foot choir] of brass strings."[7] The "smaller" *Clavesin* was probably a *Querspinett*, that is, a trapezoid-shaped harpsichord, and presumably smaller than a virginal.

We learn from a later document that "during his lifetime" the composer had already given to his younger son, Johann Christian, "3 *Clavire* nebst *Pedal*," and are informed further that at that time (November 1750), the fifteen-year-old still had them.[8] It is now thought that this "description referred to a single instrument consisting of three clavichords, each one comprised of strings, a resonance chamber, tangents and key levers. Two of them were operated with manuals and one with pedals."[9] Adlung reported that the term "clavier" was "often understood to mean primarily the clavichord."[10] He explained elsewhere how a pedal board could be played together with the manuals of a clavichord in the manner of an organ.[11] Such an instrument, like the similarly constructed pedal harpsichord, primarily served for practicing or for domestic music-making.[12]

The estate catalog reveals nothing about the specifications or builders of any of Bach's keyboard instruments. In fact, we have more information about the harpsichords (or at least the types of harpsichords) that Bach probably knew and played—and perhaps even owned—than is commonly assumed.[13] Precisely one harpsichord of Thuringian provenance and dating from the first decades of the eighteenth century is known to have survived. It is no doubt the type of instrument that Bach (and Handel) would have been familiar with during their formative years. The unique exemplar, dating from circa 1715 and by an anonymous builder, is now in the possession of the Bachhaus in Eisenach. It is a single-manual instrument with two 8-foot registers and a four-octave C–c³ compass.[14]

With but one exception Bach's pre-Köthen keyboard compositions remain within the four-octave compass C–c³. The single exception, the "Aria Variata all Man.

Italiana" (BWV 989), extends the range down to AA. Like most of the keyboard pieces in the early Bach sources, the "aria variata" does not specify an instrument. The genre of the work, however, a set of secular variations, along with the extension of the compass below C, makes it a virtual certainty that the composition was intended for a stringed keyboard, presumably the harpsichord.

Unlike the suites, the works belonging to Bach's systematic, pedagogical keyboard collections form the Köthen period largely stay within the normal C–c^3 compass. Perhaps, as Alfred Dürr suggested, this restriction reflects the range limitation of the instruments played by Bach's students and family members rather than necessarily that of Bach's own instrument.[15] Nor can it be a coincidence that the elaborate title pages on the autograph scores of both *The Well-Tempered Clavier* I (BWV 846–69) and the Inventions and Sinfonias (BWV 772–801), dated 1722 and 1723, respectively, specify no particular instrument but simply the generic clavier. Bach, no doubt, purposely left the choice among harpsichord, clavichord, and organ *manualiter* to the discretion and available resources of the player.[16]

Both the first and last volumes of Bach's monumental *Klavierübung*—containing, respectively, the six partitas (published between 1726 and 1731), and the Goldberg Variations (published 1741)—require a GG–d^3 compass. The Goldberg Variations, like the two works included in "Part 2" of the *Klavierübung* (published 1735)— the Italian Concerto (BWV 971) and the Ouverture in B minor (BWV 831)— famously prescribes a two-manual harpsichord. (Curiously, the compass of the Italian Concerto is restricted to AA–c^3 and deliberately avoids d^3.) George Stauffer conjectures that since the GG–d^3 range appears in Bach's harpsichord works for the first time in the partitas of *Klavierübung* I, the composer may well have acquired an instrument with that compass at about that time.[17]

Bach, finally, requires e^3 in the mirror fugue of the *Art of Fugue*. The pitch f^3 (along with e^3) appears only once in his works: in the second movement of the Triple Concerto in A Minor (BWV 1044)—a work, transmitted only in a copyist's manuscript, whose authenticity is uncertain.[18]

The publication of the four parts of the *Klavierübung* between 1726 and 1741 more or less coincided with Bach's activities with the Leipzig Collegium Musicum, the reputable music-making association consisting of professional musicians and university students that Bach directed from 1729 to 1737 and sporadically again from 1739 on. Among the numerous concerts offered by the Collegium Musicum, one is of particular interest. In June 1733 a local newspaper announced that "Bach's Collegium Musicum . . . [would present] a fine concert . . . with a new harpsichord [*Clavicymbel*] such as had not been heard here before."[19] Speculation abounds about the nature of this unprecedented instrument: that it was a lute harpsichord, a harpsichord with a lute stop, that it had a 16-foot register, or perhaps that it was a fortepiano from the workshop of Gottfried Silbermann.[20]

As pointed out by George B. Stauffer, although "it is highly unlikely that any period harpsichords have come down with their original strings intact" (since "the

strings were made of soft metal" and "broke frequently"), contemporary descriptions provide "evidence for brass stringing in Middle German harpsichords."[21]
Brass strings, in combination with the short string scale typical of Middle German
harpsichords, produced a relatively sustained, more "organ-like" sonority than is the
case with the more usual iron alloys of the time. Stauffer characterizes the sound
as "unusually rich and penetrating . . . ideally suited to the contrapuntal nature of
Bach's music. The strong foundation tone (which is not unlike that of seventeenth-
and eighteenth-century Thuringian organs) . . . helps to strengthen and clarify the
individual voices in polyphonic textures. In solo works, it allows inner parts to be
heard more clearly than they are on French and Italian instruments from the same
period."[22] Contemporary Thuringian organs, for their part, were distinguished by
a predilection for stops of the string family and, in general, for 8-foot and 4-foot
registers (rather than mixtures and upper voices) that resulted in a light, delicate
tone-quality.[23] This means that the characteristic timbres—and, by implication, the
sound ideals—of the harpsichords and organs that were most familiar to Bach were
by no means so different from one another as they are for the modern listener, a circumstance that must have made the idea of shared repertory for the two instruments
all but inevitable, and by no means unnatural.

Agricola informs us, finally, that Bach had once examined one of the earliest
pianofortes built by Gottfried Silbermann and had "praised, indeed admired, its
tone; but he had complained that it was too weak in the high register, and was too
hard to play."[24] He adds that years later, Bach gave his "complete approval" (*völlige
Gutheißung*) to the improvements Silbermann had made to the instrument in order
to correct these faults. In her recent monograph on the history of the instrument,
Eva Badura-Skoda devotes an entire chapter to an extensive exploration of Bach's
relationship with Silbermann, his apparent interest in the early pianoforte, and the
extent to which he may have intended its use in his music.[25]

The First Decade, circa 1703–1713:
Apprenticeship and Early Mastery

According to the obituary (published posthumously in 1754), Bach had "laid the
foundations for his playing of the clavier" at Ohrdruf, under the guidance of his
elder brother, Johann Christoph (1671–1721), with whom he lived from 1695
to 1700, following the death of their father. Although he does not seem to have
been a prodigy, and while nothing is known for certain about when Bach began to
compose, any instruction on the clavier at the time invariably entailed not only the
development of keyboard dexterity but also a variety of compositional skills such as
figured bass realization and improvisation.

In any event, by the age of eighteen Bach had begun his career as a musician and
for the next ten years served as a professional organist: first in Arnstadt (1703–7), then

Mühlhausen (1707–8), finally at the ducal court of Weimar (1708–14). With his promotion to Konzertmeister in March 1714, Bach's duties in Weimar took a new direction. In fact, however, Bach's music had already taken a profoundly new direction during the summer of 1713—in the wake of his first extensive encounter with the modern Italian concerto, an event that decisively marked a new stage in the composer's artistic development. The decade 1703–13, then, despite the changing circumstances of his employment, is best regarded as constituting a single creative period in Bach's life—the only period during which keyboard music was his central professional concern.

None of the early keyboard works reliably attributed to J. S. Bach are precisely datable. Although some of them may have been written before 1700, most were presumably composed in the decade 1703–13. Most survive in two manuscripts largely copied by, and originally in the possession of, his older brother, Johann Christoph. Both are identified today by the names of early owners. The earlier of the two, the "Möller manuscript," is roughly contemporaneous with Bach's term in Arnstadt; the second, the "Andreas Bach book," was evidently compiled during the first years of Bach's service as court organist in Weimar. The identification of the principal copyist of the volumes as Johann Christoph Bach has inspired confidence in the attributions to J. S. Bach.[26] But the virtual absence of any sources in Bach's own hand has inevitably led to problematic readings and at times conflicting versions.

Besides Bach's music, the two volumes preserve secular keyboard music by the principal German composers of the immediately preceding generations—chief among them the North Germans Böhm, Buxtehude, and Reinken and the Central Germans Kuhnau, Pachelbel, and Telemann—along with keyboard and ensemble works by leading French and Italian composers. This cosmopolitan repertoire clearly provided both the context and the stylistic models that helped shape Bach's early compositional development.[27]

Another important source for Bach's early keyboard music is the repertoire collected by the Thuringian organist, Johann Peter Kellner (1705–72).[28] The nature of Kellner's relationship to Bach is unclear, but he was probably never a student. For unlike Bach's known students, who apparently never made copies of these early works—a strong indication, incidentally, that the composer must have disowned them—Kellner was collecting them as late as the 1720s.

A hallmark of all of Bach's early compositions, an admittedly negative one, is the absence of any significant influence of the modern Italian concerto. The main influences rather are precisely those most highly represented in the Möller and Andreas Bach collections: the local traditions of Central and Northern Germany, whose keyboard forms and idioms are contrasted, and at times fused, with those of late seventeenth-century France. The early repertory in fact can be reasonably divided into two broad categories according to genre: (1) preludes (toccatas, fantasias) and/or fugues (table 5.1), and (2) a variety of multi-sectional, predominantly homophonic works: mostly suite-like collections, along with "sonatas," a set of variations, and a programmatic capriccio (table 5.2).

Table 5.1. Overview of J. S. Bach's Early Keyboard Compositions: Preludes, Fantasias, Toccatas, and Fugues

Prelude and Fugue in A Major, BWV 896	Fugue in C after Albinoni, BWV 946
Toccata in F-sharp Minor, BWV 910	Fugue in A Minor, BWV 947
Toccata in C Minor, BWV 911	Fugue in A Major, BWV 949
Toccata in D Major, BWV 912/912a	Fugue in A Major after Albinoni, BWV 950
Toccata in D Minor, BWV 913	Fugue in B Minor after Albinoni, BWV 951
Toccata in E Minor, BWV 914	Fugue in B-flat after Reinken, BWV 954
Toccata in G Minor, BWV 915	Fugue in B-flat (after Erselius?), BWV 955
Toccata in G Major, BWV 916	Fugue in G (*Machs mit mir Gott*), BWV 957
Fantasia duobus subjectis, BWV 917	Capriccio in E *In Honorem J. C. Bachii*, BWV 993
Prelude in C Minor, BWV 921	
Prelude in A Minor, BWV 922	

Table 5.2. Overview of J. S. Bach's Early Keyboard Compositions: Suites, Sonatas, Ouvertures, Variations

Ouverture in F Major, BWV 820	Sonata in D Major, BWV 963
Suite in B-flat Major, BWV 821	Sonata in A Minor after Reinken, BWV 965
Ouverture in G Minor, BWV 822	Sonata in C Major after Reinken, BWV 966
Suite in F Minor, BWV 823	Sonata in A Minor, BWV 967
Partie in A Major, BWV 832	Capriccio in B-flat Major, BWV 992
Praeludium et Partita, BWV 833	*Aria variata* in A Minor, BWV 989
	Suite in E Minor for Lute Harpsichord, BWV 996

Preludes, Fantasias, Toccatas, and Fugues

Nowhere is the evidence for a common keyboard repertory more compelling than in these interrelated genres. First of all, both *pedaliter* and *manualiter* compositions were notated in the original sources on two-stave systems; that is, there was never a separate staff for the pedal in this repertory. Moreover, several nominally *manualiter* fugues (BWV 949, 950, 955) conclude with pedal-like passages in the bass or with pedal points that not only imply organ performance but in fact are impossible to play on a harpsichord as written. More generally, there is no substantial difference between the keyboard styles of the *manualiter* and the *pedaliter* compositions belonging to this category. In illustration of this assertion, the following examples juxtapose passages from the *manualiter* and *pedaliter* repertories, organized into four functional types: (1) opening gestures, (2) continuation patterns and sequences, (3) closing gestures, and (4) fugue themes (exx 5.1 through 5.4).

In the final analysis, all of these compositions are works for "clavier." The particular medium of performance is a secondary consideration. They can be rendered appropriately, and for the most part, equally effectively, on either the organ or a stringed keyboard instrument.[29]

Bach's early preludes and fugues, whatever their medium of performance, document his emulation and assimilation of a wide range of styles from the archaic *stile antico* (in the Canzona, BWV 588), to the rather mechanical "permutation" fugue on the Reinken model (the *Fantasia duobus subiectis*, BWV 917), to rambling, quasi-improvisational *Spielfugen* in the manner of Bruhns and Buxtehude.

Although the terms "toccata," "fantasia," and "praeludium" were often used interchangeably in the seventeenth and eighteenth centuries, Bach and his contemporaries seem to have recognized certain distinctions among them. "Praeludium" (with its French and Italian cognates "prelude" and "preludio") and its synonym "praeambulum" are functional designations: they apply to any composition—short or long, simple or elaborate, homophonic or polyphonic—that serves as an introduction to another. Conversely, the terms "toccata" and "fantasia" ("fantaisie," also "fantasie") are, in principle, stylistic designations, frequently distinguishing two kinds of virtuosic display: keyboard virtuosity in the case of the toccata; compositional virtuosity in the case of the fantasia.[30]

The two surviving independent praeludia—the C-Minor, BWV 921, and the A-Minor, BWV 922—could have served either as introductions to specific fugues, from which they accidentally became separated during the source transmission, or as all-purpose preludes capable of being attached to any number of fugues sharing the same tonic. Their primitive features—repetitive, if flamboyant, keyboard-inspired formulas and sequences, short-breathed sections—suggest that they are among Bach's earliest keyboard compositions. Fugues surviving without preludes are far more numerous. With their striking subjects, characterized by repeated notes, rhetorical pauses, and uninhibited, if idiomatic, chains of melodic sequences, these compositions are often quite effective. Their stylistic limitations, however, are considerable. David Schulenberg calls attention to the rarity of real four-part writing, as well as to the "clumsy parallelisms, harsh passing dissonances, and excessively wide spacings," and suggests that these traits may be due "not so much to weak contrapuntal technique per se as to inexperience in the difficult art of writing meaningful counterpoint playable without pedals on a keyboard instrument."[31]

Of the three fugues on themes by Tomaso Albinoni: BWV 946, 950, 951,[32] the B-Minor, BWV 951—Bach's earliest fugue specifically designated as a harpsichord work—is the most impressive. To judge from the relatively numerous surviving copies and from its extensive reworkings, it is one of the few compositions from this

Example 5.1. *Manualiter—Pedaliter*: Opening Gestures. (a) Toccata in E Minor *manualiter*, BWV 914; Prelude in G Minor *pedaliter*, BWV 535

BWV 914

BWV 535

Example 5.1. *Manualiter—Pedaliter*: Opening Gestures. (b) Toccata in D Minor *manualiter*, BWV 913; Prelude in D Minor *pedaliter*, BWV 549a

BWV 913

BWV 549a

Example 5.1. *Manualiter—Pedaliter*: Opening Gestures. (c) Toccata in D *manualiter*, BWV 912; Prelude in D *pedaliter*, BWV 532

BWV 912

BWV 532

Example 5.2. *Manualiter—Pedaliter:* Continuation Patterns and Sequences, (a) Toccata in C Minor *manualiter*, BWV 911

BWV 911

Example 5.2. *Manualiter—Pedaliter.* Continuation Patterns and Sequences, (b) Toccata in D Minor *pedalite*r, BWV 565

BWV 565

Example 5.2. *Manualiter—Pedaliter*: Continuation Patterns and Sequences, (c) Toccata in C Minor *manualiter*, BWV 911; Dorian toccata *pedaliter*, BWV 538

BWV 911

BWV 538

Example 5.2. *Manualiter—Pedaliter:* Continuation Patterns and Sequences, (d) Toccata in C Minor *manualiter*, BWV 911; Toccata in C *pedaliter*, BWV 564

BWV 911

BWV 564

Example 5.3. *Manualiter—Pedaliter*: Closing Gestures. (a) Toccata in D Minor *manualiter*, BWV 913

Example 5.3. *Manualiter—Pedaliter*: Closing Gestures. (b) Passacaglia in C Minor *pedaliter*, BWV 582

Example 5.4. *Manualiter—Pedaliter.* Fugue Themes. (a) Toccata in D *manualiter*, BWV 912; Fugue in G *pedaliter*, BWV 577; Toccata in G Minor *pedaliter*, BWV 915

Example 5.4. *Manualiter—Pedaliter*: Fugue Themes. (b) Toccata in F-sharp Minor, BWV 910 *manualiter*; Toccata in F Major *pedaliter*, BWV 540

BWV 910

BWV 540

Example 5.4. *Manualiter—Pedaliter*: Fugue Themes. (c) Toccata in G *manualiter*, BWV 916; Toccata in C *pedaliter*, BWV 564

BWV 916

BWV 564

Example 5.4. *Manualiter—Pedaliter:* Fugue Themes. (d) Toccata in E Minor *manualiter*, BWV 914; Toccata in D Minor *pedaliter*, BWV 565

BWV 914

BWV 565

period to which the composer remained committed. The formal and tonal refinements of the work in its final version—a richer and more balanced harmonic plan, the inclusion of a brief recapitulation—along with its chromaticism, argue that it stands at or over the threshold of Bach's second decade of keyboard composition.[33]

Bach's seven *manualiter* toccatas have been characterized as "*Sturm und Drang* products" (Keller) and as "the culmination of Bach's early work for keyboard instruments without pedals" (Schulenberg). Evidently written throughout the course of the first decade,[34] they are impressive (if at times problematic) compositions that attest not only to Bach's mastery of the keyboard but also to his command of a wide range of musical styles that he set down, for maximum effect, in striking juxtaposition. His primary concern in this regard was evidently to explore basic compositional principles: the opposition of the improvisational and the strictly composed, of rhapsodic unpredictability and self-conscious unity.

Like their North German models, the *manualiter* toccatas consist, in principle, of five sections: three main parts separated (or linked) by two transitional episodes. The opening flourishes, or *passaggi*—which may well document actual improvisations—betray the young virtuoso composer's delight in digital virtuosity as well as coloristic and registral effect. Each toccata begins by opening the tonal space in a striking fashion: the D-Minor and E-Minor toccatas with "pedal solos" in the bass; the G-Major and G-Minor toccatas, in contrast, at the top of the keyboard, the former obsessed with repetitive scales and broken chord patterns, the latter cascading in a torrent of rapid triplets, and so on. Of the two transitional sections, the archaic style and relatively strict part writing of the first presumably form a deliberate contrast to the distinctly modern instrumental "recitative" style of the second. The fugal sections, for their part—the first normally in duple meter, the second quicker than the first and often in triple or compound meter—are rather old-fashioned: limited in harmonic scope, prone to motoric rhythms and extensive (at times excessive) sequential patterning, but also more concerned with obbligato countersubjects and double fugue techniques than would be the case later on.

Occasionally—in a manner reminiscent of the seventeenth-century variation suite—there are more or less obvious thematic or motivic similarities between the sections.[35] On other occasions the five-section schema is abandoned. In particular, the G-Major toccata, BWV 916 (like the C-Major *pedaliter* toccata, BWV 564) is in three movements, both compositions evidently the product of Bach's attempt to effect an accommodation between the stylistic worlds of the North German toccata and the Italian concerto.

Suites, Sonatas, Ouvertures, Variations

Whereas the *manualiter* preludes and fugues, at the very least, do not discourage organ rendition, there is little doubt that the works under this rubric were intended for the harpsichord. In contrast to Bach's early essays in the well-established styles and techniques of German keyboard music, the motley collection of suites and related compositions disclose his interest in more recent keyboard genres whose stylistic and formal conventions were by no means fully defined. Many of these efforts were to remain rather unsuccessful isolated experiments.

The compositions consisting largely of dances and related pieces are variously designated *Ouverture, Suite, Partie, Partita, Sonata.* The two Ouvertures—in F Major and G Minor, respectively, BWV 820 and 822—begin, as expected, with introductory movements in the familiar orchestral style that may even be transcriptions for keyboard rather than original keyboard compositions. While both works conclude with the customary gigue, they omit the other dances increasingly standard at this time among German composers of keyboard suites—allemande, courante, and sarabande—substituting others in their place.

In the G-Minor Ouverture, BWV 822, French influence, as Schulenberg observes, is apparent from the rondeau form of the gavotte, the repetition of the final phrase (a *petite reprise*) in the bourrée, and from the dotted rhythms and homophonic texture of the gigue. Similarly, the three-measure phrases of the minuet from the F-Major Ouverture, BWV 820, are characteristically French.[36] The minuet also presents less than flattering testimony to the young composer's skill at this stage, with its inconsistent textures (two or three voices), its melodic monotony, and its wavering tonal focus. (The composition is subjected to an invidious comparison with one of Mozart's earliest minuets in chapter 1.)

The Sonatas in D Major, A Minor, and C Major, BWV 963, 965, and 966, respectively—the last two arrangements of movements from Johann Adam Reinken's *Hortus musicus* (Hamburg, 1687)—are hybrid compositions that combine attributes of the toccata and the suite. They can be regarded perhaps as an early manifestation of the trend toward a *réunion des goûts*, here uniting the North German organ style with French dance music for *clavecin.* The D-Major Sonata is closest in style to the toccata, consisting of a pair of fugues separated by recitative-like transition sections. It begins, however, not with a virtuosic flourish but with a homophonic lyric movement. The final fugue, entitled "Thema all'Imitatio Gallina Cuccu," alludes to yet another keyboard tradition: the bird calls popular with seventeenth-century Italian and South German composers. The fugues in the "Reinken" sonatas, on the other hand, are sophisticated reworkings of the originals in which Reinken's "permutation" procedures of strictly invertible counterpoint are abandoned in favor of more flexible patterns.

The most well-known of the early keyboard works, the *Capriccio sopra la lontananza de il Fratro dilettissimo* (*Capriccio on the Absence of the Most Beloved Brother*), BWV 992, and the *Aria Variata* in A Minor, BWV 989, fall, respectively, toward the beginning and the end of the first decade. Each is virtually in a class by itself within the Bach canon. The capriccio, copied into the Möller manuscript around 1705,[37] is the composer's only instrumental composition with an extra-musical program— a conceit suggested by Johann Kuhnau's "Biblical" Sonatas (Leipzig, 1700)—but appropriated here to represent a purely secular, indeed mundane, event: the composer's separation from his beloved "fratro."[38]

The capriccio is notable for the expressive intensity of the first half of the work, which reaches its climax in an effectively structured passacaglia on the famous *lamento* bass (perhaps Bach's very first passacaglia). This seriousness of tone contrasts sharply with the playful character of the last two movements: the brief "aria" and the quite difficult fugue, both of which, in the same spirit as the "cuckoo" fugue of the D-Major Sonata, make use of "natural" sounds—here the octave leaps of the post horn.

The *Aria Variata*, presumably written toward the end of Bach's decade of apprenticeship and early mastery, is his only set of secular variations before the Goldberg Variations. Among the numerous textual problems posed by this composition is one concerning its dimensions and organization. In one source the work consists of ten variations; in another, only eight, arranged in a different order. Each of the variations—all but the last of which is for two voices—is an exercise in motivic and textural consistency, while the composition as a whole explores an impressively wide range of contrasting styles and affects: a set of "character" variations, then, and a precocious harbinger of the Goldberg Variations.

The First Synthesis: 1713–1723

In the summer of 1713 Bach undertook a series of arrangements of Italian concertos. This activity did not coincide with any of the familiar changes of employment in the composer's biography; nonetheless, it was arguably the most significant artistic experience of his maturity—a "watershed" event that fundamentally transformed his approach to composition. As in the case of the early works, a revision of the time-honored periodization of Bach's career is once again in order. Rather than organized in terms of "the Weimar Period, 1708–17," followed by "the Köthen Period, 1717–23," it is possible, at least from one point of view, to conceive the decade 1713–23 as a single, extraordinarily rich phase in Bach's artistic development—one marked at the beginning by the discovery of the Italian concerto and at the end by his departure to Leipzig, bringing with it the obligation to devote himself exclusively, at least temporarily, to the composition of church music. Such a division is further justified by the fact that many of Bach's keyboard compositions cannot be precisely dated either to the Weimar or the Köthen years, while work on others, though begun in Weimar, continued on into the Köthen period (and perhaps beyond).

Among the new duties connected with Bach's promotion to Konzertmeister in March 1714 was the obligation to compose a church cantata every four weeks. He continued in his post as court organist, however, and evidently managed, before leaving Weimar three years later, not only to prepare keyboard transcriptions of concertos in the Italian style but to compose several large-scale preludes and fugues, the

English Suites, and, apparently, much of *The Well-Tempered Clavier*. At Köthen the composition of solo keyboard music evidently had nothing to do with Bach's official duties as court Kapellmeister. For the most part Bach's Köthen keyboard works belonged to the private sphere: to domestic music-making with his family and especially to his activities as a teacher. His keyboard compositions from this time on took on an explicitly didactic function and were increasingly organized into sets or cycles.

In the final analysis, however, the period of artistic maturity that began about 1713 lasted in fact not for ten but rather some thirty years, during which Bach largely concentrated his efforts as a keyboard composer on the genres of the suite and the fugue. His most important contributions were to be consolidated in six substantial collections, three volumes of suites—the English and French Suites, and the Partitas (along with the Ouverture, BWV 831)—and three volumes of fugues— *The Well-Tempered Clavier* (WTC) I and II, and the *Art of Fugue* (along with the Inventions and Sinfonias). Bach regarded the two contrasting genres as forming a single integrated pedagogical program. According to Heinrich Nicolaus Gerber (1702–75), a pupil of Bach's in Leipzig from 1724 to 1727, the composer started him off on the Inventions and Sinfonias. "When he had studied these through to Bach's satisfaction, there followed a series of suites, then *The Well-Tempered Clavier*. . . . The conclusion of the instruction was thorough bass" (NBR, 322). In terms of chronology the English and French Suites, along with WTC I and the Inventions and Sinfonias, belong mainly to the decade 1713–23; the remaining compositions belong to Bach's Leipzig years.

The Concerto Transcriptions

Bach's keyboard arrangements of twenty-one concertos in the Italian style—five *pedaliter* (BWV 592–96), and sixteen *manualiter* (BWV 972–87)[39]—evidently were prepared during the period from July 1713 to July 1714 in fulfillment of a request from the young Weimar duke, Johann Ernst.[40] Whether prepared primarily for practical performance by the duke or himself, or for purposes of study, the transcriptions represent the composer's first known sustained encounter with the modern Italian concerto style.

The formal and tonal principles Bach discovered in the Italian concertos of Vivaldi, Torelli, and the two Marcellos (Alessandro and Benedetto)—in particular, the age-old principles of ritornello form now immeasurably enriched by the vastly expanded harmonic resources of functional tonality—would inform almost every work he wrote henceforth. Mastering and expanding on them and exploring their almost infinite capacity for combination with other principles of musical structure and design were destined to become a constant challenge and preoccupation in his future agenda as a composer. There were, for example, obvious correspondences between the Italian concerto and the German keyboard prelude, and between the Italian concerto and the fugue. Like many preludes, the style and the very ethos of the concerto provided an opportunity for the display of virtuosity; like many fugues, the form of the concerto was based on a principle of alternation between thematic and comparatively non-thematic sections: in the concerto between ritornello and solo, in the fugue between exposition and episode. Bach, characteristically, was interested in the potential for synthesis suggested by these connections.

Even more fundamentally, however, he was attracted to the rational tonal design and ritornello organization of the concerto that enabled the creation of unified, continuous instrumental movements on a hitherto unprecedented scale, avoiding, on the one hand, the tonal monotony and short-breathed sectionalism of, say, the variation set or the passacaglia, and on the other, the tendency, observable at times in the early toccatas—and even the early fugues—toward excessive variety and contrast at the cost of any sense of a compelling underlying unity.

Four "Great" Preludes (Fantasias) and Fugues

Among the first original fruits of Bach's study of the Italian concerto are three large-scale concertante *manualiter* works—all (coincidentally or not) in the key of A minor: the Fantasia and Fugue, BWV 904, the (Fantasia and) Fugue, BWV 944, and the Prelude and Fugue, BWV 894. *Pedaliter* organ works like these—grand in scale, virtuosic in character, concertante in style—have come to bear the epithet "great," a designation just as appropriate for their presumably contemporaneous *manualiter* counterparts.[41]

Like the toccata, the fantasia is a subcategory of prelude insofar as it usually denotes a movement preceding a fugue. But the emphasis this time is typically on compositional rather than keyboard prowess. In the Fantasia in A Minor, BWV 904/1, for example, Bach is concerned with creating an unlikely hybrid that unites the ritornello design of the modern concerto with archaic suspension-based counterpoint (*durezze e ligature*) of the *stile antico*.

The Fugue in A Minor, BWV 944—preceded in its earliest source by a miniature, ten-measure *Fantasia pour le Clavessin* in arpeggio style—is the *manualiter* counterpart of the *pedaliter* A-Minor Fugue, BWV 543. Despite its enormous length and unbroken, potentially monotonous, sixteenth-note motion throughout, it succeeds on account of its obvious virtuosity and owing to an effective concertante distinction between thematic and episodic figuration. Bach's indebtedness to the concerto is particularly clear in the ritornello structure of the Prelude in A Minor, BWV 894. Both the prelude and the fugue were later reworked as the outer movements of a true concerto: the Triple Concerto, BWV 1044 (whose authenticity as a work by Bach, however, has been challenged).[42]

The keyboard fantasia as a display of both technical and compositional virtuosity reaches its zenith in the *Chromatic Fantasia* in D Minor for harpsichord, BWV 903. As with the early Fantasia in A Minor, BWV 944, there is no ambiguity here about the intended instrument. The heading in one of the earliest copies reads *Fantasie* [*sic*] *chromatique pour le Clavecin*.[43] What defines both fantasias specifically as harpsichord compositions is no doubt their extensive, and specifically marked, arpeggio writing.

With the exception of the Goldberg Variations, the *Chromatic Fantasia* is Bach's best-known single keyboard composition; it has been endlessly performed (and analyzed) for more than two hundred years. In expression and technique it is (again with the exception of the Goldbergs) his most extravagant keyboard work; in harmony, undoubtedly, his boldest. Forkel's assertion that "this "Fantasia is unique and never had its like" (*diese Fantasie ist einzig und hat nie ihres Gleichen gehabt*) is routinely invoked. The composition, however, as Spitta was the first to observe,[44] is not altogether unlike the organ Fantasia in G Minor, BWV 542, insofar as both are unparalleled harmonic *tours de force*, whose seemingly spontaneous, "improvisational" flights of "fantasy"—rhapsodic passage work, enharmonic experimentation—are in fact subjected throughout to formal discipline of unparalleled subtlety. It is not inconceivable that both works, as Spitta suggested, were composed at about the same time—around 1720.[45] George Stauffer has pointed out similarities between the keyboard figuration preserved in an early version of the *Chromatic Fantasia*, BWV 903a, and in an early version of the fifth Brandenburg Concerto, BWV 1050a.[46]

The form of the Fantasia has been variously described as a two-part, three-part, or four-part design. A three-part "dialectical" conception seems most persuasive, consisting of a tempestuous opening toccata (to m. 49), an introspective central section, designated *Recitat[ivo]* in the early sources (mm. 49–61), and a final peroration in which the opening passage work returns and is ultimately reconciled (m. 68) with the pathos-laden rhetorical gestures of the central recitative.[47] Harmonically, the first section moves from tonic to dominant, the central section "prolongs" the dominant by means of an arpeggiation (A–E–C#), the final section returns to the orbit of the tonic in order to express a full authentic cadence: subdominant-dominant-tonic (ex. 5.5).

In its harmony the *Chromatic Fantasia* can be understood as an inquiry not only into the behavior of chromatic and enharmonic relations but into the problematic nature of the minor mode itself, whose elusiveness resides in the instability of its upper tetrachord.[48] Bach presents the issue programmatically at once in the two flourishes that open the work, which state the "melodic," "natural," and "harmonic" forms of the minor scale in close order. As a consequence of the changing inflections of the sixth and seventh scale degrees—the constantly changing combinations of half steps and whole steps, with their attendant changes in harmonic orientation—the interval of a second emerges as a unifying thematic motif, most conspicuously as a recurring, poignant "sigh" figure but also concentrated into an ornamental mordent or shaping the outline of entire phrases (ex. 5.6).

The fugue, though less celebrated than the fantasia, is as monumental in conception as the great organ fugues. For the sake of dramatic effect it abandons strict part writing at the end and indulges in massive chordal sonorities and "organistic"

Example 5.5. *Chromatic Fantasia*, BWV 903, tonal plan

Example 5.6. *Chromatic Fantasia*, BWV 903, motivic seconds

Example 5.7. *Chromatic Fantasia*, BWV 903, fugue subject

octave doubling in the bass. The unusually long and complex subject, quite unlike
the opening of the fantasia, is harmonically ambiguous at first and seems to contain
its own answer (ex. 5.7).[49]

As Hermann Keller has observed, the harmonic treatment of the subject is
extraordinary, too, in that it is used to effect modulations. The statement in measure
76, for example, begins in A minor, and ends, after passing through E minor, in B
minor[50]—a most uncommon choice of tonal goals for a composition in D minor.
No less than the fantasia, then, the fugue "is unique and never had its like."

The English Suites

Forkel's comment that these compositions "are known by the name of English Suites
because the composer made them for an Englishman of rank [*einen vornehmen
Engländer*]"[51] has not received much credence, but it should not be dismissed out
of hand. A copy once belonging to Johann Christian Bach carries the remark: "Fait
pour les Anglois" [*sic*]; moreover, in most early sources the upper stave is notated in
the treble rather than the soprano clef—counter to Bach's norm in both Weimar and
Köthen but conforming with English practice at the time.[52] At all events, the English
Suites are the earliest of Bach's three collections of keyboard suites. Considerations of
style—and the existence of an early version of the "first" suite (the Suite in A, BWV
806a) in the hand of Bach's Weimar colleague, Johann Gottfried Walther (1684–
1748)—suggest that Bach had begun to compose the suites at Weimar.[53]

The order of the dances is typical of a particularly German manifestation of the
suite tradition that extends back to Johann Froberger (1616–67). It begins with an
uninterrupted succession of the "core" dances—allemande, courante, sarabande—
and concludes with the gigue that is preceded by one or more optional dances.
Bach's immediate model for the English Suites, however, was almost certainly the six
suites by Charles François Dieupart (ca. 1667–ca. 1740), published in Amsterdam
in 1701, which have the same order and, like Bach's, begin with an introductory
movement. (Bach made copies of all six Dieupart suites in Weimar, between ca.
1710 and 1714, that is, at about the time that he seems to have been composing the
English Suites.)[54]

With the exception of the A-Major Suite, the English Suites are distinguished
by their stylistic and formal consistency.[55] The most conspicuous hallmark of the
set is the presence of a substantial prelude that is balanced, as a rule, at the end by
a correspondingly large-scale, contrapuntal gigue. Bach's recent study of the latest

Italian instrumental styles is reflected in the virtuosic and concertante style of the preludes and in their imaginative combination of fugal procedures with ritornello and da capo designs. The treatment of the core dances, on the other hand, is rather old fashioned: the allemandes are serious and essentially polyphonic; the courantes all belong to the French form—in 3/2 meter with extensive cross-rhythms; and the sarabandes closely observe the traditional rhythmic conventions of the dance, most notably the characteristically pervasive short-long rhythms.

The French Suites

The history of the French Suites is extraordinarily complex. Not only are there at least two versions of each of the six standard suites, BWV 812–17, but two further suites—the A-Minor, BWV 818, and the E-flat Major, BWV 819—are occasionally transmitted together with the French Suites in some early sources—either instead of or in addition to one or the other of the traditional six.[56] Later, more ornamented versions of the six suites are scattered in numerous eighteenth-century manuscripts of varying degrees of authority. Many of these changes and additions may reflect revisions made over time by J. S. Bach during the course of instruction; but it is impossible to determine whether all of them are authentic. Yet another version, indeed the earliest of all, has survived—at least for the first five suites. It was entered by J. S. Bach himself at the beginning of the 1722 *Clavierbüchlein* for Anna Magdalena Bach.[57]

Not even the intended order of the French Suites is altogether certain. In contrast to Bach's other collections of keyboard pieces, there is no compelling logic to the succession of keys in the standard sequence (D minor, C minor, B minor, E-flat major, G major, E major) or in any of the other successions represented in the early sources—apart from the binary division into three minor keys followed by three in the major and the scalewise descent of the first three keys. On the other hand, the number of movements increases from five (Suite 1), to six (Suites 2 and 3), to seven (Suites 4 and 5), to eight (Suite 6).

Dispensing with an opening prelude, the French Suites begin directly with the three traditional dances. The courante is represented, despite the uniformly French designation throughout, in its two opposing national styles: the older, more complex, French form, with its characteristic 3/2 meter (Suites I and 3), and the more recent, simpler, Italian form, notated in 3/4 (Suites 2, 4, 5, and 6). The collection is distinguished, finally, by the inclusion of unusual dances: the loure and the polonaise—both of which occur in none of Bach's other keyboard suites—and even a non-dance movement: the air.[58]

In contrast to the six "great" English Suites, Forkel describes these as the six "little suites" (*kleine Suiten*) and remarks that "they are generally called French Suites because they are written in the French taste. By design, the composer is here less learned than in his other suites, and has mostly used a pleasing, more predominant melody."[59] We may assume that by "the French taste" Forkel had in mind precisely the lighter, more homophonic textures as well as the more *galant* melodic writing that are the hallmarks of these suites. This style—virtually the antithesis of the English Suites—presumably reflected the taste, and very likely the influence, of the owner and dedicatee of the notebook in which the French Suites were originally inscribed: Anna Magdalena Bach.[60] In particular, the French Suites testify to her evident enthusiasm for the minuet. The dance appears in five of the French Suites— in three of them (Suites 2, 3, and 4) as a later addition. The sixth suite, for its part, includes both a polonaise and a minuet; moreover, the minuet appears after the gigue as the concluding dance of the suite—a formal device familiar from the first Brandenburg Concerto and another reflection of the French taste.[61]

The *Klavierbüchlein vor Wilhelm Friedemann Bach*

Exactly two months after his eldest son's ninth birthday, Bach began a small compilation of short keyboard pieces for him and inscribed them in a small oblong volume to which he gave the title *Clavierbüchlein vor Wilhelm Friedemann Bach*.[62] The volume enables us to reconstruct some of the first steps of Bach's pedagogical method. It begins with the rudiments—the names of the clefs and pitches—but then proceeds at once (omitting any discussion of rhythmic notation, for example) to the famous ornament table, the *Explication*, for a demonstration of how the ornament symbols are to be "properly" (*artig*) played. The (rather conservative) principles of keyboard fingering are explained next with the aid of an *Applicatio*, an extensively fingered composition, in C major and in binary form, consisting mainly of scale patterns and accompanying chords (ex. 5.8).[63]

Over the course of the following year or two the father, and occasionally the son, entered some two dozen compositions into the *Klavierbüchlein*—dances, chorale preludes, and, above all, fifteen keyboard preludes, eleven of them representing an early version of preludes from *The Well-Tempered Clavier* (see below).

Inventions and Sinfonias

After an interruption of more than a year, during which he had been preoccupied with *The Well-Tempered Clavier*, Bach returned to Friedemann's *Klavierbüchlein* and, along with his son, entered into it the Two- and Three-Part Inventions and Sinfonias.[64] The purpose of these new pieces, as Gerber's report makes plain, was to prepare the student for the preludes and fugues of *The Well-Tempered Clavier*.

In the *Klavierbüchlein* the fifteen two-part compositions are each designated *Praeambulum*, the three-part pieces *Fantasia*. Moreover, both series begin on C and are arranged as an ascending succession of seven natural keys, with natural thirds, followed by a descending succession of the eight remaining familiar keys (capital

Example 5.8. *Applicatio*, BWV 994

letters indicate major keys, lower case letters indicate minor keys): C, d, e, F, G, a, b; B-flat, A, g, f, E, E-flat, D, c. The major and minor keys on C-sharp, F-sharp, and A-flat, as well as any calling for more than four accidentals, are missing.[65]

Shortly afterward—certainly during the year 1723—Bach wrote out a new copy, renaming the two-part compositions *Inventio* and the three-part pieces *Sinfonia*, and reordering the keys of each series into a single ascending scale with the major mode consistently preceding the minor. Bach is thought to have taken the term *Inventio* from the *Invenzioni da camera*, op. 10, by Francesco Antonio Bonporti (Bologna, 1712), several of which Bach had copied out, evidently for use as figured bass exercises.[66] But Bach's Inventions have essentially nothing common with Bonporti's Corellian *sonate da chiesa* for violin and continuo, for they are premised on the fundamental equality of two voices and explore the various manifestations of imitative polyphony, canon, and invertible counterpoint. The designation *Sinfonia* for the three-part pieces is similarly curious, since it was most commonly associated at this time with instrumental ensemble music. It may have been intended to evoke its Latin cognate *Symphonia* in its archaic and most generalized sense as a concord of multiple parts. Bach also provided an elaborate title page:

UPRIGHT INSTRUCTION [*AUFFRICHTIGE ANLEITUNG*],
wherein the lovers of the clavier, and especially those desirous of learning, are shown a clear way not only (1) of learning to play clearly in two voices, but also, after further progress, (2) of dealing correctly and well with three *obbligato* parts; furthermore, at the same time not only of having good inventions but of developing the same well, and above all of arriving at a singing style in playing, all the while acquiring a strong foretaste of composition.[67]

The idiosyncratic terminology of this text has been extensively interpreted. The reference to a "cantabile style" of playing, in particular, has been variously interpreted as "lyric" and "expressive" (Spitta), "songlike" and "legato" (Keller), as well as clearly articulated, like the words of a sung text.[68] Given the strict part writing in these compositions, Bach may have had in mind a polyphonically conceived rendition, that is, one concerned primarily with the independence of each of the constituent "singing" voices.

The entire text invites exegesis. The moral tone resonating at once in the initial word "auffrichtig" ("upright," "candid," "honest," or "straightforward") is no less apparent than the intensity of the pedagogical commitment that informs the whole. Although Bach's formulations about having good "inventions," "developing" them well, and playing them in a "singing style" have obvious corollaries in classical rhetoric—*Inventio, Elaboratio* (or *Dispositio*), and *Elocutio* (or *Executio*)—precisely what Bach meant by his terms has been a matter of controversy.

Is the "invention," of the C-Major Invention, for example, the opening seven-note motive or the contrapuntal framework in which this motive is embedded?[69] Similarly, is the generating idea of the C-Minor its complex theme or the technique of strict canonic imitation that is almost invariably associated with it? The "idea" of the E-Major Invention, for its part, is surely the two-part contrary motion model that embraces both the ascending scale in the bass and the descending scale in the treble.

Apart from their observance of conventional tonal plans, the Two-Part Inventions are formally unpredictable. In all cases, the initial "invention," once formulated, is transposed, contrapuntally recombined, and extended by sequential patterning and repetition—in a word, "developed"—the artful disposition of these essentially mechanical procedures constituting, in effect, the composition.[70] Perhaps Bach called these pieces "Inventions" precisely because they largely avoid predictable formal schemata. (A traditional binary form with repeated sections appears only in the E-Major Invention.)

The Three-Part Sinfonias manage to combine fugal texture with that of the contemporary Italian instrumental trio sonata, insofar as the bass occasionally functions as a continuo-like support for two closely related treble parts. The sonata style is most pronounced in the E-flat Sinfonia, whose duetting upper parts survive in several different ornamented versions. Its rococo elegance and fundamentally homophonic texture stand in the strongest imaginable contrast to the F-Minor Sinfonia—a strict triple fugue combining *empfindsam* sigh figures, chromatic ostinati, and intensely dissonant combinations.[71]

In their stylistic and expressive range as well as their extensive appropriation of fugal procedure the Three-Part Sinfonias undeniably succeed in leading "those desirous of learning" to the threshold of *The Well-Tempered Clavier*. They fulfill this purpose so well, however, that their own claim to the status of serious artworks often remains unrecognized.

BACH'S KEYBOARD MUSIC   97

The Well-Tempered Clavier I

Bach's self-imposed pedagogical mission reached its first artistic culmination with the completion, in Köthen in 1722, of the first volume of *The Well-Tempered Clavier*. Ernst Ludwig Gerber (1746–1819), the son of Heinrich Nicolaus, relates: "According to a certain tradition [Bach] wrote his Tempered Clavier . . . in a place where annoyance, boredom, and the absence of any kind of musical instrument forced him to resort to this pastime."[72] E. L. Gerber probably had this account from his father, who presumably had heard it directly from Bach during his years of tutelage.

The disagreeable place where Bach "wrote" (*geschrieben*) the WTC—or, more likely, as Alfred Dürr suggested, the place where he conceived the plan of gathering together a number of existing preludes and fugues and augmenting them to embrace the twenty-four keys—was presumably not Köthen but Weimar, where Bach spent the last four weeks of his tenure under arrest for having "insisted too stubbornly on his release" (*seiner Halßstarrigen Bezeügung v. zu. erwingenden dimission*) from the ducal service.[73] Earlier conjecture had posited that Bach had composed, or worked on, the *Orgelbüchlein* during his Weimar detention, but it is now clear that most of the *Orgelbüchlein* chorales had been completed years earlier, perhaps 1708–10/12.[74] It is equally clear that work on the WTC must have begun long before 1722, the date on the title page of Bach's famous autograph score.

In fact, no fewer than three preliminary versions of the work survive, whose readings antedate the earliest readings of the autograph.[75] These early versions reveal that the fugues were originally designated *Fughetta*; that compositions in the minor mode with a natural third occasionally preceded their counterparts in the major mode (d-D, e-E, a-A); that several compositions (the Preludes and Fugues in C Minor and F Minor, the Preludes in A-flat Major and B-flat Minor) originally had "Dorian" key signatures; and that the D-sharp Minor Fugue, along with the Prelude and Fugue in G-sharp Minor, were originally in D minor and G minor, respectively—a strong indication that they were probably composed before Bach had conceived the idea of the WTC, and were later transposed by a half step in order to represent the more exotic keys in the collection.

The most significant differences of musical substance between the familiar and the preliminary versions of the WTC concern the preludes. New coda-like sections were added to the preludes in c, C-sharp, d, and e (in the latter the subsequent addition of an arioso melody in the right hand as well). Other preludes, too, were substantially expanded—none more dramatically than the C-Major, which increased in three stages from twenty-four to thirty-five measures.[76] The revisions bear witness, above all, to a new conception of the prelude as a genre and of its relationship to the fugue. Whereas the early versions of the preludes typically consist of undifferentiated figuration patterns that betray their origin as technical exercises, the revised versions are formally articulated by means of sectional contrasts or the introduction of subtle recapitulations of earlier passages. They are independent, self-sufficient movements and not merely prefaces to more substantial compositions.[77]

To judge from the handsome script and the elaborate title page of the 1722 autograph of the WTC, it was intended to be a clean, "fair copy" of the work. Over the course of time, however, and most likely in conjunction with his teaching activities, Bach repeatedly entered corrections into the manuscript. It is possible, in fact, to identify at least four later stages in the evolution of the work, extending over close to a twenty-year period, into the early 1740s.[78] What Bach meant by "well-tempered" in his title will probably never be definitively resolved. The only reasonably authentic opinion regarding keyboard temperament attributed to Bach is Kirnberger's comment that Bach "expressly required of him that he tune all the thirds sharp."[79] For the rest, it is likely that Bach did not have strict equal temperament in mind but was only concerned that it be possible to play in all twenty-four major and minor keys.[80]

The Well-Tempered Clavier marks the culmination of a keyboard tradition that can be traced to the Renaissance practice of performing the verses of the Magnificat in alternation between the chorus and the organ. Since the Magnificat was sung in each of the eight church modes, the *alternatim* practice precipitated the composition for the organ of cycles of Magnificat "versets" in the eight modes or "tones." The opening section of such an organ Magnificat was typically in the style of a free "intonation," or prelude, with the following versets set as brief fugues or "fughettas." The genre was particularly cultivated during the seventeenth century among South German composers. Over time the number of keys represented increased, while the number of versets or fughettas for each key decreased. By the end of the seventeenth century the number of versets was reduced to a single prelude and fughetta in each key.[81] The immediate model for the WTC was the *Ariadne Musica* (1702–15) by Johann Caspar Ferdinand Fischer (ca. 1656–1746). Fischer's collection consists of preludes and fugues in twenty keys.[82] Bach's use of Fischer's model is evident not only in the overall plan but also in the close resemblance of several fugal subjects in the two collections.

Bach's volume, however, is far more than a collection of well-crafted preludes and fugues and a demonstration of the usability of every chromatic key. It is a comprehensive survey of the most important and disparate forms and styles of the era, all developed in accordance with a single unifying compositional principle. The juxtaposition of diametrically contrasting styles and structures at the outset—in the first two fugues—can be regarded as programmatic for the entire collection. The Fugue in C Major is a "strict fugue"—a *fuga obligata*—a continuous succession of expositions without the relief of intervening episodes.[83] The diatonic subject is reminiscent of a Renaissance hexachord theme, and the conjunct linear writing generally suggests the vocal style and texture of a motet. The C-Minor Fugue, in contrast, with its clear alternation of expositions and episodes, is an example of a "free fugue," a *fuga libera*. Its disjunct melodic writing and motivic upbeat patterns are "instrumental" rather than "vocal" in style and evocative of the dance—a bourrée, perhaps—while the episodes maintain the texture of a baroque trio sonata.

Other styles and genres represented, or at least suggested, among the fugues include bourrée (C-sharp Major), seventeenth-century *stylus gravis* ricercar (C-sharp Minor), French ouverture (D), sixteenth-century *stile antico* motet (D-sharp Minor), passepied (F), and gigue (G). With respect to contrapuntal technique we find not only fugues for three or four voices but for two (E Minor) and five (C-sharp Minor) as well; stretto fugues (C, B-flat Minor), a triple fugue (C-sharp Minor), and a *fugue d'artifice* (D-sharp Minor), with its ingenious combinations and recombinations of augmentations, diminutions, stretti, and inversions.

Among the preludes the stylistic models and allusions extend from the Renaissance *intonazione* (C) to the Corellian trio sonata (B Minor), and encompass the *perpetuum mobile* (C Minor), two-part invention (C-sharp Major, F), loure (C-sharp Minor), toccata (E-flat, B-flat), sarabande (E-flat Minor), pastorale (E, also a binary sonata), aria (E Minor), Italian concerto (A-flat), and finally, the remarkable B-flat Minor Prelude, with its relentless motivic consistency and altogether original and forward-looking climactic design.[84]

The volume is also an encyclopedia of musical *affects* (in the vocabulary of the Baroque era), offering what a later age would describe as "character pieces" in which are represented every shade of expression: the playful (Fugue in C-sharp), the witty (Fugue in E-flat), the cheerful (Fugue in F), the serene (Fugue in D-sharp Minor), the sombre (Fugue in F Minor), the tragic (Prelude in B-flat Minor, Fugue in B Minor).

As to "form," the only valid generalization is that a fugue will normally maintain a strict number of voices and, rather like a chess game, will begin almost ritualistically with the constituent parts entering one by one with a statement of the subject in alternation on the tonic and its upper or lower fifth.[85] When a fugue, like the C-Minor, is based on the alternation of tonally static expositions and modulating episodes between them, then the connection with the formal rationale of the modern ritornello concerto is clear. A fugue such as the F-Major, on the other hand, adopts not only the rhythm and meter of a baroque dance (passepied) but its regular phrase periodicity and even something like its binary tonal division—if not its repetition scheme.

For all their stylistic and formal variety, however, the compositions of the WTC are based on a modern tonal structure ultimately reducible to an archetypal cadential pattern: typically I–V–vi–IV (or ii)–V–I in the major mode, or i–III–V–i in the minor. Perhaps the most impressive achievement of the work, in fact, is its fusion of the potentially antithetical principles of functional tonality and linear counterpoint.

The Second Synthesis: Leipzig, 1726–1741

The Partitas

During his first three years in Leipzig Bach was completely preoccupied with the composition of church music. But by 1726 he had begun to turn his attention once again to keyboard music, proclaiming the event with the inauguration of an ambitious publishing venture. Bach evidently took both the title *Klavierübung* (Keyboard Exercise) and the designation "partita" from a publication of his Leipzig predecessor, Johann Kuhnau (1660–1722), who published two volumes of seven suites (or *Parthien*) each, under the title *Neue Klavierübung* (Leipzig, 1689, 1692).[86] Bach's partitas were issued singly from 1726 to 1731, the serial publication concluding in 1731 with the appearance of the collected edition, designated "OPUS 1."[87]

The number of copies printed (at Bach's own expense) is unknown. The size of the initial print run for the *Musical Offering*, according to Bach himself, in a letter of October 1748 to his cousin, was "only 100," most of them given away "to good friends."[88] The print runs for the volumes of the *Klavierübung* were presumably larger. The item was expensive: individual partitas sold for at least 12 groschen each. (A groschen was worth one twenty-fourth of a thaler; 12 groschen, accordingly, was the equivalent of one-half thaler.) The complete set probably cost 3 thalers—surely an indication that the *Liebhaber* (music lovers), addressed on the work's title page and invited to "refresh their spirits" by learning to play these compositions were seriously committed and proficient. Despite its price, a second printing followed, as did a third.[89] Encouraged, no doubt, by the evident commercial success of the venture, Bach published three further volumes of the *Klavierübung* over the course of the next ten years.

The key succession of the six Partitas—B-flat, c, a, D, G, e—is ingenious (ex. 5.9). It consists of three major and three minor keys organized into two symmetrical groups of three (major-minor-minor, major-major-minor) and arranged as a succession of ascending tonics (B-flat major, C-minor, D major, E minor) intertwined with a descending series (B-flat major, A minor, G major), the intervallic distances between adjacent keys growing, accordingly, from a second to a sixth, and the tonal extremities from the first partita to the last (B-flat to E minor) separated by a tritone and belonging to different modes. Attesting to the same systematic mentality, each partita begins with an introductory movement bearing a different genre designation, the second half of the series, that is, Partita 4, initiated with an ouverture. (Bach would repeat this symbolic formal gesture at the midpoint of the Goldberg Variations.) The dances proper begin each time with the traditional allemande. In Partitas 1, 3, and 5 it is followed by a corrente; in Partitas 2, 4, and 6 by a courante. This time, in contrast to the French Suites (see above), the national distinction is properly designated throughout. The sarabandes, for their part, largely ignore the typical rhythmic patterns of the traditional dance, while the familiar optional dances (bourrée, gavotte, minuet)—a constituent of all the English Suites and half the French Suites—have been almost entirely eliminated. They have been replaced in effect by "character" pieces in binary or rondo form: rondeau, capriccio, burlesca, scherzo, aria, air.

Example 5.9. *Klavierübung* I, the tonics of the six Partitas

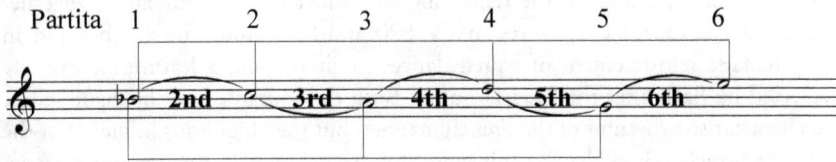

The *Italian Concerto* and the *French Ouverture*

In 1735, four years after the appearance of the collected edition of the partitas, Bach published "Part 2" (*Zweyter Theil*) of the *Klavierübung*, "consisting," according to the title, "in a Concerto after the Italian Taste and an Ouverture after the French Manner for a Harpsichord with Two Manuals" (*bestehend in einem Concerto nach Italiaenischen Gusto und einer Overture nach Französicher Art, vor ein Clavicymbel mit zweyen Manualen*).[90] Bach demonstrated the link between this volume and its predecessor not only by retaining the series title but by continuing the succession of ascending tonics represented by the first, second, fourth, and sixth partitas—B-flat, c, D, e—to the first piece in the new volume: the Italian Concerto is in F major. Although the Ouverture—perhaps planned at first (in emulation of Kuhnau's collection) as the seventh of the suites promised for the first volume—was originally in C minor,[91] it was now transposed to B minor, obviously in order to form a tritone with the F-major tonality of the concerto symbolizing the diametric opposition of the two national styles.[92] In thus juxtaposing of the Italian and French styles Bach may have been following the example of François Couperin, whose *Les goûts réunis* and *Les nations* had been published in the mid-1720s. Bach's Concerto and Ouverture represent the opposition not only of national traditions but of generational styles, as well—that is, of new and old.

The national identity of the Italian Concerto, BWV 971, is established at once by its genre. Its modernity—and to a large extent its lasting appeal—resides in its accessibility: its formal clarity and textural simplicity. The numerous two- and four-measure phrases, small-scale repetitions, frequent and emphatic cadences, contrasting solo theme, "drum bass" accompaniments, along with regular ritornello designs and recapitulations in the outer movements, are all hallmarks of the pre-Classical concerto style, as it was cultivated in the 1730s and 1740s in both Italy and Germany.

Bach's last contribution to the genre of the keyboard suite, the Ouverture in B Minor, BWV 831, on the other hand, is deliberately retrospective—just as representative of the French rococo as the concerto is of the Italian pre-Classical style. Like Bach's early keyboard ouvertures of some thirty years before, the composition dispenses with the allemande: its traditional introductory function—as in the four orchestral Ouvertures, BWV 1066–69—rendered superfluous by the presence of the introductory "ouverture" movement. The composition also follows older French practice in its separation of the remaining core movements (eliminated altogether in the early keyboard Ouvertures, BWV 820 and 822) from one another and in its systematic reinstatement of paired dances in alternation, a feature increasingly neglected by Bach after the English Suites. Both the courante and the gigue reflect the characteristic rhythms of the French manner; but the ubiquitous influence of the concerto principle is evident in this work, too, specifically, in the two outer movements: the ouverture and the concluding "echo."[93]

Most of Bach's Leipzig keyboard music was written over the course of approximately fifteen years, from about 1726 to about 1741, either in conjunction with the ongoing publication of the four volumes of the *Klavierübung* or with the compilation of *The Well-Tempered Clavier* II and the *Art of Fugue*. More precisely, with the exception of "Part 2" of the *Klavierübung*, Bach's involvement with keyboard music seems to have been concentrated at the beginning (1726–31) and the end (ca. 1738–42) of this fifteen-year period. Much of the seven-year interim was absorbed by Bach's duties in connection with the Leipzig Collegium Musicum (whose direction he had assumed in 1729) as well as by his increasing connections with Dresden.

Between the appearance of "Part 2" of the *Klavierübung* and the publication of "Part 3" in 1739, Bach completed seven harpsichord ("cembalo") concertos, BWV 1052–58.[94] Whether they—along, perhaps, with the concertos for multiple harpsichords—were written primarily for performance by the Leipzig Collegium Musicum or for Bach's recitals at Dresden is not clear. They may well have been performed at both venues. In any event, Bach's renewed interest at just this time in the genre of the concerto—specifically the then new and fashionable keyboard concerto—is attested both by the completion of the accompanied concertos and by the publication of the unaccompanied Italian Concerto, BWV 971.[95]

Characteristically, at just about the same time that Bach was revisiting the ever-modern genre of the harpsichord concerto, he also was preparing "Part 3" of the *Klavierübung* for publication, a collection mainly of *stile antico* chorale settings explicitly (according to the title page) "vor die Orgel." Nonetheless, the volume contains four Duetti, BWV 802–5, that do not require pedals, along with eight chorale settings explicitly designated *manualiter* and hence playable on any keyboard instrument. Understandably, however, the entire volume, with the exception of the Duetti, has been regarded as the exclusive province of organists.

The Well-Tempered Clavier II

Like its counterpart of 1722, the second *Well-Tempered Clavier*, compiled between 1738 and 1740, stands at the end of a period of wide-ranging stylistic assimilation that may be characterized this time as a "second synthesis," one that extended even farther afield historically: on the one hand engaging in an ever deeper exploration of the music of the past, and on the other, embracing the latest stylistic developments as advanced by a younger generation of composers. The development had begun with Bach's assumption of the directorship of the Leipzig Collegium Musicum in 1729 and with the intensification of his contacts with the Dresden court shortly thereafter.[96] The two powerful centers of musical activity in the Saxon capital—specifically, the Roman Catholic Church and the Italian opera—exerted a two-pronged influence on Bach's artistic development hardly less profound than that engendered by his exposure to the Italian concerto some two decades earlier. Through the church Bach intensified his long-standing historicizing interest in the *stile antico*; through the opera and its attendant concert life at court he expanded his familiarity with the latest musical fashions.

Bach's flirtation in WTC II with music written "according to the latest taste" (*nach dem neuesten Geschmack*, in the words of his one-time pupil Lorenz Mizler),[97] is most apparent in the preludes. Whereas only one prelude in WTC I—the last— is set with two repeated halves; ten in WTC II are so designed. Half of these (D, D-sharp minor, F minor, G-sharp minor, B-flat major), along with nine further preludes without a central double bar repetition (C, C-sharp minor, E-flat, F, F-sharp major, F-sharp minor, A-flat, A, B-flat minor)—in all more than half the preludes of the volume—are precocious explorations of the emerging pre-Classical sonata design. That is, they include clear recapitulations of the opening material, usually in the tonic, occasionally (the Preludes in C, A-flat, B-flat Minor) in the subdominant. The full "three-part" sonata form—exposition, development, recapitulation— is articulated with emphatic clarity in the "orchestral" D-Major Prelude: a veritable opera sinfonia for keyboard alone and hence in its own way a counterpart to the presumably contemporaneous Italian Concerto, BWV 971. Considering that some of these compositions must have been composed before 1740—that is, well before the publication of landmarks in the early history of the sonata such as Giovanni Platti's sonatas, op. 1, or C. P. E. Bach's "Prussian" Sonatas—it does not seem to be an exaggeration to place J. S. Bach in the vanguard of sonata composers.

Bach's indebtedness to the music of his sons' generation is apparent, too, from his appropriation of such characteristically *empfindsam* features as the expressive ornamentation of the Preludes in C-sharp Minor and G-sharp Minor, and the "sigh" figures of the F-Minor. Other preludes remain within the stylistic orbit of WTC I. The C-Major and B-Major Preludes exploit concertante writing, while the Preludes in E, F, A-flat, and B-flat evoke the pastoral style. As before, many take the Two- and Three-Part Inventions as their model, united at times with allusions to traditional dance rhythms (the allemande in the C-Minor and D-sharp Minor Preludes, the corrente in the E-Minor).

Curiously, the "rhetorical frame" of the collection seems to be inverted in comparison with that of its predecessor. WTC I begins with an intimate *arpeggiando* prelude; WTC II, in stunning contrast, opens with a monumental pedal point. But the style of the second C-Major Prelude soon evolves into decorated broken-chord patterns reminiscent of the *style brisé*. This striking reunion, at the outset, of the quintessential organ and harpsichord idioms can be taken, perhaps, as emblematic for the entire collection.[98] No less remarkable are the contrasting conclusions of the two volumes: the somber, tragic, B-Minor Fugue of WTC I vis-à-vis the playful B-Minor Fugue of WTC II, with its humorous octave leaps—an anticlimactic *dénouement* not unlike that produced by the last of the Goldberg Variations.

Modern elements are occasionally evident in the fugues as well. Schulenberg refers to the *galant* qualities of those in C, F, F Minor, and F-sharp Major and the sonata-like design of the B-flat Major.[99] Their concentration at the midpoint and endpoints of the collection is noteworthy. For the most part, however, the fugues of WTC II hold the stylistic balance to the preludes by virtue of their more conservative posture and their frequent indulgence in contrapuntal artifice. There are no fewer than three stretto fugues (D, E, B-flat Minor), four double fugues (C-sharp Minor, A-flat, G-sharp Minor, and B), and one triple fugue (F-sharp Minor). In addition, the declamatory rhetoric of several subjects—especially those in G Minor and A Minor—reflects Bach's extensive experience with choral fugues in the church cantatas of the early Leipzig period (ex. 5.10). On the other hand, the archaic stance of the fugues in D, E-flat, E, and B attests to the composer's intensified interest during the 1730s in the pseudo-Renaissance *stile antico*, the pendant to his experiments at just the same time with the *style galant* and pre-Classical style.

The history of Bach's second series of preludes and fugues in all the major and minor keys is, if anything, even more complex, its prehistory even longer, than that of the first. No fewer than nine of the forty-eight compositions from WTC II survive in discrete, earlier versions.[100] Copies of some of them, prepared by members of Bach's circle during the 1720s, suggest that Bach was contemplating a "simple" series of preludes and three-voice fugues, perhaps limited to the "white" keys with natural thirds: C, d, e, F, G, and a.[101] Moreover, unlike the first compilation, we cannot be certain that WTC II ever received its final form. Evidently working from earlier copies of the individual pieces, Bach, along with his wife, prepared a score over a period of some two or three years extending from about 1738/39 to about 1740.[102] This source, however, the so-called London autograph (a facsimile of which was published in 1980), is not an integral volume but rather an incomplete set of separate, unbound sheets, one for each prelude and fugue pair. This organization would have made it an easy matter for the composer to substitute individual items, if he so decided, without disturbing the whole.

The Fantasia in C Minor, BWV 906

On two separate occasions—the first between 1726 and 1731, the second between circa 1738 and 1740—Bach took the unusual pains of writing out a fair copy of this well-known composition. The time periods of these activities, along with aspects of the notation and the style of the composition, are suggestive.[103] In the first instance,

Example 5.10. *Well-Tempered Clavier* 2, Fugue in G Minor, BWV 885; *Well-Tempered Clavier* 2, Fugue in A Minor, BWV 889

BWV 885

BWV 889

the Fantasia could have been intended to serve as the opening movement of the second Partita of the *Klavierübung*, the C-Minor, BWV 826. If so, then the flamboyant technique of hand crossing that had been introduced in the concluding gigue of Partita 1 would have carried over to the opening movement of Partita 2. In the second instance, the bipartite sonata form of the fantasia would have recommended it as the representative of C minor in WTC II. In fact, the second autograph appends to the Fantasia the fragment of a Fugue, BWV 906/2. Assuming this conjecture is correct, it is not clear why Bach then decided to remove BWV 906 from the WTC in favor of the present C-Minor Prelude and Fugue, but the reasons may be the same as those that prompted him to abandon the highly (perhaps overly) chromatic fugue altogether, before he had finished copying it.[104]

The Final Decade

The Goldberg Variations

It is odd that the *Klavierübung*, Bach's *magnum opus* of keyboard music, does not contain a volume of fugues. Given the composer's lifelong cultivation and supreme mastery of the form—a supremacy recognized and appreciated by his contemporaries—a fugue collection certainly would have made an obvious, and fitting, conclusion to the series. In fact, during the late 1730s and early 1740s Bach was occupied not only with the compilation and composition of *The Well-Tempered Clavier* II but with the *Art of Fugue* as well. The thought is hardly outlandish that he may have intended to include one or the other (or both of them) in the *Klavierübung*. (The inclusion of both, along with the Goldberg Variations, would have brought the number of "Parts" of the *Klavierübung* to the traditional six.) For some reason, however, completion of both WTC II and the *Art of Fugue* was interrupted—perhaps, among other things, by the commission of the Goldberg Variations—and neither work reached final form.

The *Keyboard Practice Consisting in an ARIA with Divers Variations*, universally known as the Goldberg Variations, was published (most probably in the year 1741) as the final volume of the *Klavierübung*;[105] but the composition is more usually regarded as marking a new beginning, standing at the threshold of Bach's last creative period, and initiating the series of formidable, austere instrumental cycles that include the *Art of Fugue*, the *Canonic Variations on* "Vom Himmel hoch," and the *Musical Offering*. According to Forkel, the work was commissioned by the Russian ambassador to the Dresden court, Baron Hermann Carl von Keyserlingk (1696–1764), for his harpsichordist, Johann Gottlieb Goldberg (1727–56), a former Bach pupil.[106]

The Goldberg Variations constitute the largest single keyboard composition published at any time during the eighteenth century. The work is another grand Bachian synthesis—one that this time, as Manfred Bukofzer suggested, "sums up the entire history of Baroque variation."[107] The theme, a sarabande of sorts,[108] and all thirty variations are built on the same thirty-two-measure ground bass: nine variations are in the form of strict canons, each appearing (as every third number) at a different interval of imitation and systematically proceeding from the unison to the ninth. Among the remaining variations we find an *Ouverture*, a *Fugetta*, a trio sonata, several different dances, and a *Quodlibet*, or medley of popular tunes.

We also find keyboard writing of the most extravagant sort—hand-crossings, passages in thirds, trills in inner parts, rapid arpeggios and runs. Demanding and idiomatic keyboard writing at this level of difficulty can be found, if anywhere, in the works of only one other composer of the time: Domenico Scarlatti (1685–1757). Indeed, there are striking similarities between the title of Scarlatti's *Essercizi per gravicembalo* (published in London, 1738 or 1739), consisting of thirty virtuoso sonatas, and that of Bach's synonymous *Clavierübung . . . vors Clavicimbel*, consisting of thirty virtuoso variations.[109]

What is most remarkable about Bach's composition, however, is not its compositional or keyboard virtuosity but its modernity. Departing from the practice of his predecessors, Bach not only rigorously retains the regular phrase structure of the theme throughout the work but reinforces it with his variation patterns and figurations. This is accomplished, for the most part, by the direct replication of phrase units. In the first section of the first variation, for example, the pattern of the first four measures is repeated in the next four, with the right and left hands exchanging their parts. Then a new four-measure pattern is introduced at the beginning of the second eight-measure period. This, too, is repeated after four measures, again with the parts of the right and left hands exchanged. This persistent four-measure organization is maintained even in the tenth variation, the *Fugetta*.

But the phrase structure could be projected just as well by juxtaposing to the first idea another—perhaps completely contrasting—idea, of equal length. In Variation 14, for example, a long trilled note in various registers is followed by running arpeggio patterns in eighths and sixteenths (fig. 5.1). These in turn are followed by an

Figure 5.1. Goldberg Variations, BWV 988. Beginning of Variation 14. Original edition (Nuremberg, ca. 1741)

outburst of mordents alternating between the hands. There is then a rush of thirty-second notes combined with a crossing of hands, and the section ends with a flurry of thirty-second-note mordents for both hands together. Such "disorderly, excessive" variety, such sudden, capricious shifts of ideas and patterns are altogether "un-Bachian"—and altogether modern.

Even more than the keyboard virtuosity, then, the thoroughgoing periodicity constitutes a "progressive" element in the Goldberg Variations. In fact, Bach's rekindled interest in the variation form at this time, at the beginning of the last decade of his life—and for the first time since his youth—could well have been stimulated by his interest in exploring the compositional potential of this time-honored, but suddenly modern, principle of musical organization.

The *Art of Fugue*

The *Art of Fugue* owes its reputation as Bach's final composition to the circumstance that it was published posthumously and was unfinished at his death. In fact, however, the surviving autograph score reveals that most of the work had been composed by 1742, that is, within about a year of the publication of the Goldberg Variations.[110] Moreover, in its conception, the *Art of Fugue* represents the next logical step for Bach, following on the WTC and the Goldberg Variations, for it unites the basic compositional premises of both. Like the former it is a collection of fugal compositions surveying a variety of contrapuntal styles and techniques. Like the latter it not only introduces the technique of strict canon but, most significantly—and unlike all previous didactic collections of contrapuntal models (for example, Johann Theile's *Musikalisches Kunstbuch* of fifty years earlier and Johann Mattheson's quite recent *Wohlklingende Fingersprache*)—it, too, is designed as a set of "variations."[111] That is, all the contrapuncti and canons make use of the same subject, melodically embellished or contrapuntally altered though it may be from one movement to the next.

The *Art of Fugue* is not just an anthology but quite literally a *Gradus ad Parnassum* of counterpoint. The fourteen untitled movements of the original autograph version were arranged in order of increasing complexity or contrapuntal rigor: simple, double, and counter-fugues, followed by a canon at the octave, then triple fugues and mirror fugues (along with an arrangement of the mirror fugue for two claviers) followed by an augmentation canon.[112] The inclusion, specifically, of triple fugues in the collection—the first for three voices, the second for four—may have been Bach's response to a published challenge issued to him by Johann Mattheson in his *Vollkommener Kapellmeister* to produce such a composition.[113]

Owing to its tonal and thematic unity and, above all, its overarching concern with contrapuntal artifice, the style of the *Art of Fugue*, in contrast to Bach's earlier fugal collections, is relatively uniform, and frequently reminiscent of the *stile antico* (particularly so in the large note values chosen for the notation of several movements in the published version). As Schulenberg remarks with reference to the opening movements, "Many passages lack the well-defined harmonic rhythm and strong sense of harmonic directionality one expects in a late-Baroque work, and the modulatory range is very limited."[114] Yet there are modern touches even here, for example, the "sigh" figures in the augmentation canon, and the pervasive dotted rhythms in Contrapunctus 6, designated "in Stylo Francese" in the original print. Moreover, it may well be that the intense chromaticism, dissonance, and tonal obscurity of many passages in the *Art of Fugue* (for example, in Contrapuncti 3 and 13) were just as deliberately intended to be demonstrations of harmonic speculation as the elaborate canonic combinations were of contrapuntal ingenuity. They should be understood, accordingly, not as archaic relics but as a decidedly modern, even "visionary," experiment, one that Bach would resume—in the B–A–C–H episode of the unfinished fugue—when he returned to the work at the end of his life and also when he completed the last-composed sections of the Mass in B Minor (see chapter 9).

The *Musical Offering*

On July 7, 1747, some five years after he had penned much of the score of the *Art of Fugue*, Bach published a *Musical Offering to His Royal Majesty in Prussia*. The story of the work's origin is well-known. In May 1747 Bach had given a command performance at the court of Frederick the Great in Potsdam, on which occasion the king played a peculiar theme, purportedly of his own invention, on his Silbermann fortepiano and requested that Bach improvise a fugue on the subject. He also asked the composer to improvise a fugue in six parts. According to the newspaper account, Bach fulfilled the task to the king's satisfaction and to everyone's astonishment and promised to "set it down on paper in a regular fugue and have it engraved on copper."[115]

The engraving, however, included not only the three-voice fugue but also a new six-part fugue—this one, too, unlike the one he had performed in Potsdam, based on the king's subject—along with ten canons and a trio sonata, all making use of the royal theme. Bach's decision to expand the publication in this way may have been influenced by his induction, in June 1747, into the erudite Society of the Musical Sciences, founded by his former pupil Lorenz Mizler (1711–78). For that occasion, too, Bach had produced a learned work, the *Canonic Variations on the Chorale* "Vom Himmel hoch," BWV 769. Both prestigious events, then—occurring in rapid succession—would understandably have provoked a renewed interest in the compositional problems first explored in the Goldberg Variations and the *Art of Fugue*: contrapuntal artifice and thematic unity.[116]

The two keyboard fugues of the *Musical Offering* are both designated *Ricercar* in the original edition, even though the two compositions could hardly be more different.[117] Bach's interest, as so often before, was evidently in juxtaposing opposites: the three-part composition is a quite loose-textured work, intended, perhaps, to capture the character of the original improvisation. By the same token, it is also modern in style, roughly binary in form,[118] and alluding at times—as a gesture perhaps to the royal taste—to popular *galant* mannerisms such as triplets and sigh figures. The six-part setting, on the other hand, conforms to the more traditional understanding of Ricercar. It is uncompromisingly contrapuntal, although lacking the traditional artifices of canon and stretto. Except for its chromaticism, dictated by the royal subject, it is distinctly old-fashioned.[119] Finally, the three-part Ricercar, with its "sighs," arpeggios, and broken chords, is clearly music for stringed keyboard instrument—the harpsichord, if not, indeed, the fortepiano on which it originated; just as clearly, the monumentality and massive sonorities of the six-part Ricercar strongly encourage, even if they do not mandate, performance on the organ.[120]

B–A–C–H: The Revision of the Art of Fugue

Membership in Mizler's Society, along with the publication of the *Musical Offering*, may have prompted Bach's decision in the last years of his life to return to the *Art of Fugue* and to prepare it for publication.[121] In the spring of 1751 a revised and expanded version of the work was published posthumously, the task apparently carried out by Bach's son Carl Philipp Emanuel and Johann Friedrich Agricola. The edition includes four new constituent movements: a second simple fugue with inverted subject, two canons (one at the tenth and one at the twelfth), and a fragmentary fugue *a 3 Soggetti*; five movements are substantially expanded, while others appear in revised form. In addition, each movement is designated either *contrapunctus* or *canon* and in most cases carries a verbal indication of its principal contrapuntal device. Finally, the movements appear in a new sequence, and the publication ends with a completely unrelated composition—the chorale prelude on the tune "Wenn wir in höchsten Nöthen sein," BWV 668a, offered by the editors in compensation for the incomplete fugue.

As it appears in the print, the new order is at least partially corrupt, but it is clear that the expansion and the reorganization of the work reflected a new conception of its purpose, which is now more concerned, perhaps, with the representation of fugal categories than with demonstrating degrees of contrapuntal complexity.[122]

Altogether new is the addition of a fugal category that represents the *ne plus ultra* of contrapuntal complexity. Although the *Art of Fugue*, as a whole, can no longer be considered Bach's final work, that distinction may well still belong to the fugue *a 3 Soggetti*. The autograph of the legendary unfinished fugue survives on a separate sheet, written at the very end of Bach's life: sometime between August 1748 and October 1749.[123] For over a hundred years the fragment—which breaks off after a remarkably chromatic section based on the subject B–A–C–H—has been taken to be the quadruple fugue mentioned in the composer's obituary, whose missing final section was to reintroduce the main theme of the work in combination with the previous three subjects of the movement, whereupon the entire complex would be inverted.[124] Moreover, Bach's "final fugue" may not have been left unfinished by the composer. Recent speculation has plausibly suggested that Bach, contrary to the testimony of the obituary, in fact completed the final section, that it was relatively short, and was probably written on a separate sheet of paper that was lost by his heirs.[125] In its uniqueness the quadruple fugue—Bach's only fugue with four themes—has an obvious counterpart in the six-part *Ricercar* from the *Musical Offering*, his only fugue for six voices; and it may well have been his work on the latter that prompted Bach to add a similarly unique, similarly monumental, contrapuntal *tour de force* as the capstone, if not necessarily the conclusion,[126] of what the ailing master must have understood would be his *opus ultimum*.

Postscript 2019

Bach's monumental and systematic collections of keyboard music have stood at the center of the serious keyboard player's repertoire since the composer's lifetime and, beginning in the nineteenth century, have occupied an ever more prominent position in the life of the concert hall. The original version of this chapter appeared more than a quarter century ago. In the ensuing years the literature devoted to Bach's "clavier" music," already "oceanic" at that time, has steadily continued to grow.

Among the notable publications of recent decades the following (in alphabetical order) deserve special mention: Paul Badura-Skoda, *Interpreting Bach at the Keyboard*; Joseph Kerman, *The Art of Fugue: Bach Fugues for Keyboard, 1715–1750*; David Ledbetter, *Bach's Well-Tempered Clavier: The 48 Preludes and Fugues*; Siegbert Rampe, ed., *Bachs Klavier- und Orgelwerke: Das Handbuch*, 2 vols.; David Schulenberg, *The Keyboard Music of J. S. Bach*; Joel Speerstra, *Bach and the Pedal Clavichord: An Organist's Guide*; and Andrew Talle, "J. S. Bach's Keyboard Partitas and Their Early Audience." Along with the relevant discussions in Christoph Wolff's indispensable *Johann Sebastian Bach: The Learned Musician*, the chapters on the keyboard music included in Richard D. P. Jones's two-volume survey, *The Creative Development of Johann Sebastian Bach*, provide a valuable overview of the current state of research.

Adding a few hundred words, or even a few thousand words, at this juncture would serve little purpose. After all, the encyclopedic compendium, *Bachs Klavier- und Orgelwerke*, published about a decade ago, containing contributions by fifteen eminent authorities, is over one thousand pages long; David Ledbetter's study devoted exclusively to *The Well-Tempered Clavier* fills more than four hundred pages.

Perhaps a few final observations, however, contemplating Bach's relationship to the clavier could be of some interest here.

As arguably the greatest composer for the instrument in history (not to mention his status for many as the greatest composer in history *tout court*), it is fair to wonder exactly what the harpsichord meant to Johann Sebastian Bach and what purpose it served for him in his artistic mission. Like the organ, but far more intimate, the harpsichord (and perhaps, the clavichord as well), was very likely his vehicle—his "instrument." Improvising at the keyboard stimulated his imagination. More significantly, composing for keyboard instruments and performing his works at the keyboard gave him absolute autonomy and enabled the personal, direct expression, and communication, of his musical ideas. Writing for and performing at the keyboard allowed him to explore and convey, by himself, the full range of his musical imagination: from the most introspective and private to the most flamboyant and extroverted. As he wrote on the title page of his six compositions for unaccompanied violin, very likely aware of the pun created by the (deliberately?) ungrammatical Italian: *Sei solo* ("six solos," or rather: "you are alone").

Upon reflection, it is not at all surprising that Bach's keyboard works—more, perhaps, than his contributions to other genres—probe the limits. To a profound degree they are demonstrations in the sense of experiments as they test the limits of the tonal system, the tuning system, contrapuntal and harmonic limits, the physical limits of players, the technological limits of instruments.

On the latter point, Bach's keen interest in musical instruments no doubt accounts for his activity in the development of the lute harpsichord, on the one hand, and the fortepiano, on the other. He shared this commitment with one of his relatives, his cousin Johann Nicolaus Bach (1669–1753), the town and university organist at Jena, and a builder of lute harpsichords whose instruments earned the praise of Jacob Adlung.[127]

Bach's criticism and ultimate endorsement of Gottfried Silbermann's fortepianos is well-known and was cited earlier in this essay. But he is also credited with having invented a "viola pomposa," perhaps identical—perhaps not—to the violoncello piccolo called for in a number of cantatas. His prescriptions for the mysterious "corno da tirarsi" and/or "tromba da tirarsi" in other cantatas attest at the least to his interest in—and need for—trumpets and horns capable of playing chromatics.

In probing limits, Bach not only explores and demonstrates them: in the end he conquers, "domesticates," them, brings them under control, in order then to expand them. His favorite strategy of expansion, as is well-known, is synthesis: uniting, fusing, national traditions (French, Italian, and German) and/or historical traditions (*stile antico, stile moderno, style galant*), homophony and polyphony, functional tonality and modal counterpoint—often enough in the same works.

But in the final analysis, Bach's "experiments" were not merely the product of abstract intellectual speculation. Their larger purpose, one suspects, was to extend the range and depth of musical expression. From the beginning Bach's keyboard compositions were more than well-crafted, exemplary representatives of prevailing conventions and genres. They were in addition highly individual "character pieces." Consider the programmatic *Capriccio on the Absence of the Most Beloved Brother*, BWV 992. Presumably composed by 1705, it is certainly the most famous keyboard composition from Bach's early years.[128] In addition to its explicit literary program— a feature unique among Bach's keyboard works—the work is notable for its tonal audacity, progressing at one point in the second movement (a depiction of "the various casualties that could befall the friend abroad") via the circle of fifths from the tonic G minor to the key of B-flat minor. This is harmonic and tonal exploration with a personal, expressive, poignant purpose.

At the other end of his career we find what is arguably Bach's greatest harpsichord composition: the Goldberg Variations (BWV 988), published in 1741 as the final part of the *Klavierübung*. Like the two volumes of *The Well-Tempered Clavier*, it is, as a totality, encyclopedic in its far-reaching survey of styles, genres, and compositional techniques—all investigated, as is Bach's wont, according to a single unifying principle: the contrast pair of prelude and fugue in the one instance, theme and variations, along with canonic art, in the other.

As individual numbers, however, what is striking, and moving, about the constituent members of the WTC and the Goldbergs is their intensely individual character. They are "character pieces" in the most literal sense: giving expression to every mood and emotional state from uninhibited exhibitionism to the deepest, most sorrowful, most personal introspection.

To study, practice, and ultimately play one of Johann Sebastian Bach's masterpieces at the harpsichord (or any other keyboard instrument) is to become his intimate partner—one-on-one—sharing the bold compositional forays and privy to the heights and depths of expression, all fortunately set down in notation and preserved for posterity.

Chapter Six

The Minimalist and Traditionalist Approaches to Performing Bach's Choral Music

Some Further Thoughts

[If] returning from the underworld, you could see Bach (to mention him particularly, since he was not long ago my colleague at the Leipzig St. Thomas School) . . . watching over everything and bringing back to the rhythm and the beat, out of thirty or even forty musicians [*symphoniaci*], the one with a nod, another by tapping with his foot, the third with a warning finger . . .[1]

—Matthias Gesner, 1738

Thus wrote Matthias Gesner (1691–1761) in a footnote to his 1738 edition of the Roman orator Quintilian's famous treatise on rhetoric, the *Institutio Oratoria*. Gesner was the first professor of classical philology at the University of Göttingen. Previously—specifically, for the four years from 1730 to 1734—he was the rector of the Thomasschule in Leipzig; that is, he was Johann Sebastian Bach's boss, and, as this passage makes clear, he was an enthusiastic eyewitness to Bach's performances as a conductor.

If Gesner can be believed, Bach directed an ensemble of "thirty or even forty musicians." *Can* we believe him? Does it matter?

The question of the original size of Bach's orchestra and chorus has been a matter of heated debate for close to forty years now, ever since Joshua Rifkin presented a revolutionary paper entitled "Bach's Chorus" at the 1981 annual meeting of the

American Musicological Society (AMS). Rifkin argued that Bach's chorus normally consisted of a single singer on each part, literally a solo quartet: one soprano, one alto, one tenor, and one bass. It fell to me on that occasion to serve as a respondent to the bold thesis. I disagreed with my good friend Rifkin, but the discussion by no means ended on that November day in Boston. According to a bibliographical checklist devoted to the controversy compiled by Matthew Cron and published in *Bach: Journal of the Riemenschneider Bach Institute*, no fewer than fifty-four articles had appeared by the end of 1997.[2]

The AMS session was reviewed soon after the event in the *New Yorker*; Rifkin and I published an exchange of views in *High Fidelity* magazine and another in the *Musical Times* a year or so later.[3] Thereafter, having already done severe damage to a valued friendship, I vowed never again to discuss this issue in public, either in print or on a lecture podium. And—until March of 2001, when I was prevailed upon by George Stauffer (another good friend) to present an earlier version of the present paper at a symposium at the Morgan Library in New York—I remained true to that vow. Upon the urging of yet another good friend, Mark Kroll (I have been blessed with good friends), I offered the present essay for publication in the Winter 2009 issue of *Early Music America*—when the controversy seemed to have lost much of its heat—rather than leave it for eventual discovery among my posthumous papers.

The dispute over the size of Bach's chorus has not been confined to scholarly debates and publications. Historically minded musicians have lined up on both sides, performing (and recording) the concerted vocal music of Johann Sebastian either in accordance with Rifkin's one-on-a-part thesis or according to the scholarly understanding that had previously prevailed. Positions between the two camps eventually hardened, and the controversy has led to a bitter schism in the ranks of the early music community that has occasionally attracted the attention of the general media and the music-loving public and that continues to the present.

I have chosen the word "schism" deliberately, for the debate about the number of musicians who sang in Bach's chorus and played in his orchestra has often had a theological quality. In particular, the ingenious parsing of historical—dare I say, sacred—documents has played a central role among true believers who earnestly subscribe to an ethos of "authenticity" and call, among other things, for the scrupulous observance of the original performance traditions—including, not least, the size and constitution of vocal and instrumental groups. For these musicians—and their sympathetic audiences—such things matter, indeed.

To return to our eyewitness: How can we corroborate, or refute, the truth of Gesner's claim that his colleague Johann Sebastian Bach directed ensembles of "thirty or even forty musicians"? It is made, after all, in the context of a fanciful communication with a long-dead shade from antiquity (and even alludes at one point to the mythological Orpheus as though he had existed).

The crucial piece of evidence, invariably Exhibit A in any discussion of Bach's performing forces, is a memorandum in his own hand, dated August 23, 1730, and addressed to the City Council of Leipzig, the overseers to whom Bach, as the city's music director, was responsible. Bach's heading for the memorandum reads: "Short but Most Necessary Draft for a Well-Appointed Church Music with Certain Modest Reflections on the Decline of the Same" (*Kurtzer, iedoch höchstnöthiger Entwurff einer wohlbestallten Kirchen Music; nebst einigem unvorgreiflichen Bedencken von dem Verfall derselben*).[4] It is arguably the most analyzed, most disagreed-about document ever penned by a composer, with the possible exception of Beethoven's letter to the Immortal Beloved. We must briefly rehearse its contents yet again.

Ironically, Bach's intention in writing the draft was to provide clarification: he was explaining to his superiors, as simply and as unambiguously as he could, exactly what resources were necessary to meet the musical needs of the city's four principal churches. His ultimate objective was to demonstrate that he did not have those resources. But he begins his appeal by describing the facts of musical life in terms that might well have struck the councilors as insultingly rudimentary.

The opening of the document reads as follows:

> A well-appointed church music requires vocalists and instrumentalists.
> The vocalists are in this place made up of the pupils of the Thomasschule, being of four kinds, namely, sopranos [*Discantisten*], altos, tenors, and basses.
> In order that the choruses of church pieces may be performed as is fitting, the vocalists must in turn be divided into 2 sorts, namely, concertists [i.e., soloists] and ripienists [i.e., those who fill in].
> The concertists are ordinarily 4 in number; sometimes also 5, 6, 7, even 8; that is, if one wishes to perform music for two choirs [*per choros*].
> The ripienists, too, must be at least 8, namely, two for each part.

Bach later adds:

> Every musical choir should contain at least 3 sopranos, 3 altos, 3 tenors, and as many basses, so that even if one happens to fall ill . . . at least a double-chorus motet may be sung. (N.B. Though it would be still better if the classes [of the Thomasschule] were such that one could have 4 singers on each part and thus could provide every chorus with 16 persons.)

Let us pause at this point. In 1936, some forty-five years before Rifkin presented his theory to the American Musicological Society, the Bach scholar Arnold Schering published a study of Bach's Leipzig church music in which he presented, together with a mass of further evidence, what was to be the conventional understanding of the "Short but Most Necessary Draft," namely, that Bach's chorus—at least during his years as Thomaskantor in Leipzig (1723–50)—normally consisted of twelve singers: three sopranos, three altos, three tenors, and three basses.[5] One of the three in each voice category was a soloist (or concertist). His duty was to sing the solo numbers—the recitatives and arias—as well as to be one of the voices in the choral numbers and chorales, in which the remaining two singers in each voice category, the ripienists, joined in. Bach's comments also allow us to conclude that, unlike the concerted pieces, *a cappella* motets for four, five, six, seven, or eight voices were performed by the concertists, the soloists, alone. (I suspect, by the way, that the motets Bach had in mind here were those by earlier masters, composers extending back to Palestrina and Lassus, whose motets were regularly performed in the Leipzig church service of Bach's time.)

Returning to the draft: Bach reports: "The instrumentalists are also divided into various kinds, namely, string players [*violisten*], oboists, flutists, trumpeters, and drummers. N.B. The violisten include also [i.e., in addition to the violinists] those who play the violas, the violoncellos, and the bass viols." He tabulates the instrumentalists:

> 2 or even 3 for the Violino 1; 2 or even 3 for the Violino 2; 2 for the Viola 1; 2 for the Viola 2; 2 for the Violoncello; 1 for the Violon [Bass viol]; 2, or, if the piece requires, 3 for the Hautbois; 1, or even 2, for the Basson; 3 for the Trumpets; 1 for the Kettledrums. [S]*umma* 18 persons at least for the instrumental music [i.e., the instrumental ensemble, or the orchestra].

He adds: "N.B. If it happens that the church piece is composed with flutes also, . . . as very often happens for variety's sake, at least 2 more persons are needed. Making altogether 20 instrumentalists."

Now, if one adds to Bach's explicitly stated minimal cantata chorus of twelve his explicitly stated minimal orchestra of eighteen, one has thirty musicians, exactly the size of the ensemble Rector Gesner described to Quintilian. And, of course, Bach's preferred chorus of sixteen, together with the augmented twenty-piece orchestra with flutes he describes, would call for a total of thirty-six musicians.

In recent years Andreas Glöckner has drawn renewed attention to a document from the Thomaskirche archives covering the school year from Pentecost (May) 1744 to Pentecost (June) 1745. The document, though neglected, has been known to modern Bach scholarship since 1907. It lists, by name, the students who were assigned to each of the four Leipzig churches for which Bach was responsible for the Sunday service music. It reveals that seventeen students were assigned to each of the choruses for both the St. Thomas and St. Nicholas churches—the venues in which, on alternating Sundays, Bach (or a surrogate) conducted the principal music (Haupt*Music*)—typically a cantata of his own composition.[6] This seems to corroborate the numbers of choristers as described in Bach's 1730 *Entwurff*. Whether every student in each chorus in fact sang in the performances or some were just assigned a seat in the choir loft is not explicitly stated.[7]

Now Gesner tells us that sometimes "even forty musicians" participated. Perhaps even more: if Gesner had attended a performance of the St. Matthew Passion with its double chorus (i.e., some twenty-four singers) and double orchestra (without trumpets and drums, but with additional flutes, i.e., twice sixteen, or thirty-two players), he would have witnessed Bach trying to keep in order well over fifty musicians.

Moreover, we know of at least one other contemporary description of Bach conducting a cantata. A witness to an outdoor performance of Bach's (lost) cantata, *Entfernet euch, ihr heitern Sterne,* BWV Anh. 9, recalled that the composer led a group of "more than 40" musicians, evidently university students. (Another three hundred students carried torches). And, since a strong case has been made that the opening movement of the lost cantata may have been the source for the "Et Resurrexit" movement of the B-Minor Mass, this piece of evidence would seem to have relevance for determining the proper number of performers for an "authentic" rendition of the Mass.[8] Case closed.

Well, not entirely. In all fairness, I should at the least offer a summary of the counterarguments of those who subscribe to the one-on-a-part theory. But I will not—call it "disinclination"—except to mention that they largely rest on the following pillars: first, the fact that among the original performing materials for a Bach vocal composition, typically only one written part exists for each choral voice; second, the practice elsewhere in the Baroque era; third, a dazzling display of semantic and syntactical exegesis of the draft that must be read in its unabridged form to be fully appreciated. Again, I cite the bibliographical checklist mentioned earlier.

I prefer instead to suggest that in one respect both camps—the minimalists and the traditionalists—are guilty of the same offense: namely, one for which I am tempted to use the term "totalism" and to define it as a dogmatic inclination to impose a single solution, or explanation, on all situations. The minimalists maintain that essentially all of Bach's vocal music was (and therefore should be) performed by a chamber group: a chorus and instrumental ensemble of soloists. The traditionalists, for their part (largely resting their case on Bach's memorandum of 1730), maintain that essentially all of Bach's vocal music was (and therefore should be) performed by a chorus of twelve, preferably sixteen singers, and an orchestra of about twenty players.

My suspicion is that the size of Bach's ensemble was far less fixed than either camp has been willing to acknowledge but varied substantially according to circumstances. By "circumstances" I am referring not only to external, practical conditions but also to considerations of stylistic and aesthetic propriety. I certainly agree fundamentally with the traditionalists that—during Bach's Leipzig years, and thus for most of his church music—the performing forces normally consisted of a twelve- or sixteen-voice chorus and an eighteen- or twenty-piece orchestra.[9] But we cannot assume that this was always the case. There is every reason to believe that the performing forces available to Bach in Weimar, for example, were different—specifically, smaller—than they were in Leipzig. Personnel lists in Weimar mention a total of fourteen or fifteen musicians, altogether: six or seven singers, six instrumentalists, and two directors. The numbers were presumably different yet again—probably even smaller still—when Bach was employed in the small towns of Arnstadt, Mühlhausen, and Köthen. In some of these situations the "soloist presumption" (if I may call it *that*) becomes quite plausible.

But I am willing to go further still and argue that even in Leipzig the "traditionalist presumption" (if I may call it *that*) did not always prevail. Bach's vocal music, after all, belongs to a variety of categories and was written for a variety of occasions. We can readily discern several subgenres of cantata: at the one extreme we find extravagantly scored cantatas such as were performed at Christmas, Easter, and other festive occasions. Bach clearly delighted in the coloristic variety and the capacity for "big sound" at his disposal on such occasions. One need only recall the beginning of the *Christmas Oratorio*, with its audacious opening timpani solo and the ensuing rousing buildup as flutes, then oboes, trumpet fanfares, and swirling strings join in. (See chapter 8, ex. 8.1.) That all this should introduce a feeble "chorus" of less than a handful of singers is (at least for this auditor) rather hard to imagine—especially since this chorus, like most of the others in the oratorio, is little more than a simple re-texting of a movement from a secular cantata in celebration of a royal birthday that was previously performed by Bach and the Collegium Musicum most likely under lavish circumstances similar to those described above.

At the other extreme, however, we have Bach's "solo" cantatas: compositions that usually consist of a series of arias and recitatives for a single soloist throughout. A fine example is *Ich armer Mensch, ich Sündenknecht*, BWV 55, a cantata for tenor, flute, oboe d'amore, and strings. The composition contains no choral movement at all, except for the concluding simple four-part chorale, which in such a case may well not have called upon the complete twelve-voice chorus. (It may be significant that on the folder that contained the original parts, Bach describes the cantata as follows: "à 4 Voci. / ò vero Tenore solo è 3 / Ripieni." (In fact, the unavailability of a complete chorus—as this description of the vocal parts suggests—might help explain why Bach chose to compose a solo cantata that particular week in November of 1726.)

But we must keep in mind that genius, to paraphrase Stravinsky (and others), thrives on constraints.[10] Regarding constraints of size, consider the strikingly individual, and unorthodox, scorings of Bach's funeral compositions. They often suggest intimate performances held in a mourner's home or at a gravesite rather than at a church service. On these occasions Bach compensated for the lack of numbers with the imaginative use of instrumental color. The evocative and deliberately archaic scoring of the *Actus tragicus, Gottes Zeit ist die allerbeste Zeit*, BWV 106, for example—an early masterpiece most likely composed in 1707 or 1708—consists only of two recorders and two violas da gamba.

Some thirty years later Bach wrote the funeral composition *O Jesu Christ, meins Lebens Licht*, BWV 118. It is scored for four-part chorus and, like the *Actus tragicus*, calls for an archaic instrumental ensemble, consisting this time of two obbligato "litui" (which were presumably horns or trumpets of some kind) and either a brass or string group reinforcing the singers. Both funeral compositions, the *Actus tragicus* and *O Jesu Christ*, it is true, have "choruses"—choruses, I would maintain (following Rifkin here) consisting of solo voices.

But, as aesthetically satisfying, and historically probable, as solo scoring is in the genre of the funeral cantata and for the concluding four-part chorales of solo cantatas, it hardly represents Bach's normal usage. On the contrary, such compositions should be understood as occupying one end of something resembling a continuum of ensemble combinations extending from intimate, essentially private, chamber groups to the "normal," that is, the usual Leipzig Sunday cantata ensemble described in Bach's memorandum of 1730—and beyond. They clearly represent the antipode to the elaborately scored festival cantatas for the major feasts—not to mention the even more lavish secular cantatas Bach composed to celebrate the birthdays and other great deeds of the Royal Saxon family. Bach and his Collegium Musicum often performed these compositions, no doubt, with as many singers and players as he could round up—forty, fifty. One suspects that the (open) sky was the limit.

Chapter Seven

Truth and Beauty

J. S. Bach at the Crossroads
of Cultural History

During his lifetime, and for sometime thereafter, Bach was a contemporary composer. That means, among other things, that he had not yet acquired the status of immortality and was not beyond criticism. In the year 1737, at the very pinnacle of his career, and only six months after having been conferred the lofty title of "Composer to the Court Chapel of His Royal Majesty in Poland" (Compositeur *bey der Königlichen Hof*Capelle), Bach was taken severely to task, in print, by his former pupil, Johann Adolph Scheibe (1708–76), in the following terms:

> This great man would be the admiration of whole nations if [his music] had more charm, if he did not take away the natural element in his pieces by giving them a turgid and confused style, and if he did not darken their beauty by an excess of art. . . . He demands that singers and instrumentalists should be able to do with their throats and instruments whatever he can play on the clavier. . . . Every ornament, every little grace . . . he expresses completely in notes; and this not only takes away from his pieces the beauty of harmony but completely covers the melody throughout. All the voices must work with each other and be of equal difficulty, and none of them can be recognized as the principal voice. . . . Turgidity has led [him] from the natural to the artificial, from the lofty to the somber; one admires the onerous labor and uncommon effort—which, however, are vainly employed, since they conflict with Nature.[1]

Scheibe's critique, of course, is one of the most famous documents of its kind in the history of music, not least because it was far more than simply one man's opinion. It was also an ideological manifesto to which we shall return in due course.

Bach himself was by no means unaware of the unusual difficulty his music posed. Referring to his church compositions in an official document written less than a year before Scheibe's attack, Bach described them as "incomparably more difficult and more intricate" (*ohngleich schwerer und* intricater) than those by other composers.[2] It is noteworthy that Bach needed to turn to a foreign language—to Latin—in order to find the most fitting and precise description of his music. The marvelously apt word *intricat*—conveying as it does the sense of carefully gauged interconnections between constituent parts, a clockwork of sorts—does not exist in everyday German.[3]

To paraphrase Alban Berg: Why is Bach's music so hard to understand? Why is it so difficult, complex, "intricate," or, as Scheibe would have it: "turgid and confused" (*schwülstig und verworren*)? An explanation of sorts is suggested in the following conventional characterization of Bach's significance: "Appearing at a propitious moment in the history of music, Bach was able to survey and bring together the principal styles, forms and national traditions that had developed during preceding generations and, by virtue of his synthesis, enrich them all."[4]

This is a truism of musical historiography, as it was once formulated by the present writer (in 1974); but, as I have pointed out since—specifically, in "Bach the Progressive" (1976) and "On Bach's Universality" (1985)—it does not begin to do full justice to the magnitude of Bach's artistic achievement.[5] Moreover, it does not even hint at the pivotal position Bach occupies in cultural history—in the history of ideas. As the following aims to show, in Bach's case the two domains are ultimately inseparable; and, if anything, it is the latter that holds out the promise for a more satisfying answer to this question.

In the essay, "On Bach's Universality," devoted to the purely musical dimensions of this issue I summarized a description of the complex organization of the opening chorus of the cantata, *Jesu, der du meine Seele*, BWV 78, as follows:

> It is virtually impossible to imagine a grander, more comprehensive, more "universal" synthesis of historical and national styles than Bach has achieved in this movement—incorporating as it does elements of the secular as well as the sacred, the instrumental as well as the vocal; a movement whose frame of reference embraces both the Roman Catholic motet of the sixteenth century and the Lutheran chorale and whose procedures are indebted to the medieval cantus-firmus setting, the variation technique of the seventeenth-century passacaglia, and on to the modern Italian concerto and the French dance suite.[6]

Unaddressed altogether was the question as to why Bach would have felt called upon to produce such an amazingly, indeed forbiddingly complex, "intricate" composition—one easily vulnerable to Scheibe's claim that its "beauty has been darkened by an excess of art" (*ihre Schönheit durch allzugrosse Kunst verdunkelte*). Surely Bach did not lavish this effort simply in order to dazzle his listeners with a display of his compositional prowess. In the first place, it is hardly likely that anyone in the audience—that is, in the congregation—would have been able to appreciate the "incomparable" skill of the achievement. As we learn from Scheibe, his listeners were far more likely to be "confused" by this demonstration than delighted by it. Nor is it likely that the composer was indulging a purely private, personal, need to exercise his formidable powers of combination. Such a motivation was doubtless present; but it surely represented a relatively minor part of the composer's conscious objective.

It seems far more likely that the decisive explanation underlying the extraordinary complexity of a movement like *Jesu, der du meine Seele* had little to do with personal or even purely musical impulses. Rather, it must have involved larger intellectual issues informing Bach's understanding of the ultimate purpose of church music altogether, which of course was not an autonomous one.

As musical "sermons" in an orthodox Lutheran service, Bach's church cantatas were to deliver a theological message—in the words of Martin Luther, to proclaim the Word, the Truth of Christian belief.[7] At the risk of overstating the point: the primary purpose of such compositions was to serve above all else as a vehicle of theological Truth, rather than as an object of aesthetic Beauty.

This missionary objective was to be accomplished primarily by emphasizing the points of contact between the art of music and the art of rhetoric. As is well-known, Bach belonged to a tradition, extending back to Luther's time, that cultivated the referential capacity of music: its potential to convey specific meaning. Compositions were even organized into sections in the manner of formal speeches, with (to borrow the terminology of Quintilian) an introductory *Exordium*, a *Transitus* or transition to the *Narratio*, that is, the presentation of the main substance of the speech, then an *Argumentatio*, or consideration of the proposition from various points of view, and finally, a *Peroratio* or conclusion.[8]

By the seventeenth century the art of musical composition was typically referred to in the Lutheran North as *Musica poetica*;[9] for the increasing concern at this time was to develop techniques that would enable music to represent images and ideas— to function as a "language" of sorts, by finding musical equivalents, or analogies, for linguistic and poetic figures of speech. The Doctrine of Figures—*Figurenlehre*—as this practice has come to be called,[10] embraced not only metaphorical images but grammatical and rhetorical devices as well. In order to understand the "message" of a piece of music fully and accurately, it was—and is—necessary to have some familiarity with these figures of musical speech.

To return to Cantata 78: from the point of view of Bach and his Lutheran brethren, any discussion of the cantata that concentrated exclusively on its purely musical qualities completely missed the point of the piece. The proper place to begin a meaningful discussion of *Jesu, der du meine Seele* was not with an identification and enumeration of its technical devices and stylistic allusions but, simply enough, with the reading and contemplation of the text. The text of the first strophe of Johann Rist's famous chorale, which forms the basis of the opening chorus, reads as follows:

Jesu, der du meine Seele / Hast durch deinen bittern Tod / Aus des Teufels finstern Höhle / Und der schweren Seelennot / Kräftiglich herausgerissen / Und mich solches lassen wissen / Durch dein angenehmes Wort, / Sei doch itzt, O Gott, mein Hort![11]

[Jesus, who by thy bitter death, hast powerfully torn away my soul from the devil's dark domain, and saved me from the depths of despair, and hast revealed this to me in thy comforting Word, be now, oh God, my treasure!]

The verse constitutes a fairly undiluted affirmation of the central Lutheran tenet of the Theology of the Cross: the doctrine that it was Christ's suffering and death on the cross that has redeemed mankind, and that the message of salvation is revealed in God's Word alone.[12]

This is the Truth that Bach's setting was to proclaim as vividly, and as effectively, as the rhetorical resources of the *musica poetica* allowed. With respect to the movement's design, the opening and closing instrumental ritornelli can be regarded as the equivalents of the *Exordium* and *Peroratio* (ex. 7.1).

Example 7.1. *Jesu, der du meine Seele*, BWV 78/1, opening ritornello, mm. 1–9

The preliminary preview of the chorale text in the lower voices of the chorus (ex. 7.2) is like a *Transitus* to the main presentation of the chorale, which is perhaps analogous to the *Narratio* and *Argumentatio* of a speech—or a sermon. Moreover, all the compositional elements that Bach chose to incorporate in this remarkable panorama are infused with symbolic meaning.

The *lamento* bass, for example, with its descending chromatic steps (ex. 7.3), is virtually a textbook example of the *passus duriusculus* typically employed in the Baroque era to convey pain and suffering, such as Christ's suffering on the cross—or, its theological analogy, humanity's suffering in this world (or even, as the chorale text admonishes, in the next world as well).

By choosing to reiterate this motif over and over (as part of an ostinato bass)—that is, by choosing to cast the movement (on one level) in the form of a passacaglia—Bach had also found an effective way of representing the relentlessness, and the inescapability, of such suffering; and, by allowing the motif to permeate virtually

Example 7.2. BWV 78/1, mm. 17–25

Example 7.3. BWV 78/1, continuo, mm. 1–4

Example 7.4. BWV 78/1, tonal plan

every part of the ensemble, especially those of the chorus (with the exception of the soprano), he succeeded in conveying the idea of the all-pervasiveness of such suffering. Only the soprano part, bearing as it does not only the words but also the pre-existent liturgical melody of the chorale (and thus serving as the symbol of the eternal Church) is sublimely isolated and immune to this condition; the *cantus firmus* text and tune stand out like an inscription on a church portal.

Rhetorical effectiveness, in the service of theological emphasis, operates on larger structural levels of the movement, as well. Particularly compelling is the powerful harmonic shift, virtually at the midpoint of the movement, from the dark minor-mode tonalities prevailing throughout the two *Stollen* of the chorale (G minor, D minor, through m. 73) in illustration of "des Teufels finstern Höhle," to the major mode (F major, B-flat major), strategically coinciding with, and vividly representing, the words "kräftiglich herausgerissen" (powerfully torn away) at the beginning of the *Abgesang* (mm. 78–85, 99). It should not be overlooked that the words "kräftiglich herausgerissen" contain the predicate verb for this sentence—postponed by the exigencies of German grammar to the fifth line of the verse. Bach's climactic modulation to the major at this point catches and amplifies the poet's exploitation of this idiosyncrasy of the German language. In terms of the larger harmonic plan of this G-minor movement, the initially striking introduction of F major is ultimately part of an arpeggiation of the tonic triad that provides the tonal underpinnings of the movement, as illustrated in example 7.4.

As for Bach's fundamental decision to unite as many national and historical musical styles as he possibly could in this single movement, this no doubt carried symbolic meaning as well: implying that the Theology of the Cross—the belief that salvation was achieved through Christ's suffering alone—is a *universal truth*: one valid for all times and for all peoples.

In the final analysis, then, Cantata 78 is not only one of the more spectacular monuments to Bach's combinatorial genius, it is just as much eloquent testimony to his religious and intellectual heritage—in a word, to his cultural heritage. It is a work rooted in, and ultimately completely understandable only in terms of, the allegorical imagery of Lutheran theology as rendered in tones of accordance with the specifically German tradition of the *musica poetica*.

❧ ❧ ❧

The relationship between Music and Truth, however, encompassed yet another dimension. Music did not only serve, in conjunction with an explicit text (and via the symbolic conventions of the *Figurenlehre*), as a vehicle, a megaphone, for the proclamation of theological dogmas. Music's very structure, in this view, was a reflection not just of the divine order, but perhaps of the "pre-existent harmony" as described a generation earlier by Bach's compatriot, the great rationalist philosopher, Gottfried Wilhelm Leibniz (1646–1716), as has been suggested.[13]

Bach's concern about this function of his art is attested to most forcefully in the famous dictum on the thorough bass attributed to him in a manuscript copied out in the year 1738 by his pupils. While the document presumably reflects the master's teaching, the dictum is an almost verbatim quotation from a thorough bass treatise by Friedrich Erhard Niedt (1674–1717).[14] It reads: "The thorough bass is the most perfect foundation of music. It is played with both hands in such a way that the left hand plays the written notes, while the right hand strikes consonances and dissonances, so that this results in a well-sounding *Harmonie* to the Honour of God. . . . Where this is not observed there is no real music but only a devilish bawling and droning."[15] The conviction that "real music" (*eigentliche Music*) is the product of the correct application of learnable and teachable principles informs his extraordinary pedagogical commitment and is made explicit in the title pages of his didactic collections of keyboard pieces—as in the title page of the Two- and Three-Part Inventions (see chapter 5).

With his convictions about the existence of fundamental, universally valid principles—that is, "laws"—governing the operation and organization of musical phenomena, can it be that Bach—ironically, perhaps—reveals himself to be in fact (to some significant degree) a product of the Age of Reason?[16] Can it be that the Fifth Evangelist owed (almost) as substantial an intellectual debt to the Enlightenment as he did to traditional Lutheran orthodoxy? In retrospect, this intellectual synthesis (or, more properly, this spiritual reconciliation)—a phenomenon not unrelated to Bach's extraordinary achievements of musical synthesis—can be understood as all but inevitable; for God, as the Natural Theologians of the age maintained, was manifest in His work—the Universe and its Laws—as well as in His word: in the Book of Nature as well as in the Book of Scripture.[17]

Enlightenment thought, therefore (assuming that Bach was familiar with it at all), may have provided, it not exactly the impetus, at least a justification for his inborn and uniquely powerful synthesizing impulse. For synthesis, combination, and unification could readily serve not only as a fitting analogy for the proclamation of certain Orthodox Lutheran doctrines (as illustrated above in the discussion of Cantata 78); they were just as much a manifestation of one of the characteristic preoccupations of the Natural Philosophers of the period.[18]

The manifestation of Truth in the music of Bach, then, takes two forms: in his church compositions, first of all, theological Truth is proclaimed (and allegorically represented); second, Natural Truth, the operation of natural law, is demonstrated in virtually every one of his most significant works.

♪   ♪   ♪

Read against this backdrop, it is particularly ironic, at first glance, that one of the major points in Scheibe's critique of Bach is that his music is "unnatural," "artificial," and in "conflict with Nature." In fact, Scheibe's attack reveals that we have arrived at a crossroads in the history of ideas; and at its crux reside the concepts of Nature and the Natural. As we have seen, Bach's understanding of them is cast in the loftiest theological and even cosmological terms. The purpose of Art was: the Imitation of Nature—as Shakespeare put it: to hold the mirror up to Nature. For Johann Adolph Scheibe and the new aesthetic that he represented, Nature and the Natural have been reduced to considerations of amenity and grace, simplicity and immediacy. Perhaps it would be fair to say that for the new, dawning age of the *galant*—the age to be exemplified in the music of Bach's younger sons until it would be transfigured by Haydn and Mozart and ultimately transcended by Beethoven—Beauty was Truth; that is, the creation of beauty, understood as that which is pleasing (or exciting to the senses), was the true objective of art. For Bach, on the other hand, Truth was Beauty: The aesthetic experience of Beauty was the product issuing from the emulation of divine order. It is a matter of ends and means.

But there is obviously more to all of this. Bach, after all, well knew how to write music that is immediately and unproblematically beautiful: sensuous bel canto melodies, lyric and direct—and unencumbered by distracting ornaments either of the virtuosic or the contrapuntal sort. His instrumental music, especially the slow movements of his concertos, is replete with them. But there is also this less obvious, more unexpected, example: his setting of Christ's words in the Last Supper scene from the St. Matthew Passion (ex. 7.5).

George Bernard Shaw famously declared that Sarastro's arias from Mozart's *Die Zauberflöte* were the only pieces of music he knew that would not sound out of place in the mouth of God.[19] But surely the same could be maintained about this music from the St. Matthew Passion—music, which Bach in fact put into the mouth of God. The point, however, is precisely that Bach designed his magnificent melody just for this purpose: by means of an unusually euphonious, lyrical melody—distinguished by conjunct diatonic movement, sturdy, straightforward rhythm and meter, homophonic texture, and finally, the simplest, most consonant harmonization in

Example 7.5. St. Matthew Passion, BWV 244/17 (11), mm. 19b–22

the major mode—to represent (no less than the string "halo" accompaniment in the recitatives) the divine aura of Christ and to set it apart from its mundane surroundings. For, once again, such lyric beauty was not for Bach—at least not in his church music—an end in itself. It was, rather, a special effect: in essence another rhetorical figure (without question a particularly powerful one) in the arsenal of the *musica poetica*; one to be used discreetly—and strategically.

On the other hand, in much of his instrumental music—most notably in the concertos—Bach has indeed embraced the "other" conception of art: the new, and at the time, the ascendant philosophy of Beauty essentially for its own sake. And it is no surprise that these works are his most popular and that they have established themselves firmly in the modern concert repertory. They were of course written for the "delectation" of listeners who would have heard them in Bach's day as they do today: not as worshippers in a congregation but as members of a secular audience—either at court or in the bourgeois ambience, perhaps, of Zimmermann's coffeehouse.

The new aesthetic attitude was rooted not in the Protestant North but in the secular South: specifically in Italy, where the Humanist Renaissance, and not the Lutheran Reformation, formed the seedbed for an aesthetic outlook that regarded art as an immediate appeal to the senses in the service of a "human," psychological, reality and that conceived of music in particular as a language of the feelings (one magnificently well suited, by the way, for the representation of dramatic conflict)—not, as in the Lutheran world, as an agent for the affirmation of theological truths and universal, cosmological verities.[20]

"Truth and Beauty," in the final analysis, can be translated as: North and South. It is a "Tale of Two Cultures." Bach, the musical Colossus, bestrode them both.

Chapter Eight

Bach at Mid-Life

The *Christmas Oratorio* and the Search for New Paths

Only about seven years separate the creation of Bach's *Christmas Oratorio* from the onset of work on the *Art of Fugue*. The *Christmas Oratorio* was put together in the weeks before the 1734/35 Christmas/New Year's season; the manuscript containing the earliest portions of the *Art of Fugue* can be dated to around 1742. Yet the two works occupy altogether different stylistic and aesthetic worlds and seem to bear witness to a profound artistic "evolution," in a remarkably brief period of time, from a flirtation with the immediately appealing, the sensuous, and progressive in music to the uncompromisingly rigorous, serious, and timeless.

I

The *Christmas Oratorio* is Bach's last major contribution to the repertoire of German Lutheran liturgical music. By 1730, when he was just forty-five years old and was still to live for another twenty years, Bach had substantially completed what he may have expected to be his life's work as a church composer—his *Endzweck* (final goal), as he called it—namely, the production of "a regular church music to the glory of God."[1] As it happened, it had taken him little more than twenty years, rather than a lifetime, to achieve this ambitious goal. The project began when Bach had assumed the post of organist in Mühlhausen in 1707. Over the next twenty-plus years the nature of his official duties from one job to the other determined how much time and energy he would be able to devote to the *Endzweck*. At times it was sporadic; at other times (such as during his six-year sojourn in Köthen) it virtually ceased altogether. At still other times (specifically, his last few years in Weimar, 1714–17, and most especially his first few years in Leipzig beginning in 1723), the commitment was intense, indeed, even heroic: culminating in the creation of some two hundred church cantatas, along with the Magnificat, and the St. John and St. Matthew Passions. (It is tempting to think that the first version of the St. Matthew—which was written in 1727—was intended to mark the capstone and endpoint to that almost super-human achievement.) In any event, the *Christmas Oratorio*, dating from 1734/35, is a delayed outlier to the entire enterprise; for by 1730 Bach's systematic production of Lutheran church music had effectively ceased. It is symptomatic that recent discoveries have revealed that many church compositions by the Gotha Kapellmeister, Gottfried Heinrich Stölzel (1690–1749), were performed in Leipzig during the 1730s. On Good Friday, April 23, 1734, Stölzel's 1720 Passion oratorio, *Die leidende und am Creutz sterbende Liebe*, was performed in the Thomaskirche. For the 1735/36 liturgical year Bach—or perhaps a deputy—may have performed an entire annual cycle of Stölzel's cantatas. (Earlier that decade, between 1732 and 1735, an indeterminate number of Stölzel's settings of cantatas from another annual cycle also seem to have been performed in Leipzig.)[2] Bach clearly had already turned his attention in new directions.

More specifically, Bach had begun to look in two new directions, both decidedly secular in nature. In 1729 he had assumed the directorship of an amateur music-making society, the Collegium Musicum, consisting mainly of university students. He occupied this position faithfully through 1737 and took it up again, more intermittently, in 1739. We should not underestimate the importance of the Collegium Musicum for Bach's activities in the 1730s. In purely quantitative terms it was substantial. George Stauffer has demonstrated that Bach spent considerably more time conducting secular music during his ten-plus years as director of the Collegium than he had performing church cantatas over the course of his entire twenty-seven years in Leipzig as Thomaskantor.[3]

By 1730—especially after a highly unpleasant confrontation with his superiors on the Leipzig town council—Bach was ready to leave Leipzig and was literally looking in a new geographic direction as well, specifically, toward the well-endowed royal court in Dresden. Bach documented his admiration, even his envy, of the favorable musical conditions in the Saxon capital with crystal clarity in a famous memorandum that bore the provocative title: "Short but Most Necessary Draft for a Well-Appointed Church Music, with Certain Modest Reflections on the Decline of the Same."[4]

In the year 1733 Bach began to strengthen his long-standing but hitherto informal connections with the Saxon court. He took the occasion of the death in February of the elector Frederick Augustus I (as king of Poland August II "the Strong") to apply to the new monarch Frederick Augustus II (King August III) for a court title and promised "my untiring zeal in the composition of music for the church as well as for the *orchestre*."[5] He made this request in a letter dated July 27, 1733; it accompanied a gift: a set of performance materials for a newly composed work: the Kyrie and Gloria of the Mass in B Minor. Bach's ties with Dresden were to grow over the following years; and eventually, in November of 1736, he received the title of Dresden Court Kapellmeister.

Bach's new activities during this period—his connections with Dresden and his directorship of the Leipzig Collegium Musicum—reinforced one another since he found himself in both activities engaged to a large extent in related, often identical, projects such as the composition of music in honor of the royal family in Dresden or of notable middle-class burghers in Leipzig. Most of these works were performed by the Collegium Musicum.

II

This brings us back to the *Christmas Oratorio*, for almost all of the arias, duets, and free choruses (i.e., those not based on traditional chorale melodies) are not original compositions but are derived from earlier works. Most of them were taken from two compositions that were written approximately a year earlier to celebrate the birthdays of members of the Saxon royal family: *Laßt uns sorgen, laßt uns wachen*, BWV 213, performed September 5, 1733 (composed for the birthday of the Saxon crown prince, Friedrich Christian), and *Tönet, ihr Pauken! Erschallet, Trompeten!* BWV 214 (written for the birthday of Queen Maria Josepha), performed three months later, on December 8, 1733.

Bach distributed the movements derived from Cantatas 213 and 214 among the first four parts of the *Christmas Oratorio*. He also drew on two other earlier works. (The details are well-known and need not concern us here.)[6] But it is worth taking a moment to consider the opening chorus of the *Christmas Oratorio*, "Jauchzet, frohlocket" (Rejoice, exult)—one of the most brilliant and colorful compositions ever to issue from Bach's pen (ex. 8.1).

The opening words read:

Jauchzet, frohlocket, / Auf, preiset die Tage, / Rühmet, was heute / Der Höchste getan! [Rejoice, exult! Arise, praise these days; Glorify what God has accomplished today!]

The music so perfectly captures the joy and exuberance of both the text and the Christmas holiday (ex. 8.2) that it is hard to believe it was not originally written for this work but rather for the opening movement of Cantata 214, which begins (see ex. 8.3) with the words:

Tönet, ihr Pauken! / Erschallet, Trompeten, / Klingende Saiten, / Erfüllet die Luft! [Sound, ye drums now! Resound, ye trumpets! Resonant strings fill the air!]

The explicit evocation of kettledrums and trumpets in the very opening line of the work, and of the "resonant strings" in the second line abundantly explains Bach's

Example 8.1. *Christmas Oratorio*, BWV 248/1, opening

Example 8.2. Choral entry, BWV 248/1, movement 1

Example 8.3. *Tönet. ihr Pauken*, BWV 214/1, choral entry

vivid scoring of the movement, which after all offers a graphic representation—literally tone painting—of the original text, which it fits even more snugly than it does that of the *Christmas Oratorio*.

But describing the connections between the two versions of this movement is not really the main point of this comparison, which is rather this: anyone would think that the opening words of Cantata 214, "Tönet, ihr Pauken," must have been the inspiration for Bach's stroke of genius—to begin a work commanding the kettledrum to sound literally with a kettledrum solo. And of course they were—eventually. But that was not Bach's original idea. It was an afterthought. The first draft of the movement, which still survives in Bach's composing score of the cantata, certainly has a great deal in common with the final version (ex. 8.4).[7]

Both readings have the same key (D major), the same meter ($\frac{3}{8}$), the same orchestration, and the same character. Even the melodic and rhythmic motifs were largely the same. But the inspiration of letting the timpani begin alone and having the other instruments enter in carefully calibrated stages, creating that exhilarating step-by-step buildup of rhythmic energy and excitement, was not there. It may be enlightening to speculate about why it was not.

Such a theatrical gesture, one suspects (one that was guaranteed to delight—and surprise—his audience), did not come very naturally to Johann Sebastian Bach. The creator of some of the most complex (and serious) music ever written was surely reluctant to "stoop" (we think) to opening a serious large-scale work so sensationally. He eventually did it, presumably, not only because it perfectly captured the imagery of the text but also because he knew it would make a surprising, audience-pleasing effect.

Example 8.4. *Tönet, ihr Pauken*, BWV 214/1, rejected draft

Mozart often remarked that music had to make an "effect." "Effect" was one of the most important concepts in his aesthetic vocabulary; the term appears a number of times in his letters.[8] But it is not a term that one associates with the aesthetic outlook of Johann Sebastian Bach. We perhaps all too readily assume that flamboyant effect and immediacy of appeal—essentially for their own sakes—must have been unnatural, almost immoral, motivations for Bach (especially after he had outgrown his youthful career as an organ virtuoso); but they did belong to the aesthetic values of the new, modish style of music (and life) cultivated and appreciated at the Dresden court and increasingly everywhere.

In other respects as well, the opening chorus reflects the new *galant* aesthetic. It is predominantly homophonic with some fairly "unthreatening" stretches of counterpoint. Melody and harmony are mostly diatonic and straightforward. The phrasing is quite regular, frequently falling into clear two- and four-measure groups, and sixteen- and thirty-two measure sections.

As for the *galant* values of charm and immediacy of appeal: nowhere has Bach written a more charming, more appealing composition than the sinfonia that opens "Part 2" of the *Christmas Oratorio*. The scoring famously features two transverse flutes and a quartet of exotic oboes: a pair of oboes d'amore and another pair of oboes da caccia. Again, as he had done with the opening of "Part 1" of the oratorio, Bach offers here an exquisite tone painting, one that this time evokes a pastoral ambience for the adoring shepherds (ex. 8.5).

The sinfonia, however, does not seem to have been adapted from a pre-existing secular work. As far as we know, it was newly composed for the oratorio. But it may well have been inspired by a pre-existing secular work—one written not by Bach himself but by a younger Italian contemporary, Pietro Locatelli (1695–1764).

Locatelli's Concerto grosso in F Minor, op. 1, no. 8 (composed by 1721), was one of the compositions Bach performed with the Collegium Musicum. He performed it at least three times, the first time around 1734, that is, in the same year as the *Christmas Oratorio*. Locatelli's concerto ends with a movement marked "pastorale." Like Bach's sinfonia it is in the major mode and in a gentle, lilting 12/8 meter; the melodic writing is sweet, even innocent; and there are delicate exchanges between the string soloists and the tutti ensemble (ex. 8.6).

All this has led to the plausible speculation that Locatelli's pastorale may have inspired Bach's decision to compose a pastoral sinfonia for the *Christmas Oratorio*.[9]

Incidentally, Bach's colorful quartet of oboes, like that drum solo in the first movement, documents Bach's intensified interest at the time in the emerging art of orchestration and in exploiting this resource to a degree only occasionally observed before in his career. He experimented with a similarly imaginative instrumental combination the year before. The "Quoniam" of the B-Minor Mass is scored for bass voice accompanied by four low instruments: an obbligato horn, two bassoons, and the basso continuo.

Example 8.5. *Christmas Oratorio*, BWV 248/10, Sinfonia, mm. 7–10

Example 8.6. Locatelli, Concerto grosso in F Minor, op. 1, no. 8 (1721), Pastorale, mm. 1–4

III

The *Christmas Oratorio* marks the high point—although definitely not the end-point—of Bach's flirtation with the progressive style.[10] He did not abandon this direction entirely, but he did turn now (or rather: returned), with a renewed sense of purpose, to the musical traditions that were more congenial to his inborn gifts as a consummate master of the complex arts of polyphony.

This redirection—this course reversal—took place almost immediately after the performance of the final part of the *Christmas Oratorio* on January 6, 1735. His very next composition was composed for the Fourth Sunday after Epiphany, which fell on January 30, less than four weeks later. This was a regular Sunday cantata, *Wär Gott nicht mit uns diese Zeit* (Were God not with us in this time), BWV 14. It was written to fill a gap in the cycle of chorale cantatas that Bach had composed exactly ten years earlier, in the years 1724–25. It is, if anything, old-fashioned rather than progressive: rigorously, even defiantly, contrapuntal and complex.

The opening movement dispenses with the concerto-inspired instrumental ritor-nello typical of most of Bach's chorale cantatas. It has, rather, the archaic form of the chorale motet: each line of the chorale cantus firmus—typically intoned in long notes in the soprano voice—is preceded by a fugue-like pre-imitation in the three remaining voices of the chorus. Often enough the pre-imitation develops motives derived from the chorale melody. In the present case, all four choral parts participate in the pre-imitation, while the cantus firmus melody is intoned by instruments—two oboes and a horn in unison—in augmentation. Bach, then, has expanded the con-trapuntal fabric from four to five independent parts. He has added another level of complexity as well: the four-part pre-imitations of each chorale line are constructed as a counter-fugue, each entering part sings the motivic idea of the previous part in inversion. If the motive in the first voice (whose contour, once again, is taken from the chorale melody) ascends, then the answering voice descends. Bach maintains this challenging pattern throughout the movement (ex. 8.7).[11]

Bach's growing interest in such archaic styles and techniques is dramatically docu-mented in a recently discovered, altogether unique, source, one in which we observe Johann Sebastian working out traditional exercises in strict counterpoint together with his oldest son, Wilhelm Friedemann.[12] They are literally working side by side—on the same page. Handwriting and paper analysis dates the manuscript approxi-mately to the years 1736 to 1738, a time when Friedemann was in his mid-twenties and employed in Dresden as the organist of the Sophienkirche. Since the paper is of Dresden manufacture, one assumes that the exercises were written out during one of J. S. Bach's visits to the Saxon capital—perhaps during his visit in early December 1736, when he officially accepted the appointment as Dresden Court Composer (and marked the occasion with a recital inaugurating the new Silbermann organ at the Frauenkirche).

Example 8.7. *Wär Gott nicht mit uns diese Zeit*, BWV 14/1, mm. 1–15

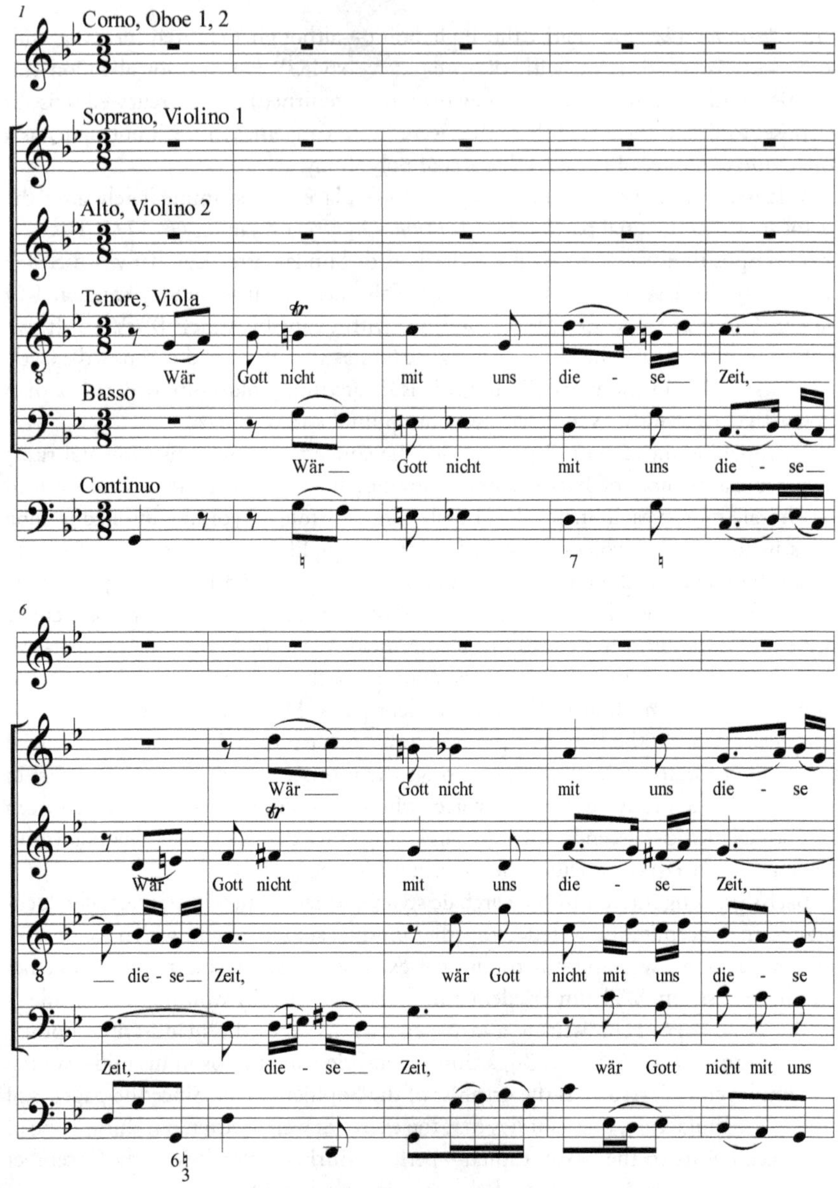

Example 8.7.—*(concluded)*

The entries on the sheets show Bach and his son working out problems in double and triple counterpoint, inventing contrapuntal exercises in augmentation, diminution, inversion and stretto; exploring the idiosyncrasies of the old church modes, and wrestling with difficult-to-answer fugue subjects.[13]

These exercises were not by any means mere abstract theoretical puzzles but rather quite practical issues of the kind that Bach was to face repeatedly in the music contained in "Part 3" of the *Klavierübung* and in the *Art of Fugue*. As Peter Wollny, who brought the manuscript to light, suggests, the exercises reveal that Bach was tackling these problems seriously by the mid-1730s. Indeed some of the exercises use a theme that is the prototype of the *Art of Fugue* subject (ex. 8.8).[14]

We must backtrack a bit. Just three months after Bach completed the *Christmas Oratorio* in January 1735, he marked his fiftieth birthday. The significance of this event—a landmark for anyone—must have been considerably greater for Bach, owing to the fact that his father, Johann Ambrosius (1645–95), his mother, Elisabeth (1644–94), and his brother, Johann Christoph (1671–1721), all died at the age of fifty.

This poignant fact may help explain why at just this time, around the year 1735, Bach compiled a family genealogy and began to put together a collection of music composed by his ancestors—known today as the *Alt-Bachisches Archiv*.[15] At this

Example 8.8a. J. S. Bach, exercise in diminution canon

Example 8.8b. *Art of Fugue*, BWV 1080, subject

time Bach also began to look back on his own achievements to date: he revised a number of his own earlier works and organized them into systematic collections. The fair copy of the St. Matthew Passion, the "Great Eighteen" organ chorales, originally composed during the Weimar period, and also the second volume of *The Well-Tempered Clavier* were the most significant products of this retrospective project. All this genealogical, collecting, and revising activity abundantly attests to Bach's desire to refresh and reassess his connection with the musical traditions of his ancestors—and to rededicate himself to perfecting them further.

IV

Bach's evolving aesthetic reorientation received a powerful, perhaps decisive, external impetus in the year 1737 as a consequence of the severe criticism leveled at the composer by Johann Adolph Scheibe. Some of its implications were discussed at the outset of chapter 7. At this point it is more pertinent to note that the critique ignited an intense controversy. There was a lively exchange in the musical press over the next several months, and lingering contributions to the issue appeared years later.[16] The chief protagonists were Scheibe and Bach's defender, the jurist (and sometime rhetorician), Johann Abraham Birnbaum (1702–48). Lorenz Christoph Mizler (1711–78) and Christoph Gottlieb Schröter (1699–1782) also contributed to the debate.[17] Bach himself, as we have seen, had already acknowledged—a year before all this commotion had broken out—that his church compositions were, in his words, "incomparably more difficult and more intricate" (*ohngleich schwerer und intricater*) than those by other composers.[18]

Whether, as it seems, Bach and his supporters misconstrued Scheibe's remarks and reacted with undue vehemence is beside the point: it is clear that Scheibe's comments stung the perhaps overly sensitive, battle-scarred composer—and that they also encouraged him to dig in his heels. There can be little doubt that the Scheibe controversy, coming less than a year after Bach's bitter turf battle with the rector of the Thomasschule, Johann August Ernesti (1707–81)—the "prefects' dispute" (*Präfektenstreit*), which played out in August and September 1736, had aggravated further Bach's growing estrangement and alienation from his official duties in Leipzig. (By the mid-1740s Bach seems not only to have increasingly absented himself from Leipzig for weeks at a time but may have effectively ceased conducting the Sunday church services entirely.)[19]

Bach's immediate response to Scheibe's criticism was not a literary piece but a musical one. It was actually addressed even more directly to another essayist. In 1739 Johann Mattheson (1681–1764), arguably the preeminent German music theorist of the time, published his monumental treatise, *Der vollkommene Capellmeister*. On page 441 of the tome he made the following appeal to the Thomaskantor: "Of double fugues with three subjects, there is, as far as I know, nothing else in print but my own work [*Die wolklingende Fingersprache* (1735, 1737)], which I, out of modesty, would commend to no one. On the contrary, I would much rather see something of the same sort published by the famed Herr Bach in Leipzig, who is a great master of the fugue [*ein grosser Fugenmeister*]."[20]

Gregory Butler has made a compelling case that Bach must have been familiar with this passage before its publication.[21] While one need not agree with Butler that the term "Fugenmeister" was meant derogatorily, one can nonetheless agree with him that Bach took up Mattheson's invitation to construct and publish such a fugue and that he would have meant it to serve as well as (in Butler's words) "a published musical rebuttal to Scheibe's criticisms."[22]

Butler has plausibly identified Bach's great five-voice Fugue in E-flat, BWV 552, the concluding item in "Part 3" of the *Klavierübung*, as the composer's response to Mattheson—and Scheibe. He observes that "no other fugue of Bach's quite resembles this one in its structure. . . . Is it a double or a triple fugue? In fact, it is a double fugue with three subjects as specified by Mattheson, that is, a fugue in which there are three distinct subjects and in which the first subject combines in double counterpoint with each of the two other subjects but never with both" (exx. 8.9a–d).[23]

Scheibe's critique and the ensuing controversy it unleashed—together with Mattheson's challenge—can only have strengthened Bach's determination to abandon the effort to ingratiate himself to potential patrons and the larger public by catering to the vagaries of taste, to acknowledge his true calling and strongest gifts, and to devote himself instead ever more totally to what he increasingly recognized to be the lasting verities and values of his art.

"Part 3" of the *Klavierübung*, published in 1739, is mostly devoted to the traditional repertoire of the organ chorale. But "traditional" hardly begins to describe the

Example 8.9a. Fugue in E-flat, BWV 552/2, Principal subject, mm. 1–9

Example 8.9b. Fugue in E-flat, BWV 552/2, Second subject, mm. 37–41

Example 8.9c. Fugue in E-flat, BWV 552/2, Second subject + first subject, mm. 58–64

backward-looking character of the collection, which is notable for its exploration of the ancient church modes, the sixteenth-century "Palestrina" style of contrapuntal writing (i.e., the *stile antico*), and for the extensive use of canonic procedures. The volume, in short, forms the gateway to Bach's ensuing collections of serious, demanding contrapuntal *tours de force*.

But it might be more appropriate to refer to what "Part 3" of the *Klavierübung* achieved not so much as forming the "gateway," but as opening the "floodgates." In the years following the publication, Bach produced a steady "flood" of formidable contrapuntal masterpieces gathered together into monumental collections. The final volume of the *Klavierübung*, the Goldberg Variations, appeared in 1741. Along with its tribute to modern keyboard virtuosity, the Goldberg Variations recorded Bach's interest in systematic canonic procedures. And, again, during the late 1730s and early 1740s, Bach was occupied not only with the compilation of the second volume of *The Well-Tempered Clavier* but also with the *Art of Fugue*, the latter representing, as described in a previous chapter, the next logical step for Bach, uniting the compositional premises of both *The Well-Tempered Clavier* and the Goldberg Variations.[24]

The 1730s, then, were a time of artistic crisis for Johann Sebastian Bach. The decade began soon after Bach had achieved his presumed *Endzweck*: the creation of a comprehensive repertoire of sacred music for the Lutheran church. In the immediate

Example 8.9d. Fugue in E-flat, BWV 552/2, Third subject, mm. 82–90

aftermath the composer experienced a dramatic drop in productivity, a demoralization, and a conflict with the church authorities. By the end of the decade, however, Bach had completed and published the third and fourth parts of the *Klavierübung* and was well along with the composition of the second volume of *The Well Tempered Clavier* and the *Art of Fugue*.

On closer inspection we can see that the decade of the 1730s—actually a "long" decade spanning some dozen years from 1729 to 1741 or 1742—was almost evenly bisected into two equal parts. During the first half dozen years, from about 1729 to 1735, Bach assumed the directorship of the Collegium Musicum and became involved with modern secular instrumental music and with secular and sacred vocal music for the Dresden court. This period, which culminates in the composition of the *Christmas Oratorio*, is marked musically by Bach's engagement or "flirtation" with the new *galant* style.

The second half dozen years of the long decade began immediately after the completion of the *Christmas Oratorio* in January 1735, which was shortly before the composer turned fifty. It ends with the composition of the major portion of the *Art of Fugue*. Musically, it was at first a time of consolidation—pulling together (and revising) previously written works into systematic collections (the eighteen great organ chorales, volume 2 of *The Well-Tempered Clavier*). That is, it began as a retrospective taking stock of where Bach had arrived in his compositional development—and what was left to do. By its end these half-dozen years witnessed a renewed commitment to the contrapuntal tradition and the ethos of uncompromising musical craftsmanship.

The discussion of Bach's keyboard works in chapter 5 recounts that during the fifteen years or so from around 1707 to 1723, Bach had famously succeeded in creating a synthesis of the leading national traditions of his age: the organ and church music of Germany (toccatas, fantasias, etc.), the concerted instrumental music of Italy (the Brandenburg Concertos), and the secular keyboard music of France (the French and English Suites). The discussion then proposed that by the same token, the dozen years or so of the "long decade" from around 1729 to 1742 could be profitably understood as a second synthesis, one in which Bach expanded his horizons in greater historical (rather than geographic) directions to embrace both the ancient (the *stile antico*) and the most recent (the *style galant*). On the one hand, Bach was interested in emulating, absorbing—and surpassing—the new impulses of his sons' generation; on the other hand, he was intent on looking backward and embracing the stylistic conventions and aesthetic values of his musical ancestors, which for him were moral values as well. Common throughout was the restless quest for new stimuli, new impulses, new paths. Chapter 9 argues that in his last years Bach managed to extend his historical reach considerably farther—forward and backward—with the composition of the final movements of the Mass in B Minor.

Chapter Nine

Bach at the Boundaries
of Music History

Preliminary Reflections on the B-Minor
Mass and the Late-Style Paradigm

Beethoven famously declared that Bach's name was a misnomer: "His name ought not to be Bach [brook] but *Meer* [ocean]."[1] Who would disagree! It is no surprise that the oceanic, qualitative immensity of Bach's achievement is matched by a comparably oceanic, if quantitative, immensity of the literature devoted to it—and to the composer himself. The indispensable on-line database, *Bach Bibliography*, compiled by Yo Tomita (Queen's University, Belfast) under the auspices of the Bach-Archiv, Leipzig, records, at present (2018), some 73,000 publications devoted to the composer and his works. About the B-Minor Mass the bibliography reveals that it is easily Bach's most written-about work. So much has already been said about it that it is hard to imagine that there is still more to add. In the twenty years from 1997 to 2017 over 150 publications devoted to the Mass had appeared—easily outpacing the number devoted to the St. John and St. Matthew Passions in the same time span (110 and 106 publications, respectively). As for Bach's instrumental works: there had been an even hundred dedicated publications to *The Well-Tempered Clavier*, and a mere twenty-one to the Brandenburg Concertos in that period. These statistics, incidentally, did not include all the discussions of these works in general treatments of Bach's music.

The extensive scholarly attention to the Mass reflects its immense, long-standing popularity with the musical public—a popularity readily explained: it is in the supra-national Latin rather than German and sets a universally familiar, effectively supra-denominational (if undeniably religious) text. The composition, moreover, taken as a whole (and in contrast to the Passions, for example), is colorful, lively, and—measured against the composer's own standards—much of the time remarkably euphonious, even jubilant. None of this, of course, denies its pervasive seriousness and—once again, measured against the composer's own standards—extraordinary compositional complexity.

The B-Minor Mass's immediacy of appeal is an anomaly among late works by great composers. Thanks to Theodor Adorno, the concept of "late style" in music has largely come to be equated with that of Beethoven. Indeed the very term, "late style" (*Spätstil*), was coined by Adorno in his 1937 essay, "Spätstil Beethovens," and pursued by him further in his "Verfremdetes Hauptwerk: Zur Missa Solemnis" (1959).[2] Beethoven's *Missa Solemnis*, according to Adorno, was the exemplar of the "alienated master-piece." Edward Said, in his posthumous volume, *On Late Style* (2006), observes that Beethoven's late works, in Adorno's view, are "bristling, difficult, unyielding." Indeed, "constitutively alienated and alienating: difficult, forbidding works like the *Missa Solemnis* and the *Hammerklavier* Sonata are repellent to audiences and performers alike."[3] Elsewhere Said hastens to point out, however, that there are other, quite different, manifestations of a late style in the works of other masters—not only composers but artists and writers, as well: "a new spirit of reconciliation and serenity," or perhaps a spirit "not so much . . . of wise resignation as a renewed almost youthful energy that attests to an apotheosis of artistic creativity and power."[4]

Late style could be either reactionary and retrospective—as in Heinrich Schütz's late Passion settings—or experimental. Wagner moved in both directions in his late works: on the one hand, the retrospective *Meistersinger* (1867) with its reintroduction of closed forms and rediscovery of diatonicism along with academic counterpoint; and, on the other, the futuristic *Parsifal* (1882), in which a medieval tale is wrapped in an experimental post-Romantic, arguably post-tonal, musical vocabulary.

The late works of J. S. Bach, while they of course have been the objects of serious study for as long as musicians and scholars have been interested in the life and music of J. S. Bach, have not (as far as I can tell) played much of a role in more general discussions of the late-style phenomenon per se—perhaps because so much of it fails to fit comfortably into any one of the prevailing paradigms. Like Wagner, Bach, too, moves in both directions in his late works—usually within the same works: the Goldberg Variations, the *Musical Offering*, and, most dramatically, in the B-Minor Mass. Part of the mundane explanation for this, perhaps, is that his two great patrons in his last period were the Catholic elector in Dresden and the atheist king in Berlin. Their sudden importance in the composer's affairs attests to the fact that, after 1736, Bach increasingly lived in a form of interior exile in Leipzig. Alienated by the recently imposed academic reforms at the Thomasschule that significantly reduced the role of music in the curriculum, he effectively abandoned the composition of German Lutheran church music entirely—a matter touched upon earlier.[5] In this connection, Said informs us that lateness, among other things, "is a kind of self-imposed exile." He invokes Adorno's claim that it results in a music that is "episodic, fragmentary, riven with . . . absences and silences." Said emphasizes "the sense of apartness and exile and anachronism, which late style expresses."[6]

Bach's Mass in B Minor is, of course, not only a late work: it is probably Bach's very last work, completed in the last months—or even weeks—of his life. But no one would describe it in the way Adorno and Said describe Beethoven's *Missa solemnis*. The B-Minor Mass shows no signs of fragmentation and disintegration. It is, if anything, a miracle of integration. Its compelling sense of unity is particularly miraculous in light of the well-known fact that its component sections were written over the course of some thirty-five years beginning in Bach's Weimar period and are almost all reworkings of material that originated in different contexts.[7] Unquestionably, though, the kaleidoscope of styles in the Mass is symptomatic of late style insofar as it represents a distanced overview, a recapitulation.

Ernest May has suggested that the Mass is "arguably the greatest work by the greatest classical composer of all time," invoking, among other authorities, the Swiss publisher Hans Nägeli's famous subscription announcement in 1818 for the first edition of the Mass as "the Greatest Musical Work of Art of All Times and Nations."[8] The claim has been challenged. The late conductor, and Bach venerator *nonpareil*, Craig Smith (1947–2007), insisted (and was willing to defend the proposition) that the St. Matthew Passion was not only J. S. Bach's greatest work but indeed the greatest human accomplishment of all time—eclipsing all others.[9] The biologist Lewis Thomas, author of *Lives of a Cell*, for his part, maintained that the best way to inform other civilizations in space about the achievements of humankind would be "to send music. . . . I would vote for Bach, all of Bach, streamed out into space, over and over again. We would be bragging of course."[10] (In fact, the *Voyager* spacecraft, launched in 1977 to outer space, carried a musical disc. The first human music placed on it is Bach's Brandenburg Concerto No. 2, BWV 1047. Two other works by Bach are included (although not the Mass in B Minor): the Gavotte en Rondeau from the solo violin Partita in E, BWV 1006/3, and the Prelude and Fugue in C Major from *The Well-Tempered Clavier* II, BWV 870. Bach is the only composer—West or East—on the disc honored with three compositions.)

❧   ❧   ❧

It seems that almost anything one wishes to claim about the B-Minor Mass is true—just as virtually anything one wishes to claim about its creator, J. S. Bach, is true: that he was a reactionary, a conservative, a progressive, a modernist, an anti-modernist, a radical, a bigot, a pragmatist, an amoral opportunist. While not everyone will be able to agree on any one of these characterizations of the composer, everyone, surely, will agree on the encyclopedic scope of the Mass in B Minor and acknowledge that it contains multitudes. It displays, after all—in exemplary form—just about every style, genre, and national tradition of musical composition found in Mass settings during the composer's lifetime.

Bach's interest in and fascination with Latin church music and the sixteenth-century *stile antico* in his last decades (a topic increasingly investigated nowadays),11 is a bit analogous to Richard Strauss's obsession with the eighteenth century—an obsession he carried throughout his life but increasingly so in his last years.[12] Both cases can be understood, among other things, as symptomatic of a withdrawal from, an escape from, the realities of the contemporary scene into the past: Strauss's attempt—along with purely aesthetic considerations (his rejection, for example, of the direction of the Second Viennese School)—to ignore the Nazi barbarism that had enveloped his world, Bach's rejection of the encroaching rationalist attitude of the Enlightenment threatening to topple the pillars of his world, namely, the centrality of music and religion. Much like Strauss, Bach, too, after 1736 (as mentioned earlier), increasingly lived in a form of self-imposed interior exile in Leipzig. To some extent, then, Bach's late-period Latin works might also attest—like Beethoven perhaps, after all—to an attitude of defiance.

Unlike Strauss's infatuation with the eighteenth century, however, Bach's engagement with Latin church music and the *stile antico* was not just—or perhaps even primarily—an escapist retreat into the past. In contrast to his earlier German cantata and Passion settings, which are personal and dramatic—focused on the subjective believer and his god—his late Latin settings are supra-personal. It is one thing, as in the Passions, to dramatically depict the suffering on the cross (along with the events leading up to it), to empathize with the reaction of the witnesses to it, and to reflect upon its meaning. It is another thing, as in the Mass, to declare that you believe—as a matter of doctrine—in the incarnation, the crucifixion, and the resurrection. The affirmative character of the Mass, then, proclaims a confident serenity, which suggests in turn that its composer—at least for the purposes of this project—has moved beyond the personal, subjective ego struggle. As Robin Leaver puts it, "For Bach, the shift in emphasis from German to Latin was momentous. . . . His perspective changed from the homiletical to the liturgical. Cantatas . . . originally conceived as sermons . . . were reworked to become liturgical prayers and praises directed to God."[13]

There is another way to regard the Mass, namely, as part of the encyclopedic project that increasingly occupied Bach in his last decades—an enterprise revealed of course not only in the Mass but also in the "Eighteen Great Organ Chorales," *The Well-Tempered Clavier*, the Goldberg Variations, the *Musical Offering*, and the *Art of Fugue*. But is this encyclopedic project, paradoxically, not, at least to some degree, a precocious manifestation of something quite modern—namely, the spirit of the Enlightenment as it is demonstrated in Denis Diderot's *Encyclopédie*, a work, after all, that began to appear in 1751, that is, literally only months after Bach's death?

One is tempted, however—and not simply in order to be contrarian—to advocate for the "de-contextualizing" of the Mass in B Minor. Bach's *opus ultimum* extends the historical frame of reference he first systematically explored in the 1730s both forward and backward: now embracing on the one end Gregorian chant and, on the other, a postmodern, speculative harmonic vocabulary beyond the known limits of his time. The opening movement of the Credo section of the work emphatically cites the familiar Gregorian melody at the outset (ex. 9.1).

At just about the midpoint of the Confiteor movement Bach presents the underlying chant melody as a canonic cantus firmus at the fifth between the bass and the alto (ex. 9.2).[14]

On the other hand, the futuristic thrust of the Credo section as a whole—and of the entire work—becomes manifest in the final measures of the same movement, the Confiteor (which, incidentally, along with the Et incarnatus, are the only movements of the Mass almost certain to have been newly composed at the end of Bach's life). Specifically, in the transition to the final movement of the Credo, a jubilant "Vivace e allegro," Bach prematurely anticipates its first four words, *et expecto resurrectionem mortuorum*, but ventures into a disorienting, hitherto virtually unexplored musical world—one not explored, perhaps, since the harmonic audacities of Carlo Gesualdo (ex. 9.3).

The passage explores, and exploits, ambiguous chromatic and enharmonic progressions that verge on the post-tonal. This is Bach the Futurist, the Visionary: the unmoored harmonic groping, the "triadic atonality" (to borrow an apt term coined by Edward Lowinsky to describe the wilder music of Gesualdo),[15] deployed to evoke the moment of the soul's transfiguration as it "expectantly" and perhaps (as suggested by Joel Lester) with more than a touch of apprehension—even fear—seeks the light and clarity of the eternal life to come.[16] The notoriously heavily corrected autograph score—virtually indecipherable at times—reveals that the passage, even at a quite late stage in its genesis, posed apparently unprecedented difficulties to the composer.[17] The harmonic language here leapfrogs decades, even generations, into the future of music history, bypassing the modern, that is, contemporary, language and conventions of his own time and even those of his sons' generation. It has progressed beyond progressive or even radical. Yet at the same time such visionary speculation, *musica speculativa*, reveals, paradoxically, a medieval mindset—at least as much as a radical/revolutionary one. Perhaps we should just call it "timeless."

Example 9.1. Mass in B Minor, Credo, BWV 232/13, mm. 1–8

Example 9.2. Mass in B Minor, Confiteor, BWV 232/20, mm. 71–78, with interpolated chant melody

Example 9.3. Mass in B Minor, Confiteor, BWV 232/20, mm. 121–46 + Et expecto, BWV 232/21, mm. 1–2

Chapter Ten

Father and Sons

Confronting a Uniquely
Daunting Paternal Legacy

In his provocative essay, "Carl Philipp Emanuel Bach and the Aesthetics of Patricide," Richard Kramer remarks, "Everywhere, Emanuel felt the need to speak of his father. In his music, he fails to do so. The patrimony is not acknowledged there."[1] Kramer demonstrates this in a perceptive analysis of one of Emanuel's challenging keyboard compositions, the Sonata in C Major, H. 248 (1775).

Coping with that patrimony could not have been a picnic for the male offspring of Johann Sebastian Bach. The towering shadow cast by J. S. Bach on the lives, careers, and ambitions of all five of them was undoubtedly overwhelming.[2] Kramer's comment invites us to ponder the various tactics and strategies these uniquely privileged—and uniquely challenged—offspring developed to come to terms with that intimidating legacy. He has also offered an intriguing way to assess and understand the meaning of the careers of the Bach sons: namely, by determining the degree to which—and the manner in which—they succeeded in emerging from their father's shadow. Much of what follows will be conjectural; but very little is not conjectural in historical or biographical writing concerned with comprehending the meaning of events centuries old. On the other hand, much of it will be a matter of reasonably "connecting dots"—that is, documented facts—which we may have become overly reluctant to connect or account for in rather obvious ways.

Bach and His Sons

According to at least one eighteenth-century author, there was an abundance of mutual disdain between Johann Sebastian Bach and his musical sons. Carl Friedrich

Cramer (1752–1807), the editor of the important *Magazin der Musik*, personally knew both Philipp Emanuel and Friedemann.[3] In his autobiography, written in 1792–93, Cramer mentions: "The old Sebastian had three sons. He was satisfied only with Friedemann, the great organist. Even about Carl Philipp Emanuel he said (unjustly!): ''Tis Berlin blue! It fades!'—Regarding the London Chrétien, [Sebastian] Bach was wont to cite the verse by Gellert: 'The boy is sure to thrive owing to his stupidity!' In fact, among the three Bach sons this one had the greatest success.—I have these opinions from Friedemann himself."[4]

Cramer goes on to report that Sebastian "rejoiced over his son Friedemann with whom the organ died out, so to speak. 'This is my beloved son,' he used to say, 'who pleases me well.'"[5] This is clearly a quotation of Luke 3:22, which describes the heavenly voice that was heard at the baptism of Jesus: "Thou art my beloved Son; in thee I am well pleased" (*Du bist mein lieber Sohn, an dem ich Wohlgefallen habe*). What should be made of the fact that Johann Sebastian Bach here cites the bible in such a way that he compares himself to God the Father and Friedemann to Jesus? Is this blasphemy, or self-deprecating, ironic humor?

All these remarks are rather flattering to Friedemann, so it is no surprise to learn that he, and not Emanuel, was Cramer's source for these self-serving comments. But there is a problem with many, if not all, of these quotations from Cramer: Wilhelm Friedemann Bach, as we shall see shortly, was a liar!

Wilhelm Friedemann Bach

The great mystery in the life of Friedemann—Sebastian's oldest son and allegedly his favorite—is this: why did he fail so miserably? As David Schulenberg remarks at the beginning of his indispensable study of Friedemann's music, he was "a brilliant disappointment or underachiever"; "he enjoyed early success but, *for unknown reasons*, quit a respectable position as organist during his middle years."[6] Schulenberg has no hesitation in dismissing the "unfortunate . . . facile but largely groundless psychologizing" that "continues to color present-day views of the composer and his music," insisting that "psychological speculation can lead *only* to *doubtful* presumptions and hypotheses."[7] Are *plausible* presumptions and hypotheses so unimaginable that they should not even be sought? Must repeated observations of, say, manifestly self-destructive behavior be merely inventoried with no further attempts at understanding?

As is well-known, Friedemann's life poses an array of intriguing questions. Here are a few of them: Why, in 1762, did he turn down a magnificent job, offered to him on the proverbial silver platter, namely, that of Kapellmeister in Darmstadt? Why did he throw away his job in Halle just two years thereafter, at a time when he had no other job prospects, only to linger there unemployed for another seven years? Why, in the late 1770s, did he destroy his chances in Berlin by clumsily intriguing against Johann Philipp Kirnberger (1721–83) at court?[8] Kirnberger, a devoted student and champion of Johann Sebastian Bach, had been eager to help Friedemann in his dire circumstances. Is it unreasonable to see in Friedemann's conspiring against a fellow student of his father's and attempting to replace him in the favor of Princess Anna Amalia, as some form of sibling rivalry? According to Kirnberger, even Philipp Emanuel—at least around 1779—distanced himself from Friedemann: "And his brother in Hamburg also will have nothing to do with him."[9]

Kirnberger was one of the great collectors and preservers of Sebastian Bach's musical legacy and did more than almost anyone else, next to Philipp Emanuel, to promulgate Johann Sebastian Bach's aesthetic and compositional principles and teaching method. Friedemann, for his part, was one of the great squanderers and losers of his father's musical legacy. Actually, within fewer than ten years of Sebastian's death his favorite son had begun selling off the master's music manuscripts. This activity had started not, as is commonly thought, in the mid-1770s, when he was thoroughly desperate and indigent, but well before—during his Halle years—admittedly also a period of great financial difficulty.[10]

Long before that, in 1733, Sebastian had helped Friedemann—arguably, to an unseemly degree—get his first job as organist at the Sophienkirche in Dresden. Sebastian ghostwrote the job application in his son's name (two applications, actually) and even forged Friedemann's signature on them.[11] Could not Friedemann, at the age of twenty-three, compose his own job application letters? It is also almost certain that at his audition Friedemann played one of his father's masterpieces: the great G-Major Prelude and Fugue, BWV 541.[12] Whether this fact was made known to the audition committee, or whether Friedemann played BWV 541 in addition to, or instead of, compositions of his own, is unknown.

It is known that Friedemann falsely claimed to have authored his father's organ transcription of Vivaldi's Concerto in D Minor, BWV 596. The claim is made on his father's autograph manuscript, a document penned when Friedemann was around five years old. At the top of the first page of the score, following the work heading (in J. S. Bach's hand), Friedemann wrote: "by W. F. Bach in the hand of my father" (*di W. F. Bach / manu mei Patris / descript*).[13]

Martin Geck suggests that we must not judge Friedemann too harshly for this, remarking that collaborative work among Bach family members was common, and we would be well advised "to leave the whole matter in semi-darkness."[14] This, surely, is an example of what could be called "Friedemann apologetics." In recent years one can detect an effort to rehabilitate Wilhelm Friedemann Bach's reputation by dismissing not only nineteenth-century fictionalized depictions of his life and character (epitomized by unfounded claims that he was an alcoholic) but even eighteenth-century and contemporary accounts as romanticized fantasies and exaggerations. The pendulum of the undeniably necessary corrective when considering Friedemann's life and character has perhaps, in the present emphatically nonjudgmental age, swung too far in the opposite direction.

Example 10.1a. W. F. Bach, exercise in counterpoint (Dresden, ca. 1736–39)

Example 10.1b. J. S. Bach, exercise in counterpoint (Dresden, ca. 1736–39)

A remarkable document, dating from the mid-1730s, helps illuminate the relationship between Sebastian and Friedemann. In it we literally observe Bach and his son collaboratively—or perhaps competitively—working out problems in double and triple counterpoint, augmentation, diminution, inversion, and so on. With some embarrassment we witness Friedemann struggling with—and Sebastian completing with effortless insouciance—these tricky exercises in sixteenth-century style (exx. 10.1a, b).

It seems that Sebastian "treated" Friedemann to this diversion (rather than, say, taking out a deck of cards) when he went to Dresden for a visit around 1736 or so.[15] We can imagine how enjoyable Friedemann might (or might not) have found this friendly contest of musical wits. Was Sebastian at all aware of Friedemann's certain humiliation, or was he simply clueless?

The Darmstadt episode alluded to earlier is quite perplexing. In 1746, after thirteen years in Dresden, Friedemann resigned his position in order to take a better one: that of organist and director of church music at the Liebfrauenkirche in Halle. In 1762, following the death of Darmstadt court's long-serving Kapellmeister, Christoph Graupner (1683–1760), Friedemann received a firm offer to replace him. Apparently, as was the case in Halle, the Darmstadt position, too, was offered to Friedemann on the basis of no known audition. This position was better than the respectable Halle job Friedemann had been occupying, increasingly unhappily, since 1746. It was so desirable, in fact, that in 1723 Graupner had turned down the Leipzig Thomas Kantorate in order to remain in Darmstadt. Graupner had been persuaded to stay by an altogether irresistibly generous counter-offer from his patron,

Count Ernst Ludwig.[16] Only thereafter was the Leipzig position offered to, and of course accepted by, J. S. Bach.

Friedemann dragged out the negotiations with Darmstadt for so long that the offer was eventually withdrawn. (This did not prevent him, however, from describing himself some years later, in 1767, as "the recently appointed Kapellmeister to the landgrave of Hesse-Darmstadt.")[17] A doctrinaire Freudian might suggest that Friedemann let the job slip through his fingers because he could not allow himself to exceed his father. It is as if Friedemann had been determined to commit career suicide, thus dashing his father's high expectations of him. But is not such self-inflicted failure on the part of a formidably talented child not merely a self-destructive act but also an act of spite, or retribution, against the parents for some perceived wrong or injury?

The Darmstadt incident, in any event, marked the turning point in Friedemann's fortunes. Two years later, in 1764, he suddenly resigned his job in Halle. No precipitating cause or dispute is known. Friedemann evidently had inherited his father's temperament but not his survival instinct. He apparently stayed on in Halle with no official or visible employment other than taking on private pupils. Perhaps, as has been surmised, he may, like the legendary Flying Dutchman, have journeyed for some seven years as a traveling virtuoso to places like Vienna, Russia, and the Baltic states, until, in 1770 or 1771, he showed up in Braunschweig as a freelance organist.[18]

In the end Friedemann entered upon a wandering life, supporting himself by selling his wife's property, giving organ recitals, teaching, and selling (or trying to sell or at least rent out) his father's music manuscripts. In doing the latter was he perhaps symbolically erasing his father's legacy (or at least casting off his own personal connection with it) while at the same time attempting to ensure that Sebastian—his formidable father—materially continued to support him?

It is not easy to avoid entertaining Freudian notions when pondering Wilhelm Friedemann Bach. Martin Geck who, as we have seen, was something of an apologist for Friedemann, concludes his discussion of his tragic existence by introducing a famous Freudian term: he wonders whether perhaps "the father may have cast his eyes all too insistently on him—not only during his lifetime but also, in the sense of a superego [Über-ich]—even after his death."[19] An overzealous superego does not seem to have been Friedemann Bach's main problem.

Even David Schulenberg, an outspoken skeptic about Freudian approaches to biography, almost succumbs to the temptation when he addresses the Plümicke episode. The dramatist Carl Martin Plümicke (1749–1833) wrote in his memoir-cum-history, *Entwurf einer Theatergeschichte von Berlin* (1781), that he had "undertaken in the years 1778 and 1779 for Herr (Wilhelm Friedemann) Bach, who is famous for his great musical genius, the preparation of a serious opera (after Marmontel): *Lausus und Lydie.* . . . But it remained unfinished owing to the illness of the composer and until now has not been printed."[20] Martin Falck cataloged the opera as the last numbered item (number 106) in the catalog of Friedemann's works appended to his monograph.[21]

It is easy to imagine that Wilhelm Friedemann, in Berlin, and in increasingly desperate straits at just that time (owing to the Anna Amalia-Kirnberger fiasco, which unfolded between February 1778 and 1779), would have been more than receptive to Plümicke's initiative, had he not been indisposed by "sickly circumstances" (*kränkliche Umstände*)—in a word, by illness.[22]

Whether the initiative originated with Plümicke or with Friedemann himself, there is yet another reason to think that the opera's plot would have had special appeal and meaning for Wilhelm Friedemann. Ultimately deriving from Virgil's *Aeneid*, the original story recounted the rivalry between the virtuous Laurus and his tyrannical father for the love of Lydia. It ends with Laurus sacrificing his life defending his malevolent father. In Marmontel's version, son and father were reconciled before the end.

Discussing this episode, Schulenberg, like Geck in a different context, introduces a famous Freudian notion, but only to dismiss the notion. He writes: "It is not necessary to imagine that some latent Oedipal urge impelled Friedemann to this subject. Still, without making any anachronistic or simplistically Freudian assumption, it is *reasonable to suppose* that the relationship between Friedemann and his father was the source of profound tensions; these might have been expressed by his taking an interest in Marmontel's story."[23] Before proceeding any further, it is necessary to point out that Schulenberg has misunderstood Plümicke's text by construing it to claim that the impetus for the opera had come not from the librettist but from Friedemann. Schulenberg writes: "Evidently in 1778, four years after coming to Berlin, Friedemann had 'engaged' [*unternahm*] the playwright and historian Carl Martin Plümicke to prepare for him a libretto based on Marmontel's moral tale," and so on.[24] The original text is obscure on this point, since *unternahm* means "undertook" (not "engaged"), while the pronoun "he" (*er*) in this instance is a self-reference to Plümicke, not to Friedemann Bach. The rest is inference. In any event, I wish to expand on Schulenberg's "reasonable supposition" by exploring what may have drawn Wilhelm Friedemann Bach to this particular story and not some other treatment of the archetypal conflict between father and son.

We can begin by noting that Friedemann's mother, like Sebastian's in his time, died when the boy was not yet ten years old (in July 1720). Perhaps the death was even more traumatic in Friedemann's case than in Sebastian's, since Friedemann's father was not there to share the boy's grief or provide comfort when the tragedy struck. Johann Sebastian Bach was away at the time, having accompanied his patron, Prince Leopold, to Karlsbad, and only learned about his wife Maria Barbara's death and burial when he returned home to Köthen. Is it unreasonable to suppose that Sebastian's absence may have further exacerbated the boy's sense of abandonment during those painful days?

Barely one and a half years later, in December 1721, Johann Sebastian took a new wife: the twenty-year-old court singer Anna Magdalena Wilcke (1701–60), a woman sixteen years Sebastian's junior—and just nine years Friedemann's elder. Thereafter, except for a year spent in nearby Merseburg (1726–27) taking violin instruction from Johann Gottlieb Graun (1702 or 1703–71), Bach's oldest son would continue to live in the household with his father and young stepmother for another twelve years, that is, throughout his adolescence and early adulthood. By the time the twenty-three-year-old had finally left home for Dresden in 1733, Anna Magdalena was herself only thirty-two. (By then, incidentally, she had given birth to nine children with a tenth child on the way.) Rather than (or in addition to) resisting a latent Oedipal urge directed against his father, can Friedemann have been battling with stressful guilt-inducing feelings directed toward his stepmother? To repeat a familiar refrain: we shall never know.

Finally, what, if anything, should be made of the fact that Friedemann waited until he was forty-one years old (and Johann Sebastian had very recently been safely laid to rest) to marry? His wedding took place on February 25, 1751, barely seven months after his father's burial. His bride, the daughter of his landlord in Halle, was a woman he had known for some five years, since his arrival in 1746.[25]

Carl Philipp Emanuel Bach

In his analysis of Emanuel's C-Major Sonata Richard Kramer seems to imply that under the surface there is evidence of defiance and subversion directed at the heart of Johann Sebastian Bach's aesthetic legacy. Like Kramer, one can describe this posited rejection of the artistic ethos that Bach had presumably imparted to his sons as aesthetic patricide, or, more flippantly, "killing Sebastian." Exactly what were the aesthetic premises of Bach the Father that Emanuel was repudiating? Before addressing that question directly, it will be helpful to provide some further context.

Whether or not Philipp Emanuel had set out to commit "aesthetic patricide," he certainly made no effort to "bury" his father, that is, to consign him to oblivion, to expunge his shadow and his memory as completely as possible. In Emanuel's case, quite the contrary obtains: he made every effort to keep J. S. Bach's memory and his legacy alive. One need only mention his role in the publication of Sebastian's four-part chorales, the *Art of Fugue*, his coauthorship of an obituary for his father, his informative letters to Johann Nikolaus Forkel, Sebastian Bach's first biographer; and above all, his systematic collection and preservation of his share of Sebastian's musical legacy, not to mention his public performances of his father's church music.

On a relatively trivial level, Emanuel Bach may have been asserting his professional independence from his father by failing to follow in his "footsteps" when it came to mastering the organ pedals: the skill that was perhaps the principal source of Sebastian's towering reputation throughout the eighteenth century. In 1733 Emanuel unsuccessfully applied for the organist post at the Wenzelskirche in Naumburg. Twenty years later, in 1753, he was again unable to obtain an organist post, this time in Zittau. Finally, in September 1772, it was no doubt with embarrassment bordering on humiliation that the Bach son had to find a surrogate—a dilettante, at that—to demonstrate the glories of the Hamburg organs to the visiting Charles Burney. As recounted by David Yearsley:

> When Burney came to Hamburg and marveled at its organs in 1772, . . . this second son of J. S. Bach did not—could not!—demonstrate any of the city's organs for his visitor. . . . Burney writes, . . . "M. Bach has so long neglected organ-playing, that he says he has lost the use of the pedals, which are thought so essential throughout Germany, that no one can pass for a player worth hearing, who is unable to use them." . . . One should not underestimate the irony and indignity of a Bach son finding himself in arguably the greatest organ city in Europe and not feeling himself able to do justice to its organs. . . . [Emanuel] was surrounded by an embarrassment of riches yet plagued by an embarrassing lack of ability to enjoy them. As the ardent admirer of C. P. E. Bach, the poet Matthias Claudius, put it soon after Bach's arrival in Hamburg, . . . "Bach does not play the organ at all and must endure an array of criticisms."[26]

Yearsley goes on to suggest that "such feelings of inadequacy at the ultimate Bachian instrument must also color the 'Comparison of Bach and Handel,' a document almost certainly written by C. P. E. Bach in response to Charles Burney's account of the Handel commemorations of 1784 which praised Handel above Bach."[27]

Turning to the infinitely more substantial aesthetic issues at play in trying to understand the relationship between Sebastian and Emanuel Bach, it is important to remember, first of all, that the strongest motivation driving a younger artist to follow a different direction from the older generation is surely that of basic self-assertion. It is a matter of psychic survival; but it also seems, at least in the Western tradition, something like a natural law of artistic history. Carl Philipp Emanuel Bach certainly did not reject *in toto* the implicit artistic credo informing his father's works: those being a commitment to uncompromising high-quality craftsmanship, the avoidance of the slick, the easy, the conventional, and the audience-pleasing. A consequence almost automatically flowing from that largely unspoken commitment was a definite, if not necessarily articulated, embrace of originality. But this leads to a paradox: namely, the more Emanuel or any of Bach's sons cultivated originality and individuality the more they subscribed to and emulated, rather than rejected, a fundamental aesthetic premise of their father.

Consider in this connection a remark by Karl Friedrich Zelter (1758–1832)—a musician, one-time director of the Berlin Singakademie and, most famously, a close friend of Goethe's—that is notated in the margin of his copy of Forkel's biography of J. S. Bach: "Seb[astian] Bach was an original, because he was unlike anyone else. If [Forkel's] assessment is correct [i.e., his comment that 'Friedemann approached the nearest to his father in the originality of all his thoughts'], then the son who came closest to him necessarily must have been the less original, i.e., the unoriginal one; and this is how we see Friedemann Bach, without intending to diminish his achievement."[28] Zelter was surely right: to the extent that Friedemann and Emanuel cultivated originality and individuality, they were, to the same extent, in one fundamental respect—namely, the sharing of a governing artistic ethos (and despite superficial differences in style dictated by contemporary taste)—proclaiming themselves to be not rebels but rather their father's acolytes.

There can be little question that much of Emanuel's music, and certainly much of his keyboard music, altogether embodies the Sebastianian principles of originality, expressivity, and seriousness. In one respect, however, he most decidedly and perhaps defiantly took a stylistic path that, at the very least, would have puzzled Sebastian: namely, his frequent refusal—arguably Emanuel's trademark—to subscribe to the cardinal Sebastianian aesthetic principle of unity. Philipp Emanuel explicitly acknowledges this when he writes in his autobiography almost as an afterthought (i.e., after presenting his catalog of works), the following:

> Since I have never cared for excessive uniformity [*Einförmigkeit*] in composition and in taste, since I have heard so much and such diverse good music, and since I have always believed that one should accept whatever is good, wherever it might be and even if it only occurs in small doses in a piece, this all, together with my God-given natural talent, has led to the diversity [*Verschiedenheit*] in my works which others have observed.[29]

In this explicit, publicly announced repudiation of "Einförmigkeit" (uniformity, or perhaps monotony), can it be that Emanuel was programmatically distancing himself from that compelling sense of logical consistency, unity, and coherence that are the hallmarks of his father's music, in order to embrace and advocate something very different indeed?

There seems to be a contradiction, incidentally, between Philipp Emanuel's urbane and sophisticated personality and the unbridled, erratic, seemingly irrational style that informs so much of his instrumental music. It is as if, in his instrumental music (especially his keyboard fantasies), he were wearing a mask: one of the *empfindsam* (sensitive), ostentatious, proto-Romantic, nonconformist. Instead of inexorable unity there is the spontaneous and unpredictable: the sudden, striking contrast. The explicit purpose was to move the heart, to express the composer's feelings (i.e., his *Empfindungen*) and to awaken those of the listener: "to set the heart in motion" (*das Herz in Bewegung setzen*).[30] Sebastian Bach, however, claimed far more modestly only that his keyboard music was "written to refresh the spirit" (*zur Gemüths-Ergoetzung verfertiget*).[31] Emanuel Bach, of course, shared his new expressionistic—or is it an exhibitionistic?—outlook (what music historians have variously dubbed, depending on the nature of the sentiments being expressed, the *Sturm und Drang* or *Empfindsamkeit* movement) not only with his brother, Wilhelm Friedemann, but with his entire generation, at least in the German-speaking world.

This was their new governing aesthetic principle, representing vis-à-vis Johann Sebastian Bach and his generation (in Kramer's formulation) "the aesthetics of patricide." No one practiced it more imaginatively or radically or compellingly than Carl Philipp Emanuel Bach.

In the most literal sense, it is clear that Philipp Emanuel Bach, far more than his father, was the "learned musician": an intellectual, a correspondent of Diderot's, and a friend of Lessing's. He demonstrated his learning most spectacularly with a lasting contribution, what is arguably his greatest achievement, to a field his father never entered: the writing of a scholarly treatise. If Sebastian had ever seriously contemplated doing such a thing—and he had been compiling materials at least since the early 1740s, possibly for a projected textbook, or instruction manual, on traditional counterpoint—he clearly never brought it to completion, as had his son.[32] Emanuel's treatise can be regarded as a monument to his father, founded as it is, to a considerable degree, on Sebastian's methods. But it also proclaims the advent of a new style grounded in a new aesthetic. The work, in short, is a testament to both and, as such, reflects perhaps both explicit allegiance and implicit rebellion.

Emanuel's impressive circle of acquaintances in Hamburg, along with his extensive correspondence, reveal that he was adept at making friends. Johann Sebastian and Friedemann Bach, however, were far more adept at making enemies. Not that Emanuel invariably pleased. While Princess Anna Amalia, King Frederick's sister, was one of Emanuel's greatest patrons, bestowing on him the title of "honorary Kapellmeister" [Kapellmeister von Haus aus] after he had left Berlin for Hamburg,[33] Frederick the Great himself (at least according to Zelter) "had a personal dislike of [eine persönliche Abneigung gegen] Emanuel Bach and for that reason did not appreciate this great artist according to his just deserts."[34]

Zelter reported this information in his biography of Karl Friedrich Fasch (1736–1800), who was no doubt the source for the assertion. Fasch was surely a credible one: he had joined the Prussian court in 1756 as a harpsichordist, thus becoming an immediate colleague of Emanuel Bach's, and remained at the court until his death in 1800. He was also, apparently, Emanuel's good friend. In August 1758, during the Seven Years' War, Emanuel Bach and Fasch, along with their families, took refuge in Zerbst with the latter's father, Kapellmeister Johann Friedrich Fasch (1688–1758), to escape the threatened Russian invasion of Berlin. They remained in Zerbst until early December. On the other end of the thread, K. F. Fasch's relationship to Zelter was just as close. In 1791 Fasch founded the Berlin Singakademie; Zelter, his student, was not only a member of the group but became its director after Fasch's death.

In 1755, two years after the publication of the treatise, Emanuel failed to step into his father's shoes as Thomaskantor, that is, as director of church music for the city of Leipzig. Later, Philipp Emanuel did, of course, manage to fill his godfather Georg Philipp Telemann's shoes when he inherited Telemann's position as director of church music for the city of Hamburg. (This time, one of his rivals for the position, incidentally, was his half-brother, Johann Christoph Friedrich.)

One can say that in a nontrivial sense Emanuel had two fathers: his natural father and his godfather. He was evidently very fond of Telemann and had a warm, filial, relationship with him.[35] Conversely, he had no mother. His true mother, Maria Barbara Bach (1684–1720), died when he was six. Despite long-standing claims to the contrary, there is no reason to think that Emanuel neglected his widowed stepmother, Anna Magdalena.[36] In addition to whatever help he may have provided, she also had other resources: among them potential income from serving as the sales representative in Leipzig for publications of works by her late husband and her stepson, Emanuel. In June 1751 an advertisement in the Leipzig newspapers announced a subscription for the *Kunst der Fuge* and indicated that copies could be procured in Leipzig from "Frau Wittbe Bachin." The announcement was presumably drafted by Emanuel Bach. From 1752 until the end of her life Anna Magdalena was responsible as well for the Leipzig distribution of Emanuel's keyboard treatise. Emanuel also contributed from 1772 on, well after Anna Magdalena's death in 1760, to the financial support of his surviving sister and half-sisters. At that time, however, his own economic circumstances in Hamburg were much better than they had been in Berlin during the time of his stepmother's widowhood and that of the Seven Years' War.[37]

In the particular case of Emanuel, the impulse toward filial piety seems to have been considerably stronger (perhaps even suspiciously so) than any conventional, generational, rebellious impulse. Emanuel was surely far too intelligent and too intellectually honest not to have realized that his father was the greater composer. This must have been more than a little deflating and must have generated some inevitable sense of resentment. But he was manifestly talented and resourceful enough to establish his own musical identity and to enjoy a successful career with, if anything, more worldly acclaim and prestige than his father had ever enjoyed during his lifetime. Perhaps Emanuel's extraordinary commitment to the preservation and cultivation of his late father's musical legacy was to some significant degree an act of compensation (and expiation) for his having undeservedly (as he might have thought) surpassed his father in gathering up the coin of worldly success.

Admittedly, that may be putting it too strongly. One hint as to how Emanuel Bach may have measured himself against his father is provided by the gala concert he produced in Hamburg in April 1786, just two years before his death. The program, one of the earliest historical concerts, far from burying Sebastian's music, dramatically "resurrected" it by including the complete Credo from the B-Minor Mass. This was without question an act of profound filial veneration and perhaps marks the beginning of a serious posthumous revival of Sebastian's church music altogether, well before Mendelssohn's revival of the St. Matthew Passion. Also on the program were two numbers from Handel's *Messiah*: the aria "Ich weiß, daß mein Erlöser lebt" (I know that my Redeemer liveth) and the "Halleluia" chorus. But the concert concluded with two works of Emanuel's: his Magnificat, Wq 215, composed in 1749 (and almost certainly performed in Leipzig before the death of his father, presumably in his presence);[38] and the grand double-chorus work, *Heilig*, Wq 217, the composition Emanuel was convinced would be his swan song and would serve "the purpose that I may not be forgotten too soon after my death."[39] May we infer from Emanuel's readiness to place his compositions before the public, along with the greatest masterpieces of G. F. Handel and J. S. Bach, that he was altogether confident that his work would comfortably hold its own in their company? And was he perhaps just as confident, too, that he fully belonged in the same pantheon as their authors?

ૐ   ૐ   ૐ

It is altogether appropriate, and not just for the sake of completeness, to include at this juncture discussion of two musical sons of Sebastian who have understandably always played minor roles in the Bach family saga.

Johann Gottfried Bernhard Bach

Emanuel's younger brother, Johann Gottfried Bernhard, was born to Maria Barbara in 1715.[40] In many respects his fate parallels that of Friedemann, but worse. A source of endless pain, embarrassment, and heartbreak to his father, in May 1739 Bernhard allegedly died of "fever" at age twenty-four, shortly after matriculating at the University of Jena the previous January and after having botched organist positions at both Mühlhausen and Sangerhausen. These two jobs, by the way (and certainly not coincidentally), were ones that Sebastian had held, or almost held: his later personal connections with the two towns were almost certainly instrumental in securing both organ positions for his son.[41] Bernhard's behavior in Sangerhausen elicited from Johann Sebastian the most personal and poignant confession he ever set down on paper. On May 24, 1738, that is, just a year before his son's untimely, perhaps suspicious, death, Sebastian wrote a letter to the Sangerhausen town councilor, Johann Friedrich Klemm (1706–67), in response to the news that Bernhard had disappeared from his post and had left unpaid debts behind. The letter reads, in part:

> With what pain and sorrow . . . I frame this reply. . . . Upon my (alas! misguided) son I have not laid eyes since last year. . . . At that time I duly paid not only his board but also the Mühlhausen draft [i.e., debt] (which presumably brought about his departure at that time) but also left a few ducats behind to settle a few bills, in the hope that he would now embark upon a new mode of life. But now I must learn again, with greatest consternation, that he once more borrowed here and there and did not change his way of living in the slightest, but on the contrary has even absented himself and not given me to date any inkling as to his whereabouts.
>
> What shall I say or do further? Since no admonition or even any loving care and assistance will suffice any more, I must bear my cross in patience and leave my unruly

son to God's Mercy alone. . . . I am fully confident that you will not impute the evil conduct of my child to me. . . . I most obediently request Your Honor to have the goodness to obtain precise information as to his whereabouts . . . so that one last effort may be made to see whether with God's help his impenitent heart can be won over and brought to a recognition of his mistakes.[42]

As in the case of Friedemann, Sebastian seems, at the least, to have played too large and dominating a role in Bernhard's professional life. The consequence was disastrous, and it is hard not to wonder whether Bernhard's manifestly self-destructive behavior was in part an act of spite and punishment directed at what he had perceived as an outsized, overbearing father.

Johann Christoph Friedrich Bach

In his autobiography cited earlier, C. F. Cramer altogether dismissed Johann Christoph Friedrich (the "Bückeburg") Bach, when he wrote about Sebastian: "He had three sons: Christian Bach, Carl Philipp Emanuel Bach, and Friedemann Bach; (the fourth in Bückeburg I don't count among them, since he does not really belong to the [true] 'Bachs!')."[43] Friedemann himself, however, considered Christoph Friedrich to be the "best keyboard player [*den stärksten Spieler*]" of the four brothers, who "could play his father's keyboard compositions most proficiently [*am fertigsten*].[44]

Johann Christoph Friedrich Bach was apparently a congenial individual with solid but limited talents. Thanks undoubtedly, in no small part, to his father's letter of recommendation sent to Count Wilhelm von Schaumburg-Lippe in December 1749 (some seven months before the composer's death), he was fortunate to find a congenial prince in whose service he spent his entire career.[45] Born in 1732, the same year as Joseph Haydn, Christoph Friedrich led a "Haydnesque" existence, arguably the ideal eighteenth-century musician's life. He thus succeeded, more than any of his brothers, in realizing his father's fond fantasy, namely, what Sebastian had found for a while and had hoped to have found forever in Köthen and in Prince Leopold.[46] Christoph Friedrich's position at Bückeburg seems to have been a fairly close copy of Sebastian's position at Köthen. And just as Sebastian had considered leaving it to become organist at the Jacobikirche in Hamburg when economic conditions in Köthen had begun to deteriorate, Christoph Friedrich too, at one point during the hard times of the Seven Years' War, applied for, and was offered, an appointment as organist in Altona (now part of Hamburg but at the time a Danish town). In the end, however, he remained in Bückeburg.[47]

Around ten years later, Christoph Friedrich applied unsuccessfully for the Hamburg position that went to his brother Carl Philipp Emanuel. In 1778, after passing through Hamburg to pay a call on Philipp Emanuel, Christoph Friedrich visited his brother Christian in London for several months, leaving his son, Wilhelm Friedrich Ernst (1759–1845), to study there for some three years with the youngest son of Sebastian.

Unlike the grim and vindictive Friedemann, the altogether realistic and unpretentious Friedrich was able not only to acknowledge and appreciate but even to celebrate the success of his brothers Emanuel and (especially) Johann Christian, just as he could recognize the talent of Mozart. He demonstrated his appreciation of the latter by putting on a performance of *Die Entführung aus dem Serail* at the Bückeburg court.[48]

Johann Christoph Friedrich Bach lived in Sebastian's household until he left for Bückeburg just before his eighteenth birthday in June of 1750, shortly before his father's death in July.[49] Thus, unlike his younger brother Christian, he did not go off to live with his older brother Emanuel. He plays no discernible role in any primal Oedipal scenario.

Johann Christian Bach

The same could be said of Johann Christian Bach. According to a rumor apparently begun by the British Bach champion Samuel Wesley (1766–1837), Johann Christian referred to his father as "the old wig."[50] Whether or not he ever actually said that, it seems clear that Christian Bach, the greatest master of the "gentle affections" (the *affetti amorosi*), who in his music largely rejected excessive complexity in favor of accessibility and amiability, was (at least from the Sebastianian perspective) the greatest radical and the true aesthetic patricide.

Christian not only "killed" Johann Sebastian aesthetically, he effectively "buried" him quite completely by obliterating virtually all traces of him not only in his music but in his life. It was, however, an act of silent annihilation, not vociferous rebellion. Only Christian managed to escape his father's orbit completely, with death as his greatest ally. The other brothers followed in their father's footsteps, serving as musicians at court or municipal directors of church music. Indeed, Friedemann and Emanuel, like their father, pursued both these career paths. But Christian succeeded in separating himself totally from Johann Sebastian Bach geographically, culturally, and, in terms of music, stylistically and aesthetically.

There are few if any obvious traces of Sebastian's stylistic influence in Christian's music, not even in his polyphonic church music, which, written in Italy under the aegis of Padre Martini, is modeled on the *stile antico*. We find virtually none of the "luxuriant" late Baroque counterpoint (to use Bukofzer's apt term) of what could be called the *stile Sebastiano*.[51] Christian does, however, make an overt reference to the opening theme of the first movement of his father's Sonata in G Minor for Viola da Gamba and Obbligato Harpsichord, BWV 1029—transposed to C major—in his early song, "Mezendore," Wb H1 (ex. 10.2), and, in his violin sonata in B-flat

Example 10.2a. J. C. Bach, "Mezendore" ("Herr Nicolaus Klimm erfand"), Warb H1 (Berlin, 1756), mm. 1–4

Example 10.2b. J. S. Bach, Sonata in G Minor for Viola da Gamba and Obbligato Harpsichord, BWV 1029, movement 1, mm. 1–2

Major, op. 10, no. 1, of 1773, Wb B2, to the opening of the Partita in B-flat Major, BWV 825, from the *Klavierübung* I (ex. 10.3).[52] Otherwise, for all intents and purposes, Johann Christian Bach evidently came not at all to praise his father, let alone to venerate him; he came to bury him—that is, to ignore him completely—pure and simple.

After Sebastian's death, Christian spent his late teen years with Emanuel in Berlin, where he undoubtedly took the opportunity to experience Italian opera. According to Ernst Ludwig Gerber, "Various female Italian singers, whose acquaintance he had made [in Berlin], awakened in [Christian] the desire to see Italy."[53] Whether he did so with his brother's approval and encouragement is by no means certain. Indeed, it is not altogether clear what Emanuel's role was at the court of Frederick the Great with respect to the Berlin *Hofoper*. He certainly was not engaged to compose Italian opera seria, which was largely the responsibility of Carl Heinrich Graun. Nor did he evidently have an explicit dispensation excusing him from performing in the orchestra pit, as did Johann Joachim Quantz.[54]

One assumes that, as one of the court's two harpsichordists, he was regularly obliged to play continuo in opera performances at the newly built opera house in Berlin. But neither in his autobiography of 1773 nor in his *Versuch*, does Emanuel Bach explicitly refer to his participation in opera performances. He calls attention rather

Example 10.3a. J. C. Bach, Sonata No. 1 in B-flat for Violin and Piano, op. 10, no. 1, Warb B2, Allegro (London, ca. 1773), mm. 1–5

Example 10.3b. J. S. Bach, Partita No. 1 in B-flat, BWV 825, Praeludium (Leipzig, 1726), mm. 1–2

to his performing in the king's chamber music sessions at his several residences.[55] That is perhaps indicative; for it is quite certain, as Mary Oleskiewicz has documented, that Emanuel Bach took part specifically in the performance of small-scale comic intermezzi at Sanssouci, Potsdam, and Charlottenburg.[56] Such explicit testimony does not seem to be available, however, with regard to Emanuel's role in the great Berlin opera house.

What does seem certain is that Emanuel was not pleased with the music his half-brother ultimately created, nor with developments in Italian opera, at least at the time of his brother's successes. He reportedly told Matthias Claudius shortly after he settled in Hamburg in the late 1760s that "at bottom my brother's most recent music is nothing. It pleases the ear but leaves the heart empty. That is my opinion of the new music and the new comic music, which, Galuppi told me, is now fashionable in Italy, too."[57]

If the great mystery in Wilhelm Friedemann's life is why he failed so miserably, then the great mystery in Johann Christian's life is how he became so successful, or more specifically, how he got to Italy (i.e., in the manner described by Gerber or otherwise), how he became an opera composer, and how, while serving as a young, newly minted church organist at no less a venue than the Milan Cathedral, he managed to garner some extremely prestigious opera commissions from both Turin and Naples.

Unlike his brothers and his father, Christian succeeded in going abroad. The other brothers dutifully followed their father's career path in not doing so. Ironically, this is a testimonial to Christian's Sebastianian sense of purpose, mission, and independence; it suggests that he was, after all, most like Johann Sebastian in this one fundamental way. There is also an irony in that Christian had gone to Italy to fulfill an (unspoken) purpose, or *Endzweck* (to use his father's powerful term), which he as a young man had famously used at a similar point in his career to proclaim his ultimate goal of performing a "regular church music" (*regulirte* kirchen *music*)— a Lutheran church music, needless to say—"to the glory of God."[58] In Christian's case it was the very secular goal of becoming an opera composer. The irony is all the richer, when one recalls that Christian had at first become a church organist like his father and his half-brother, Wilhelm Friedemann—but in the service of the Roman Catholic Church.

Christian's half-dozen years in Italy from 1755 to 1761, are intriguing in a number of ways, many of which suggest that his repudiation of his father's legacy was profound indeed. To begin with, there were his studies with Padre Martini who was not only obviously a father surrogate of sorts but also the aesthetic antipode to Sebastian (insofar as Martini's Palestrinian ideal of counterpoint played a respected, but definitely subordinate, role in J. S. Bach's contrapuntal universe). In this connection it is worth observing that, once he left the country of his birth, Christian composed church music in Latin, operas in Italian and French, and songs in English, but, apparently, nothing in German[59]—that is, nothing in the language central to his father's vocal music legacy. Evidently, neither the biblical texts of Martin Luther nor the verses of the great hymn poets of the sixteenth and seventeenth centuries—often the animating impulse of J. S. Bach's inspiration—played any role for Christian Bach during the years of his artistic maturity.

At least as stunning as Christian's neglect of his mother tongue, and perhaps even more poignant, was his conversion from his father's—indeed from his forefathers'—deep-rooted Lutheran heritage to Roman Catholicism. As insincere and opportunistic as his conversion might have been, could there have been any more profound expression of—if not aesthetic, then, certainly, spiritual—patricide? When annotating his copy of the Bach family Genealogy for J. N. Forkel, circa 1774–75, Emanuel Bach added the following to the entry on Johann Christian: "[He] is now in England in the service of the Queen—between us, he has managed differently from honest Veit." As Hans T. David and Arthur Mendel observed in the original edition of *The Bach Reader* (an observation retained by Christoph Wolff in *The New Bach Reader*), "Philipp Emanuel's remark: 'between us, he has managed differently from honest Veit' [*inter nos, machte es anders als der ehrliche Veit*] has been interpreted as a disapproving allusion to Johann Christian's having embraced Roman Catholicism." The editors proceed, it is true, to express their doubts as to that interpretation, preferring rather to see Emanuel's comment as an expression of pride in Christian's great success in England.[60] The earlier understanding is far more persuasive. Veit Bach, as reported by J. S. Bach in the very first sentence of the Genealogy, was honored by his descendants for having "had to flee Hungary in the sixteeenth century on account of his Lutheran religion."[61] Moreover, if Emanuel Bach was "expressing pride in the success and fame" of his half-brother, as David and Mendel suggest, then it is difficult to fathom why he thought it was necessary to whisper his pride—*inter nos*—to Forkel.

To follow up with another paradox, Charles Burney points out yet one more similarity between Johann Sebastian and Johann Christian Bach: both were "deprived" (to use Burney's word) by their father's death when they were still young. Both then went off to live with a much older brother: Sebastian with Johann Christoph Bach (fourteen years his senior) and Johann Christian with Carl Philipp Emanuel (twenty-one years his senior). As with Emanuel, Burney also makes a case for Christian as an original innovator:

> [J. C.] Bach seems to have been the first composer who observed the law of *contrast*, as a *principle* [original italics]. Before his time, contrast there frequently was in the works of others; but it seems to have been accidental. Bach in his symphonies and other instrumental pieces, as well as his songs, seldom failed, after a rapid and noisy passage to introduce one that was slow and soothing. His symphonies seem infinitely more original than either his songs or harpsichord pieces, of which the harmony, mixture of wind-instruments, and general richness and variety of accompaniment, are certainly the most prominent features.[62]

Once again: a son of Johann Sebastian Bach demonstrated, by virtue of his extraordinary craftsmanship and originality, that—despite the outward appearance (or sound) of things—in the final analysis he was his father's authentic artistic heir.

We can conclude with a final irony. Johann Christian Bach went to Bologna, studied with Padre Martini, and soon thereafter shed all traces of his father's musical idiom. A few years later Wolfgang Amadeus Mozart went to Bologna, studied with Padre Martini, and discovered the music of Johann Sebastian Bach (some of which Martini, a true admirer of J. S. Bach, may have acquired from J. C. Bach). Over the remaining decades of his life he absorbed its lessons into his own works and triumphantly demonstrated its enduring, "unkillable," relevance to posterity.[63]

Chapter Eleven

Johann Christian Bach and Eros

Much about the life of Johann Sebastian Bach's youngest son remains obscure. Factual lacunae, contradictions, ambiguities, along with insinuations touching on his private life punctuate the biographical record almost from the very beginning.

Uncertainty concerning certain basic facts about Johann Christian Bach begins as early as the testimony of a firsthand source one would have considered unimpeachable, namely, Carl Philipp Emanuel Bach. Emanuel, it will be recalled, had taken in his fifteen-year-old half-brother to live with him in Berlin following the death of their father in July 1750. Who would know better than Emanuel the year in which Christian left his home? In Emanuel's annotation of the family Genealogy he remarks that Christian "traveled in the year 1754 to Italy" (*reiste ao. 1754 nach Italien*).[1] His claim, understandably, was dutifully repeated later by reliable eighteenth-century writers such as Ernst Ludwig Gerber.[2]

Along with the question of when Johann Christian left for Italy one can ask the connected question: how did he get there, that is, under what circumstances? Here, again, early commentators have something to say. Johann Nikolaus Forkel provides the intriguing detail that Christian, while living with Emanuel in Berlin, had "made the acquaintance of many female Italian singers, one of whom talked him into going to Italy with her" (*er mit vielen italienischen Sängerinnen bekannt wurde, deren eine ihn beredete mit ihr nach Italien zu gehen*).[3] And Gerber's dictionary informs us, likewise, that "the acquaintance with various female Italian singers awakened in him the desire to see Italy" (*in ihm die Bekanntschaften verschiedener ital. Sängerinnen die Lust erweckten, Italien zu sehen*).[4]

Charles Sanford Terry, while citing these early sources, was apparently the first person to question both the dating of Christian's departure and the prevailing explanation behind his decision to head for Italy, an explanation that had evolved in a curiously colorful fashion since the time of Forkel and Gerber.[5] Terry cites a nineteenth-century writer, one Elise Polko, who claimed that Christian, "repelled by

the prospect of passing his life as an organist in some obscure German community
. . . found relaxation under the *beaux yeux* of Benedetta Emilia Molteni (1722–80),
prima donna of the Berlin Opera." Polko reported further that Molteni married
Johann Friedrich Agricola (1720–74), Frederick the Great's court composer, but that
"the pair were hindered by their coachman's death from starting a honeymoon in
Italy. Christian snatched his opportunity, concealed his round and boyish face under
a false beard, secured the place of the dead Jehu, and drove Emilia and her husband
to Milan, only removing his disguise on Italian soil." Terry describes this tale as a
"farrago of fiction" and deems it "unsurpassed for audacious invention."[6]

Terry explains that, while it is true that Emilia Molteni and Agricola were married, the marriage had taken place in 1751, that is, "some years before Christian's
alleged exploit." He does acknowledge that "in the face of more contemporary references, the implication of impetuous gallantry [cannot] be evaded. Christian was an
engaging fellow, good-looking, eager, with a gift for making friendships which captivated both sexes equally and, in after life, made him 'der Liebling der Engländer'"
(quoting, in German, a phrase from Forkel).[7] But he emphatically defends the reputation of his hero, insisting that any claim "that [Christian's] life was immoral at any
period of its duration is an innuendo no evidence supports."[8]

We learn all this titillating gossip and speculation as early as page 11 of Terry's
biography. On the following page the author declares: "If [J. C. Bach] entered Italy
with Molteni, or another, the association was due to her art rather than the enthral-
ment of her graces." As to when this all happened: by chapter's end Terry proposes
the year 1756, rather than 1754, for Christian's departure for Italy. He proposes,
namely, that the journey took place in the wake of the closure of the Berlin Opera
in 1756, that is, upon the outbreak of the Seven Years' War. Moreover, he suggests
that Christian may have indeed accompanied a prima donna back to Italy. It was not
Emilia Molteni, however, but rather Giovanna Astrua (1720–57), who, according to
Terry, returned to Turin in that year, outfitted with a pension from King Frederick in
the amount of 1,000 Reichsthaler. As a consequence of his redating, Terry is obliged
to question not only C. P. E. Bach's 1754 dating for Christian's Italian journey but
also the accuracy of the date 1755 found on the title page of volume 1, part 6 of
F. W. Marpurg's *Beyträge*, since Marpurg states therein that Christian had "recently
traveled to Italy" (*ist vor kurzem nach Italien gereiset*). Terry's conclusion at the close
of his opening chapter: "If Christian accompanied her [Astrua], a love-intrigue
becomes a companionship of mutual accommodation. He was recently turned
twenty and not indifferent to feminine charm. But for the moment, art was his only
loadstone, Italy his single mistress."[9]

In the meantime, all this chronological speculation has become moot: Hans-
Joachim Schulze demonstrated in the 1980s that J. C. Bach probably left for Italy
not in 1754 (as per C. P. E. Bach and Gerber) or in 1756 (as per Terry) but in the
late spring or summer of 1755. He adduces evidence indicating that the 1755 date
appearing on the title page of volume 1, part 6, of Friedrich Wilhelm Marpurg's

Historich-kritische Beyträge zur Aufnahme der Musik, accurately documents the year of the events it records (if not the year in which it was issued). One of those events refers to J. C. Bach, noting that he had "recently left for Italy" (*ist vor kurzum nach Italien gereiset*). In addition, Schulze notes that in a later publication—the *Legende einiger Musikheiligen* (Breslau, 1786)—Marpurg reported that Johann Christian Bach had attended the first performance of Carl Heinrich Graun's *Der Tod Jesu*, an event that took place in Berlin on March 26, 1755.[10]

ᵇ ᵇ ᵇ

Confident now that the year of Christian's arrival in Italy has at last been resolved, we can consider some of his activities there and how they have been represented both by his contemporaries and by modern observers. Karl Geiringer, in his well-known monograph, *The Bach Family*, notes that Johann Christian (now having renamed himself "Giovanni") "had the good fortune to become the protégé of a wealthy Italian nobleman, Count [Agostino] Litta of Milan."[11] Geiringer also informs us that "the relationship between the two men was of the friendliest nature," and wishes us to know that the count referred to the gifted young composer, in a letter of August 1757 addressed to Christian's mentor in Bologna, the legendary music scholar and pedagogue Padre Giovanni Battista Martini (1706–84), as "his 'beloved Giovannino.'"[12] This is not quite accurate: the Italian original reads "*nostro* [i.e., not "mio"] *amatißimo Giovannino Bach*" (i.e., "our most beloved Johnny Bach").

Whether the undeniable amorous warmth of the sentiment should be construed as an implicit confession of a homoerotic attraction or simply as an effusive literary flourish between male friends of a kind not uncommon among the aristocratic classes of the time must be left to the judgment of the reader. At all events, at the time of that letter, Count Litta (born March 13, 1728) was not yet twenty-nine years old, Christian (born September 5, 1735) was not yet twenty-two. By then the youngest son of Johann Sebastian Bach had probably been living in the count's residence for some two years.

Geiringer reports, however, that "as early as January 1757 we see [Christian] writing to the Padre [not from his home base in Litta's Milan but] from Naples. . . . What he did in Naples," Geiringer teases, "is unknown."[13] Geiringer's arguably suggestive claim of ignorance may be true in the narrowest sense; but it is also true that Christian mentions in the same letter, dated January 18, 1757, that he was in Naples with the permission of his patron. As translated by Terry: "Chevalier Litta's particular favour granted me another month's stay here."[14]

Christian may well have been in Naples in order to explore the opera scene there; but it is also conceivable that he was there less for professional than for personal reasons. Geiringer cares not to speculate. He does note that four years later, during the period 1761–62, Bach was in Naples once again and that this time his activities are readily accounted for: He was fulfilling two operatic commissions for the Teatro di

San Carlo—commissions sparked by the success of an opera composed the previous year for the Teatro Regio in Turin. "Giovanni," in Geiringer's words, "spent glorious months in Naples," adding that "he had been absent for a whole year. . . . Count Litta, who had to hear various not unjustified criticisms of his protégé's behavior, was getting restive."[15]

Geiringer omits a number of details that may have accounted for Litta's "restiveness." A more recent Christian Bach biographer, Heinz Gärtner, provides them. Gärtner reports that Christian "had fallen in love with the dancer Colomba Beccari, an affair in which the public took a lively interest. The authorities were displeased, claiming that his affair gave rise to idle gossip. A government official summoned him and issued a reprimand." Other contemporary reports alleged that Christian "had been observed 'joining female singers in the box reserved for them.' Once more he was instructed, through the theater secretary, that this was inappropriate." We learn that on yet another occasion an "official reminded him . . . 'in his own interest,' that 'His Majesty had repeatedly given an order, even to the officers of the royal guard, forbidding them to flirt backstage with any female cast members during the performance.'"[16]

Perhaps it was these reputed Neapolitan antics that were upsetting Count Litta. But perhaps his consternation had mainly to do with Christian's prolonged absence from his duties as second organist at the Milan Cathedral, a post he had obtained in June 1760 in return for having converted to Roman Catholicism—thanks, no doubt, in no small part to the count's exertions on his behalf.[17] In a letter dated April 7, 1762, to Padre Martini, Litta—this time indeed referring to Johann Christian as "il mio Bach"—writes, "Yet he would be unwise to forfeit a position that pays him 800 lire a year. . . . It therefore behooves him to show himself industrious, rather than acting in such a way that the person who recommended him for this appointment regrets having done so. People here are beginning to complain, especially the high clergy."[18]

We still lack important information about Christian's Italian period. We do not know how this Lutheran-turned-Catholic church organist and counterpoint student of Padre Martini became an opera composer at all—a remarkably successful one at that—from the very beginning: one who somehow managed to establish connections with the larger Italian opera scene while serving since 1760 as second organist at the Milan Cathedral. Specifically, we do not know for certain how, almost immediately after assuming that modest organist post at the age of twenty-five, he had managed to nail no fewer than three prestigious opera commissions (all, as it happened, settings of librettos by Metastasio), beginning in December 1760 with an opera for the Teatro Regio of Turin (*Artaserse*) and continuing with two further operas for Naples: *Catone in Utica* (1761) and *Alessandro nell'Indie* (1762).

Christian, as indicated earlier, no doubt became acquainted with the Italian opera while still living in Berlin with Carl Philipp Emanuel in the years following his father's death. Philipp Emanuel himself, however, apparently had no official connection with the Berlin court opera. He was, rather, one of Frederick the Great's chamber musicians. Moreover, he may even—for personal, professional, aesthetic, or moralistic reasons—have discouraged or frowned upon Christian's attending opera performances.[19] But he evidently could not prevent him from doing so.

While it is not certain how Christian obtained the Turin commission in the first place, it could well have resulted from the favorable reception of some substitution arias he had composed for singers he had met in Bologna. The arias were inserted into operas composed by others. In any case, reports of the success of the Turin operas inspired the director of the Naples theaters, Bernardo Tanucci (1698–1783), to extend the Naples invitations.[20] Christian arrived in Naples auspiciously—bearing a glowing letter of introduction to Tanucci from Count Karl Joseph Firmian (1716–82), the Austrian governor of Lombardy, mostly known today for the important and positive role he played in Mozart's life but at the time a noted patron of the arts in general and a close friend, among others, of the great art historian Johann Joachim Winckelmann (1717–68).[21]

In January 1762, shortly after the premiere of the second of his Naples operas, Christian accepted a position at the King's Theatre in London, settled there, and—apart from occasional sojourns in Mannheim and Paris in connection with operatic and other commissions—effectively remained there for the rest of his relatively short life until his death twenty years later on January 1, 1782.

* * *

John Christian Bach arrived in London during the summer of 1762.[22] Over the course of his London years an "intimate friendship" (Geiringer's characterization)[23] developed between him and his fellow countryman, Carl Friedrich Abel (1723–87), an outstanding composer and pre-eminent virtuoso on the viola da gamba who had moved to London some three years earlier, that is, in the spring of 1759. Abel, however, was not only Bach's fellow countryman: his father, Christian Ferdinand Abel (1682–1761), a violinist (and sometime gamba player himself), had been a close colleague of Johann Sebastian Bach's at Köthen, where Carl Friedrich was born in 1723.

According to Charles Burney, Abel the younger was "a disciple of Sebastian Bach." Ernst Ludwig Gerber claimed that Abel, "as a pupil at the Thomas School in Leipzig probably enjoyed instruction from the great Sebast[ian] Bach" (*genoß, als Thomas-Schüler zu Leipzig, wahrscheinlich den Unterricht des großen Sebast. Bach*).[24] Although there is no documentary evidence that Abel was ever an enrolled pupil at the Thomas School, he was certainly in Leipzig on October 13, 1743, where he gave a gamba recital during the inaugural season of the Großes Concert—the precursor of the Leipzig Gewandhaus Orchestra. Immediately thereafter he took a position at the Dresden court, where he remained for the next fifteen years. Whether he and Christian Bach had any contact in Germany before Christian left for Italy in 1755, is not known for certain.

At all events, by late 1763, by which time they had begun (or possibly renewed) their association in London, Christian Bach was twenty-eight years old, Abel forty. They presented their first joint concert in London in February 1764 and initiated their celebrated Bach–Abel concert series in January 1765. The series continued for sixteen years—through May 1781. For most of that time they shared a succession of bachelor apartments.[25] Exactly how long they lived together, and when they ceased to do so, is a matter of dispute. The entry on Abel in *The New Grove Dictionary of Music and Musicians*, claims that "after sharing a home for many years they had found separate residences in 1771."[26] Stephen Roe, however, suggests that they shared lodgings "for at least ten years," lasting until January 1773.[27]

Fast forward to November 1772, when Bach was in Mannheim for the rehearsals of his new opera, *Temistocle*. The visit may also have been significant for a more personal reason. Geiringer relates that the composer "who had so far been a confirmed bachelor, unresponsive to the lovely prima donnas with whom he was working, was captivated by beautiful Elisabeth Augusta Wendling, the young daughter of his host [the famous flautist Johann Baptist Wendling (1723–97), well-known from the Mozart biographical literature], and he proposed to her. She refused to marry a man 20 years her senior, but later did not mind becoming the mistress of the Elector, who was even 9 years older than Bach."[28] A well-known source for this information was Mozart's mother. She included the rumor in a postscript to Wolfgang's letter to her husband Leopold from Mannheim, dated November 20, 1777, and, accordingly, written some five years after the incident would have taken place. Frau Mozart no doubt had heard the story, or something like it, from one of the Wendlings.[29] She gives no reason, such as age (the reason suggested by Geiringer), for Augusta's alleged rejection of Bach, mentioning only that the Wendlings "have an only daughter who is very beautiful and whom that Bach in England wanted to marry."[30]

Whatever the veracity of his alleged proposal to Augusta Wendling, Christian, upon returning to London after the *Temistocle* performances, "looked around" (Geiringer) "for a suitable wife, and found her in the Italian singer, Cecilia Grassi, whom he had known for years"[31]—at least since 1766 when she was engaged in London for the upcoming season as the *prima donna seria*; but, as Stephen Roe suggests, he "may well have been already acquainted with Cecilia Grassi, if only by name, by the time [he] left Italy after July 1762."[32]

Roe, unfortunately, was no more able than previous scholars to determine exactly when Cecilia Grassi was born or precisely when her marriage to Bach took place. He discounts Terry's assertion of 1746 as the year of her birth and suggests that a "birth date of somewhere between 1730 and 1735 is most likely: she was perhaps the same age, or a little older than her husband."[33] As for the wedding date: Roe conjectures that although "so far no external records of their marriage have been discovered in any British archives"—a circumstance already lamented by Terry—the marriage presumably "took place at some stage between mid 1776 and early 1778 when Cecilia Grassi had effectively retired from her career as a singer." If true, then both Cecilia

Grassi and John Christian Bach would have been anywhere between thirty-eight and forty-one years old at the time of their wedding—uncommonly old in any case for a newlywed woman in the eighteenth century. Roe suggests, finally, that the couple probably moved into new lodgings at No. 3 New Cavendish Street at about the time of their marriage. In any case, it was to be the house "where [Bach] almost certainly died."[34]

❧ ❧ ❧

Considerable confusion and speculation (sordid speculation, at that) prevails concerning the nature of the relationship among the three *dramatis personae*: Bach, Abel, and Cecilia Grassi, during the years leading up to the marriage—whenever that event may actually have taken place. Terry relates that the memoirist Henry Angelo (1760–1839) "makes the incredible statement that [soon after her arrival in London in 1766] Cecilia forthwith became Abel's mistress, and that he established her in Frith Street."[35] According to Angelo (as related by Terry), "Abel had many Gainsboroughs. . . . Several of them . . . Abel parted with 'for the indulgence of that vanity which led many a wiser man than Abel to keep a mistress.' They decorated the drawing room of his Dulcinea, who, 'though no beauty, was a wit.'" Terry also cites Angelo's claim that "after Abel's death, 'his Dulcinea going abroad, she parted with . . . this collection of Gainsborough's, which were sold by auction.'"[36]

Terry finds it "impossible to reconcile Angelo's statement with the known facts of Cecilia Grassi's career." Angelo, we learn, also claimed that "the liaison continued till Abel's death. That event took place in 1787, five years after Cecilia became Bach's widow. She must therefore have been Abel's mistress while she was Bach's wife, an inference vetoed by the relations of the two men, and by the consideration Cecilia received from the Queen when her husband died. . . . Apart from his virtuosity, Abel was remembered for his drunken habits and generous nature." Terry's explanation: "It is probable that, after Bach's death, [Abel] gave Cecilia the shelter of his house till she returned to Italy." Finally, he adduces another diarist—and sometime pupil of Christian Bach—"Mrs. Papendiek, who knew Cecilia well, expressly speaks of her as 'of good character and well-regulated conduct.' Certainly [Terry concludes] she would not have so described her if Cecilia's relations with Abel were as Angelo's hazy recollection imagined them."[37]

Stephen Roe, too, emphatically discounts Angelo's story, noting that after Abel's death in 1787 the sale of his effects "seems to have been arranged by his brother for the benefit of his family." He then adds a *coup de grâce*: "Angelo's grasp of detail does not anyway inspire confidence: he refers to Johann Christian throughout as 'Sebastian Bach,' an unnerving blunder."[38]

Returning to the indelicate question of Mme. Grassi's physical appearance: Geiringer, perhaps paraphrasing Angelo's remark that she was "no beauty," comments that "Cecilia was not beautiful" (p. 414). It is more likely, however, that his authority for this was not the highly questionable Henry Angelo but rather the altogether estimable Charles Burney. Burney had actually put the matter even more indelicately, apparently finding it worth noting—and reporting to the world—at the very outset of his discussion of her in his *General History of Music* that "Mrs. Bach" was both "inanimate on the stage, and far from beautiful in her person." He does go on to praise her "truth of intonation, with a plaintive sweetness of voice, and innocence of expression that gave great pleasure to all hearers who did not expect or want to be surprised."[39]

At this juncture, one cannot help but wonder that John Christian Bach, at the height of his fame, fortune, and popularity as one of the most celebrated figures on the London cultural scene, a man renowned as much for his charm and amiability as for his talent, was content to choose for his wife a woman *d'un certain âge* whose lack of beauty was striking enough to draw public comment from the likes of Charles Burney, and whose vocal gifts, according to the same authority, gave pleasure only to those "who did not expect or want to be surprised." (Stephen Roe, for his part, cites another contemporary witness who described her voice toward the end of her career as "being a tenor, which is very singular and I think disagreeable.")[40]

Terry also wondered about this. He mentions that Mrs. Papendiek thought that it might have been "Cecilia's savings, some £2000, that attracted him"; but he dismisses this explanation. His own conjecture reads: "If Cecilia's moderate attractions could not secure a husband, nor her savings contribute to his relief, a practical reason for their partnership may be found in her ability to assist him in labour from which his income chiefly was derived."[41] The implication of either speculation, surely, is that Cecilia Grassi's attractiveness to J. C. Bach lay in the support she could provide to him in his career, whether by participating in the Bach–Abel concerts, by giving instruction to his pupils (specifically mentioned by Terry in this connection), or by contributing material, that is, financial, support.

Can one be forgiven for wondering whether we are dealing here not (*pace* Henry Angelo) with a *ménage à trois* but rather with a *mariage blanc*? The Bachs, after all, married late and had no children. Indeed, one's suspicions about the extent of an erotic attachment (if any) between Mr. and Mrs. Bach are fueled further by the following account reported by none other than Wolfgang Amadeus Mozart. In the summer of 1778 Mozart and Christian Bach were both in Paris at the same time: Mozart as part of his six-month sojourn in the French capital in the hope of landing a position, Bach in order to audition singers for the upcoming production of his opera *Amadis de Gaule*.

In a letter to Leopold from St. Germain, dated August 27, 1778, Mozart informs his father that "Tenducci is here too. He is Bach's bosom friend" (*der herzensfreünd von Bach*).[42] Giusto Ferdinando Tenducci (ca. 1735–90), exactly Bach's age, was a renowned soprano castrato. In the same letter Mozart informs us that Tenducci "is *very* fond of me" (Mozart's own emphasis in the original: "weil er mich *sehr* liebt") and that Wolfgang was writing a *scena* for him—a work (K. 315b), which, if it was ever completed, is now lost. Tenducci's career, like that of C. F. Abel, was more than a little flamboyant, marked by a number of scandals including doing time in debtor's prison. (Christian Bach himself loaned him money more than once.)[43] Although a castrato, Tenducci not only was married (since 1766) but reportedly sired two children with his wife. The legendary Casanova, moreover, an undisputed expert in such matters, would have us know that Tenducci's nickname was "Triorchis," that is, triple-testicled. (It is not clear whether this was meant literally or metaphorically—or how Casanova happened to know.)[44]

One must not read too much into Mozart's use of the word "herzensfreünd" or the phrase "weil er mich *sehr* liebt." After all, in the same letter he famously tells Leopold—and us—referring to Christian Bach: "I love him . . . with all my heart" (*ich liebe ihn . . . von ganzem herzen*).[45] As is well-known, the use of such extravagant emotional language (encountered above, as well, in the letters of Padre Martini and Agostino Litta re J. C. Bach) to characterize close friendships among men was not at all unusual at the time. Conceding all that, is it not curious, nonetheless, that in 1778 Christian Bach—not only a relatively recently married man but one whose wife was a professional, accomplished singer of some standing—had chosen to travel to Paris to oversee the preparations for his new opera in the French capital not with her but rather with his *herzensfreünd*, the scandal-prone Tenducci? Mozart suggests that Bach wanted the colorful castrato's help in auditioning singers. But surely Mrs. Bach, the former *prima donna seria* of the London opera, would have been just as helpful in that regard.

❧   ❧   ❧

Cecilia Grassi and Christian Bach were married for some four to six years (depending on the unclear date of their wedding) until Bach's death on New Years Day, 1782, at the age of forty-six. The marriage, as mentioned earlier, was without issue. According to a contemporary diarist, incidentally—cited by Stephen Roe[46]—Charles Burney, in addition to disparaging Cecilia Grassi's appearance also predicted that she would "bring no children." (What could he have been thinking?) By the time of his death John Christian Bach's esteem in London's musical life had been on the wane for some seven years. His star was being eclipsed by the arrival of new talents in the city who were capturing the imagination and enthusiasm of the public: above all the opera composer Antonio Sacchini (1730–86) and the keyboard virtuoso Johann Samuel Schroeter (1753–88). Moreover, owing to having made unsuccessful investments and having been defrauded by a housekeeper, he had acquired enormous debts—amounting to some £4,000. One suspects that the enormous stress of these compounded psychic blows and financial burdens led to the rapid deterioration of his health and premature death. (Contemporary documents attributed his death to "una malatia di petto" as well as "a galloping consumption."[47]

Abel apparently never married—or so one infers from the fact that, after his death his effects were inherited by his younger brother.[48] Moreover, according to the *New Grove Dictionary* entry for Abel he was "good friends with the Mannheim violinist Wilhelm Cramer (1746–99), and the two shared an apartment before Cramer's second marriage, from 1776 to about 1779"—that is, very possibly from just about the time of Bach's marriage to Cecilia.[49] (We also read in the same source that "it was at this time that Abel showed signs of the illness that was to kill him [some ten years later]; it was apparently brought on by rich living and in particular by an over-indulgence in drink, but it seems impossible to link this with any tragedy in his life (as has been suggested)." That is, according to the authors of the Abel entry in the *New Grove Dictionary*, we should attach no significance to the emergence in Abel of malignant symptoms of ill-health and self-destructive behavior at just about the time of Bach's marriage to Cecilia.

Abel continued the Bach–Abel concerts after Bach's death, but, to cite the *New Grove* account once again: "Strangely, Bach's widow declined Abel's public offer of assistance. Possibly the relationship between Bach and Abel had by then become no more than a business matter; after sharing a home for many years, they had found separate residences in 1771 [*sic*] and unlike his flamboyant partner, Abel seems to have led a quiet and well-ordered life."[50] Strangely, this description of Abel's lifestyle contradicts the description the same authors would provide just two pages later in the same article with that reference to "rich living" and "an over-indulgence in drink."

One can readily imagine other explanations for Mrs. Bach's decision to reject Abel's offer of financial support. C. S. Terry, as we have seen, was able to call on two contemporary witnesses—Mr. Angelo and Mrs. Papendiek—to challenge the suggestion that the relationship between the two musicians "had by then become no more than a business matter," which does not seem to be much of an explanation at all. Would it really have been "strange" for Cecilia Grassi, now the widow Bach, to have declined "a public offer of assistance" from Abel if—admittedly a colossal "if," indeed—she had once upon a time been Abel's mistress (as Mr. Angelo alleged), or if Abel "was remembered for his drunken habits," as Terry summarizes the situation— and as Knape, Charters, and McVeigh seem, at least some of the time, to concede? For we also learn from Mrs. Papendiek, via Terry, that after the death of his longtime partner and roommate, John Christian Bach, Abel had "lost also much of his power of exertion from grief, and often had recourse to stimulants that overdid his intention."[51] If so, Mrs. Bach may well have been reluctant to accept assistance from someone whose excessive grief at the death of her husband, she may have thought, was quite inappropriate for anyone other than his lawfully wedded spouse to feel, much less to display.

At the very least, we also learn from Mrs. Papendiek, via Terry, that Abel, "by reason of his failing . . . was 'not received in the higher circles of society as a visitor,' and when the end came, was buried 'without any honours conferred by the profession, but followed to his grave by a few select friends, of whom Mrs. Papendiek was one.'"[52] This claim, incidentally, is emphatically rejected by Knape, Charters, and McVeigh. They insist that: "Up to the time of his death Abel maintained a highly respected position in London society, at court, in the homes of the nobility, in fashionable circles, and among his fellow musicians; the several obituaries were unanimously laudatory."[53]

⁂　⁂　⁂

The demise of the two main protagonists offers a suitable opportunity to break off this inquiry—one provoked by the occasionally contradictory (occasionally self-contradictory), often bizarre, often evasive contemporary and modern accounts bearing on the life and character of one of the most celebrated and important musicians of the mid-eighteenth century. What, if anything, can we conclude from it?

Numerous contemporary documents—above all, letters and memoirs from personal acquaintances—testify unambiguously that Johann Christian Bach was a most attractive individual: attractive, indeed, to members of both sexes. They reveal just as clearly that he, in turn, was charmed by, and attracted to, them. As a young man on the make and on the go in Italy he charmed and infatuated not only a number of female singers and dancers but also his early patron Count Litta. He apparently even cast a similar spell on his famous mentor, the sage and saintly Padre Martini, as well. It may well be, however, that Bach's relationship with Carl Friedrich Abel, his countryman, colleague, business partner, and longtime roommate, was the most significant of his life. Their association must be described as more than merely close. It was an extraordinarily devoted, intense—"intimate"—friendship. In contrast, one suspects that Bach's dealings with the irresponsible, flamboyant, high-voltage castrato Ferdinando Tenducci had more the character of a daring adventure: an escapade—perhaps a momentary escape from what one suspects may have been ultimately a platonic marriage to the famously plain-looking and unexciting *prima donna seria*, Cecilia Grassi.

Inconclusive? Of course! The "true" nature of Christian Bach's erotic life—specifically, the extent to which he may have engaged in physical sexual activity, if any at all, with Litta, Abel, Tenducci, or any other men—would have taken place as covertly as possible and is therefore inevitably unknowable. Such activity, had it been known at the time, was not only illicit: it was potentially a capital offense.[54]

On the other hand, there are powerful counter-indications suggesting that the conjugal relationship of J. C. Bach and Cecilia Grassi was at the least an affectionate one. In the words of Stephen Roe, Cecilia was "the keeper of the Christian Bach flame and keeper of his heritage,"[55] to whom he left "all his worldly goods" in a will drawn up on November 14, 1781—a document that notably included the phrase (in a scribe's hand), "my dear wife, Cecilia Bach late Cecilia Grassi."[56] Whether that phrase represented a heartfelt declaration of love or only legal boilerplate cannot be determined. But there is now no doubt, thanks to the research of Stephen Roe, that Bach's widow took an active role in settling her late husband's affairs.[57]

On July 1, 1782, six months after her husband's death, Cecilia returned to Italy. It is now known—refuting the traditional understanding alleging the contrary (and deriving from the account of Mrs. Papendiek)—that she ultimately returned to England, where she died on February 2, 1791, and was buried in the same church-yard, St. Pancras, as her husband.[58]

❧ ❧ ❧

The source of Christian Bach's personal appeal obviously lay not only in his musi-cal talent but just as much in his character. In his music Bach was acknowledged above all else as the master of the *affetti amorosi*—the gracious, gentle, "affections." They can be described further as amiable, tender, ingratiating. His allegros, for their part, are typically spirited and sparkling, light-hearted, and with an infectious immediacy of appeal. It seems that his personality embodied the same qualities. The famous Gainsborough portrait of the composer captures all of them while at the same time revealing him to have been an elegant, refined, handsome, gentleman: one unabashedly fond of the finer things—in a word (the word actually used by an early biographer)—a "sensualist."[59] It is understandable that he inspired affection—and perhaps considerably more—in his friends, male and female.

Where, then, resided his strongest, most meaningful attachments and desires—spiritual, emotional, erotic: with men, with women, both? The answer, of course, is that we shall never know.

Chapter Twelve

Bach and Mozart

Styles of Musical Genius

Johann Sebastian Bach and Wolfgang Amadeus Mozart represent the antipodes of eighteenth-century musical genius. According to the traditional view, Bach's music was the culmination of the so-called Baroque era during the first half of the century; Mozart's, conversely, was the culmination of the antithetical Classical style, during the second half.[1] The antithesis is not just a technical matter of the contrast between the late Baroque and high Classical styles. It extends into their personal lives as well. We know almost nothing about Bach's private life; we know almost too much about Mozart's. Bach was an orphan; Mozart was all-too-much the son of an autocratic father. Bach was the product of the Lutheran tradition of northern Germany. Mozart was born into the Catholic tradition of Austria; but he clearly belonged even more to the secular, aesthetic, tradition that had its origins in Renaissance Italy. These starkly contrasting personal backgrounds inevitably affected their existential values: their understanding of their "purpose in life," their artistic missions. This understanding, in turn, inevitably touched on the purpose and, ultimately, the meaning of their music. Why did Bach and Mozart bother to compose at all? What did the effort and the resulting work mean to them? What were their fundamental objectives as artists?

I should like to begin exploring these issues somewhat indirectly. Rather than talking immediately about Bach or about Mozart, let us consider Mozart's Bach—a matter we shall consider even more extensively in chapter 14. As it turns out, Mozart instinctively understood a great deal about the creative impulse informing the music of Bach. In April of 1789, on the occasion of his visit to Leipzig (and his performance on the organ of the Thomaskirche—Bach's own organ), Mozart experienced a close encounter of the revelatory kind with the church music of J. S. Bach. The event was recorded by Friedrich Rochlitz (1769–1842), a pupil at the Thomasschule at the time of Mozart's visit, and later the founding editor of the influential Leipzig journal *Allgemeine Musikalische Zeitung*. Rochlitz writes:

On the initiative of the late [Johann Friedrich] Doles, then Kantor of the Thomas-Schule, the choir surprised Mozart with a performance of the double-chorus motet, *Singet dem Herrn ein neues Lied* [BWV 225], by Sebastian Bach. . . . Hardly had the choir sung a few measures when Mozart sat up startled; a few measures more and he called out: "What is this?" [*Was is das?*] And now his whole soul seemed to be in his ears. When the singing was finished he cried out, full of joy: "Now, there is something one can learn from!" [*Das ist doch einmal etwas, woraus sich was lernen läßt!*].[2]

J. S. Bach, no doubt, would have been most gratified at Mozart's reported response to his music. For it was Bach's explicitly stated intention to have his music serve as an object of study. On the title page of *The Well-Tempered Clavier* Bach had declared that this monumental collection of superbly crafted preludes and fugues was "for the Use and Profit of the Musical Youth Desirous of Learning" (*Zum Nutzen und Gebrauch der Lehr-begierigen Musicalischen Jugend*), and he ended the title of the *Orgelbüchlein* with the telling rhyme: *Dem Höchsten Gott allein zu Ehren / Dem Nechsten, draus sich zu belehren* (In Praise of the Almighty's Will / And for my Neighbor's Greater Skill). Bach, then, certainly thought of himself very much as a teacher.[3]

Mozart, for his part, hated to teach. He declared to his father: "Giving lessons . . . is no joke. . . . You must not think that this is laziness on my part. No, indeed! It just goes utterly against my genius [his word] and my manner of life."[4] Of course, Mozart is talking about giving keyboard lessons; Bach was teaching, above all, through the example of his compositions. Nonetheless, it is clear that there was a vast distance between the self-proclaimed artistic missions of J. S. Bach and W. A. Mozart.

There is more to be learned from Mozart's contact with Bach. The episode in the Thomaskirche did not represent his first serious encounter with the music of the Thomaskantor. That had occurred almost twenty years earlier.[5] But it was resumed with particular intensity about a year after Mozart had settled in Vienna. On April 10, 1782, Mozart reported home to his father: "I go every Sunday at twelve o'clock to the Baron van Swieten, where nothing is played but Handel and Bach. I am collecting at the moment the fugues of Bach—not only of Sebastian but also of Emanuel and Friedemann."[6] Indeed, under the auspices of the Baron Gottfried van Swieten (1733–1803), formerly the Austrian ambassador to Prussia and later the prefect of the Imperial Library in Vienna, Mozart, in April 1782, had embarked on a study of the fugues of J. S. Bach, most notably those of *The Well-Tempered Clavier*.[7]

Even more than in the case of the motets, the formidable and uncompromising preludes and fugues of *The Well-Tempered Clavier*, as Mozart undoubtedly recognized, constitute an art of *revelation*. They were never meant to be merely listened to, but rather to be played—and studied. In fact, Bach's most devoted admirers today, as in the past, developed their admiration of his music by playing or singing it themselves and thereby entering actively into an aesthetic realm of a particularly sublime, transcendental sort. This is a quite different experience from that of allowing oneself to be emotionally moved by more worldly, or "human" sentiments transmitted, that is, communicated, by intermediaries: by professional interpreters.[8] For Mozart, on the other hand, music was, above all else, an art of communication and expression; and what it communicated and expressed was the "thoughts and feelings" of the composer. In a famous passage he had once confessed to his father: "I cannot write in verse, for I am no poet. I cannot arrange the parts of speech with such art as to produce effects of light and shade, for I am no painter. Even by signs and gestures I cannot express my thoughts and feelings, for I am no dancer. But I can do so by means of sounds, for I am a musician."[9] In further contrast to Bach's explicit conviction that music must teach was Mozart's conviction that music must please. For Mozart it was part of the very definition of music. "Music . . . must never offend the ear, but must please the listener, or in other words must never cease to be music. . . . The Janissary chorus [from *Die Entführung aus dem Serail*] is . . . all that can be desired, that is, short, lively and written to please the Viennese."[10] Mozart also revealed to his father with reference to the "Haffner" Symphony: "I have composed my symphony in D major, because you prefer that key."[11] Whereas Bach composed the preludes and fugues of *The Well-Tempered Clavier* for the noble didactic purpose described earlier of instructing "the musical youth desirous of learning," the impetus behind the composition of Mozart's very Bachian fugue in C, K. 394, was a desire to please his wife.[12]

By no means, however, should Mozart's desire (indeed, his need) as a composer to please his audience be understood as pandering. Quite the contrary: if he was to compose a short, lively Janissary chorus to please the Viennese, then it would be a first-class Janissary chorus. Quality was not to be sacrificed for the sake of appeal. Nor need it be. Mozart would have both. As he explained in 1782, with reference to his recently completed piano concertos, K. 413 to 415, "[There are passages] here and there from which the *connoisseurs alone* [emphasis in the original] can derive satisfaction, but these passages are written in such a way that the less learned cannot fail to be pleased, though without knowing why."[13] It was, for Mozart, a matter of honor. As he declared, "I am really unable to scribble off inferior stuff."[14] Similarly, if he wished to make a favorable impression on the preeminent composer of Europe, Joseph Haydn, with a series of string quartets, then he would invest (as he reported in the dedication appended to the original publication) "long and laborious study" to produce string quartets of the very highest quality.[15] The ambition (or compulsion), then, to please provided Mozart with a simply enormous artistic agenda. After all, the only way he could hope to please, variously, his wife, his father, Baron van Swieten, the Viennese audience, Emperor Joseph, and Joseph Haydn was to be the universal musician he was.

As striking as Mozart's desire to please was his high esteem for what he called "effect." "Ah, if only we had clarinets too [i.e., in Salzburg, as they had in Mannheim]! You cannot imagine the glorious effect of a symphony with flutes, oboes and clarinets."[16] "My new Haffner symphony [K. 385] has positively amazed me, for I had forgotten every single note of it. It must surely produce a good effect."[17]

Bach's music was little concerned with either of Mozart's declared objectives, appeal or effect. Bach's music by and large was not intended or expected to appeal to a concert audience in the modern sense. Bach had little occasion—although there was some—to write what we may call "public" (or, more precisely: "entertainment") music. Admittedly, his most popular compositions today, by far, are his instrumental concertos, especially the Brandenburg Concertos. This is completely understandable; for in them we find an emphasis not only on virtuosity and exuberant technical display but also on an intensity and immediacy of expression that strikes a sympathetic listener as "personal" in tone and feeling. It is unclear how many such compositions Bach wrote. At all events, hardly two dozen concertos survive.[18] On the other hand, he composed hundreds of church cantatas, close to two hundred of which survive. These compositions, however, for all their superb technical craftsmanship and profound expressivity, were primarily intended not for the "delectation" of a concert public at all, but rather for the "edification" of a church congregation. They may even have been conceived for, and dedicated to, the ultimately exclusive audience: for the majority of Bach's cantata manuscripts close with the inscription *SDGI* (Soli Deo Gloria): "To God alone the glory."[19] All of this has been deliciously summarized by the Swiss theologian (and passionate Mozart enthusiast) Karl Barth in his famous *bon mot*: "It may or may not be the case that when the angels make music in praise of God they play Bach; but I am sure that when they are by themselves they play Mozart—and then God, too, is especially eager to listen in."[20]

We are now ready, I think, to reframe the questions I posed at the outset rather more specifically, as follows: Why did Bach perceive his music as "revelation"? Why did he conceive his artistic mission as one of teaching his neighbor and of praising God? Why did Mozart, on the other hand, understand his art as self-expression? Why did he feel obliged to please and impress his listeners? What, in a word, were the deeper forces driving the creativity of Bach and Mozart?

Let me turn first to Mozart whose life is less enigmatic than that of Bach, largely because it was so well documented from the beginning by the principals themselves. Indeed, there is probably more material of this kind bearing on Mozart than there is for any other artist before the nineteenth century. Over 1,200 original copies of letters survive from Mozart and his immediate family alone. Furthermore, Mozart's father, Leopold, kept every document relating to his son, and saw to it that—at least during Wolfgang's childhood (i.e., when Leopold was on hand himself)—virtually every fact and movement of the boy was duly recorded, sometimes unduly exaggerated, either in a diary or in the form of extensive letters to acquaintances back in Salzburg, describing their experiences on their European tours.

The irony is that many of the most crucial pieces, especially those pertaining to Mozart's maturity, are missing. This is exactly the opposite of the usual situation. With most great figures of history we know little about their childhood but quite a bit about their adult years; for it is normally not obvious that a child is going to be a great man some day. With Mozart the case was the reverse. Leopold Mozart recognized Wolfgang's extraordinary musical talent and was convinced that he was going to be a great musician. Moreover, he planned to write a biography of his phenomenal child himself and, therefore, recorded everything. Finally, Wolfgang was more famous and celebrated as a child prodigy than as a man—known (and reported on) throughout Europe from London to Naples, Paris to Prague. As a consequence, material bearing on Mozart's childhood abounds. For our present purpose this constitutes, needless to say, an unalloyed boon. Childhood, after all, is the crucible of personality; and in the case of an artist, the seedbed of creativity.

But it really does not take exhaustive familiarity with Mozart's biography to recognize that by far the two most significant facts of his childhood were, first, his extraordinary musical talent, a natural gift perhaps unmatched in history, and second, the extraordinarily powerful presence of his father.

One can readily imagine that, with the exception perhaps of Franz Kafka, no great artist has ever had to cope with such a formidable father. Moreover, in Mozart's case, the life, talent, and fortunes of the son had become the father's all-consuming obsession. Mozart had clearly learned at a most early age that his enormous musical talent was a source of unbounded pride and pleasure to his parents whose praise and delight in his abilities were of course a source of great encouragement and gratification to himself. (By the age of six, it had literally become Mozart's profession to please and delight others beside his parents with his talent.) Conversely, it must soon have become evident to the boy that he could appease his father, ward off his displeasure, by means of, perhaps only by means of, his musical accomplishments. There is every reason to suspect that Leopold made it clear to the boy that parental approval, and implicitly parental love, too, largely depended on his continued musical performance and production. We can be sure that Wolfgang quickly learned this lesson. No doubt he soon discovered as well that he could always reassure himself, as well as relieve pent-up emotional pressures, by drawing on the resources of his extraordinary creative talent. In short, music and composition had become for Mozart, in the language of the psychologist, an effective "ego defense": a source of self-esteem, a means of winning approval.

Such patterns of behavior, as they continue into adult life, can become a hallmark of the "depressive" personality, one unduly dependent on the opinions and approval of others, and therefore given to behavior designed to ingratiate oneself with others, potentially at the cost of suppressing one's own individuality.[21]

Mozart has in fact been diagnosed as an individual with mild "manic-depressive" or "cyclothymic" tendencies.[22] This, of course, is not to say that he suffered from an emotional disorder in any significant clinical sense. But such ugly, clinical, terminology has come to serve, in the modern era, as our preferred vocabulary for describing, understanding, and categorizing human nature. This is an enterprise that has engaged mankind since antiquity, when Hippocrates divided members of the species according to the four temperaments, the choleric, the sanguine, the phlegmatic, and the melancholic, and attempted to explain their behavior in terms of the preponderance of one or the other of the bodily fluids.

I am convinced that Mozart did not suffer from any serious pathological condition. The composer could hardly have been unaware of the phenomenal quality of his artistic achievements, for they were repaid, often enough, in the coin of worldly success: fame and money. And it would hardly have been "abnormal" if such "ego reinforcement" at times produced a "manic" state of triumphant elation—and even excessive exuberance. Indeed, it is difficult to imagine how it could have failed to do so. As for his bouts of sadness: Mozart himself was convinced that there was "always an [external] cause" for them. And there is evidence that he was not altogether wrong. Most but not all of the severe emotional difficulties he experienced can be associated with stressful circumstances of the moment: the death of his mother, loneliness, paternal browbeating, financial worries, separation from his wife. Yet there is no denying that he was especially sensitive to the opinions of others. He claimed not to care, but he clearly did. On August 8, 1781, he wrote to his father: "I played to [Countess Thun] what I have finished composing [from the first act of *Die Entführung*] and she told me afterwards that . . . what I have so far written cannot fail to please. But on this point I pay no attention whatever to *anybody's praise or blame*—I mean, until people have heard and seen the work *as a whole*."[23] Two years later he asked his father, "Please send me, if possible, the reports about my concert."[24] In the face of truly severe criticism, such as he experienced at the time of his break with his patron and protector, the formidable and frugal Prince-Archbishop of Salzburg, Hieronymus von Colloredo (1732–1812)—with whom the Mozarts had had a difficult relationship for years—Mozart not only lost his ability to work but even suffered physical collapse. From Vienna, May 12, 1781, he wrote:

> All the edifying things which the Archbishop [Colloredo] said to me during my three audiences . . . all the subsequent remarks which this fine servant of God made to me, had such an excellent effect on my health that in the evening I was obliged to leave the opera in the middle of the first act and go home and lie down. For I was very feverish, I was trembling in every limb, and I was staggering along the street like a drunkard. I also stayed at home the following day, yesterday, and spent the morning in bed.[25]

His moods of depression could also become intense. On June 27, 1788, he wrote to his fellow Mason and creditor, Michael Puchberg (1741–1822), "If such black thoughts did not come to me so often, thoughts which I banish by a tremendous effort, things would be . . . better."[26] On July 7, 1791, just five months before his death, Mozart confessed to his wife, who was taking a cure at the time: "I can't describe what I have been feeling—a kind of emptiness, which hurts me dreadfully—a kind of longing, which is never satisfied, which never ceases, and which persists, nay rather increases daily. . . . Even my work gives me no pleasure."[27] But it is important to add, as does Mozart, that the reason for this particular bout of melancholy was his separation from Constanze.

The recognition of Mozart's mildly manic-depressive temperament—let us just call it his "moodiness"—helps explain other features of his behavior. For example his scandalous, and rather "manic," delight in scatological language. There is a series of letters Mozart wrote to his first cousin Maria Anna Thekla Mozart (1758–1841), whom he called "Bäsle" (little cousin), the daughter of Leopold Mozart's brother, that contains almost nothing but obscenities of this sort.

But it is important to realize, first of all, that there was a sociological context for the "Bäsle" letters. Crude scatological language was by no means taboo in the eighteenth century among the European middle class. Body parts and functions were called by their vernacular names, not their Latin euphemisms. The words were used openly and naturally, even between men and women. Talking about the excretory functions in the late eighteenth century, it seems, was a bit like talking about one's diet today—or perhaps about one's analysis—and really no more gauche. I would like to stress two further point about the "Bäsle" letters. First, their obscenities are almost exclusively scatological; they contain very few sexual references, and those few are hedged in *double entendre*. The second point is this: Bäsle must have been amused by them.[28] This observation, as obvious as it is, emphasizes the fact that, once again, Mozart wished to please his audience. He seems to have been adept at adjusting his language and his behavior, like his music, to suit the occasion. In general, he knew how to "behave," or, put another way, he knew how to "act" properly. This ability, I believe, holds the key not only to much of Mozart's personality but also to much of his art. Mozart, apparently, for the reasons we have been discussing, was a role-player throughout his life—a perpetual actor. This may also explain in part why he was a great dramatist. Mozart was able to create such credible characters on stage, characters ranging from Monostatos and Papageno to Sarastro, from Zerlina to the Countess, because he possessed an almost limitless capacity to empathize. And this capacity, I submit, derived from the fact that he was obliged to play an exceptionally wide range of roles in his own life—especially in his childhood.

Mozart, after all, in addition to the powerful and no doubt oppressive omnipresence of his father, did not grow up like other children, developing his personality under stable circumstances in a more or less stable circle of peers. On the contrary, he was constantly on the move, especially during the ten formative years from 1763 to 1773, that is, between the ages of seven and seventeen. He was performing all the time—and not only on stage as a pianist. He was also performing a constantly changing role in a constantly changing social context: now at the court of Maria Theresa or George III or Louis XVI; now in the often colorful company of actors and singers; now among his fellow musicians at home in Salzburg—men, perhaps, of dubious character and etiquette; each time Mozart "fit in."

In a word, he was accommodating. As with his music, Mozart behaved in the manner he thought would best please his comrades and companions of the moment. With Bäsle he was the vulgarian. With his billiard and bowling companions he played the clown and prankster. With his pupils—mostly women—he may occasionally have played the seducer. With his wife Constanze the role had many facets. On the one hand, there was the purely physical, robust, lovemaking. But Mozart also played another part with her. Constanze had been shabbily treated by her mother, and it is clear that Mozart thought of himself as her protector and savior. At court, so far as is known, his manners were beyond reproach; he was a convincing courtier. With his father, Wolfgang was by turns the affectionate child, the gentleman of lofty moral principles, the bold rebel, even the mature, reflective man of thought. With his brethren from the Masonic lodge, Mozart was the high-minded humanitarian.

Finally, this ability to adjust, to assume many roles, has its counterpart in Mozart the musician. Mozart was the ultimate eclectic. He was at home, like no other musician in history, with literally every genre and style of his time: the concerto, the symphony, the opera, church, keyboard, and chamber music. His achievements in each were supreme but most impressive perhaps in opera, where his ability as a person to absorb and empathize with such a range of human behavior fused with his unlimited technical resources and stylistic range as a musician and composer.

❧ ❧ ❧

It seems possible, then, to fit together a picture of Mozart the man that not only does justice to even the less flattering facts of his life but seems to harmonize with his profile as a composer. Can the same be done in the case of J. S. Bach?

In stunning contrast to the situation with Mozart, we know relatively little about the private life of J. S. Bach.[29] Nonetheless, there is no doubt that whereas the decisive fact about Mozart's childhood, and perhaps for his personality, generally, is that he was the son of an overwhelming and formidable father, the decisive fact about Bach's childhood, already emphasized in earlier chapters, is that he was an orphan before his tenth birthday. We can also wonder about the quality of parental, or at least maternal, attention he had received in his earliest childhood. Bach was the youngest of eight children. It is likely that childhood sickness was always present in the household. We know that death was a not infrequent visitor. Just two months after Bach was born a brother died at the age of ten. Exactly one year later, a sister died at the age of six.[30] Shortly after the death of the *pater familias*, Ambrosius Bach, the family broke up and Sebastian went off to live with his oldest brother and protector, Johann Christoph.

In short, whereas the child Mozart suffered under the threat of the withdrawal of parental love, the child Bach experienced the actual deprivation of his parents. And this catastrophic deprivation—along with others, real or imaginary (as the story of Johann Christoph and the hidden manuscript reveals)—engendered in him, as suggested earlier (chapter 1), an attitude of "basic distrust" toward a treacherous world, predisposing him to religion, especially to the Lutheran religion with its message of personal faith and salvation, combined with a determined rejection and distrust of the vain and deceptive pleasures of what he may ultimately have regarded as a meaningless world.

The temperament that Bach seems to have developed, potentially vulnerable to a powerful sense of apathy, futility, meaninglessness, should perhaps be dubbed "the Sebastian complex." At all events, in order to prevent this discussion from taking on an unduly clinical tone, I shall adopt the conceit of designating the two temperaments I have been describing up to now henceforth as the "Mozartean" and "Bachian."

Unlike the Mozartean personality, the Bachian is typically an introvert, detached and isolated, inclined to keep his fellow man "at arm's length," and evincing an air of coldness, superiority, and aloofness. He is reluctant to become emotionally involved with others. In this connection it is good to recall Bach's letter to his childhood friend, Georg Erdmann. As recounted in chapter 2, it is in essence a business letter in which Bach, increasingly frustrated with his situation in Leipzig, asks his friend to help him find a new position. As we have seen, the letter mentions Bach's family but reveals virtually nothing about the affective relationships among the members of his family. His family, it seems, was an extension of his profession—his "calling."

It is not difficult for this absence, distrust—perhaps even abhorrence—of intense personal emotional involvement, such as we detect in Bach, to enhance the sense of meaninglessness I referred to before. Nor is it difficult to understand how a formidably gifted individual like Bach could find in his own creativity the compensating resources to create meaning.

The recourse to art, then, on the part of the talented and creative individual of Bachian disposition has an altogether different motivation from that of an individual of Mozartean temperament. A Mozart hopes to win approval (and love) with his display of talent and by providing pleasure. A Bach hopes, in the absence of any perceived meaning in the outer world, to create for himself his own world of meaning, and to proclaim it—to reveal it—to others: disciples, congregants.

It is hardly surprising that the Bachian temperament is observed more frequently in brilliant scientists than in artists. In a provocative study entitled *The Dynamics of Creation* (1972), the British psychiatrist Anthony Storr suggests that both Albert Einstein and Isaac Newton had "an intense need to create an all-embracing, explanatory scheme which would alleviate the discomfort of living in an arbitrary or contradictory world." Storr adds that Isaac Newton, "like many a prophet, seems to have been convinced that he had a direct personal relationship with a God who inspired him." In other words, when the Bachian temperament appears in individuals "of religious bent," they are, according to Storr, "apt to substitute a relation with God with the human contacts they find so difficult."[31] This is more than a little reminiscent of J. S. Bach's practice of signing his church compositions *Soli Deo Gloria*.

The strong representation of scientists (rather than artists) of genius possessed of what I have been calling the Bachian personality gives us an important clue as to the musical consequences of Bach's psychological predisposition. For Bach, music was destined to be far more than a mere object of aesthetic beauty. Rather it was, in two respects, a revelation—a manifestation—of truth. First of all, his church cantatas, in connection with their liturgical texts, were designed to serve as explicit vehicles of theological truth. Second, and more significantly, for Bach all "real" music, in its very substance and structure, bore witness to the divine order itself.[32]

Bach's synthesizing impulse had for him (as for Newton and Einstein) deep psychological sources. Synthesis and unification were, at the same time, a characteristic preoccupation of the philosophers and scientists of the Enlightenment. The ultimate significance of the work of Isaac Newton—for which he was duly celebrated during his own time—is that he had discovered in the laws of gravity the "unifying principle," the underlying unity that lay behind the new discoveries about the natural world that were being amassed in the course of the seventeenth century.[33] Compare Bach's achievement in *The Well-Tempered Clavier* with that of Newton. On the one hand, the work embodies a fusion of the potentially antithetical principles of functional tonality and linear counterpoint; on the other, it constitutes an "encyclopedic" survey of the most diverse forms and styles of the era—dances, arias, motets, concertos—all developed in accordance with a single "unifying" compositional principle: that of the fugue (see chapter 5). The parallel with the achievement of Newton is both palpable and profound.

It was certainly palpable to Johann Wolfgang von Goethe who exclaimed after he had heard the fugues of *The Well-Tempered Clavier* for the first time, it was "as if the eternal harmony were conversing within itself as it may have done in the bosom of God just before the Creation of the world."[34] Goethe was more right than he could have imagined. God's bosom indeed! It seems to me that it is by no means inappropriate to picture Bach the orphan, the "fatherless father" (literally, the father of twenty children, figuratively, in his role as teacher, the father of dozens of students and disciples), feeling himself, for the reasons we have been discussing, predestined to don the mantle of the lawgiver and understanding his personal destiny to be nothing less than that of a Godlike maker of worlds—worlds, to be sure, of musical sounds that not only bore witness to, but indeed emulated, the divine order itself.

What we witness in the case of both Bach and Mozart is the auspicious intersection of personality and history. Bach was born under the old aesthetic dispensation, according to which the purpose of art was the imitation of nature: Truth was beauty; that is, the aesthetic experience of beauty was the product issuing from the contemplation, or emulation, of divine order. For Mozart and his contemporaries, on the other hand, nature and the natural were redefined and understood in terms of amenity and grace, simplicity and immediacy, and personal self-expression. For composers of the Classical period, beauty was truth; that is, the creation of beauty, understood as that which is pleasing (or "effective," i.e., exciting to the senses) was the true objective of art. Despite their tragic personal destinies, Bach and Mozart each enjoyed the immensely good fortune of appearing at precisely the right time and place in history not only for the optimal cultivation of their prodigious natural gifts but for the expression of their particular spiritual needs, as these needs emerged from the crucible of their childhood experiences. The lesson seems to be this: for there to be art of the highest order there has to be a congruence of historic and personal circumstances—a perfect union of style and genius. There is more than one road to Parnassus.

Chapter Thirteen

Mozart and *Amadeus*

During the annual meeting of the American Musicological Society (AMS) in the year 1996, the society sponsored a first-ever panel devoted to exploring a new discipline within our discipline, namely, film as musicology (*ossia:* musicology as film criticism). I was asked to consider Milos Forman's cinematic version of Peter Shaffer's sensational play *Amadeus*.[1] It was certainly about time for such an effort, considering how many times members of our profession had been asked: "Was Mozart really like that?" or "Were there really such creatures as castrati—and were they really like *that?*" In short: Hollywood had discovered the romance of music history and had become infatuated with it (if not necessarily with us). But before true love could take hold with its new object of desire, Tinseltown evidently was convinced that cosmetic surgery was necessary—minor or major (no pun intended) as the case may be. But since, for the love object, the more radical the surgery, the greater the risk of disfigurement, perhaps fatally so, it would seem to have fallen to music scholars, if to anyone, to be on guard—prepared to do battle, if necessary, but not to assume that they are destined to be up against an inevitably hostile antagonist.

I suggested to my colleagues that before any of us were tempted to seek the thrilling rush of the sense of intellectual and moral superiority by bashing Hollywood for falsifying the facts of music history (and in the process perhaps risking no little embarrassment), we would do well to pause for a moment and consider: what would we think of, say, any historians of ancient history who would rake Shakespeare, or Handel, over the coals for what they had done to the historical Julius Caesar? If their gripe were solely with the undisputed circumstance that hard facts had been disregarded, rearranged, deliberately distorted, or even completely made up, well, then, I think we might be inclined to dismiss the criticism, to put it mildly, as missing the point. The poetic license, after all, is a license, if not to kill, then at least to maim, the literal truth. Such criticism would also fail to acknowledge the manifestly different purposes of historiography and dramaturgy.

The aesthetic, and indeed the moral, point, from a musicological perspective, when considering the genre of the music-historical film should be the same as that informing our attitude toward its counterpart and antecedent: the venerable—if frequently suspect—historical novel. And it is the same attitude, really, that should steer our judgment of Shakespeare or Handel or any lesser mortal who chooses to "do a number" on Julius Caesar—or on the kings of the Houses of Lancaster or York. Namely: if, armed with the shield of their poetic licenses, they are going to trash the facts of history and, along the way perhaps, cast a baleful light on the reputations of great and famous men, then they had better be prepared to redeem the historiographical insult with a sufficient portion of poetic truth, justice, or some other compelling form of adequate compensation.

Hollywood, admittedly, is not Handel. And while, by the same token, Peter Shaffer, the author of both the play and the film script of *Amadeus*, may not be Shakespeare, everyone, surely, would readily agree that he is not a mere opportunistic purveyor of tabloid titillation, either, but a thoughtful dramatist who deserves to be taken seriously.

Unlike the other works discussed at the AMS panel, by 1996 *Amadeus*, and the controversy and hand-wringing it precipitated, were overly familiar and quite stale. The play had been around for more than fifteen years. It opened in London in 1979 and in New York a year later, was published in book form in 1981, and appeared as a movie directed by Milos Forman in 1984. The film world's collective verdict on the movie reverberates in the fact that it won eight Academy Awards in 1984, including Best Picture.

Members of the musicological community, however, had considerably more trouble with it, owing, of course, to all those historical "mistakes" or, if one prefers, "liberties." In response to the challenge the film presented in that respect, the October 1984 issue of the journal *Eighteenth-Century Life* published a set of three short essays under the rubric "Film Forum: *Amadeus*," consisting of "*Amadeus* and Authenticity," by Jane Perry-Camp (Florida State University), "*Amadeus*: From Play to Film," by Mark Ringer (UCLA), and "*Amadeus* and the World of Milos Forman," by J. L. L. Johnson (College of Charleston).[2] Perry-Camp's "*Amadeus* and Authenticity" was able to report on the "lists upon lists" of factual errors that had already been drawn by then, recited many of those errors, and added quite a few more, suggesting that "*Amadeus*' historical mistakes and semi-mistakes are legion."[3] The interested reader can consult the lists in her article.[4] Though Perry-Camp was largely negative in her evaluation of the film and even worried about its ultimate cultural impact—concerned that Mozart here "is once again the victim of commercial interests"[5]—she does make an important concession (or confession) when she remarks that "there is one overwhelming salvaging force in *Amadeus*: Mozart's music."[6]

As with Salieri, *Amadeus* indeed may make confessors of us all. I confess that I admire almost everything about both the play and the quite different film. As I admitted to my colleagues at the outset of the AMS symposium: I had come to praise *Amadeus* not to bury it. I found the play, with its emphasis on what Mark Ringer described as the "*theomachia* between Salieri and the Big Guy Upstairs,"[7] both dramatically effective and intellectually provocative—and an undeniably significant addition to late twentieth-century theater. As for the film: as Shaffer once explained in an interview, the main protagonist there was no longer Salieri; it was, rather, Mozart's *music*.[8] One of his central objectives in fact was to saturate the film with it.

In both its stage and film versions *Amadeus*, of course, is a work of the imagination. The author has felt free to shift the chronology, to fuse the facts into new configurations, and to augment them for dramatic effect. There is nothing wrong with this, simply because, in this instance, it works so well. In art, success—artistic success, whether or not it is accompanied by commercial success—is its own justification. It would be carping and pedantic to accuse Shaffer of distorting the facts; it would be absurd to accuse him of not knowing them. Shaffer knew the facts and exactly what he was doing with them. Moreover, there is no need to correct the record or offer a defense of Mozart: for the facts of the matter are readily available. Whoever is interested in pursuing them should get hold, first of all, of Otto Erich Deutsch's *Mozart: A Documentary Biography*.[9] It seems likely that Deutsch's book, along with an edition of the Mozart letters, served as one of Shaffer's principal sources.[10] As a theatergoer, I applaud Shaffer's extensive familiarity with the events of Mozart's life and, even more, his eloquent and perceptive homage to Mozart's music.

We can begin with the music. Who has not been impressed by Salieri's impassioned, vivid description of the slow movement of the Serenade for Thirteen Wind Instruments, K. 361, featuring an unforgettable squeezebox image (ex. 13.1)?

> Extraordinary! On the page it looked like nothing. The beginning simple, almost comic. Just a pulse—bassoons and basset horns—like a rusty squeezebox. Then suddenly—high above it—an oboe, a single note, hanging there unwavering, till a clarinet took over and sweetened it into a phrase of such delight! This was no composition by a performing monkey! This was a music I'd never heard. Filled with such longing, such unfulfillable longing, it had me trembling. It seemed to me that I was hearing a voice of God.

As to the composer—specifically, Shaffer's perpetuating the myth of Mozart's effortless composition in the scene where Constanze shows Salieri her husband's manuscripts who swoons while contemplating their impeccable notation (probably my favorite scene in the movie): Let us not, in our pleasure at having established in recent years the full extent of the numerous sketches and drafts in Mozart's hand, proceed to debunk the myth of effortless composition categorically.[11] The fact remains that Mozart's manuscripts are all-too-often all-too-clean for comfort. I remember studying in amazement bordering on disbelief, and a sense of the eerie, the autograph of the Piano Concerto in E-Flat, K. 482, and realizing that, with respect to the compositional process, it contained nothing of interest. Indeed, there were almost no corrections of any kind, not even minor ones.[12]

Example 13.1. Mozart, Serenade in B-flat, K. 361, movement 3, mm. 1–5

I "confess" that I love that scene because it forces us all to confront the unsettling conundrum of artistic creativity of the highest imaginable order. Indeed, it seems reasonable to understand *Amadeus*, as much as anything else, as presenting a symptom of our need to account for the achievements of the great: to explain and comprehend what made these, our fellow creatures, so extraordinary. Perhaps this need is even greater now than ever before, since, in a secular age, our greatest figures have in a real sense become our gods. And when there are gods and mysteries—that is, major unanswered questions—there will be myths.

The "new mythology" is a reflection not of Romantic idealization, which saw the artist as a flawless and perhaps a tragic hero, but rather of the age of modern psychology and iconoclasm. We now see the blemishes on the portrait with microscopic clarity. Mozart the man was not a porcelain angel. According to the new mythology, he was not particularly admirable at all. Ironically, the Mozart of Romantic myth lives on nonetheless—not only in *Amadeus* but in our most sophisticated biographical studies. We still prefer to cast Mozart in the story of his life as a largely innocent victim, be it of the Archbishop of Salzburg, of his rival Salieri, or of his father Leopold.

It is not necessary to be a drama or film critic to realize that Shaffer's play (and the movie) are primarily about Salieri, and that in them Mozart is Salieri's obsession. Consequently, unlike *Immortal Beloved, Impromptu,* or *Farinelli* (and apart from all questions of aesthetic taste or historical truth), *Amadeus* belongs only to a limited extent to the traditional, sentimental Hollywood genre of musician's biography. It is a fable—a fable about God's capricious apportionment of talent among his creatures: specifically, his incomprehensible favoring of the most decidedly undeserving. In Shaffer's fable we do not see the historical Mozart objectively, nor even through the author's eyes, but only through the eyes of Salieri—as Shaffer imagines Salieri to be for his own dramatic purposes. And according to Shaffer's bitter, envious, and resentful Salieri, Mozart was an obnoxious brat with an obnoxious laugh who did not know how to behave or dress and who seemed to find infinite infantile pleasure in uttering scatological words.

Granting all that, Shaffer's play, apart from its dramatically legitimate manipulation of the facts, does raise important issues regarding Mozart's personality that must concern anyone interested in the composer's biography.

ᴈᴥ ᴈᴥ ᴈᴥ

In trying to understand or portray any important individual, we inevitably begin with the primary sources: the letters, original documents, and reminiscences of those who knew him. In Mozart's case there is a wealth of such material. In fact, there is an overabundance of it—probably more than for any other artist before the nineteenth century. As reported earlier (chapter 12), over 1,200 letters from Mozart and his immediate family survive from the period of the composer's lifetime. The vast majority of them pertain, most unusually (but understandably), to his childhood—owing primarily to his fame as a prodigy and his ambitious father's scrupulous record keeping and reporting—while for the man Mozart there are substantial gaps in the epistolary record. Here, too, though, the reasons are not difficult to discern. First of all, during the last ten years of his life—that is, for most of his adulthood—Mozart largely remained in Vienna; as he did not travel extensively, he had little occasion to maintain an extensive correspondence. It is symptomatic that not a single first-hand letter exists between Mozart and the librettists of his greatest operas: Lorenzo Da Ponte (1749–1838), the librettist of *The Marriage of Figaro, Don Giovanni*, and *Così fan tutte*; and Emanuel Schikaneder (1751–1812), the author of *The Magic Flute*.[13] Second, whereas Leopold Mozart and others carefully preserved any letter from Wolfgang, Wolfgang himself was not so conscientious. Thus, not a single letter survives from his wife Constanze to the composer. It is even possible that certain documents were deliberately destroyed. Constanze is suspected of having destroyed a large number of letters written to Wolfgang by Leopold—letters in which he is critical of her or her family and voices his objections to the idea of their marriage. She may well have destroyed other documents, too, that, in her opinion, shed an unfavorable light on Mozart or herself. In any case, no letters from Leopold Mozart, or from Wolfgang's sister, Nannerl, addressed to the composer, survive from his Vienna period.

This absence of documentation makes it impossible to give definitive answers to such important questions about Mozart's life as the nature and extent of his contacts with Joseph Haydn, or with other figures in his last years. We can only speculate about the most significant question facing the biographer of Mozart: what caused the rapid deterioration in his financial situation—and apparently in his career, generally—during the last six years of his life? As late as March 1785, Leopold Mozart reported to Nannerl that his son was living comfortably and had some 2,000 gulden to his name. By November—eight months later—Wolfgang was borrowing money. What had happened in the interim?

As indicated earlier, when we do not have facts about the lives of great individuals, they are replaced—as the *Amadeus* phenomenon abundantly demonstrates—with myths. It is a symptom of the vitality of our worship of the great that the mythology concerning them is not a static, closed one—an "ancient" mythology—but rather quite alive and, accordingly, constantly changing. The current Mozart mythology is almost the exact opposite of that of a hundred years ago. The Mozart myth of the "old testament"—the one that prevailed before the appearance of *Amadeus*—was, in principle, an idealization. Once again: for the Romantic sensibility, Mozart, like his music, must have been a paragon. The man must have consisted either entirely of virtues, or he possessed, at worst, a few rather attractive, easily excusable frailties such as naiveté, or vulnerability. Most important, there could not be any fundamental contradiction between the essence of the work and the essence of the man. There had to be an essential harmony between the two. And, since Mozart's work was judged to be complete, flawless, perfectly proportioned—"classic," in the sense of pure Apollonian beauty—the man behind the work had to be something like that: serene, harmonious, virtuous, worthy of adulation and emulation. To the extent that he suffered, he must have been a mostly innocent victim: misunderstood, betrayed. If certain facts contradicted this view, they were minimized or discreetly suppressed.

According to the new Gospel according to Peter Shaffer (and others), Mozart was hotheaded, spoiled, immature, infantile, uncouth, vulgar, weak in character, perhaps a compulsive gambler, perhaps anal-erotic. But the stature of the music has remained untouched. The resulting irony is that our empirical, proudly un-Romantic age, with its abhorrence of such notions as Inspiration, the Transcendental, and the Sublime, is confronted with a particularly confounding enigma: the discomforting disharmony between the man and his achievement.

🐦   🐦   🐦

What, then, do we really know for certain about Wolfgang *Amadé* Mozart? At the mere mention of his name we encounter a myth, an old one but one still with us. General usage will have it that the composer's real name was Wolfgang Amadeus Mozart. That, *pace* Shaffer, is a myth. The point may be trivial—what's in a name, after all?—but it is indicative of the problem. Mozart was actually baptized Joannes Chrysostomus Wolfgangus Theophilus Mozart. In his youth he signed his name simply "Wolfgang Mozart." His father often referred to him in letters to third parties as "Wolfgang Gottlieb"—Gottlieb being the German equivalent of Theophilus ("beloved of God"). From about the age of twenty-two on, Mozart regularly signed his name as "Wolfgang Amade Mozart"—with or without an accent (going in either direction, grave or acute) over the final "e." Only twice in his life, in 1774 and in 1779—and both times in a jocular context—did Mozart use the name "Amadeus."[14]

It is interesting for the myth-making process that the name "Amadeus" begins to make its appearance literally at the moment of Mozart's death: on the death certificate, on the estate documents, in the newspaper obituaries. It only became established as the standard, indeed official, name of the composer because the Leipzig publishers Breitkopf & Härtel chose it when they began to publish a complete edition of Mozart's works in 1799. The name, however, is symptomatic. The Latin form clothes the man in an aura of classical purity and universality: more lofty, and more bloodless, than his own choices of Amade, Amadeo, or, often enough, no middle name at all. One would be hard put to think of any other composer after 1600 to have been posthumously given a Latinized name.

Having touched upon the subject of Mozart's death, this is perhaps the appropriate moment to air the question of its cause. We do not know for certain what Mozart died of. The death certificate lists the cause of death as "severe miliary fever" (*hitziges Frieselfieber*).[15] It is not clear what was meant exactly by that term in the eighteenth century. We do know that it was not a clinically precise term even then.

It presumably meant even less than "the flu" means today. At this time the prevalent view is that Mozart most likely died of inflammatory rheumatic fever—the result of a streptococcal infection that usually attacks both the joints and the heart. Mozart had had three bouts with rheumatic fever as a child, which presumably had permanently weakened his heart. In the autumn of 1791 there was an outbreak of the disease, and a considerable number of people besides Mozart fell victim to it. On November 20, the pain and swelling in the joints forced Mozart to bed; two weeks later, on December 5, he died. It is not inconceivable that the immediate cause of Mozart's death was the bleedings he was subjected to by his doctor.[16]

After this survey of the vital statistics of baptism, christening, and death, we can proceed to a description of Mozart's physical appearance and try to visualize him externally before attempting to probe deeper. Franz Xaver Niemetschek (1766–1849) knew Mozart personally. In his biography of the composer, originally published in Prague in 1798, he tells us:

> There was nothing special about the physique of this extraordinary man; he was small and his countenance, except for his large intense eyes, gave no signs of his genius. His glance was unsteady and absent-minded, except when he was seated at the piano; then his whole face changed. . . . His small build [*der kleine Wuchs seines Körpers*] was due to the overtaxing of his brain in his youth and the lack of exercise in his childhood. He was, however, born of good-looking parents and is himself said to have been a beautiful child; but from the age of six he was permanently in a sitting posture, and he was also beginning to write at that time, too.[17]

It is clear, too, that Mozart was a nervous man. His sister-in-law, Sophie Haibel née Weber (1763–1846), reported that Mozart was always "playing the piano" on other things, "on his hat, pockets, watchband, tables, chairs."[18] And it may be that the composer suffered from "his small build." It was in compensation for this insecurity, perhaps, that he set great store on clothes. Mozart's interest in clothes is amply documented. Muzio Clementi (1752–1832), the composer and keyboard virtuoso who engaged in a piano competition with Mozart in the Hofburg on Christmas Eve 1781 at the behest of Emperor Joseph II, later remarked that when he saw Mozart for the first time he was convinced that "to judge by the man's elegant clothes, that he must have been the imperial valet."[19] And the singer who created the role of Don Basilio in the first performance of *Figaro*, the Irishman Michael Kelly (1762–1826), recalled in his memoirs that Mozart appeared at the dress rehearsal in a red robe trimmed with fur.[20] Finally, we have Mozart's own testimony—in the form of a letter addressed to the Baroness von Waldstätten, one of his patronesses in Vienna in the early 1780s. On September 28, 1782, Mozart wrote to her inquiring about a "beautiful red coat which attracts me enormously . . . I must have a coat like that, for it is one that will really do justice to certain buttons which I have long been hankering after. . . . They are mother-of-pearl. . . . I should like all my things to be of good quality, genuine and beautiful."[21]

We must return to the matter of Mozart's death. The reason there has been so much morbid fascination with it has little to do with the fact that Mozart died so young. (Schubert died at an even younger age—thirty-one—and that fact has not aroused so much interest.) It is rather that rumors began early on to the effect that Mozart was poisoned—either accidentally (from an overdose of mercury, the leading treatment at that time for syphilis), or deliberately—by a rival: specifically by Antonio Salieri.[22]

Salieri was just five years older than Mozart. He was born on August 18, 1750, in the Veneto region of Italy, but had been living in Vienna since he was sixteen. In 1774, at the age of just twenty-four, he was appointed "Court Composer and Conductor" of the Italian opera at the Viennese imperial court. That is, he had been occupying one of the leading musical positions in Europe for seven years by the time Mozart moved to Vienna in 1781. Seven years later, in 1788, Salieri assumed the even loftier title of "Court Kapellmeister"—a position he held for the next thirty-six years, until a year before his death on May 7, 1825. In 1823 a rumor circulated that Salieri, who was suffering from a violent illness at the time and had expected to die, had confessed that he had poisoned Mozart. Whether he actually made the confession is not known. But the rumor circulated, and was even reported to the deaf Beethoven in one of his conversation books.[23]

In Shaffer's play, once again, we only see Mozart through the eyes of Salieri. But In the case of Salieri, unlike that of Mozart, it is not easy to keep close tabs on Shaffer. Salieri's life and character have not yet been subjected to very much scholarly investigation. Accordingly, Shaffer's guess as to what Salieri was really like, and his attitude toward Mozart, is as good as anyone else's. It is certainly easy to imagine that Salieri, only a few years older than Mozart, recognized and felt threatened by the young man's superior talent. It is clear that, with his influence at court, Salieri was in a position to help Mozart, had he chosen to. But he chose not to. There is no unambiguous evidence, however, that Salieri ever actively plotted against Mozart. Nonetheless, Mozart's friends and relatives did suspect the Italian. Leopold Mozart was convinced that Salieri was behind the intrigues impeding the rehearsals of *The Marriage of Figaro* in 1786; and Mozart's sister-in-law reportedly once commented, after Mozart's death, that "Salieri couldn't stand Mozart."[24] On the other hand, it seems that, on the surface, relations between the two men were at least correct. Mozart did take Salieri (and Salieri's much-favored pupil, Caterina Cavalieri (1755–1801), the singer who created the role of Constanze in *The Abduction from the Seraglio*) to a performance of *The Magic Flute*, as Shaffer portrays. On the following day, October 14, 1791, in the last letter surviving from his hand, Mozart wrote to his wife:

> You can hardly imagine how charming they were and how much they liked not only my music, but the libretto and everything. They both said it was an *operone*, worthy to be performed for the grandest festival and before the greatest monarch, and that they

would often go to see it, as they had never seen a more beautiful or delightful show. [Salieri] listened and watched most attentively, and from the overture to the last chorus there was not a single number that did not call forth from him a bravo! or bello![25]

❧ ❧ ❧

Amadeus has caused a sensation, of course, because it depicts Mozart as an infantile, foul-mouthed vulgarian who did not know how to behave (or dress) and who seemed to find endless pleasure in uttering four-letter scatological words. It was evidently new to much of the general public that Mozart used such language; but it has been long known by musicians and scholars that this was the case. The depiction dismayed, confused, and fascinated audiences—and captured their imagination. People were understandably skeptical and wanted to know if there was any truth to this portrayal. It was hard for them to imagine that Mozart used such foul language—the language that erupts in the letters Mozart wrote to Maria Anna Thekla, the daughter of Leopold Mozart's brother, that is to say, his cousin, whom he called "Bäsle," that is, "little cousin."[26] The letters are undeniably tasteless. What is one to make of them? How has our profession come to terms with them?

Let us count the ways (as the player in *Hamlet* might have described them, if his interest in genres had been directed to modern intellectual fashions rather than Elizabethan dramatic forms): the characterological, the psychoanalytical, the sociological, the cultural-linguistical, the clinical-pathological.

The sociological (or perhaps the cultural-linguistical) explanation may be the most enlightening. As mentioned earlier (chapter 12), it was not unusual in the eighteenth century—at least in the German-speaking world—to refer to body parts and functions by their vernacular names. The letters of the Mozart family contain numerous references of this kind.[27] Mozart uses the words in letters to his father and mother. In fact, the only surviving letter written by Mozart directly and exclusively to his mother consists of nothing but a doggerel poem made up of scatological couplets. He wrote it, incidentally, in January 1778, at just the same time he was composing his dissonant letters to Bäsle. The remarkable document reads (in part):

> O, mother mine! / Butter is fine. / Praise and thanks be to Him. / We're alive and full of vim. / . . . Besides, to people I'm tied / Who carry their muck inside / And let it out, if they are able, / Both before and after table. / At night of farts there is no lack, / Which are let off, forsooth, with powerful crack. / The king of farts came yesterday / Whose farts smelt sweeter than the May. . . . But now I really must rest a bit / From rhyming. Yet this I must add, / That on Monday I'll have the honor, egad, / To embrace you and kiss your hands so fair. / But first in my pants I'll shit, I swear. / Adieu Mamma / Your faithful child, / With distemper wild / Trazom.[28]

Mozart's mother, for her part, concludes the earliest extant letter of hers to her husband, dated September 26, 1777, as follows: "Keep well, my love. Into your mouth your arse you'll shove. I wish you good night, my dear, but first shit in your bed and make it burst."[29]

It is surely undeniable, however, that the letters Mozart sent to his Bäsle—especially during the time span 1777–78, when he was twenty-two years old and she was turning twenty—decisively crossed most anyone's threshold of good taste. Nonetheless, it seems possible to absorb Bäsle's letters into a coherent portrait of Mozart's personality and character, one that manages to account for a number of facts and attitudes that at first seem contradictory. Such a portrait, moreover, need not be ruinous to Mozart's personal reputation—not that it is at all necessary to offer an apology. If Mozart should turn out to have been an insufferable boor, posterity would surely be able to learn to live with the fact while continuing to cherish his music. It has, after all, made such adjustments often enough in the case of other great creative artists.

Most significant is the fact that the Bäsle letters are fairly concentrated in time. Five of Mozart's nine surviving letters to his cousin were written at just the period—between October 1777 and February 1778—when Mozart fell seriously in love for the first time in his life. He was ready to give up everything then in order to go to Italy with Aloysia Weber (1760–1839), his voice pupil and the sister of the woman he would ultimately marry. Perhaps more consideration should be given to what may be a direct link between the outburst of crude language in the Bäsle letters and Mozart's infatuation with Aloysia Weber. Perhaps the letters constituted an important outlet for sexual tensions that may have been plaguing Wolfgang at the time. We know that Mozart's sexuality was strong (at least we have his word for it). In a letter to his father written at the time of his betrothal to Constanze he wrote:

> The voice of nature speaks as loud in me as in others, louder perhaps, than in many a big strong lout of a fellow. I simply cannot live as most young men do in these days. In the first place, I have too much religion, in the second place, I have too great a love of my neighbor and too high a feeling of honor to seduce an innocent girl; and, in the third place, I have too much horror and disgust, too much dread and fear of diseases and too much care for my health to fool about with whores. So I can swear that I have never had relations of that sort with any woman.[30]

Thus Mozart—on December 15, 1781, one month short of his twenty-sixth birthday.

As for Mozart's scatological language, it never erupted again in the same way. There are of course occasional vulgarities scattered throughout his letters; and he did write those obscene canons. But this was all harmless fun, unlikely to raise any eyebrows in the early twenty-first century or the late eighteenth.

The fact that the Bäsle letters contain almost no sexual references suggests that their scatology may have been a rather bizarre form of "sublimation" for the erotic impulses directed toward Aloysia that Mozart was trying to control at that time. This further suggests, incidentally, that Mozart observed a taboo when it came to sexual obscenities. There are some erotic letters from Mozart, however. They were written to Constanze over the space of a month and half in the spring of 1789 when he was on a concert tour to Dresden and Berlin. They testify to a remarkable "development" in the composer's amorous inclinations. On April 8, 1789, on the road to Prague, Mozart is the gallant, romantic, cavalier: "How are you? I wonder whether you think of me as often as I think of you? Every other moment I look at your portrait—and weep partly for joy, partly for sorrow. Look after your health, which is so precious to me and fare well, my darling! . . . Adieu. I kiss you millions of times most tenderly and am ever yours, true till death."[31] On April 13 his informality returns. A playful scherzo follows the *moderato affettuoso*:

> If I were to tell you all the things I do with your dear portrait, I think that you would often laugh. For instance, when I take it out of its case, I say, "Good-day Stanzerl!—Good-day, little rascal, pussy-pussy, little turned-up nose, little bagatelle. Schluck and Druck." And when I put it away again, I let it slip in very slowly, saying all the time, "Nu, Nu, Nu!" with the peculiar emphasis which this word so full of meaning demands, and then just at the last quickly, "Good night, little mouse, sleep well." Well, I suppose I have been writing something very foolish (to the world at all events); but to us who love each other so dearly, it is not foolish at all.[32]

On April 16 there is a *serioso*: "Dear little wife, I have a number of requests to make. I beg you . . . in your conduct not only be careful of your honor and mine, but also to consider appearances. Do not be angry with me for asking this. You ought to love me even more for thus valuing our honor."[33] On May 19, from Leipzig we have the introduction to the finale:

> Oh, how glad I shall be to be with you again, my darling. But the first thing I shall do is to take you by your front curls; for how on earth could you think, or even imagine, that I had forgotten you? . . . For even supposing such a thing you will get on the very first night a thorough spanking on your dear kissable little arse, and this you may count upon. Adieu, Ever your only friend and your husband, who loves you with all his heart.
>
> W. A. Mozart.[34]

Finally, on May 23, from Berlin, the descent from Parnassus is completed. The curtain-closer is now *a tempo*:

> On June 1st I intend to sleep in Prague, and on the 4th—the 4th—with my darling little wife. Arrange your dear sweet nest very daintily, for my little fellow deserves it indeed, he has really behaved himself very well and is only longing to possess your sweetest . . . [in Emily Anderson's words: "Each dotted passage represents a word which has been blotted out in the autograph."] Just picture to yourself that rascal; as I write he crawls on to the table and looks at me questioningly. I, however, box his ears

properly—but the rogue is simply . . . and now the knave burns only more fiercely and can hardly be restrained.[35]

This is Mozart at his most unbuttoned in matters sexual. These letters abundantly attest to Mozart's warmly affectionate and sexually robust relationship with Constanze. But they also suggest that it may have been based on little more than the couple's shared uninhibited sensuality.

This last observation is important on a broader level. As Hermann Abert emphasized, Mozart was a "sensual" individual in the most literal meaning of the word. His relation to experience was direct—through the senses, and not, say, through contemplation.[36] This fact helps explain his evidently limited interest in politics, philosophy, books, and poetry (except for librettos) as well as his enthusiasm for theater and horseback riding. It also accounts for his interest in people and his skill at observing them and characterizing them. Mozart was remarkably observant; his letters are full of assessments and verbal caricatures of the people he met on journeys, especially opera singers. His remarks on such occasions are often biting, stingy with praise, usually objective but occasionally moralistic or judgmental.[37]

Let us return once again to the Bäsle letters. They were tailored to appeal to the taste of their recipient. Contrary to the impression created by *Amadeus*, there does not seem to be any occasion on which Mozart made a fool of himself in public. Moreover, as suggested earlier (chapter 12), not only did he know how to "act" properly but his experience as a role-player along his ability to empathize—a consequence of his unusual childhood—may well hold the key to his greatness as an opera composer.

It is conceivable that play-acting had become such a normal pattern in Mozart's behavior that it would have been impossible to say—perhaps even for him to say—when he was "himself." There are of course many people who feel that they are always playing a role, never being "themselves." It is a common malady. Mozart may have been such an individual. It is easy to imagine that such turbulence in the life of any young child and early adolescent as Mozart had experienced during the decade of his Wunderkind years of interminable traveling and performing variously—whether on stage or at court—would have made it formidably difficult to develop a "well-focused" personality.

For many Mozarteans (scholars and lay admirers alike), even more repellent than the scatological utterances emanating from the mouth of Shaffer's/Salieri's Mozart was that infuriating laugh. To begin with, in contrast to the potty-mouth language, there is no historical evidence for this idiosyncrasy. We simply have no contemporary testimony at all as to how Mozart sounded when he laughed. But despite the lack of documentary substantiation, one can find a plausible dramatic rationale for this persistent, gratingly irritating attribute attached to the play's antihero (not inappropriately for a musician, a sounding attribute—a leitmotif). A moment's reflection reveals that it must represent—that it must *be*—the mocking laughter of the gods: laughter directed toward all us common mortals who have been spitefully, maliciously denied the fire of creative genius. Indeed, Salieri himself informs his confessor (and us) of this painful fact. He recalls the incident at the carnival when Mozart, after having delighted everyone present with a grotesque imitation of the sourpuss court composer at the keyboard (concluding the wooden composition with a resonant perfect authentic fart), bursts yet again into hysterical laughter. Salieri's observation: "That was not Mozart laughing at me, Father. That was God. That was God laughing at me through that obscene giggle. Go on, Signore, laugh, laugh."

If there was a "true" Mozart who revealed himself at all in a social context, it may have been the man who evidently shared few, but highly treasured, hours with Joseph Haydn. The friendship the two men are known to have felt for one another (despite the fact that they were a generation apart in age) must lead us to conclude that it was nourished not only by mutual recognition of and admiration for each other's genius but also by deep affection. Perhaps Haydn embodied for Mozart admirable qualities both as a musician and as a person he sought in vain in his flesh-and-blood father; perhaps Mozart, for the childless Haydn, represented the gifted son he may have wished he had. It is noteworthy that paternal imagery, along with emphatically repeated declarations of profound friendship, pervades Mozart's famous dedication of his string quartets to the old master. The dedication begins: "To my dear friend Haydn, / A father who had resolved to send his children out into the great world took it to be his duty to confide them to the protection and guidance of a very celebrated Man, especially when the latter by good fortune was at the same time his best Friend. Here they are then, O great Man and my dearest Friend. . . ." The document continues:

> May it therefore please you to receive them kindly and to be their Father, Guide and Friend! From this moment I resign to you all my rights in them, begging you however to look indulgently upon the defects which the partiality of a Father's eye may have concealed from me, and in spite of them to continue in your generous Friendship for him who so greatly values it, in expectation of which I am, with all my Heart, my dearest Friend, your most Sincere Friend / W. A. Mozart.[38]

(Joseph Haydn, incidentally, is a character notably, if understandably, absent altogether from Peter Shaffer's drama.)

At the conclusion of a probing consideration of the relationship between Mozart and Haydn and of the contents of the quartet dedication, Maynard Solomon writes: "The imagery seems to resonate with Mozart's very personal yearning for an ideal paternal/filial harmony, for a vigorous, creative, and accepting musical father. For it is not only Mozart's 'sons' but himself whom he entrusts to Haydn's care. In consigning his musical children to his friend (and Masonic brother) Mozart conscripted Haydn to become his father, while at the same time he validated his own claims to creative fatherhood."[39]

❧ ❧ ❧

For the purposes of the musicological panel in the year 1996, the "correct" understanding of Mozart's foul language or how he laughed was of little import. What was important to members of the profession was to acknowledge that the film stimulated widespread and intense general interest in two Mozart phenomena: the man and his music. Almost at once Mozart became—at least for a while—the most popular, most well-known, most purchased, and, very possibly, the most truly enjoyed of the classical composers: readily displacing Beethoven, Tchaikovsky, or anyone else who, before 1980, might have disputed his claim to that position.

Furthermore, since people were baffled and could not get enough of the movie, or of Mozart, or his music, they turned to the members of the musicological profession for answers and guidance. In 1984 or 1985 (that is, just a year or two after the movie had opened), after I had presented a talk about it and its relation to "the facts," a young woman in the audience made a confession of her own, namely, that she had by then already seen the film some thirty-five or forty times and that it was consuming her. Indeed, she indicated that it had given her life new meaning. Although she had absolutely no musical background, she now knew that she needed to find out as much about Mozart as she possibly could. As she put it—quite spookily—she wanted to devote her life to him. (She wanted to know, in a word, whether she should become a musicologist.) Potentially more significant: Anecdotal chatter suggested that in the wake of *Amadeus*, enrollments in college music courses nationwide, especially courses about WAM himself, saw unprecedented increases—at least for a while.

By 1991 the Mozart mania had, if anything, increased even more. At a conference inspired by the major Mozart event of that year, the bicentennial commemoration of his death, someone asked why Mozart was receiving all this attention, especially from the popular media. One of the panelists conceded that it was something of a puzzle. Another helpfully suggested: "It's that movie, of course—still."

That movie, then, had become the most potent ally of the musicological profession—arguably the most potent ally of everyone engaged in the enterprise of cultivating and promulgating classical music—performers, scholars, and teachers. So, two thumbs up here for *Amadeus*—even if the possibility cannot be dismissed that in the end it will be understood to constitute only another chapter in the ongoing effort to account for one of the most formidable creators in human history—another layer in the secular mythology.

Chapter Fourteen

Bach and Mozart's Artistic Maturity

In the annals of musicological writing few questions have been rehearsed so often, or for so long, as that of Mozart's relationship to Bach and the significance of that relationship for subsequent music history. The traditional, and still predominant, understanding of Mozart's relationship with Bach, reduced to its essentials, runs as follows. About a year after he had settled in Vienna, and by early 1782 at the latest, Mozart came to know the music of J. S. Bach during the course of his weekly Sunday musical matinees at the home of Baron Gottfried van Swieten (1733–1803). This exposure and confrontation, this *Auseinandersetzung*, with the music of Bach profoundly and permanently influenced, indeed virtually transformed, Mozart's style and even reshaped his fundamental understanding of the nature and potential of music. The result was a major aesthetic and stylistic breakthrough—one that effected a synthesis of the "learned" and the "galant," of Bachian counterpoint and complexity and rococo "naturalness" and immediacy. The result was nothing less than the creation of the Viennese Classical Style.

This familiar argument, a virtual truism not only of Mozart biography but of music history and still by far the prevailing view, has in fact been challenged and by some distinguished authorities. Sides have been taken. Since the question has become controversial, a brief review of the history of the historiography is in order. The first attempt to assess the larger historical importance of Mozart's Bach reception—as opposed simply to noting that Mozart knew and admired Bach's music—was offered by one of Mozart's own acquaintances, the Abbé Maximilian Stadler (1748–1843). In his *Materialien zu einer Geschichte der Musik*, compiled between 1815 and 1829, Stadler remarks: "Owing especially to those works of his written during the last ten years in Vienna, Mozart propelled himself to such heights that he was acknowledged, not only in Vienna but throughout Germany, indeed throughout all of Europe, as the greatest master, *one who united within himself Sebastian Bach's art, Handel's strength, Haydn's most witty clarity and charm*."[1] Since then, all has been Variations on the Theme. For example, Constanze Mozart's second husband, Georg Nikolaus Nissen (1761–1826), clearly appropriating Stadler's insight, wrote the following in the *Anhang* to the first full-length biography of Mozart (published in 1828):

> After [composers], with the exception of but a few masters, and in the interest of achieving a light, popular, sentimental style had distanced themselves ever more from the thoroughness of old Sebastian Bach, Mozart appeared, who, filled with deep admiration for Bach, combined in his own compositions Italian charm, German strength, and most notably Bachian art (specifically with respect to richness of harmony, melodically informed bass lines, and contrapuntal treatment, altogether); and along with Joseph Haydn he founded a new epoch in the art of music, the one with which the modern style began.[2]

In the twentieth century, Hermann Abert devoted an entire chapter of his monumental Mozart biography to demonstrating the same proposition. The chapter is titled "Profound Changes in Style: The Influence of J. S. Bach, G. F. Handel, and C. P. E. Bach" (*Die große Stilwandlung unter dem Einfluß Seb. Bachs, Händels und Ph. E. Bachs*).[3]

The thesis attained its classic—or perhaps one should say, its Romantic—formulation in Alfred Einstein's *Mozart: His Character, His Work*, in a chapter entitled "Mozart and Counterpoint." Einstein writes: "For Mozart the encounter with [Bach's] compositions resulted in a revolution and a crisis in his creative activity." He continues: "Mozart was never completely finished with this experience, but it enriched his imagination and resulted in more and more perfect works."[4]

In recent years the theme has been echoed and developed further by, among others, Charles Rosen, Ludwig Finscher, and Robert L. Marshall. Early in *The Classical Style*, Charles Rosen observes: "In spite of Mozart's acquaintance with later composers who tried to continue the contrapuntal tradition, a remarkable development comes over his work from the moment he begins to know the music of Johann Sebastian Bach."[5]

According to Ludwig Finscher:

> Mozart's decisive breakthrough to the classical style, his contribution to the elaboration of this style as a synthesis which one can, with some justification, describe as a Universal style, one in which the historically older idea of a synthesis of national styles was lifted, this breakthrough took place not in the symphony, indeed not really in any particular genre, but primarily in the context of a biographical situation, in which Mozart's lifelong practice of coming to terms with various stylistic models culminated in the confrontation, practically simultaneously, with two artistically overwhelming impressions: the encounter with Bach and Handel in the house of Baron van Swieten and the encounter with Haydn's String Quartets, opus 33.[6]

Elsewhere Finscher puts it more cogently: "The year 1782 [thanks to the encounter with Bach, Handel, and Haydn's op. 33 string quartets] thus becomes an epochal year, indeed the year in which the classical style was born—and presiding over the birth are Bach and Handel."[7]

As for Marshall, his essay, "Bach and Mozart: Styles of Musical Genius," originally opened with this form of the conventional wisdom: "It is well known that Mozart was profoundly impressed by, and influenced by, the music of Johann Sebastian Bach. Indeed, his mature style is unimaginable without it."[8]

This view, although it is the prevailing opinion, is not unanimous. Several eminent Mozarteans have questioned the ultimate importance of Mozart's Bach experience. The challenge was apparently first issued by Stanley Sadie in a brief article, "Mozart, Bach and Counterpoint."[9] Sadie asks: "Did Mozart's contact with Bach, as Einstein claimed, really cause a 'revolution and a crisis in his creative activity'?" After considering the well-known fugal examples Sadie concludes that "Mozart undoubtedly had the utmost reverence for Bach as a supreme master of his craft; but I fancy he would have been amused, or perhaps mildly offended, at the notion of anyone so absurdly out of date affecting his music in anything more than the most superficial ways."[10]

There is at least a trace of debunking skepticism, too, in Neal Zaslaw's comment, early in his magisterial study of Mozart's symphonies: "Much has been made of Wolfgang's encounter in the early 1780s with J. S. Bach's contrapuntal style, but sufficient recognition has not always been given to the fact that Wolfgang grew up surrounded by composers who prided themselves on their command of the *stile antico*."[11] This comment, by the way, is in effect the only substantial reference at all to J. S. Bach in Zaslaw's massive volume. Finally, Ulrich Konrad, in his comprehensive investigation of the Mozart sketches, cites and essentially endorses Sadie's position:

> Let the opinion at the least be voiced that the constant emphasis on both Constanze Mozart's alleged passion for fugues, which is supposed to have stimulated her husband, as well as the encounter of the composer with the music of Johann Sebastian Bach— which, especially in the German-language literature has virtually taken on the aura of a mythos—that these observations do not essentially advance the goal of an objective assessment of the historical and, above all, the musical implications of Mozart's contrapuntal thought.[12]

Despite such recent doubts, however, the familiar, traditional understanding, at least in this writer's opinion, still retains its validity. However, as the reservations that have been raised concerning the "mythos" (in Konrad's characterization) make clear, a number of qualifications are called for.

In the first place, it is, at best, misleading to draw a close parallel between Mozart's confrontation with the music of Bach and Handel, and J. S. Bach's encounter with sixteenth-century polyphony. When Bach embarked on his serious investigation of the *stile antico* in the mid-1730s, Palestrina had been dead for close to 150 years; when Mozart began his systematic study of J. S. Bach, Bach had been dead for just over 30. The relation between Bach and Mozart, in short, is not at all analogous to that between Bach and Palestrina. Bach belonged to the generation of Mozart's grandparents and was the father of one of Mozart's mentors, Johann Christian Bach. By the same token, Bach's music, for Mozart, was not representative of a historical style (not yet) nor part of a historicizing movement as it was to be for Beethoven. Bach's music represented a *stile antico* for Mozart no more, perhaps, than the music of Bartók or Stravinsky represents a *stile antico* for us.

❧ ❧ ❧

Johann Sebastian Bach's name appears in the Mozart family correspondence for the first time in Wolfgang's famous letter of April 10, 1782, to his father, cited earlier, in which he reports on his Sunday matinees at the home of Baron van Swieten.[13] It is hard not to get the impression from the standard biographical literature that these visits marked the beginning of Mozart's serious encounter with the music of Bach. But it seems clear from the way Mozart introduces the names of Bach—father and sons—that they were not unfamiliar to Leopold and needed no particular identification or further description. On the contrary: Mozart's knowledge of Bach's music most likely antedated the Van Swieten sessions by well over a decade. Moreover, the constellation of evidence for this contention actually begins, not surprisingly, with Leopold Mozart.

In the early 1750s, Leopold Mozart had connections with at least one important member of the Berlin Bach circle: Friedrich Wilhelm Marpurg (1718–95). Marpurg's connections with Bach are well-known. Most notably, he was the author of the preface to the second edition of the *Art of Fugue* (published in 1752); and in his *Abhandlung von der Fuge* (1753/54) he drew extensively on the music of J. S. Bach for his examples. As for Leopold Mozart's connections with Marpurg: In 1756 Marpurg had published a favorable review of Leopold's violin treatise in his *Historisch-Kritische Beyträge zur Aufnahme der Musik*; in the following year, and in the same journal, he printed Leopold's "Report on the Present State of the Musical Establishment at the Court of His Serene Highness the Archbishop of Salzburg in the Year 1757."[14] It seems safe to assume that Marpurg had commissioned the contribution from Leopold a year or so earlier.

Whether or not Leopold's connections with Marpurg involved the music of J. S. Bach is not known. But it is a possibility. It is even possible that Leopold had become aware of Bach's music considerably earlier than the 1750s, namely, as a student in his native Augsburg. During Leopold's youth, the Kantor of the Protestant church in Augsburg, St. Anne's, was Philipp David Kräuter (1690–1741). According to his own testimony, Kräuter, a native of Augsburg, had been a pupil of Johann Sebastian Bach's in Weimar in 1712 and 1713.[15] Several scholars have suggested that Leopold "doubtless" heard performances by Kräuter in Augsburg in his youth and they "probably" included music by J. S. Bach.[16] Most recently, however, research in the Augsburg church archives bearing on Kräuter's musical activities there has revealed that he performed cantatas by Bach's contemporaries Telemann, Erlebach, Stölzel, and J. F. Fasch but so far has uncovered no evidence that he ever performed the music of his teacher.[17]

Finally, in addition to Marpurg in Berlin and, perhaps, Kräuter in Augsburg, Leopold had also had some contact with one of Bach's leading champions in Leipzig: Lorenz Christoph Mizler (1711–78). As is well-known, Mizler, in the year 1747, inducted J. S. Bach (whom he described as his "good friend and patron") into his *Korrespondierende Sozietät der Musicalischen Wissenschaften* as its fourteenth member. Considerably less well-known is the fact that in 1753 Mizler had at the least considered extending an invitation of membership into his prestigious society to Leopold Mozart.[18]

As for Wolfgang, it seems reasonable to assume, in light of Leopold's likely acquaintance with J. S. Bach's music, that he had exposed Wolfgang to it as a young child. And, if not Leopold in Salzburg, then surely Johann Christian Bach in London. Indeed, our suspicions concerning an early Wolfgang Mozart–Sebastian Bach connection rise above the level of circumstantial evidence and assume something resembling documented verification in the following passage from Franz Niemetschek's *Life of Mozart*. Referring to the Mozarts' grand tour to Paris and London in 1764 and 1765, Niemetschek reports: "In Paris and London, pieces by Handel and Bach were placed before him [Wolfgang], which to the astonishment of all experts he was immediately able to perform with accuracy and with proper expression."[19] (Of course, we cannot be altogether sure that by the late 1790s the "Bach" Niemetschek had in mind, with his conjunction of the names of Handel and Bach, was Johann Sebastian.)

Finally, evidence of a more tangible, and audible, sort is provided by a musical composition: Mozart's fragmentary (but almost finished) Fugue in G Minor for "Clavier," K. 401/375e.[20] Whether this piece is for organ or piano or harpsichord, for two hands or four hands, has been a matter of dispute. What has never been in dispute is the manifest Bachian influence to be seen and heard in it (ex. 14.1).

It is hard to imagine how Mozart could have composed, or even have imagined composing, such an atypical piece—moreover, a contrapuntal *tour de force* of the first order: a counter-double fugue, that is, a double fugue whose two subjects are inversions of one another—if he had remained in sublime ignorance of the *Art of Fugue* or *The Well-Tempered Clavier*. The idea is even more inconceivable, given the frequently observed and, indeed, impossible-to-overlook similarities between Mozart's subject and those of both the B-flat Minor Fugue from book 1 of *The Well-Tempered Clavier* and the *Art of Fugue* (ex. 14.2).

The connection is especially strong with the *Art of Fugue*, since, in addition to the family resemblance of the subjects, the same compositional techniques are explored. Indeed, it seems to have been Mozart's objective to "trump" his model, insofar as his fugue unites within a single composition the "agendas" of no fewer than three of

Example 14.1. Mozart, Fugue in G Minor, K. 401, mm. 1–11a

Example 14.2. (a) Bach, *Well-Tempered Clavier* 1, Fugue in B-flat Minor, BWV 867/2, subject; (b) Bach, *Art of Fugue*, BWV 1080/1, subject

Bach's pieces from the *Art of Fugue*: two of the simple fugues based, respectively, on the *rectus* and *inversus* forms of the subject, along with the Contrapunctus No. 5 (in the numbering of the original edition) in which both forms are combined (see ex. 14.3).[21]

So "Bachian" is this fugue, and so impressive—if admittedly rather dry and "academic" in its technical mastery—that it has been confidently dated by all commentators (until fairly recently) to Mozart's Vienna period and specifically to Mozart's "Bach year," 1782. It is now known, however, that the work was composed a full decade earlier than that. Wolfgang Plath demonstrated some forty years ago, on the

Example 14.3a. Bach, *Art of Fugue*, BWV 1080, opening of Contrapunctus, 1, 3, and 5

Example 14.3b. Mozart, Fugue in G Minor, K. 401, mm. 1–3, 46–48, 81–84

basis of the handwriting in the autograph, that the composition was in all likelihood composed in the late summer of 1772.[22] Mozart scholarship, it seems, has not yet fully come to terms with the implications of this discovery, the most significant of which, clearly, is that Mozart not only knew, but had already begun his confrontation—his *Auseinandersetzung*—with J. S. Bach's most significant and challenging contrapuntal keyboard music by the early 1770s. This, of course, again raises the question as to the source of this exposure. If it was not the good Baron van Swieten, then who? Evidence already presented above strongly suggests both Leopold and J. C. Bach as plausible intermediaries. But an even more likely candidate is worth consideration.

It is known that Padre Giovanni Battista Martini (1706–84), who among other things was the teacher of Johann Christian Bach in the late 1750s and an admirer of Johann Sebastian Bach during the composer's lifetime, owned a fragmentary but musically complete copy of a print of the *Musical Offering* as early as April 1750. He also possessed a manuscript copy of much of the E-Minor Partita, from *Klavierübung* I,[23] and most likely *Klavierübung* III as well. (At all events, he quotes the opening of *Dies sind die heilgen zehn Gebot*, BWV 678, in his *Storia della Musica*.)[24] Therefore, it would have been altogether consistent with his interests as a contrapuntist (and with his passion as a bibliophile) for him also to have acquired a copy of the *Art of Fugue*—through J. C. Bach or others—well before the visit of the Mozarts to Bologna in 1770.

It is important to keep in mind that Mozart's involvement with the fugue in the early and mid-1770s, while, on the one hand, remarkable and perhaps unique with respect to its specific evocation of J. S. Bach and in its breathtaking display of the most sophisticated contrapuntal virtuosity, was, on the other hand, symptomatic of the newly kindled infatuation with traditional fugal procedures among Austrian composers at the time. Hitherto largely a specialized stylistic device, mainly identified with music for the church and ritualistically associated with a few traditional moments in the Mass and elsewhere, the new phenomenon, as is known, now introduced contrapuntal and fugal procedures into secular instrumental ensemble music as well. It also had aesthetic and ideological connections with the so-called *Sturm und Drang* episode of the mid-1770s. Its full dimensions, at least for the chamber music of the period, have been copiously documented by Warren Kirkendale.[25]

Among the best-known manifestations of this trendy contrapuntal fashion are the "learned," and not a little pretentious, fugal finales in three of Haydn's String Quartets, op. 20 (composed 1771), and, in emulation of them, Mozart's String Quartets in F Major and D Minor, K. 168 and K. 173, respectively, composed in late summer 1773. These compositions, however, for all their fugal expositions, stretti, inversions, and retrogrades, have essentially little, if anything, to do with J. S. Bach. They reflect, rather, textbook models and are more than a little dependent on conventional thematic and contrapuntal formulas, such as the descending chromatic *soggetto* of Mozart's K. 173 or the subject of Haydn's F-Minor Quartet finale (ex. 14.4). (The latter archetype is clearly discernible as well, to a greater or lesser degree, in the subjects of Bach's *Musical Offering* and Mozart's K. 401.)

However, one important literary source, technically and ideologically, for this renewed interest in the venerable, if nearly moribund (but not yet quite extinct), strict, or learned, style in composition does exhibit specific connections to J. S. Bach: the writings of the Berlin theorists Marpurg and, especially, Johann Philipp Kirnberger (1721–83), whose advocacy of the *Kunst des reinen Satzes* caught fire during the 1770s in Vienna. There was, then, in this respect, a transmission to Mozart, along with other Austrian composers, of what we may describe as a specifically Bachian ethos, regarding "serious" or "strict" composition.

Most important and obvious is the fact that the more imaginative composers of the time recognized the aesthetic potential of transforming a textbook thematic stereotype—for example, in the minor mode, a popular four-note motif constructed from two pairs of pitches: the first pair representing the tonic chord with a leap (up or down) from tonic to dominant (or vice versa), the second pair representing the dominant (perhaps with the downward leap of a diminished seventh from the sixth degree to the leading tone)—if one were to remove it from the domain of the merely pedagogical and aim to release its inherently powerful expressive properties. Doing so could introduce into the sphere of the hitherto innocuous symphony, for example, in place of the routine major-mode arpeggio fanfares in the opening allegros that passed for "themes," a more serious, more intense, more personal thematic statement. An example that comes readily to mind is the opening of Mozart's precocious Symphony in G Minor, K. 183/173dB, composed by October 5, 1773 (ex. 14.5).

Example 14.4. Haydn, String Quartet, op. 20/5, finale, opening theme

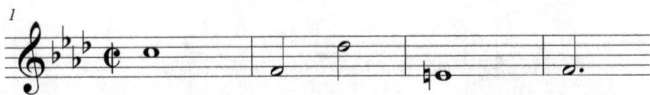

Example 14.5. Mozart, Symphony in G Minor, K. 183/1, opening theme

We owe, then, to this retrospective return to late Baroque melodic convention the invention of something quite new in symphonic writing: what we may call the "Passionate Allegro Theme." There was also the recognition of the dramatic, even heroic, potential of such an academic contrapuntal device as stretto, if strategically introduced (perhaps in the course of a development section). An example can be found in the same movement (ex. 14.6).

Broadly speaking, these symptoms of the *Sturm und Drang* phenomenon are perhaps best understood as part of a general reaction against (or impatient boredom with) the facile, *galant*/rococo, minimalist aesthetic that had permeated and dominated European musical culture for some fifty years, since the 1720s. It is easy to see how this style would not wear well in the long run and could not satisfy any formidably equipped composer—a Haydn or a Mozart. By the 1770s the complex, intellectually challenging, deeply expressive music of Bach was literally waiting to be (re)discovered. Its (re)discovery was perhaps as inevitable as anything in history, or at least in art history, can ever be: the most gifted composers of the 1770s and 1780s were under-challenged and undernourished, and they were thirsting for such nourishment and challenge as the music of Johann Sebastian Bach could provide. This was true, too, of course, not only for composers but also for the most thoughtful connoisseurs: a Baron van Swieten, for example.

***

All of the foregoing notwithstanding, I do not wish to disavow the conventional wisdom proclaiming the signal importance of the year 1782 and of the weekly performances at the home of Baron van Swieten. The conventional wisdom is correct: the significance of those sessions cannot be overestimated; they were of decisive

Example 14.6. K. 183/1, mm. 87–93

importance for Mozart's later artistic development. But our understanding of the precise nature of their significance, and of the ways in which Mozart henceforth approached and appropriated the music of Bach needs to be, if not altogether reevaluated, nonetheless modified.

The year 1782 does indeed represent the period, if not of Mozart's first encounter, then of his first extended, intensive, and systematic study of the keyboard music of J. S. Bach, along with the oratorios of Handel. Mozart wrote to his sister on April 20, 1782, that "The Baron van Swieten . . . gave me all the works of Handel and Sebastian Bach to take home with me (after I had played them to him)."[26]

During his years in Berlin as Habsburg "ambassador extraordinary" to the Prussian court (1770–77) van Swieten belonged to the circle of Princess Anna Amalia (1723–87). Like the princess, he was a pupil of Kirnberger's, through whom—and also through none other than Anna Amalia's brother, Frederick the Great, himself—van Swieten became a fervent admirer of the music of J. S. Bach. He later became close to C. P. E. Bach in Hamburg. We know that the works in the baron's possession included the Two- and Three-Part Inventions, the French and English Suites, the partitas, a copy containing the fugues of *The Well-Tempered Clavier*, the *Musical Offering*, "Part 3" of the *Klavierübung*, the six organ sonatas, BWV 525–30, arranged for two claviers—even a copy of the Magnificat prepared from the original autograph, which had been in C. P. E. Bach's possession.[27]

Mozart's reignited confrontation with the music of J. S. Bach, begun under the aegis of van Swieten, passed through at least three—actually four—distinct phases that may be characterized as transcription, imitation, assimilation and synthesis, and transcendence.

Stage 1: Conscientious, indeed reverential, transcription. This consisted of making arrangements of Bach's fugues, taken mainly from *The Well-Tempered Clavier* (but from other sources as well), for strings: quartet and probably trio (perhaps also string quintet). K. 405, which survives in Mozart's autograph, consists of five four-part fugues from Book 2 of *The Well-Tempered Clavier*, arranged for string quartet. They are the first five four-part fugues from the set: namely, those in C minor, D major, D-sharp minor (here in D minor), E-flat major, and E major.

Another series, K. 404a (whose authenticity has been challenged but is largely accepted) consists of six three-part fugues arranged for string trio. This time they are all provided with newly composed preludes, most of them presumably by Mozart. Three are from *The Well-Tempered Clavier*. From Book 1: no. 8 in D-sharp Minor (here in D Minor); from Book 2: nos. 14 in F-sharp Minor (here in G Minor) and 13 in F-sharp Major (here in F Major). The group also contains Contrapunctus 8 from the *Art of Fugue*, preceded by the F-Major Adagio from the D-Minor Organ Trio, BWV 527, which serves as a prelude to the Contrapunctus; also movements 2 and 3 from the C-Minor Organ Trio, BWV 526, presented here as a prelude and fugue; finally, a fugue by Wilhelm Friedemann Bach with a newly composed prelude by "Mozart." It is worth observing that all the arrangements are scrupulously literal—reverential, one might say—and that they include items from the organ trios, which we know were in van Swieten's possession, as well as a fugue from the *Art of Fugue*, which we otherwise do not know for a fact to have been in van Swieten's collection.[28]

Stage 2: After faithful transcription Mozart proceeded to stylistic imitation. The best-known example, and the only Bachian composition of this period that Mozart managed to complete, is the Prelude and Fugue in C Major, K. 394/383a. This is the work that is accompanied by the famous letter to his sister Nannerl, in which Mozart relates:

> My dear Constanze is really the cause of this fugue's coming into the world. . . . As she had so often heard me play fugues out of my head, she asked me if I had ever written any down, and when I said I had not, she scolded me roundly for not recording some of my compositions in this most artistic and beautiful of musical forms, and never ceased to entreat me until I wrote down a fugue for her. So that is its origin.[29]

Two points are worth noting about this passage. First, Mozart claims that while he had "often" played "fugues out of my head," he had never "written any down." Apparently he had completely forgotten about K. 401. Second, Stanley Sadie has

taken Mozart's claim that he wrote this composition to please his wife as an indication that the composer himself was not particularly enthusiastic about fugal writing.
Sadie comments:

> It would . . . seem that the prospect of pleasing his fiancée and paying his respects to
> van Swieten rather than any profound impact made by the music of Bach or Handel,
> lay behind the countless fugues which he started during 1782—started, but did not
> finish; for to Mozart these were nearer to technical experiments than to genuine artistic
> expression, so the spur to complete them was absent. (Almost everything he wrote for
> Constanze, incidentally, was left unfinished.)[30]

It is worth remembering, however, that in his letter to Nannerl, Mozart refers to
fugue as "this most artistic and beautiful of all musical forms" (*das künstlichste und
schönste in der Musick*)—a characterization strongly suggesting that the composition
of K. 394 represented more than merely a wish to oblige Constanze or van Swieten.

As for Mozart's fugue, it is clear that he derived the subject from the C-Major
Fugue of *The Well-Tempered Clavier*, Book 1. In effect, Mozart detached the four
opening notes from the beginning of Bach's subject and appended them to the end
(ex. 14.7).

The fugue is an imitation; but perhaps it should more properly be considered
an homage to J. S. Bach. As a composition, the work is less than altogether successful. Apart from the rather wooden, regular two-measure phrases throughout (a
point already observed by Edward Lowinsky), the appoggiaturas of the countersubject are unprepared and unmotivated; they seem to have been introduced only for
the sake of creating a dissonant "Bachian" effect.[31] Similarly, the later sequential
chain of fourths, especially in the stretti in diminution, is quite awkward. In effect,
while Mozart may have managed to capture the surface of Bach's fugue, he missed
its essence.

Stage 3: Assimilation and synthesis. The ultimate artistic accomplishment of
Mozart's 1782 encounter with Bach was to find a way to incorporate the stylistic
vocabulary and technical complexity of Bach's music into the framework of his own
personal instrumental idiom. This Mozart achieved by the end of 1782. He knew
that he had made a decisive advance. On December 28, 1782, Mozart wrote to his
father: "I should like to write a book, a short introduction to music, illustrated by
examples."[32] At just that time he was putting the finishing touches on the first of the
six string quartets he would eventually publish and dedicate to Joseph Haydn: the
Quartet in G, K. 387, which bears the date "li [*sic*] 31 de decembre 1782" at the top
of the autograph score. The G-Major Quartet is Mozart's first mature masterpiece
in the genre of the string quartet. Within the previous six months Mozart had completed two other "watershed" masterpieces in his career: the Piano Concerto in A,
K. 414/385p, the first of the mature Viennese piano concertos; and *Die Entführung
aus dem Serail*, the work that had preoccupied him for an entire year (from July 30,
1781). It is easy to imagine that when Mozart reflected on what he had achieved in

Example 14.7. (a) Mozart, Fugue in C Major, K. 394/2, subject; (b) Bach, *Well-Tempered Clavier* 1, Fugue in C Major, BWV 846/2, subject

these works he concluded that he had something of value to say on the subject of music. (So why not write a book!)

What he had achieved in the G-Major Quartet—most spectacularly and famously so, in the last movement—was a reconciliation, a rapprochement, of the antithetical polyphonic and homophonic principles of the fugue and the sonata. I deliberately refrain from calling it a "synthesis": It is not, strictly speaking, a synthesis, since the two idioms appear programmatically in stark alternation from section to section throughout the movement. But by introducing the two idioms into the same movement Mozart demonstrated the effectiveness, the viability—the validity—of strict fugal procedure for the contemporary Classical style (ex. 14.8).

The principal lesson for Mozart of the encounter with the music of Bach through the stages of transcription, imitation, and assimilation was not only that it made available an enormous expansion of stylistic and technical resources. Most important, all this Bachian armory was in the service of a profoundly deepened understanding of the nature of musical expression. Finally, as the G-Major Quartet had at least suggested, these resources had the capacity of being effectively subsumed within the prevailing contemporary instrumental idiom.

After 1782 Mozart made ever more natural, more self-confident use of the compositional resources he had appropriated from Bach. Contrapuntal sophistication and harmonic subtlety were henceforth something self-evident: *eine Selbstverständlichkeit.* The transparent and kaleidoscopically changing textures of even the most modest pieces, such as the miniature divertimenti for three basset horns, K. 439b, are so exquisite and refined that they could, and should, serve as late eighteenth-century instructive counterparts to Bach's Three-Part Inventions, that is, as models of the Classical-era ideal of strict part writing (ex. 14.9).

Another striking example of what could be termed "Classical counterpoint" is the opening theme of the Serenade in E-flat for Wind Instruments, K. 375, again with its iridescent transparency and understated, ever-changing, quasi-polyphonic dialogue taking place below the theme (ex. 14.10).

Example 14.8. Mozart, String Quartet, K. 387, finale, mm. 1–23

Example 14.9. Divertimento for Three Basset Horns, K. 439b, Minuet, mm. 1–30

Example 14.10. Serenade in E-flat for Wind Instruments, K. 375, movement 1, mm. 1–17

Mozart continued to imitate Bach, that is, to challenge—and, if possible, surpass—J. S. Bach on his own terms: to indulge his own propensity (no doubt acquired from the example of Bach) for overt exhibitions of compositional bravado. By the fall of 1787 he was prepared to unleash them in a veritable fireworks display of contrapuntal virtuosity in two towering masterpieces: the dance scene from the first act finale of *Don Giovanni* (premiered on October 29, 1787), in which three orchestras play three dances simultaneously in three different meters, and the contrapuntally saturated coda of the fourth movement of the "Jupiter" Symphony (dated August 10, 1788), in which the five themes of the movement are continually combined and recombined in mutually invertible counterpoint, much in the manner of a Bachian permutation fugue (ex. 14.11).

It is tempting to suggest that Mozart consciously derived the "Jupiter" coda from the example of Bach's permutation fugue.[33] But I have not found any evidence that Mozart was familiar with any of Bach's strict permutation fugues. As for the dance scene from *Don Giovanni*, I know of no such *tour de force* involving conflicting meters in the music of Bach. What is most miraculous is that both escapades—the dance scene and the symphony coda—while challenging the technical and aesthetic limits, and no doubt the intellectual capacities of the contemporary audience, manage nonetheless to remain within the basic stylistic context of the late eighteenth century.

That the stages of Mozart's Bach "reception"—transcription, imitation, assimilation/synthesis, and (if one is willing to accept my gloss on the "Jupiter" and *Don Giovanni* examples) transcendence—represent a conceptual, not a chronological, progression, is made clear by Mozart's journey to Leipzig in 1789. The visit precipitated yet one more systematic phase of largely derivative stylistic imitation. It was during this visit that Mozart heard Bach's motets: *Singet dem Herrn* for certain, probably *Jesu, meine Freude*, and perhaps others as well, performed by the choir of the Thomasschule. Mozart's reaction was witnessed by Friedrich Rochlitz, who later described it in a famous anecdote, part of which was cited earlier (chapter 12). Rochlitz's report continued:

> [Mozart] was told that this School . . . possessed the complete collection of his motets and preserved them as a sort of sacred relic. "That's the spirit! That's fine!" he cried. "Let's see them!" [*Das ist recht, das ist brav—rief er: zeigen Sie her.*] There was, however, no score of these songs; so he had the parts given to him; and . . . Mozart sat himself down, with the parts all around him . . . and, forgetting everything else, did not get up again until he had looked through everything of Sebastian Bach's that was there. He requested a copy, valued it very highly, and, if I am not very much mistaken, no one who knows Bach's compositions and Mozart's *Requiem* will fail to recognize . . . the study, the esteem, and the full comprehension of the spirit of the old contrapuntist achieved by Mozart's versatile and unlimited genius.[34]

Example 14.11. Mozart, Symphony no. 41 in C Major, K. 551, "Jupiter," finale: five themes employed contrapuntally in the coda

Bach's immediate influence upon Mozart's late vocal music is evident not only in the fugal choruses of the Requiem but most notably, as is well-known, in the episode for the "armed men" from the act 2 finale of *Die Zauberflöte*. The music for this scene is set in the style of a Bach chorale prelude and even uses the melody of the Lutheran chorale "Ach Gott, vom Himmel sieh darein" as a cantus firmus. Moreover, as Reinhold Hammerstein has observed, its counterpoints closely resemble elements from the movement "Gute Nacht, o Wesen" from Bach's motet, *Jesu, meine Freude*, BWV 227 (ex. 14.12).[35]

I suspect that Mozart was inspired to set the scene in this fashion after studying those parts for the "complete collection of [Bach's] motets" (*die vollständige Sammlung seiner Motetten*) mentioned by Rochlitz that were preserved in the Thomasschule; for among them were not only the sources of *Singet dem Herrn* and *Jesu, meine Freude* but also a set of parts for Bach's chorale cantata *Ach Gott, vom Himmel sieh darein*, BWV 2, whose opening movement is set in motet style.

It was, in fact, not unusual at the time for motet-style choruses from Bach's cantatas to be preserved together with the manuscripts of the motets proper. Particularly pertinent in this respect is a mid-eighteenth-century score manuscript miscellany [D B, Am. B. 12–14], copied in Berlin and belonging to the collection of the Princess Anna Amalia—and thus surely available to Baron van Swieten, too—that unites the opening chorus of *Ach Gott, vom Himmel* with the equally motet-style opening chorus of *Aus tiefer Not schrei ich zu dir*, BWV 38, and the motet *Jesu, meine Freude*, BWV 227.[36]

At the end of Mozart's life the example and challenge (or provocation) of J. S. Bach make their appearance not only in the context of such major compositions as *Die Zauberflöte* and the Requiem, but even in the unlikely arena of a piece for a mechanical clock. The so-called Fantasy in F Minor, K. 608, composed in March

Example 14.12a. *Die Zauberflöte*, act 2: scene of the armed men, mm. 1–15

Example 14.12a.—*(concluded)*

die - se Stra - ße   voll Be - schwer   -   den,

1791, is in many respects Mozart's boldest effort at unabashed Bachian style imitation.[37] The piece's ritornello, with its heavy downbeat chords and contrasting dotted figures, seems to contain an allusion to the E-Flat Prelude from *Klavierübung* III, published in 1739, which Mozart surely got to know through van Swieten (ex. 14.13).

The ritornello alternates here with a number of episodes, two of which are complete fugues that are based on the same theme and are studded with inversions, stretti, and harmonic, indeed, enharmonic audacities that propel the first fugue of this F-minor composition into the key of F-sharp minor, whereupon the ritornello reappears in that key. Complementing the reference of the ritornello theme to that of Bach's *Klavierübung* prelude, Mozart's fugue theme, for all the Bachian artifice of its ensuing treatment, has in fact been borrowed from George Frideric Handel. It is effectively a condensation (or reduction) of the double subject of the opening fugue from Handel's only authentic, published collection of such pieces, the *Six Fugues or Voluntarys [sic] for the Organ or Harpsichord* (ex. 14.14).[38]

More important than his witty thematic allusions to both Bach and Handel is the fact that Mozart seems to have striven here not only to emulate but to trump the structural conception underlying the prelude and fugue from the *Klavierübung*. Bach's prelude and fugue are, typically, autonomous, self-contained compositions: in fact, in the original edition of the *Klavierübung* they are placed, respectively, at the beginning and end of the compilation, and thus emphatically separated from each other by no fewer than twenty-five intervening compositions. Mozart, in contrast, by inserting the fugues as episodes between the ritornelli of his fantasy, has managed to combine the major premises of Bach's prelude—the ritornello form and regal character—with the idea of a multi-sectional fugue that is the central premise, and the hallmark, of Bach's grandiose concluding work into a single continuous composition.

Example 14.12b. "Gute Nacht," from *Jesu meine Freude*, BWV 227/9, opening

Example 14.13a. Bach Prelude in E-flat, BWV 552/1, mm. 1–10

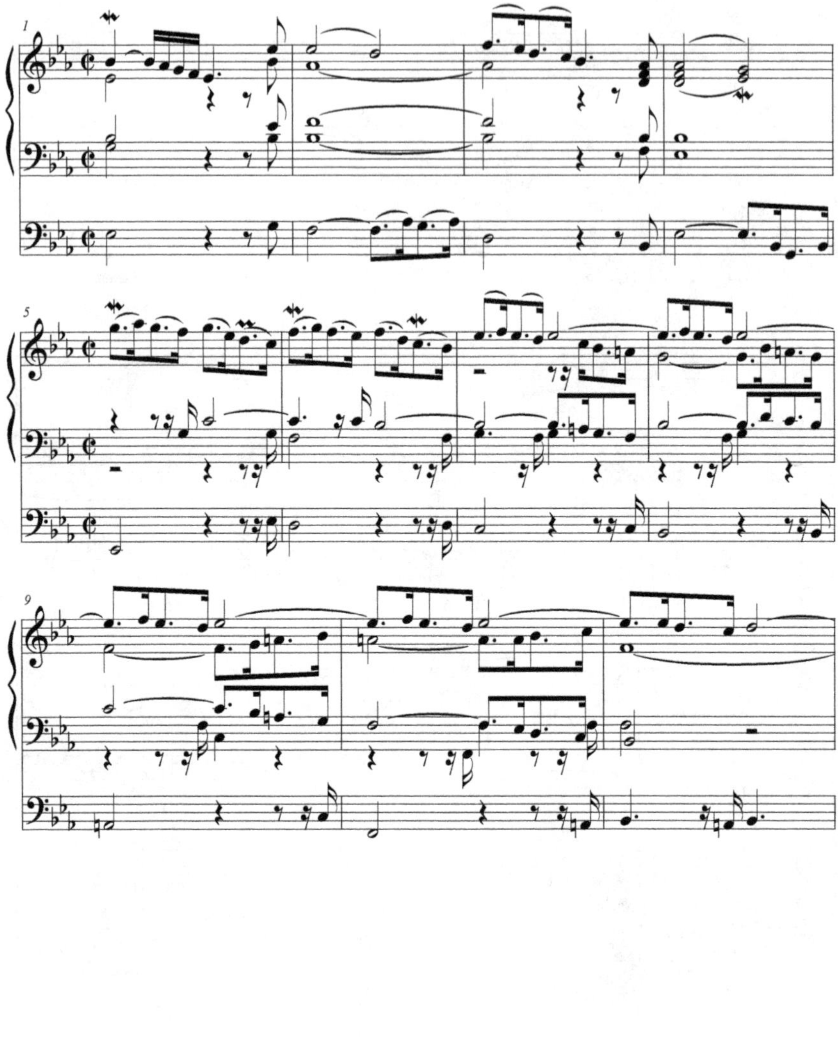

Example 14.13b. Mozart, Fantasia in F Minor for Mechanical Organ, K. 608, opening

Example 14.14a. Handel, Fugue in G Minor, HWV 605, mm. 1–12

Example 14.14b. K. 608, mm. 13–21

The fantasy, then, not unlike the finale of the G-Major String Quartet, K. 387, programmatically unites within a single movement two contrasting compositional models or principles—this time both intimately associated with the figure of Johann Sebastian Bach, and both, at least since Bach, traditionally regarded as polar antitheses: those of prelude and fugue. That Mozart saw fit to do this by means of a fugue theme stolen from Handel is all the more piquant.

Of course, the whole notion of such combinatorial virtuosity—the synthesis and unification of opposites, the idea of a universal music as constituting a musical universe—all this, too, is an essential part of Johann Sebastian Bach's legacy to Wolfgang Amadeus Mozart.[39]

ᴥ   ᴥ   ᴥ

Mozart's encounter with Johann Sebastian Bach was, in the end, energized not only by the sense of *discovery*—of the archaic, the alien, the Other—but also by a sense of *recognition*: the recognition in Bach's music of the successful fulfillment and embodiment of many of his own artistic impulses. In the uncompromising, intricate stylistic and expressive musical idiom of Johann Sebastian Bach, Mozart had not just discovered the Other; more significantly, he had come to recognize a hitherto largely unacknowledged and undeveloped part of his own musical personality. It was a matter, if anything, of *self*-discovery.

Chapter Fifteen

Mozart's Unfinished

Some Lessons of the Fragments

I

Mozart has left a long trail of unfinished compositions. They come in all sizes and, variously distributed, at all times throughout the course of his creative life. Between the 626 whole numbers of the last version of the Köchel catalog (Köchel 6), published in 1964, there are listings for more than 120 fragmentary pieces—that is, about one for every five completed works. But that number does not convey the full picture, since there are no fewer than 33 fragmentary works that have regular "Köchel" numbers—works like the Requiem, K. 626 and the C-Minor Mass, K. 427/417a. The number 33, then, should really be subtracted from the 626 and added to the 120, bringing the proportions—in round numbers—to something like 600 to 150, or one fragment for every four completed works. Some forty years after the appearance of Köchel 6, the *Neue Mozart-Ausgabe* published a facsimile edition of the surviving fragments reflecting the results of the extensive handwriting and paper investigations undertaken in the intervening decades. The volume includes a tabulation that effectively confirmed the earlier assessment. According to the latest research, the total number of known Mozart fragments now stands at 159.[1]

There are unfinished pieces in the "London Sketchbook" dating from the year 1764, when Mozart was eight years old;[2] others continue to appear up to the very end with the Requiem. But the fragments are by no means evenly distributed throughout the composer's life. The years 1777 to 1779 were the critical years of Mozart's travels to Mannheim and Paris, the first extended journey without his father and one during which he experienced his first serious, and frustrating, love affair (with Aloysia Weber—see chapter 13), along with continual professional disappointments in Paris, and, above all, the death of his mother there in early July 1778. This may help explain the appearance of the first substantial unfinished works at this time. Although no fragments survive from 1777, among the six extant torsos from the years 1778–79 we find a Singspiel (*Zaide*, K. 344/336b), a church piece (a thirty-four-measure Kyrie fragment in E-Flat, K. 322/296a, dated to early 1779),[3] and a couple of remarkable concertos for multiple soloists (to which I shall return).

Mozart's first months in Vienna, beginning in March 1781, constituted another crucial turning point in his life. This time the incompletion rate was high: during the following nine months, until the end of that year, there is one unfinished composition for every two completed works (6:12). Physical and emotional stress may hold the explanation. This was the period just following the premiere of *Idomeneo*, which took place in Munich in January 1781. It was no doubt a time accompanied by feelings of exhaustion, exhilaration, letdown. The premiere of *Idomeneo* was followed by six months of perpetual crisis, marked by the adjustment to life in Vienna and the painful process of breaking with Salzburg—a process that, on the one hand, severely damaged Mozart's relationship with his father and, on the other, culminated not in marriage but rather in his ignominious "divorce," sealed with a kick to the rump, from the service of the archbishop. Of course, this was a blessing only barely disguised, and Mozart knew it.

Not surprisingly, the greatest concentration of fragments dates from the composer's first half-dozen years in Vienna. During this period (1781–87) there are traces of over ninety unfinished compositions—twenty in the year 1782 alone, most of them evidently following the premiere of *Die Entführung aus dem Serail*, K. 384, on May 29 and embracing his marriage to Constanze Weber on August 4. In contrast, for the entire early period—the sixteen years from 1764 to 1780—there are only some thirty such documents altogether.

Over the course of the last four years of his life, from 1788 on, Mozart managed to complete around ninety compositions (K. 533 to 626), and managed *not* to complete some twenty-five further works, for a completion ratio of just over three to one. According to his own thematic catalog, in the year 1788 Mozart succeeded in finishing some thirty dated compositions.[4] According to the latest research, it is also the Viennese year with the smallest number of unfinished compositions: just two.

In pondering such statistics one must keep in mind that many of Mozart's works, finished as well as unfinished, cannot be definitely dated. Moreover, even if we had precise dates for every composition, knowing the mere number of works composed in a given period of time still would not mean very much, since a little contredanse counts as "1" (e.g., K. 534), as much as does *Don Giovanni* (K. 527). And, indeed, the same point should be made about the unfinished works. They range in substance and content from the notation of a brief thematic idea of perhaps two or three measures to torsos of gigantic dimensions like the C-Minor Mass and the Requiem. While some fragments do no more than record the most embryonic of beginnings, others preserve nearly complete compositions—compositions that may even be performable in whole or in part.[5] This is clearly so in the case of multi-movement compositions—operas, concertos, sonatas, along with the Mass and the Requiem—in which some of the individual numbers were completely finished. There is one intriguing implication of this: namely, it is conceivable that a composition listed in

Köchel 6 as an independent, single-movement piece—say, a rondo (or an andante) for flute (or violin, or piano)—may actually be the only finished movement of what Mozart originally had intended as a full-size concerto or sonata.[6]

Given their numbers, it is perhaps not very surprising that virtually every compositional genre is represented among the fragments: church music, German and Italian operas, concert arias, Lieder, symphonies, along with chamber music, concertos, sonatas, and pieces for a colorful variety of instrumental combinations and soloists. The only form that is absent altogether is the opera seria. But this is readily explained: Mozart only took up the composition of a serious opera when he had received a firm contract—entailing a firm deadline, on the one hand, and a lucrative fee, payable upon delivery, on the other. Works of that kind always took highest priority and were not readily set aside.

For the rest, we can detect several distinct patterns of distribution of the unfinished works among the various musical genres. There are a striking number of woodwind pieces. There are also a considerable number of unfinished church pieces—mostly the opening measures of Kyrie settings. As Alan Tyson has shown, many of these date not from the Salzburg period but from the later Vienna years. He suggests that they originated around 1788.[7] Similarly, there are numerous contrapuntal and fugal drafts that are now known to date from many different times, rather than to be concentrated, as previously thought to be the case, in the year 1770, on the one hand (in connection with Mozart's studies with Padre Martini), or, on the other hand, around the year 1782: the time when Mozart is supposed to have been strongly encouraged by both his wife Constanze and by Baron van Swieten to write fugues.[8]

II

From a purely musical point of view an intriguing collection of incomplete compositions consists of the scores of some half-dozen instrumental compositions, mostly concertos, that had reached an advanced stage of formation before they were set aside. There can be no doubt that Mozart had been seriously committed to these pieces. They first appear in 1778 and reappear sporadically throughout the Viennese period.

Concerto for Piano, Violin, and Orchestra in D Major, K. 315f

The first substantial torso belongs to a double concerto—for piano, violin, and orchestra in D major—which Mozart began in November 1778 in Mannheim on his journey home from Paris. The movement extends for 120 measures and constitutes the composer's longest incomplete work up to this time (ex. 15.1).

Example 15.1. Concerto for Piano, Violin, and Orchestra in D Major, K. 315f, mm. 1–4

Mozart intended it for himself and for the excellent Konzertmeister of the Mannheim Orchestra, Ignaz Fränzl (1736–1811).[9] The heading on the first page of the autograph manuscript is complete except for the date—an indication that Mozart was entirely confident about the prospects for the work.[10] The substantial opening ritornello is completely scored. (At seventy-four measures it is the longest Mozartean concerto ritornello except for that of the C-Major Piano Concerto, K. 503.)[11] With the entry of the solo, however, the accompaniment is missing. The draft contains all or most of the thematic material of exposition; it also prepares for the modulation to the dominant, finally breaking off upon the arrival of the pivotal "V of V" (dominant of the dominant) harmony, the threshold of the new key.

The draft of the double concerto is an example of what may be called "block" or "sectional" composition. In each formal section Mozart first enters the melody or principal motivic parts, then the bass, then the filler parts. He evidently proceeds then to finish the scoring of the drafted section before moving on to the next.

Sinfonia Concertante for Violin, Viola, Cello, K. 320e

Probably no more than a year later, sometime in the course of 1779, Mozart began to compose another multiple concerto, equally ambitious in scope and content, this time 134 measures in length. It was to be a sinfonia concertante for violin, viola, cello, and orchestra. It was written soon after his return to Salzburg, almost certainly at about the same time as the famous (and finished) Sinfonia Concertante in E-Flat for Violin and Viola, K. 364/320d.[12] It carries the adjoining number 320e in *Köchel 6* (ex. 15.2).

As in K. 364, the viola part is transposed and intended for *scordatura* tuning; this time the transposition is a whole tone lower. As in the Double Concerto, K. 315f, the opening ritornello is again completely scored; and once again, upon the solo entry the accompaniment is missing. This time, however, the solo parts are continued through the presentation of the secondary theme in the dominant and on to the soloists' closing theme. But the autograph breaks off before the cadence. In effect, however, the entire exposition has been notated: the arrival in the dominant this time is not only prepared, as it is in K. 315f, but confirmed. But once again only the opening ritornello is fully scored. This is, then, another example of "block" composition.

The two concerto drafts share approximately the same formal, and even temporal, dimensions: in performance they each last about four minutes and continue to the change of key—stopping either at the threshold of the dominant or just crossing over it. This much of the form was evidently necessary, but also sufficient, to enable Mozart to fix and secure the viability of the new composition: defining and recording its principal thematic material along with its first significant modulation in anticipation of its completion at some future date.

Example 15.2. Sinfonia Concertante for Violin, Viola, Cello, K. 320e, mm. 1–10.

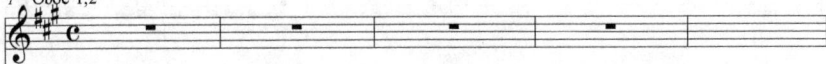

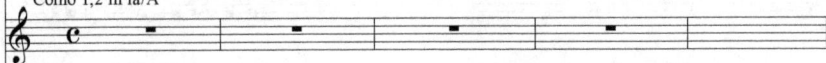

Example 15.2.—*(concluded)*

Horn Concerto in E-Flat, K. 370b, K. 371

In March 1781, at the very beginning of his Vienna period, Mozart began work on a horn concerto. Its unfinished state reveals that his compositional procedures changed in two respects. First of all, in contrast to the two preceding works, we now have material for two movements—both of them incomplete. Interestingly enough, the second movement, a rondo, is more complete than the first. Mozart, then, apparently did not compose the movements in consecutive order; nor did he feel constrained to complete one entirely before moving on to the next.

It is difficult to know exactly how much of the first movement, K. 370b, was written, because the manuscript was cut up into numerous pieces and eventually scattered around the world.[13] Most likely, the entire movement was drafted. The entire opening ritornello, the solo exposition, the dominant tutti, the brief development section, and most of the recapitulation are present (ex. 15.3).

Example 15.3. Horn Concerto in E-flat, K. 370b, mm. 1–15

Example 15.3.—*(concluded)*

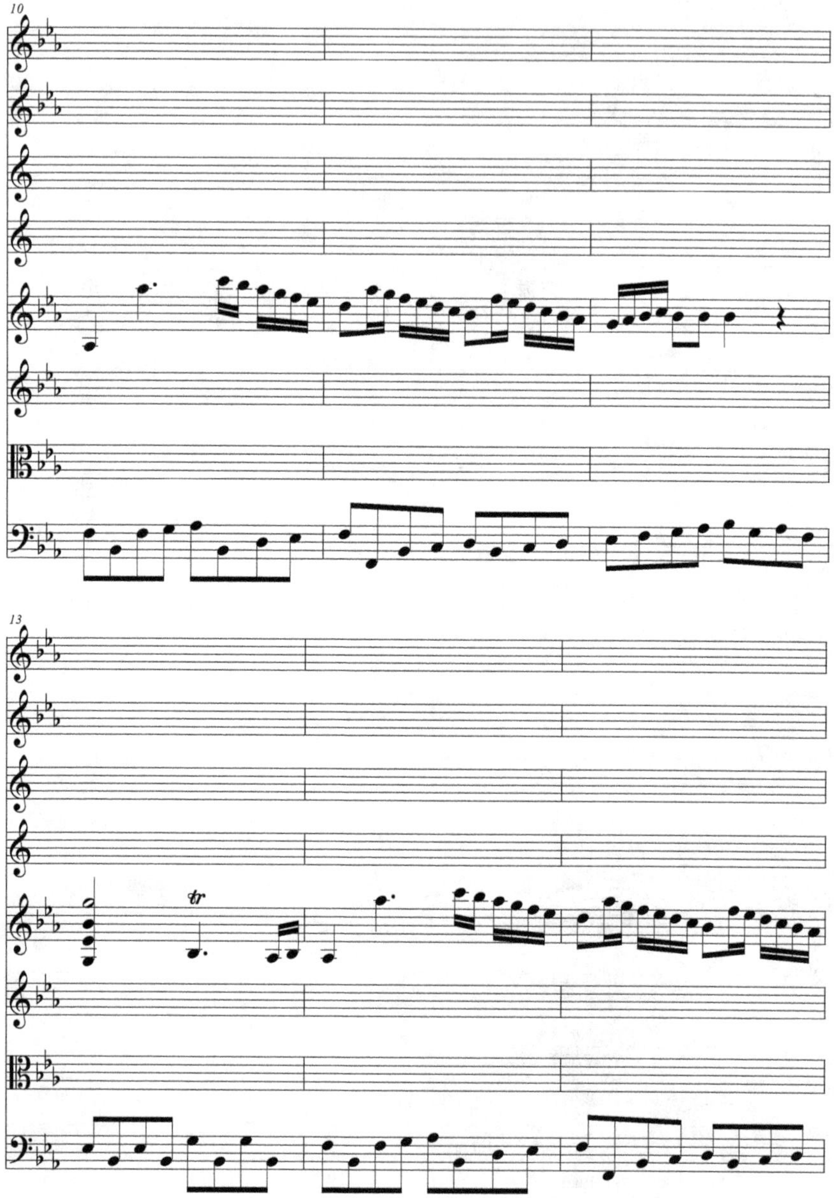

Unlike the Double and Triple Concertos, K. 315f and 320e, however, the movement is nowhere fully scored—only the principal parts are notated: melody plus bass, along with any motivically active accompanirnent.[14]

The second difference between this draft and those of the two pre-Vienna concertos is this: in the earlier concertos Mozart apparently composed section by section in fully scored "blocks": finishing each formal section before beginning the next. Here he is composing "horizontally": entering the principal melodic or thematic parts (plus bass) for the whole movement before filling in the remaining accompaniment—a quite different compositional method often described as the creation of a "continuity draft."

The autograph for the second movement, the Rondo, K. 371, contains a heading with composer's name and the date: "21 de mars 1781" (ex. 15.4).

The presence of the date suggests that Mozart considered this piece in effect "composed," even though it was not completely scored. The movement is indeed complete, however, in the sense that the notation reaches the end. It is in fact a combination of "block" and "horizontal" composition. The first two refrains of the rondo were completely scored; for the solo episodes and remaining refrains only the principal parts were written down.[15]

Concerto for Basset Horn in G, K. 621b

Finally, a draft survives for a Concerto for Basset Horn in G Major, dating from 1787 or 1788.[16] The draft extends for a full 199 measures (ex. 15.5).[17]

Although it is not completely notated, it may have been completely composed. First of all, the score breaks off at the end of a full double leaf, or bifolio. That is, it may well have continued on a new leaf, now lost. Second, it is virtually identical to the Clarinet Concerto in A, K. 622, which, of course, was completed—some three years later, at the very end of Mozart's life.[18] The basset horn concerto can be taken as ideally representing the one pole of Mozart's compositional method: what I have been calling "horizontal" composition.[19]

What all these compositions have in common, apart from their outstanding quality and unfulfilled promise, is their less-than-conventional choice of soloist or combination of soloists.[20] It is clear—and sometimes specifically documented—that Mozart enthusiastically embarked on these compositions with a particular performer (and perhaps even a particular performance) in mind. It is just as clear that at some point his expectations were dashed, whereupon he set the piece aside—no doubt with the firm intention of resuming work whenever an opportunity for a performance should present itself.

III

Considerably more, of course, could be said about Mozart's approach to the task of composition. The principal tangible evidence bearing on this question continues to

Example 15.4. Horn Concerto in E-flat, K. 371, mm. 1–13

Example 15.5: Concerto for Basset Horn in G, K. 621b, mm. 1–10 be that provided by the autograph manuscripts of the music.[21] But Mozart's letters and other contemporary testimony shed valuable light on the question, as well. They testify, first of all—if the composer is to be taken at his word—to his need and desire for congenial circumstances, peace of mind, and adequate time to plan and to contemplate. In a letter to his father from Paris, dated July 31, 1778, Mozart declared, "I love to plan works, study, and meditate."[22] Some five years later, in a letter to his father from Vienna, dated July 5, 1783, he remarked, "I prefer to work slowly and with deliberation."[23] Mozart, however, rarely had these amenities—time least of all. He no doubt composed at his legendary breathtaking speed out of necessity, not inclination.[24]

It is important, at all events, to distinguish the act of composing—inventing—from the act of writing down music. When the creative challenge was relatively unproblematic—as, for example, in the composition of simple recitatives or ball-room dances—then the act of conception and the activity of writing for Mozart were virtually simultaneous. As he reported to his mother from Milan on October 20, 1770, while he was at work on his opera *Mitridate*, "I cannot write much [i.e., to her at the moment], for my fingers are aching from writing [composing] so many recitatives."[25] On the other hand, Mozart's most significant works were the product of a shorter or longer period of intense gestation—much, perhaps most of it, internal rather than on paper, but no less intense for that: the grander the conception, the more intensive the preliminary planning. According to Mozart's widow, Constanze, "When some grand conception was working in his brain, he was purely abstracted, walking about the apartment, and knew not what was passing around."[26] But even after such internal preparation there was often the need for further working out, this time on paper. This was notably the case when Mozart determined to raise the professional stakes for himself—namely, by publishing the composition. On such occasions, it would seem that the degree of his artistic self-criticism was heightened—or, perhaps, that the level of his personal self-confidence was lowered. This may help explain why the original manuscripts for compositions intended for publication—compositions, that is to say, that Mozart wished not only to present to contemporary audiences but to preserve in relative permanence (in effect "for posterity")—by and large contain a significantly greater concentration of reworked and rejected passages than do the manuscripts of more "occasional" works (works like the concertos discussed here) that were intended perhaps for but a single performance. The heavily corrected manuscripts of the six celebrated string quartets Mozart was soon to publish—with a dedication commending these spiritual offspring to his revered older colleague, Joseph Haydn, and the "fruit," in Mozart's words, "of a long and laborious study"—provide perhaps the most dramatic example of Mozart exercising (or laboring under) his severest powers of self-criticism.[27]

To return to the unfinished concertos: our examination of the manuscript scores of this handful of musical fragments suggests one final general point about Mozart's compositional procedures. Whether he adopts the "block" approach typical of the pre-Vienna works in this genre or the "horizontal" approach occasionally encountered during the Vienna period—and these, along with a continuum of mixtures and combinations of the two, represent his usual methods in the larger instrumental forms—it appears that the creative act was always driven forward, step by step, along the unfolding form. Mozart, unlike Haydn, did not construct formal models or composition plans—plotting out in advance an opening idea in one corner of his score, a second theme somewhere else, or perhaps mapping the harmonic design of a development section by marking the cadence tones but leaving the connecting links (the transitions between these strategic points) to be added later on.[28] In a real sense, the act of composition for Mozart seems rather to have been a very fluent thing, indeed a "stream" of consciousness, or at least of artistic instinct wherein, as far as one can see, one thing (i.e., one musical idea), literally led to the next. After his death, Mozart's widow remarked that Mozart composed music as if he were writing a letter.[29] This may be what she meant.

Epilogue (*ossia* Postmortem)

Had Mozart Lived Longer: Some Cautious (and Incautious) Speculations

I

When Mozart died at 12:55 on the morning of December 5, 1791, the score of the Requiem lay unfinished on his desk. In addition, the torsos of over 150 further unfinished works were scattered in his Vienna apartment. Some were the briefest jottings; others represented substantial portions of incipient masterpieces. Among them one finds virtually every musical genre of the late eighteenth century: compositions for the church, German and Italian operas, concert arias, Lieder, symphonies, chamber music, concertos, sonatas, and pieces for a colorful variety of instrumental combinations and soloists.[1] Many of these works would certainly have been completed had Mozart lived longer.

Mozart's remarkably long list of unfinished works reflects the poignant fact that his life itself was unfinished—cut off at the height of his powers at the age of not quite thirty-six. It is hard to disagree with the common view that Mozart's early death was probably the most tragic single event in the history of music. And it is understandable that music lovers in their more morbid and whimsical moments wonder: What if he had lived longer? For obvious reasons scholars and biographers are less likely to permit themselves to entertain speculations on a question of this kind. But what if one were to take the question seriously for a moment? Doing so not only has its idle fascination but also its share of surprises and ironies.

To get things started, let us first consider another intriguing hypothetical proposition—in fact the exact converse of our chosen question—namely, what if Mozart had died even earlier, say, when he was Franz Schubert's age? Here there is no need for speculation. Franz Schubert (January 31, 1797, to November 19, 1828) died two months before his thirty-second birthday. If Mozart had died at Schubert's age, he would have departed this world in November 1787. His last work would have been *Don Giovanni*, K. 527, completed October 28, 1787. This means that the last hundred-plus compositions listed in the Köchel catalog would never have been written: among them the operas *Così fan tutte*, *La clemenza di Tito*, and *Die Zauberflöte*, and also the Clarinet Quintet, the Clarinet Concerto, the last two piano concertos, the "Prussian" string quartets, the last three symphonies, and, of course, all of the Requiem.[2]

On the other hand—what if Mozart had lived on? We have some concrete data to work with in attempting to answer responsibly this manifestly unanswerable question. Needless to say, certainty about Mozart's likely activities in his "afterlife" is greatest for the period immediately after his death and grows ever more tenuous as one peers further into the years that follow. The first thing Mozart would have done, of course, was complete the Requiem. He had the strongest incentive to do so: a firm commission of a lucrative fee of apparently 50 ducats.[3]

Before he had retired to what was to be his deathbed on Sunday, November 20, 1791, the composer had invested some five weeks of concentrated work on the Requiem. During that time he had managed to finish entirely only the first of the fifteen projected movements of the work. But he had almost completed the second and had also entered the principal vocal and instrumental parts of seven further movements into his working score. Given Mozart's pace, he would, had he lived, doubtless have completed the Requiem in less than four weeks—that is, well before his thirty-sixth birthday on January 27, 1792.

With the completion of the Requiem we exhaust what can be asserted with virtually complete certainty about Mozart's "posthumous" activities. But it pays to carry on.

II

In December 1790, the impresario Johann Peter Salomon (1745–1815) traveled to Vienna from London with a double objective. In the words of an obituary for Salomon published in London:

> He determined to engage Haydn and Mozart, not only to write exclusively for him, but to conduct their compositions in person. For this purpose he went to Vienna, where after several interviews with both these great musicians, it was mutually agreed that Haydn should go to London the first season [i.e., 1791], and Mozart the next [i.e., 1792]. They all dined together on the day fixed for the departure of the travelers; Mozart attended them to the door of their carriage, wishing them every success, and repeating, as they drove off, his promise to complete his part of the agreement the following year.[4]

Mozart had long wished to travel to England. He had spent fifteen enjoyable and productive months there as a child (from April 1764 to August 1765), almost the entire time in London. And he made it clear on several occasions in later years that he harbored a great fondness for the British, describing himself at one point as "an out-and-out Englishman" (*ein ErzEngelländer*).[5] (He seems, incidentally, to have sympathized with the British at the time of the American Revolution.)[6] In the early 1780s Mozart had taken some English lessons; and during the years 1786 and 1787 he began to form serious plans, through the agency of some English friends, to visit England and to secure either an opera contract or a concert tour in London. In short, Mozart must have accepted Salomon's invitation with great enthusiasm.

As it turned out, Haydn was asked to stay on in London for a second season; and the absence of any communication between Salomon and Mozart during the course of the year 1791 suggests that no firm plans for Mozart to visit England during 1792 were ever developed. Mozart's long-sought visit, then, had been postponed; but we can be quite certain that it ultimately would have materialized. Had Mozart not died in the meantime, he would presumably have been invited for the 1793 season—as was in fact Haydn, perhaps only because Mozart was no longer alive.[7] And, as in the case of Haydn, perhaps, the deteriorating political situation in Europe at the time, owing to the shock waves of the French Revolution, would have impelled Mozart as well to postpone his visit until 1794.[8]

But Mozart may well have traveled elsewhere: perhaps to Amsterdam, or Hungary, or Russia. We know that in September 1791 Count Razumovsky discussed the prospect of inviting Mozart to Russia with Prince Gregor Potemkin,[9] and that in December Mozart had received an annuity of 1,000 gulden from a group of Hungarian nobles, and an offer of an even greater sum had arrived from Amsterdam.[10]

In the meantime Mozart would have begun to reap the benefits of the colossal success of his last opera, *Die Zauberflöte*, which premiered on September 30, 1791, with Mozart conducting. Although its initial reception was lukewarm, *Die Zauberflöte* soon gained enormous popularity.[11] We can be sure that the librettist, Emanuel Schikaneder, who was also the enterprising managing director of the Theater auf der Wieden, the house where *Die Zauberflöte* was performed, would have been keen to capitalize on the work's success and would have contracted Mozart for a series of *Singspiele* for the ensuing seasons, surely one per year at the least. It seems safe to assume that Mozart would have produced these works over the following five or six years (interrupted, of course, by his trip to London at some point during the mid-1790s), while continuing to produce other operas whenever an attractive commission came his way. As for their subject matter, at some point in the mid- or late 1790s Mozart would have composed *Der Zauberflöte zweiter Teil* to a libretto by Johann Wolfgang von Goethe. In 1794 Goethe had heard a performance of Mozart's *Zauberflöte* in Weimar, where he directed the court theater and opera, and soon thereafter set to work on a sequel. He prepared a draft of *Der Zauberflöte zweiter Teil* in 1795–96 and tried, without success, to stimulate interest in it among composers in the years immediately following.[12] Mozart, of course, would not have shared their problem of following in the footsteps of the composer of *Die Zauberflöte*.

Eventually Mozart would have composed a serious or "heroic" *Singspiel* similar in character to Beethoven's *Fidelio*, which premiered in 1805. The text would have been another work of Goethe's: *Faust*. In later years Goethe lamented that he could find no composer adequate to the task of setting *Faust* to music. He once remarked to Eckermann, who had urged him not to despair of finding appropriate music for his masterpiece: "It is absolutely impossible. . . . The music has to be in the character of *Don Giovanni*; Mozart would have had to compose *Faust*."[13] We may safely postulate that Goethe would have prevailed on Mozart to compose a Singspiel on *Faust* within, say, a year or two following the publication of part 1 of the immortal drama in 1806—the performance taking place either in Schikaneder's Theater auf der Wieden in Vienna or, more likely, at Goethe's court theater in Weimar.

We have to reckon, then, with the loss of a *Faust* opera with music by Mozart as well as a sequel to *Die Zauberflöte* with a text by Goethe. Moreover, at some point Mozart would almost certainly have composed an opera on a Shakespearean theme. An admirer of William Shakespeare, he alluded to *Hamlet* more than once in his letters,[14] and his wife remarked that "Mozart was fond of reading and well acquainted with Shakespeare in the translation."[15]

More significantly, Italian operas and German *Singspiele* based on Shakespeare had been popular in Vienna for quite some time. A successful Singspiel by Georg Benda entitled *Romeo und Julie* was presented in Vienna in 1783—that is, early in Mozart's Viennese period. In December 1786, *Gli equivoci*, based on *The Comedy of Errors*, was set to music by one of Mozart's English friends, Stephen Storace (1762–96). The libretto was by Lorenzo Da Ponte, the librettist of Mozart's *Le nozze di Figaro*, which premiered in Vienna earlier that same year. The enthusiasm for Shakespeare held throughout the following decade. In 1799 Antonio Salieri offered an operatic version of *Falstaff*. We are justified, then, in lamenting the loss of a Shakespearean opera from Mozart's pen.[16]

III

To return to Mozart's postponed English journey: had Mozart gone to London, he would no doubt—like Haydn—have been commissioned by Salomon to compose, among other things, six new "London" symphonies on the grandest scale. Moreover, had Mozart gone to London specifically for the 1794 season, it seems quite possible that Haydn, then sixty-two years old and weary, would not have undertaken (or even have been invited for) his second London tour of 1794–95, for which he composed his six last symphonies. In short, had Mozart lived, posterity might have inherited six more symphonies by Mozart—and six fewer by Haydn.

The interconnected affairs of Mozart and Haydn would have been altered in another respect. In April 1787 the seventeen-year-old Beethoven had arrived in Vienna to study composition with Mozart. In fact he had an audition with Mozart on that occasion. But before he could arrange for lessons, the young student suddenly had to return to Bonn to attend to his sick mother. Beethoven returned to Vienna in November 1792 and remained there for the rest of his life. Since Mozart was dead, he arranged to take composition instruction from Haydn and studied with him for about a year—that is, until Haydn set off in January 1794 on his second London tour. At all events, Mozart had been especially impressed with Beethoven's improvising abilities in April 1787. He allegedly remarked to a friend at the time, "Keep your eyes on him; some day he will give the world something to talk about."[17]

It seems safe to conclude, therefore, that Mozart would have agreed to take on Beethoven as his pupil. Moreover, as in the case of another of Mozart's particularly talented pupils, Johann Nepomuk Hummel (1778–1837), Mozart may have offered to Beethoven an opportunity to live in his home where (as Hummel's father reported in his son's case) he would "have everything free, lessons, lodgings, food."[18] Beethoven's lessons with Haydn were less than altogether successful.[19] Whether he would have fared any better with Mozart—and whether the experience would have done his own compositional development good or ill—is beyond even idle conjecture.

Mozart's excursion to London could well have led to the composition of other major works besides the symphonies for Salomon. One of the lingering questions about Mozart's "afterlife" is whether he would ever again have collaborated with Lorenzo Da Ponte (1749–1838), the brilliant librettist of *Le nozze di Figaro* (1786), *Don Giovanni* (1787), and *Così fan tutte* (1790). At first blush, the answer would seem to be no. For Da Ponte, who had settled in Vienna in 1783, had become involved in various scandals and was dismissed from his position as Imperial Court Poet by order of the emperor and, in the spring of 1791, was obliged to flee Vienna.[20]

Following his dismissal from the Viennese imperial court in 1791, Da Ponte traveled about Europe but finally settled in New York in 1805. After helping to introduce Italian opera to the New World (among other things he produced *Don Giovanni* there in 1825), Da Ponte ultimately became the first professor of Italian language and literature at Columbia University. Between his departure from Vienna in 1791 and his arrival in New York in 1805, Da Ponte spent most of his time in London, where he continued to produce serious and comic opera librettos. Among them was *La scuola de' maritati*, based on Shakespeare's *The Taming of the Shrew*, set to music in 1795 by Vicente Martin y Soler.[21]

In London Mozart would undoubtedly have renewed his acquaintance with his old English friends, the composers Thomas Attwood (1765–1838, his former pupil) and Stephen Storace; Storace's sister, Nancy (1765–1817), who had created the role of Susanna in the 1786 premiere of *Figaro*; and the Irishman, Michael Kelly (1762–1826), who had created the role of Don Basilio in the same opera. All these individuals were engaged at the time at the King's Theatre. With these connections,

Mozart surely would have endeavored and succeeded in securing an opera commission. If so, there is every reason to believe that he would have collaborated again with his greatest librettist, Da Ponte, on another opera. (Perhaps this would have been Mozart's Shakespearean opera—an opera buffa, of course. It would have been Da Ponte's third libretto drawn from the works of the Bard.)[22]

For the rest, Mozart in London, like Haydn before him, would have deepened his acquaintance with, and his admiration for, the oratorios of George Frideric Handel with similar consequences, no doubt, for his later activities. Perhaps, too, he would, like Haydn, have received an honorary doctor of music from Oxford University.

IV

Mozart would probably have been back in Vienna well before the end of the 1790s. Throughout the decade, except for the journey to London, he would have continued to compose instrumental music and also—more intensively than at any time since he had left Salzburg—church music. That Mozart cultivated a lifelong interest in church music is amply attested. Constanze claimed that church music was "his favorite genre" (*dieß sein Lieblingsfach sey*).[23] Until recently it seemed that Mozart had virtually abandoned church composition once he had settled in Vienna in 1781. It turns out, however, that several unfinished church compositions that had always been assumed to belong to the Salzburg period actually date from late in the Vienna years—the period after 1787.[24]

In 1790 Mozart emphasized his skills as a church composer in support of a petition for an appointment as second court Kapellmeister, and just one year later he offered his services to the municipal council of Vienna as an (unpaid) assistant to the ailing Kapellmeister of St. Stephen's Cathedral, Leopold Hofmann (1738–93).[25] Upon Hofmann's death in 1793 Mozart would finally have succeeded to the position of Kapellmeister of St. Stephen's and finally begun to indulge his talents as a church composer. His efforts in this respect would have been further stimulated by his exposure to Handel's oratorios in London. And it seems virtually inevitable that Mozart, too, like Haydn, would have been commissioned to compose secular oratorios on the Handelian model. After all, the texts for both Haydn's *Die Schöpfung* (1798) and *Die Jahreszeiten* (1801) had been prepared by Baron Gottfried van Swieten, the director of the imperial library in Vienna and one of Mozart's patrons.

As for instrumental music, Mozart's brilliant career as a piano soloist had reached its zenith in Vienna in the mid-1780s—specifically in the years 1784 to 1786, during which he had composed no fewer than twelve extraordinary piano concertos. During the remaining five years of his life, however, only two further piano concertos followed. It is unlikely that Mozart would have composed many more in later years. The Vienna public, as Mozart predicted, had tired of him in the role of piano virtuoso.[26] (Moreover, he had no doubt tired of it himself.)

But Mozart certainly would have composed more chamber music. In 1789 he had been commissioned by King Friedrich Wilhelm of Prussia to write six string quartets. He had only managed to complete three of them by the time of his death: the quartets, K. 575, K. 589, and K. 590. Since Mozart allegedly was paid 100 *friedrichsdors* for the first of these, he would surely have completed the commission. In fact, sketches for further quartets belonging to this series survive.[27] Similarly, of six piano sonatas commissioned by the Prussian Princess Friederike at the same time as the string quartets, Mozart had completed only one: the Sonata in D Major, K. 576. Again, though, there is evidence that he had begun to compose others.[28]

Whether Mozart would have composed further symphonies after the "Jupiter" Symphony—beyond the six he would have written for London, of course!—is not clear. Haydn wrote no further symphonies after his return from London, although he continued to compose for another eight years and lived for another fourteen. Moreover, except for the last three symphonies, all written in the summer of 1788, Mozart had composed no symphonies at all during his Vienna years specifically for Viennese performance. The "Haffner" Symphony, K. 385 (1782), was written for Salzburg, while the "Linz," K. 425 (1783) and "Prague," K. 504 (1786) symphonies were composed for the cities from which they derive their nicknames. On the other hand, Mozart's last three symphonies are thoroughly innovative works that signal a significant departure in his stylistic development, one that we can well imagine he would have wanted to pursue. And there is no telling how Mozart would have responded to the symphonies of his former pupil Beethoven, which had begun to appear in the year 1800.

V

We have been able to construct a scenario that reasonably postulates some of Mozart's likely activities for barely a decade following his death in December 1791. Soon after the turn of the new century, Mozart would have just turned forty-four. His mother (1720–78) had lived to be fifty-eight, his father (1719–87) sixty-eight, his sister (1751–1829) seventy-eight. Had Mozart, like his father lived to be sixty-eight, he would have died in 1824, just three years before Beethoven, and would have heard, and been influenced by, the latter's music. Conversely, Beethoven would have heard (or at least studied) and, just as likely, been influenced by Mozart's compositions of the 1790s, 1800s and 1810s, and early 1820s.

What the effects of this mutual stimulus would have been on the work of both artists we cannot begin to imagine: more piano sonatas from Mozart, perhaps; maybe more operas from Beethoven. In 1819, Mozart, along with Beethoven and several dozen other prominent Viennese composers (including Franz Schubert and Franz Liszt), would have been invited by the publisher Anton Diabelli (1781–1858) to contribute a variation on a waltz theme of Diabelli's for a projected publication. Mozart (like Schubert, Liszt, and all the others) would surely have composed only one—not, like Beethoven, thirty-three.

VI

It is tempting to think that genius never ceases to create and grow. We are strongly inclined to assume that Mozart, arguably the most formidably gifted musical genius in history, would have continued to compose—and to produce masterpieces of the highest order—for as long as he lived: into his sixties, his seventies, and beyond. But a moment's reflection reveals that this need not be the case. Gioacchino Rossini (1792–1868) effectively ceased composing in 1829, at the age of thirty-seven. Rossini, one can object, was not a genius of Mozart's stature. Then consider the case of Albert Einstein (1879–1955). One of the seminal thinkers of all time, Einstein effectively ceased producing significant work by 1925, when he was just forty-six. Einstein, one can object, was a natural scientist, not an artist; the creative rhythm is not the same. Then consider, finally, the case of William Shakespeare (1564–1616). Around 1610, at the age of just forty-six, Shakespeare completed *The Tempest* and retreated to Stratford-on-Avon, successful and fulfilled, to spend his remaining years tending his garden.

But perhaps the *dénouement* in Mozart's case would have been entirely different. Mozart was one of the most widely traveled individuals of his time. It has been precisely calculated that of the 13,097 days of his life (thirty-five years, ten months, nine days), 3,720 (ten years, two months, eight days) were spent traveling.[29] He visited—or at least spent some time in—no fewer than 202 towns and cities, extending alphabetically from Aachen to Zurich and geographically from Amsterdam in the north to Pompeii in the south, London in the west, and Vienna in the east. But despite the obvious discomforts in the eighteenth century, Mozart proclaimed his need to travel—that it was, in fact, a necessary stimulus to his talent. He once confessed: "A fellow of mediocre talent will remain a mediocrity whether he travels or not; but one of superior talent (which without Impiety I cannot deny that I possess) will go to seed if he always remains in the same place."[30]

By 1810, Mozart would have essentially remained in the same place, Vienna, for close to thirty years. So it is not altogether outlandish to imagine that around then the fifty-four-year-old composer and Freemason—long since disgusted with the ever more intolerant, more repressive, political atmosphere in Vienna and the ever more alien social and cultural climate in post-revolutionary Napoleonic Europe—would have received an invitation from his old acquaintance and his best librettist, Da Ponte, asking him to join him in the New World to help establish an Italian opera in New York, and that Mozart would have accepted the invitation!

Perhaps, like Da Ponte, he would have decided to remain in New York and, once again like the clever poet, entered the groves of academia, becoming Da Ponte's colleague at Columbia University and respectably ending his days as a professor of music—his first regular job.

Notes

Prologue

1. Dahlhaus 1985, 1986. All citations from that chapter in the following are taken from the Harriss translation.
2. The headings, respectively, of chapters 8 and 9 in Bukofzer 1947.
3. The Gluck and Haydn quotations appear together in Blume 1970, 28.
4. See the excerpts in Treitler 1998, 670–82.
5. Herbert Dieckmann, "Diderot's Conception of Genius," cited by Edward E. Lowinsky in "Musical Genius: Evolution and Origins of a Concept" (1964), reprinted in Lowinsky 1989, 46.
6. An even earlier harbinger perhaps can be observed in the transition passage from the "Confiteor" to the "Et expecto" movements of Bach's B-Minor Mass. See chapter 9 in this volume.
7. In this connection, see Subotnik 1991.
8. Downes 1961, 279.
9. "Bach the Progressive" (1976) and "On Bach's Universality" (1986), both reprinted in Marshall 1989.
10. Eggebrecht 1970.
11. I would emphasize now, more than three decades after this essay was written, that Mozart (and Haydn) eventually produced another grand synthesis by incorporating into the works of their maturity the sophisticated polyphonic procedures of the Baroque masters—above all, of course, those of Bach and Handel. See chapter 14 in this volume.
12. For an opposing view of the century to that proposed here, see Webster 2003.

Chapter One

This essay is an extended version of the keynote address presented, under a different title, at the biennial meeting of the American Bach Society in April 2000 in Washington, DC. It is also an outgrowth of the author's review of Wolff 2000, which appeared in the *New York Review of Books* (Marshall 2000).

1. Soon after the appearance of the last of the 104 volumes of the NBA in 2007, Bärenreiter-Verlag announced the launch of a *Neue Bach-Ausgabe—Revidierte Edition*. The new project, which published its first volume—a new edition of the Mass in B

Minor in 2010—plans to release approximately fifteen volumes in the series at the rate of one or two per year.

2. Dürr 1977 (originally published 1951), Dürr 1976 (originally published 1957, and Dadelsen 1958.

3. Blume 1962, 1963.

4. A complete critical edition of these sources up to the year 1800 appears in three supplementary volumes of the NBA: the *Bach-Dokumente* (BDOK I, II, and III). Since the publication of the BDOK volumes, discoveries of further documents have been reported and published in the principal organ of Bach research: the *Bach-Jahrbuch* (BJ). English translations of the most important Bach documents are available in NBR.

5. Not surprisingly, our knowledge of the chronology of Bach's works has been further refined and extended in the decades since the work of Dürr and von Dadelsen in the 1950s. See Glöckner 2008, also the chapter "Life and Works 1685–1750" in Leaver 2017, 487–539.

6. These carry the numbers 1081 to 1120 in the second edition of the BWV. The most well-known are the fourteen canons on the first eight bass notes of the aria from the Goldberg Variations, BWV 1087, and thirty-one organ chorales included in the "Neumeister" manuscript of Yale University, BWV 1090–1120. See Wolff 1985.

7. The "Calov" Bible commentary—an edition of the scriptures from the year 1681 with copious interpretative commentaries by the influential Orthodox Lutheran theologian Abraham Calov (1612–86)—turned up during the 1960s at Concordia College, St. Louis, Missouri. Two editions of the relevant material, with substantial commentaries, have been published: Cox 1985 and Leaver 1985. A luxurious, three-volume facsimile edition of the complete work was published in the Netherlands in 2017 (Calov 2017).

8. In addition to the critical reports to the individual volumes of the NBA, see Marshall 1972.

9. Controversy surrounds, for example, the authenticity of Bach's most famous organ composition, the Toccata and Fugue in D Minor, BWV 565 (well-known from its use in Walt Disney's *Fantasia*). There is even a question as to whether it was originally an organ piece. See Williams 1981; Claus 1998; Wolff 2000, 72, 511–12; and Williams 2003, 155–59.

10. The literature on these topics is too vast even to attempt an adequate summary. Some notable contributions are Prinz 2005 (instruments), Haynes 1985, 2002 (pitch); Dreyfus 1987a (continuo practice), F. Neumann 1978 (ornamentation), Butt 1990 (articulation), P. Badura-Skoda 1993 (keyboard performance), and Marshall 2008 (tempo). Finally, there is the copious literature on the proper size of Bach's chorus, a controversial topic seriously reopened for the first time in forty-five years by Joshua Rifkin at the annual meeting of the American Musicological Society in Boston in 1981 and continuing to this day. For specific references, see chapter 6 in this volume.

11. See, respectively, Geiringer 1966, Marshall 1989, McClary 1987, Marissen 1995, Chafe 1991, and Dreyfus 1996. Well ahead of the game, Heinrich Besseler had proposed a view of Bach as a pathbreaker in the mid-1950s. See Besseler 1955.

12. One notable publication of recent years has actually served to increase our ignorance about the composer's whereabouts. In 2015 Michael Maul announced the discovery of a document revealing that for a period of two years in the mid-1740s Bach had apparently

abandoned his regular church duties in Leipzig. What he was doing instead is not clear. See Maul 2015.

13. Certainly the ambitious recent biography by John Eliot Gardiner (Gardiner 2013) constitutes a serious effort from any point of view. The present writer would like to think that Gardiner's approach to his subject—at least to some limited extent (the treatment, perhaps, of Bach's early life)—was a response to the challenge put forth when the original form of this essay was published in 2001. See also my review of Gardiner's book (Marshall 2014).

14. See BDOK I–III and NBR.

15. Some decades ago the US Bach scholar Arthur Mendel was asked by a film producer to serve as an expert consultant for a projected movie about Bach. Mendel advised him not to bother: you could not make a film about Bach's life. There was nothing exciting about it—except for the making of the twenty children, and you could not show that (back then).

16. Christoph Wolff's comprehensive and indispensable biography (Wolff 2000) represents the capstone of this tradition. See the present writer's review of Wolff's study cited at the outset of this chapter.

17. Freud's studies of Leonardo (1910), Michelangelo (1914), and Dostoyevsky (1928) are reprinted in Freud 1989. See also Erikson 1962 (on Luther), 1969 (Gandhi); Solomon 1998 (Beethoven), 1989 (Schubert), and 1995 (Mozart); Feder 1992 (Ives). See also Ostwald 1985 (Schumann).

18. BR, 51; NBR, 44.

19. See "Zipfel," in Grimm and Grimm 1984, vol. 31 (originally 15), 1548.

20. Forkel 1802, 3; English translation in NBR, 417–82. The passage cited appears on p. 424.

21. The Quodlibet is published in NBA I/41, edited by Andreas Glöckner (2000). The first edition, edited by Max Schneider, was published shortly after its discovery (Bach 1931). The facsimile edition of the composition (Bach 1973) includes a complete, if euphemistically rendered, English translation of the text by Charles Sanford Terry. The German original is printed in Neumann 1974, 248–49. Günther Kraft (Kraft 1956) attempted to identify and decipher the musical quotations and allusions to Thuringian folk songs as well as the numerous topical and familial references contained in the text.

22. The German original is reproduced (in facsimile only) in the NBA edition of the Anna Magdalena notebooks, NBA V/4, edited by Georg von Dadelsen (1957), 130. The translation of the first verse appears in the standard English edition of Philipp Spitta's classic biography (Spitta 1951, 2:152).

23. See chapter 2 in this volume.

24. This was the period of Bach's sojourn in Lübeck, from November 1705 to February 1706, to see and hear Dieterich Buxtehude (1637–1707). The minutes of the rebuke are published in NBR, 46–47.

25. Letter of June 25, 1708. NBR, 57. The original reads "wiedrigkeit" and "verdrießligkeit." BDOK I, 19–20 (original orthography; see preface).

26. See the pertinent documents in NBR, 118–25 (regarding the 1725 altercation with the university over the authority to direct—and be paid for—the so-called New Service at the University church); 137–38 (regarding the 1728 controversy regarding the authority

to choose the hymns for the Leipzig church service); and 172–85 (regarding the 1736 dispute with the rector about the authority to appoint the choir prefect).

27. NBR, 145. ["Mit dem *Cantor* Bachen habe Er geredet, der aber schlechte lust zur arbeit bezeige." BDOK II, 206.]

28. NBR, 152. ["daß . . . [ich] fast in stetem Verdruß, Neid und Verfolgung leben muß." BDOK I, 67.]

29. NBR, 158. ["ein und andere Bekränckung unverschuldeter weise . . . empfinden müßen." BDOK I, 74.]

30. The nature of Bach's relationship to Martin Luther is explored further in chapter 3.

31. Bach's mother was buried on May 3, 1694; his father remarried on November 27, 1694, and died on February 20, 1695. For an alternative view of the significance of Bach's status as an orphan, see Botwinick 2004.

32. The story makes its first appearance in the obituary for Bach written by Carl Philipp Emanuel Bach and Johann Friedrich Agricola and published in 1754 in Lorenz Mizler's *Neu-eröffnete Musikalische Bibliothek*. Johann Nikolaus Forkel repeated it in his 1802 biography of Bach. See NBR, 299, 425.

33. See C. P. E. Bach's letter to Forkel dated January 13, 1775. NBR, 398–99.

34. NBR, 425.

35. Reproduced in NBR, 283–94. ["Ursprung der *musicalisch-Bachi*schen *Familie*." BDOK I, 255–61.]

36. The anthology was published in a modern edition in 1935, reprinted 1966). Schneider 1966.

37. The reader lacking German will forgive this pun. ("Bach" is the German for brook or stream, "Quelle" the German for source, both literally and figuratively.)

38. NBR, 283. [der *lutheri*schen *Religion* halben aus Ungern entweichen müßen. BDOK I, 255.]

39. Bach's relationship with Martin Luther is explored further in chapters 3 and 7.

40. Hanns Bach (1555–1615) may have been a relative of Vitus, who died in 1619. According to Karl Geiringer, he was a carpenter by trade, a *Spielmann*, and court jester to the Duchess of Württemberg in Nürtingen. C. P. E. Bach owned two portraits of him— very likely inherited from his father and thus strong evidence that Sebastian was well aware of Hanns's existence and his rather embarrassing claim to fame and had deliberately omitted him from the genealogy, for in one of the portraits Hanns wears the jester's jingling bells on his right shoulder. A panel above his head bears a verse inscription: "Hie siehst du geigen / Hannsen Bachen / Wenn du es hörst so / mustu lachen. | Er geigt gleichwol / nach seiner art, / Und tregt ein hipschen / Hanns Bachen Bart." As it was translated by Henry S. Drinker: "Hans Bach, the fiddler, has a style / That when you hear him, you must smile; / It is indeed unique and weird, / In keeping with his Hans Bach beard." The second portrait is bordered by a Latin inscription reading, "Hans Bach, famous and amusing court jester, jocular fiddler, a diligent, upright, and religious man" [Hans Bach: Morio celebrius et facetus: fidicen ridiculus: homo laborios[us] simplex et pius]. See Geiringer 1954, 9–10, and Plate IV (opposite p. 32); also Richards 2012, 1:41; 2:23.

41. NBR, 291. ["ist auch der Musik zugethan. Hat sich aber niemalen zu einer *function* begeben, sondern sein meistes *Plaisir* in Reisen gesuchet." BDOK I, 260.] The family members were numbered in the Genealogy by Bach himself.

42. Erikson 1962, 52–53. The current layman's term for this is "negative role model."
43. See Freyse 1956.
44. The Arnstadt consistory minutes of February 21, 1706, relate that Bach had "hitherto made many curious *variationes* in the chorale, and mingled many strange tones in it, and that the Congregation has been confused by it." NBR, 46. ["in dem *Choral* viele wunderliche *variationes* gemacht, viele frembde Thone mit eingemischet, daß die Gemeinde drüber *confundiret* worden." BDOK II, 20.]
45. The example is reproduced from the NBA IV/3 (1961), 14–15. The editor, Hans Klotz, claims that the sources for BWV 715 seem to argue for a Weimar origin of the work. See NBA IV/3, KB (1962), 11.
46. Letter of August 15, 1736, to the Leipzig Town Council. NBR, 176. Bach introduced the phrase in the course of his quarrel with the rector of the Thomas School regarding the appointment of the choir prefect. The German original reads "ohngleich schwerer and *intricat*er." BDOK I, 88. It is noteworthy that Bach had to resort to Latin to find the appropriate adjective to describe his music.
47. NBR, 42. The speculation, first proposed by Spitta, that the "fratro" (n.b., not "fratello") was Bach's brother Johann Jacob, was first called into doubt by Wolff, who has suggested that a spiritual "brother"—namely, Georg Erdmann (1682–1736), Bach's classmate in both Ohrdruf and Lüneburg and, in October 1730, the recipient of one of the composer's few truly personal letters—may have been the dedicatee of the capriccio. See Wolff 2000, 74–75.
48. Kübler-Ross 1969.
49. Cox 1985, 19.
50. Ibid., 20. Cox's translation is appropriated here with slight modification. ["Wenn du nun wollest einen Fürsteher . . . aus dem, den du weist, daß er aus angebornen Haß dein Verderben suche, das ist nicht allein unehrlich und ungeschickt, sondern auch narrisch, und Frevel, und eine Versuchung Gottes." Ibid., facs. 84] The biblical text of Deuteronomy 23:3–4 reads as follows in the King James version: (verse 3) "No Ammonite or Moabite shall enter the assembly of the Lord; even to the tenth generation none belonging to them shall enter the assembly of the Lord for ever; (verse 4) because they did not meet you with bread and with water on the way, when you came forth out of Egypt, and because they hired against you Balaam the son of Beor from Pethor of Mesopotamia, to curse you." Calov's point seems to be that just as the Ammonites and Moabites were not elevated, since they demonstrated their hostility toward the Israelites, so should no one be raised to a position of authority who has demonstrated his hatred for those he would rule. More precisely: no one should accept as his leader anyone who has demonstrated such hatred.
51. A third brother, Johann Günther (1653–83), was "ein guter *Musicus*" as well as "a skillful builder of newly invented musical instruments" [ein geschickter Verfertiger verschiedener neu *inventi*rten musikalischen Instrumenten]. The three brothers, nos. 13–15 in the Genealogy, were the sons of the Arnstadt organist, Heinrich Bach (1615–92, no. 6), himself the brother of Sebastian's grandfather, Christoph Bach (1613–61, no. 5). See NBR, 288; BDOK I, 258.
52. NBR, 57; BDOK I, 19–20.
53. See "Endzweck" in Grimm and Grimm 1984, vol. 3, col. 468. The entry cites Kant's definition: "Der zweck, welcher die unumgängliche und zureichende bedingung aller

übrigen enthält, ist der endzweck" (capitalization thus in the original): "that purpose which encompasses the absolutely necessary and sufficient condition for all others, is the *Endzweck.*" The precise meaning of this elusive phrase is explored further at the beginning of chapter 3.

54. BDOK I, 21. The rather understated translation in NBR (p. 58) reads: "Since he could not be made to stay, consent must doubtless be given to his dismissal."

55. The Ouverture is transmitted in the "Andreas Bach Book," a major source of Bach's early keyboard works. See the discussion in Hill 1987, 336–37, 416–20. The movement is reproduced here from NBA V/10, edited by Hartwig Eichberg (1976), 47.

56. The example is reproduced from NMA IX/27/1, edited by Wolfgang Plath (1982), 94. The composition, which is transmitted entirely in the hand of Wolfgang, is now thought to have been composed by him in 1764—not two years earlier (as had been maintained by his sister, writing many decades later. It has accordingly been renumbered as K. 1e in the sixth edition of the Köchel catalog (Köchel 6). See Plath's foreword to the NMA edition, xxi.

57. See MDB, 455 and Marshall 1991, 3–4.

58. See chapter 14, example 14.7.

59. The example is reproduced from the NBA I/35, edited by Alfred Dürr (1963), 17.

60. Even before the publication of Gardiner's Bach biography mentioned earlier, path-breaking work addressing biographical issues from a political and economic perspective had been offered by Ulrich Siegele. See especially his three-part article Siegele 1983, 1984, 1986 (summarized and updated in Siegele 1997); also Siegele 1999.

Chapter Two

1. NBR, 151–52; original German text in BDOK I, 67–70. See also the facsimile edition of the letter, edited by Nathan Notowicz (ca. 1960), in Bach 1960.

2. On Anna Magdalena's musical and family background, see Schubart 1953, also Schulze 2013. The most comprehensive biography of Bach's second wife is Hübner 2004. See also Yearsley 2019. On her life after the death of Johann Sebastian, see Spree 2019.

3. Schubart 1953, 29; Hübner 2004, 38.

4. Gerber [1790] 1977, 1:76.

5. Unfortunately, not even a portrait of Anna Magdalena survives—although it is known that an oil painting of her once existed and was in the possession of C. P. E. Bach. It may have been executed in September 1732 when Bach, together with Anna Magdalena, journeyed from Leipzig to Kassel in order to examine and give a recital on the newly completed organ in St. Martin's Church. On the way he may have passed through the town of his birth, Eisenach, and arranged at that time for the Eisenach cellist and court painter, Antonio Cristofori (1701–37), to execute the portrait. See Maul 2011.

6. See NBA V/5, edited by Wolfgang Plath (1962). See also the facsimile edition (Bach 1959), edited by Ralph Kirkpatrick. Bach's keyboard works and his pedagogical method are discussed at length in chapter 5.

7. The often-fraught nature of this double role is explored further in chapter 10.

8. On the physical state of the notebook, see NBA V/4, KB, edited by Georg von Dadelsen (1957), 8, 22, and 26–27.

9. Ibid., 25.

10. Arnold Schering had already made this point. See the foreword to his edition of the notebook (Bach 1935, ii).

11. See the facsimile edition, edited by Georg von Dadelsen (Bach 1988).

12. Curiously, the various polonaises contained in the *Klavierbüchlein* are not discussed in Paczkowski 2017.

13. By Schering (Bach 1935, ii).

14. The vocal line of the "Aria di Giovannini" ("Willst du dein Herz mir schenken"), BWV 518, is notated in the treble clef. It was entered in the notebook some time after 1725 by an anonymous scribe (designated "Anonymus L 24" in the NBA catalog of Bach copyists) otherwise unknown in the Bach sources. Both the unique hand and the treble-clef notation argue against Bach's authorship of this song. See NBA V/4, KB, 113–16; also NBA IX/3, edited by Yoshitake Kobayashi and Kirsten Beisswenger (2007), 104.

15. English translation in BR, 97–98. The translation does not appear in NBR. The remaining five strophes of the poem, written in an unknown hand from the second half of the eighteenth century, are preserved on a separate sheet of paper that was bound into the notebook at a later time. See NBA V/4, KB, 60.

16. Cantata 82 was originally composed for the Feast of the Purification of Mary, on February 2, 1727. It survives also in versions for soprano (ca. 1730) and mezzo-soprano (ca. 1735). See Dürr 1976, 94. The notebook version postdates the earliest cantata version and was copied by Anna Magdalena sometime before 1733. See NBA V/4, KB, 106.

17. Wollny 2002b, esp. 33–36.

18. NBA V/4, KB, 89–90.

19. According to Hans-Joachim Schulze, the cantata was probably written around 1747 for a former student at the University of Leipzig. Schulze 2010, esp. 79–88.

20. Since no original sources for the cantata survive, its date of composition is unknown. The preponderance of opinion, largely based on stylistic evidence, has favored a Köthen origin. See the discussion in Dürr 1971, 2:700–702; and NBA I/40, KB, edited by Werner Neumann (1970), 14–16.

21. See Schulze 1979, 54–58.

22. Ibid., 50

23. The late features of Anna Magdalena's handwriting here, and the essential agreement of her version of the "aria" with that published around 1741 suggest that it may have been copied at about the same time.

24. F. Neumann 1985, esp. 290–92.

25. Unfortunately, Bach did not think of providing the composer's first name; and it is not certain whether the reference is to Georg Böhm (1661–1733), the Lüneburg organist with whom Bach evidently studied in his youth, or some less well-known composer with the same surname.

26. The title page of the principal source—penned by Bach's godson, Johann Ernst Bach (1722–77)—containing Bach's keyboard arrangements of concerti by various composers, BWV 592 and 972–82 (Deutsche Staatsbibliothek mus. ms. Bach P 280) reads *XII CONCERTO [sic] di VIVALDI*, although at least five of the originals are by other

composers: Alessandro Marcello (BWV 974); Torelli (BWV 979); Benedetto Marcello (BWV 981); and Duke Johann Ernst of Weimar (BWV 982 and 592). See the entries for these works in BWV.

27. For the handwriting identifications see Schulze 1963/64.
28. The poem is reproduced, translated, and discussed in chapter 1.
29. See NBA V/4, KB, 72.

Chapter Three

1. An English translation of the complete text of Bach's letter of resignation (actually a request for dismissal) is printed in NBR, 57; the German original in BDOK I, 19.
2. Siegele 1978, 313–15.
3. Daniel R. Melamed persuasively argues that a surviving inventory of the Mühlhausen Blasiuskirche music library allows us to identify the "choicest church compositions" Bach presumably had at his disposal at the time, some (or many) of which he may personally have acquired. The collection consisted mostly of printed works by leading seventeenth-century German masters, among them Heinrich Schütz. See Melamed 2002.
4. Wolff, "Chronology and Style in the Early Works: A Background for the Orgel-Büchlein," (1988), reprinted in Wolff 1991, 299. For the most comprehensive consideration of the work's genesis, see Stinson 1996.
5. The most complete discussion of the collection appears in Stinson 2001.
6. The connection, in particular, of the very last, "eighteenth," composition, the "deathbed" chorale, *Vor Deinen Thron tret ich hiermit*, BWV 668, to Bach's original conception, has been a matter of debate. It was entered into the original autograph manuscript as a late addition, in fragmentary form, in the hand of an anonymous copyist. See Stinson 2001, 34–38.
7. The trumpets, which double the oboes, published in earlier editions of the work, are only found in posthumous manuscripts of the work and were evidently added by Wilhelm Friedemann Bach. See NBA I/31, KB, edited by Rempp (1987).
8. Another example of such retrospective writing is the opening movement of *Wär Gott nicht mit uns diese Zeit*, BWV 14, discussed in chapter 8.
9. Bloom 1973, 5.
10. See chapter 14.
11. Bloom 1973, 11.
12. That, in fact, is the subtitle of Geiringer 1966.
13. Schweitzer 1964, 1:3.
14. Bloom 1973, 52.
15. Ibid. (Bloom's translation). Goethe made the remark in the course of a conversation on December 17, 1824, with his close friend, the statesman Friedrich von Müller (1779–1849). The original reads: "Gehört nicht Alles, was die Vor- und Mitwelt geleistet, dem Dichter von Rechtswegen an? Warum soll er sich scheuen, Blumen zu nehmen, wo er sie findet? Nur durch Aneignung fremder Schätze entsteht ein Großes." The comment was in response to apparently widespread charges at the time accusing Lord Byron of plagiarism. See Goethe 2017, 5:119.

16. For C. P. E. Bach's comment, made in reply to an inquiry from the early Bach biographer Johann Nikolaus Forkel, see NBR, 398.

17. The music library of the Michaeliskirche in Lüneburg, where Bach spent two years (1700 to 1702) as a student and chorister, contained copies of some thirty Schütz compositions. The library of the Mühlhausen Blasiuskirche, for its part, contained a copy of Schütz's famous *Psalmen Davids* of 1619. See Wolff 2000, 58; Melamed 2002, esp. 215.

18. In this connection it is important to point out as well that, although C. P. E. Bach does not mention the fact, his father was certainly aware of the music of his greatest contemporary, George Frideric Handel. Bach copied out the performance parts of Handel's cantata *Armida abbandonata*, HWV 105, in 1731, and in the late 1740s, the score of the "Brockes" Passion, HWV 48. (See Beißwenger 1992, 289–94.) Moreover, Bach made at least two unsuccessful attempts to meet Handel during the latter's visits to Halle: in June 1719, and again in June 1729 (Wolff 2000, 207–9). Conversely, there is no evidence that Handel was familiar with any of J. S. Bach's music.

19. Leaver 1978, 11–12.

20. In his letter of October 28, 1730, to his friend Georg Erdmann. NBR, 152; BDOK I, 67.

21. See Leaver 1983, 14n9. By the same token, Bach may have been reluctant to reveal to his friend Erdmann the full extent of his Leipzig income. Eberhard Spree suggests that Bach's annual income, including revenues from private lessons, instrument and music rentals, additional performances, and other sources—at least by the late 1740s—may well have been around 1,400 thalers, or about twice the sum the composser had cited to Erdmann in 1730. See Spree 2019, 48.

22. Ibid., 42, which also reproduces and transcribes Bach's receipt. Incidentally, this document evidently contains the only surviving written reference to Martin Luther in Bach's hand.

23. Freud 1939, 136–40.

24. Ibid., 138.

25. Ibid., 140 (emphasis added).

26. Schalk 1988, 34. The original reads: "Die Musica ist eine schöne herrliche Gabe Gottes, und nahe der Theologie. Ich wollt, meiner geringen Musica nicht um was Großes verzeihen. Die Jungend soll man stets mit fleis zu dieser Kunst gewöhnen, denn sie macht feine geschickte Leute." Luther [1566] 1912, 490 (No. 968). For a description of Bach's copy of the *Tischreden*, see Leaver 1983, 59.

27. Luther [1538] 1965, 324. The original Latin text in Luther 1538 [1914], 372–73.

Chapter Four

1. Taruskin 1995, 357–58.

2. Marissen 1998. In the preface to a later essay collection, Marissen reports, "over the past several decades, I have delivered hundreds of general public lectures on Bach and Lutheranism, mostly in pre-concert talks." Although he does not specify exactly how many of them were devoted to the matter of anti-Judaism in the St. John Passion one presumes that it must have been a considerable number. See Marissen 2016a, 14.

3. R. Erickson 2011.
4. A substantial excerpt, in English translation, of this document appears in Smither 1977, 110. My thanks to Robin Leaver and Michael Marissen for bringing the Luther source to my attention.
5. On the meaning of *hoi Ioudaioi*, see Marissen 2016, 128–30, 152.
6. Bail 2006.
7. Private communication from Rumscheidt to the author.
8. Marissen 2016.
9. For a review of the varying interpretations of this characterization, see Leaver 2013, 21–38.
10. See Erickson 2009, especially the section "Jews and Judaism in Bach's World," 28–32.
11. Birnbaum defended Bach against the criticism leveled against him by Johann Adolph Scheibe (1708–76), an episode touched upon later in this volume (chapter 8). Regarding Birnbaum's religion: in January 2015 Dr. Jörg Hansen, director of the Bachhaus Eisenach, informed the present writer in a personal communication, "Johann Abraham Birnbaum's grandfather, . . . also named Johann Abraham Birnbaum (1644–1704), . . . was a lawyer and Saxon politician. . . . The great-grandfather was a medical doctor at the Saxon duke's court and named Abraham Birnbaum (1612–99). His father in turn was Joachim Birnbaum (b. 1586), and his grandfather, Abraham Birnbaum (1545–1635). (I found the last two on a genealogy website http://gedbas.genealogy.net/person/ancestors/1125697424). If this is correct and there was a conversion, as indeed the name suggests, it would most likely have already occurred in Luther's time."
12. The facsimile of the passage is reproduced in Cox 1985, col. 1098 (facsimile 163).
13. Leaver 1985, 93–98. The German original in Cox 1985, 22. For an alternative interpretation of Bach's markings in the Calov Bible commentary, see Marissen, 2018.
14. On the First *Jahrgang* as a cycle, see the discussions in Gardiner 2013 and Chafe 2014.

Chapter Five

1. It is datable to the obituary for Bach published in 1754 by Carl Philipp Emanuel Bach and Johann Friedrich Agricola. See the English translation in NBR, 296–307 (esp. 303–4).
2. This can be the case in harpsichord pieces, as well—as the seven-measure-long sustained bass note in the opening measures of the sarabande from the third English Suite, BWV 808/4, attests.
3. NBR, 251–52.
4. Rampe 2016, 171–72.
5. NBR, 152. Bach's actual income at the time of his death was probably considerably higher.
6. Wolff 2000, 412.
7. NBR, 366. Agricola's comment appears in an editorial note published in the influential treatise, *Musica mechanica organoedi*, by Jacob Adlung (1699–1762), which was published posthumously in 1768. Howard Schott reasonably suggests that one of the two lute harpsichords listed in Bach's estate catalog would have been the instrument heard

by Agricola, who had studied with Bach from 1739 to 1741. See Schott 2007, 23. It seems just as reasonable to assume that the other was the work of Bach's cousin, Johann Nicolaus Bach (1669–1753), son of the "profonder Componist" Johann Christoph Bach (1642–1703) and himself both a composer and instrument maker. See the Postscript to this chapter.

8. NBR, 255–56. ["Und weiln der jüngste Herr Sohn, Herr Johann Christian Bach 3. *Clavire* nebst *Pedal* von dem *Defuncto* seelig bey Lebzeiten erhalten und bei sich hat." BDOK II, 504.]
9. Spree 2019, 103.
10. Adlung [1758] 1953, 568.
11. Adlung [1768] 1961, 2:158–62.
12. Marshall 1989, 280–81; also Speerstra 2004, 26, 46.
13. For a summary of the present state of our knowledge in this regard, see Marshall 2019.
14. See Rampe 2016, 172, which includes a photograph of the instrument.
15. Dürr 1988, 222.
16. Marshall 1989, 291.
17. Stauffer 1995, 303–4.
18. Dürr 1988, 229.
19. NBR, 156.
20. Stauffer 1995, 298–300.
21. Ibid., 317.
22. Ibid., 317–18. The use of brass strings throughout the compass also implies tuning at a low chamber pitch. Personal communications from Paul Guglietti and Mark Kroll. On pitch in Bach's keyboard music, see Marshall 2019, 268–69.
23. See Faulkner 1991, also Cornell 1991.
24. NBR, 365. ["Er hat den Klang desselben gerühmet, ja bewundert: Aber dabey getadelt, daß es in der Höhe zu schwach lautete." BDOK III, 194.]
25. E. Badura-Skoda 2017, 150–81.
26. Schulze 1984.
27. See Hill 1987 and Hill 1991. The secular repertory of the Möller and Andreas Bach volumes was surely complemented by a similar collection of chorale settings. Some of its contents may survive in the "Neumeister" collection, containing thirty-eight chorale preludes by the young Bach (thirty-three hitherto unknown), along with chorale settings by Bach's ancestors and others. See Wolff 1985.
28. Many survive in a single large volume, evidently gathered and bound together only after Kellner's death. See Stinson 1989a.
29. The strongest argument for a preferred harpsichord rendition can be made in the case of the Toccata in G Major, BWV 916. An early copy, now lost but attributed to Bach's pupil, Heinrich Nicolaus Gerber, bore the title *Concerto seu Toccata pour le Clavecin*.
30. The use of the term "capriccio" for BWV 993 is an anomaly: the work is a fugue and altogether different in design from the *Capriccio on the Absence of the Most Beloved Brother*, BWV 992. See below.
31. Schulenberg 2006, 61. See also Stauffer 1980 regarding Bach's early organ preludes.
32. The subjects are all taken from Albinoni's Trio Sonatas, op. 1 (Venice, 1694).
33. See the analysis of the two versions in Schulenberg 2006, 72–76.

34. Keller 1950, 63; Schulenberg 2006, 97. It is tempting to connect the individual toccatas, on the basis of their ranges, with Bach's organs at Arnstadt, Mühlhausen, and Weimar, and thus create the framework for a chronology. But such an enterprise is ultimately inconclusive. See the argumentation in Marshall 1989, 283–87.
35. For example, between the two fugues of the D-Minor, between the "arioso" and final fugal sections of the F-sharp-Minor, or the characteristic neighbor-note pattern in three of the four sections of the E-Minor Toccata.
36. They are an example of the so-called *Menuet de Poitou*. See Little and Jenne 2001, 71–72.
37. Hill 1987, 126.
38. The long-standing assumption, first advanced by Philipp Spitta, has been that the object of this distant precursor of the "Lebewohl" Sonata was Bach's older brother Johann Jacob. Both the identity of the "fratro" and the date, however, have recently been called into question. Hill 1987, and, especially, Wolff 1992.
39. Seventeen, if one includes the questionable Concerto in G Major, BWV 592a. See Schulenberg 2006, 136–37.
40. Schulze 1984. Only shortly before, in February 1713, Bach had begun to employ the latest Italian operatic forms in his vocal music; the recitative and the da capo aria make their first appearance in the "Hunt" Cantata, *Was mir behagt*, BWV 208.
41. Schulenberg 2006, 141, plausibly suggests that the *manualiter* compositions may all date from the late Weimar period. For other datings, see Stinson 1989b.
42. NBA VII/3, KB, edited by Dietrich Kilian (1989), 47–48.
43. As copied by Johann Tobias Krebs (1690–1762), a Weimar pupil of Bach's. A second copy in the same ms. (Berlin State Library *mus. ms. Bach* P 803) has the same title. See Zietz 1969, 67, 71, 94–98.
44. Spitta 1962 3:181–82.
45. Peter Williams has noted stylistic similarities between the opening flourishes of the organ fantasia and those found in the unaccompanied violin sonatas of 1720 (Williams 2003, 88). But George Stauffer has suggested a considerably earlier dating for BWV 542/1, namely, ca. 1708–12. Curiously, Stauffer's argument, though based entirely on stylistic analysis, does not mention the work's astonishing enharmonic writing. See Stauffer 1980, 109–10.
46. The date of the early version of the concerto has been associated with the 1719 purchase of a harpsichord by the Berlin maker, Michael Mietke, for the Köthen court. See Stauffer 1989, esp. 175–81.
47. Bach may have borrowed the idea of an instrumental recitative from the slow movement of Vivaldi's "Grosso Mogul" Concerto, a work that he had transcribed for organ, BWV 594. See Schulenberg 2006, 150.
48. This may also explain the absence of a flat in the key signature of the original manuscripts of the *Fantasia*—but not the fugue.
49. See Marshall 1989, 49, for more on the theme's complex structure.
50. Keller 1950, 161.
51. As translated in NBR, 468. Forkel 1802, 56.
52. NBA V/7, KB, edited by Alfred Dürr (1979), 86–91.
53. Ibid., 85–86.
54. See NBA IX/2, edited by Yoshitake Kobayashi (1989), esp. 38, 45.

55. Whether the Suite in A Major, even in its revised form, was conceived from the outset as part of the set is not altogether certain. Not only is it the only suite to make use of the contra octave, it is also superfluous to the key scheme of the remaining suites: A minor, G minor, F major, E minor, D minor. (See Eppstein 1976, esp. 36 and 48.) Moreover, in the earliest known copy, the Suite in A Minor, that is, the second suite, originally bore the designation "Svit. 1re." See NBA V/7, KB, 86.

56. See NBA V/8, edited by Alfred Dürr (1980).

57. See NBA V/4, KB, edited by Georg von Dadelsen (1957), and Dadelsen 1957; also chapter 2 in this volume.

58. The loure appears in the unaccompanied Violin Partita in E, BWV 1006, the polonaise in the first Brandenburg Concerto, BWV 1046, and the Orchestral Suite in B Minor, BWV 1067.

59. NBR, 469. ["Man nennt sie gewöhnlich Französische Suiten, weil sie im Französischen Geschmack geschrieben sind. Seinem Zweck nach ist hier der Componist weniger gelehrt als in seinen anderen Suiten, und hat sich meistens einer lieblichen, mehr hervor-stechenden Melodie bedient." Forkel 1802, 56.]

60. Both of Anna Magdalena's notebooks evidently bear witness to her decidedly French taste in music. See chapter 2 in this volume.

61. On the numerous special problems posed by the minuet movements in the French Suites, see NBA V/8, KB, edited by Alfred Dürr (1982), 81–84.

62. The volume has been published in a facsimile edition (Bach 1959). See also the critical edition, NBA V/5, edited by Wolfgang Plath (1962), and chapter 2 in this volume.

63. Bach's fingering method is discussed at length in Faulkner 1984, 21–38. See also Marshall 2019, 275–77.

64. Since Forkel, the three-part pieces are usually referred to as "Inventions" as well.

65. Except for the absence of F-sharp minor, the keys are the same as those described by Johann Mattheson in *Das neu-eröffnete Orchestre*, published in 1713. (See Franklin 1989, 255.) The seven ascending two-part inventions may well all have been composed at an earlier time than the remaining compositions. See NBA V/5, KB.

66. Schulenberg 2006, 187 and 468n57.

67. As translated in NBR, 97–98, including some emendations suggested by Laurence Dreyfus (Dreyfus 1996, 1). ["Auffrichtige Anleitung, Wormit denen Liebhabern des *Clavires*, besonders aber denen Lehrbegierigen, eine deütliche Art gezeiget wird, nicht alleine (1) mit 2 Stimmen reine spielen zu lernen, sondern auch bey weiterer *progreßen* (2) mit dreyen *obligaten Partien* richtig und wohl zu verfahren, anbey auch zugleich gute *inventiones* nicht alleine zu bekommen, sondern auch selbige wohl durchzuführen, am allermeisten aber eine *cantable* Art im Spielen zu erlangen, und darneben einen starcken Vorschmack von der *Composition* zu überkommen." BDOK I, 220.]

68. Butt 1990.

69. Dreyfus 1996, 10–14.

70. Ibid., 20–22.

71. Chafe 1991, 43–51, offers an allegorical interpretation of this extraordinary composition.

72. NBR, 372. ["hat er nach einer gewissen Tradition, sein Temperirtes Klavier . . . an einem Orte geschrieben, wo ihm Unmuth, lange Weile und Mangel an jeder Art von musika-lischen Instrumenten diesen Zeitvertreib abnöthigte." BDOK III, 468.]

73. Dürr 1984, 7. Another possibility suggested by Dürr is Karlsbad, where Bach sojourned with Prince Leopold for about five weeks in 1718 and again in 1720. For the original wording of the ducal arrest warrant, see BDOK II, 65.
74. Wolff 1991; Stinson 1996.
75. See Dürr 1984, and NBA V/6.1, KB, edited by Alfred Dürr (1989).
76. See White 1992.
77. See Dürr 1984, also Riedel 1969, and Brokaw 1986.
78. See the commentary by Walter Dehnhard in his edition of the work (Bach 1977), also Dürr 1984.
79. NBR, 368; BDOK III, 304. It is important to note that at the time, all "good" temperaments, not just equal temperament, tuned the thirds sharp. See Barbour 1947, esp. 71.
80. A number of possible systems have been proposed. For an overview, see Lindley 1980a, 1980b; also Marshall 2019, 268.
81. Constantini 1969.
82. See the modern edition, edited by Ernst von Werra (Fischer 1965). Fischer omits five keys: C-sharp major, E-flat minor/D-sharp minor), F-sharp major, A-flat minor/G-sharp minor), and B-flat minor—that is, all keys of five or more accidentals, with the exception of B major. On the other hand, he includes E-Phrygian as the twentieth key.
83. So designated by Friedrich Wilhelm Marpurg in his *Abhandlung von der Fuge* (1753). Cited in NBR, 359.
84. Besseler 1955.
85. Some of Bach's early fugues, like Handel's, begin with a double subject, in which the initial thematic idea (subject) is directly answered by a different one (countersubject). See Marshall 2019, 287–89.
86. Bach, too, it seems, may have planned to include a seventh suite. According to a newspaper announcement published in 1730 for the fifth partita, two more were to follow. See BDOK I, 202.
87. The composition of the partitas, however, may well have considerably antedated their publication. This is known to be the case for Partitas 3 and 6 (in A Minor and E Minor, respectively), for which early versions were entered by J. S. Bach—as fair copies—at the beginning of the 1725 *Clavier-Büchlein* for Anna Magdalena Bach.
88. NBR, 234.
89. See NBA V/1, KB, edited by Richard D. Jones (1978), 17–18. A comprehensive discussion of the publication history of the partitas of *Klavierübung I* appears in Talle 2003, 32–54.
90. BDOK I, 235. For the date see NBA V/2, KB, edited by Christoph Wolff (1981), 17.
91. Ibid., 48.
92. Bach's willingness to transpose the Ouverture a half step down from the three-flat-key of C minor to the two-sharp-key of B minor strongly suggests that he set little store in the theory of *Tonartencharakteristik*, which argued that each key had its own inherent and distinct affective character. See Steblin 2002. Rita Steblin does not discuss the challenge to the theory of key characteristics posed by the numerous examples of compositions existing in different keys usually a half or whole step apart.
93. Dreyfus 1987b.
94. Eva Badura-Skoda explores the possibility that Bach may have had the fortepiano in mind for one or more of the keyboard concertos in Badura-Skoda 1991. See also

Badura-Skoda 2017. At all events, the original autograph scores for all seven concertos explicitly designate the solo instrument as "cembalo." See NBA VII/4, edited by Werner Breig (2001), 20.

95. See Wolff 1991, 223–38, also Schulze 1981. Jane R. Stevens argues that several of Bach's accompanied concertos for one or more harpsichords—in addition to the C-Major Concerto for Two Harpsichords, BWV 1061, for which the fact is established (see NBA VII/5, KB, edited by Karl Heller and Hans-Joachim Schulze (1990), 75)—may, at some earlier stage, have been unaccompanied keyboard concertos. See Stevens 2001.

96. Marshall 1976.

97. See NBR, 350; BDOK II, 336. Although Mizler was specifically referring to a secular cantata (now lost), it is worth noting that this remark in defense of his teacher was made in 1738, that is, at just about the time Bach was assembling WTC II and during the time of the Scheibe controversy. See chapters 7 and 8 in this volume.

98. Bach may originally have planned to open WTC II with a surviving version of the Prelude in C-sharp Major, BWV 872a/1, notated in C major and in an *arpeggiando* style quite similar to that of BWV 846/1.

99. Schulenberg 2006, 246, 260.

100. Brokaw 1985.

101. Hofmann 1988.

102. Franklin 1989.

103. See the commentary in Marshall 1989, 193–200.

104. For two interesting completions of the fugue, see Cone 1974 and Schulenberg 2006, 155–58.

105. It is curious—and perhaps significant—that Bach did not follow the precedent he had established when he designated the two volumes of the series following the partitas as "Zweyter Theil" and "Dritter Theil," respectively. The composer decided in the case of the Goldbergs *not* to designate them as constituting a "Vierter Theil" of the *Klavierübung*. For the problems of dating the publications, see NBA V/2, KB, edited by Walter Emery and Christoph Wolff (1981), 94.

106. NBR, 464–65; Forkel 1802, 51–52.

107. Bukofzer 1947, 297.

108. Bach's authorship of the theme has been challenged by Frederick Neumann. See Neumann 1985 and the responses in Marshall 1989, 54–58, and Schulenberg 2006, 377; also this volume, chapter 2

109. Historical and geographical circumstances by no means preclude Bach's having known Scarlatti's music. See Marshall 1989, 46–48.

110. Specifically, the first nine pieces were entered by 1742, the five remaining pieces by 1746. See Wolff, "The Compositional History of the Art of Fugue" (1983), reprinted in Wolff 1991, 265–81, 424; also Kobayashi 1988.

111. Regarding Theile, see Carl Dahlhaus's preface to the modern edition (Theile 1965); regarding Mattheson, see Stauffer 1983. See also Snyder 1980 for a possible precedent in Buxtehude for Bach's mirror fugue.

112. Wolff 1991, 274, and Schulenberg 2006, 400.

113. Butler 1983a.

114. Schulenberg 2006, 404.

115. See NBR, 224, 302–3, 430, for the original newspaper account along with those published in the obituary and in Forkel's biography.
116. Whether the constituent movements of the collection were intended to be arranged in a specific order, however, has been a matter of controversy. See U. Kirkendale 1980; Wolff 1991, 239–58; and Marissen 2016b.
117. On the contemporary definitions of *Ricercar*, see Wolff 1991, 324–29.
118. Schulenberg 2006, 393.
119. For an opposing stylistic analysis of the ricercars, see Marissen 2016b.
120. In addition to the two ricercars, the NBA suggests realization of two two-part canons on the harpsichord. See NBA VIII/I, edited by Christoph Wolff (1974), 48, 54, 70, 78.
121. The title *Kunst der Fuge* may not have been Bach's: it appears on the title page of the autograph in the hand of his son-in-law, Johann Christoph Altnikol (1720–59). Conceivably, Bach's own title could have been *Clavierübung letzter Theil.*
122. Wolff 1991.
123. Kobayashi 1988.
124. NBR, 304; BDOK III, 86. Gustav Nottebohm was the first to propose this solution. See Wolff 1991, 259–64. But see the recent controversy in Milka 2014, Büsing 2015, Daniel 2016, and Büsing 2016.
125. Wolff 1991; and Butler 1983b. For a recent completion, see Schulenberg 2006, 422.
126. Gregory Butler has suggested that the quadruple fugue would have been the fourteenth and final fugue followed, in the publication, by the four canons. See Butler 1983b.
127. Adlung [1768] 1961, 2:135–36.
128. See also the discussion of the piece earlier in this chapter.

Chapter Six

1. NBR, 328–29. The original Latin text in BDOK II, 331–32.
2. Cron 1997: 77–81.
3. The pertinent citations (after Cron): (1) Joshua Rifkin, "Bach's Chorus," paper read at the 1981 Annual Meeting of the American Musicological Society (Boston: the initial presentation of Rifkin's thesis with Robert L. Marshall serving as respondent); (2) Nicholas Kenyon, "Musical Events," *New Yorker* (December 14, 1981): 199–98; (3) Rifkin, "Bach's 'Choruses'—Less Than They Seem?" *High Fidelity* 32 (September 1982): 42–44; (4) Marshall, "Bach's 'Choruses' Reconstituted," *High Fidelity* 32 (October 1982): 64–66, 94 (reply to [3]); (5) Rifkin; "Bach's Chorus: A Preliminary Report," *Musical Times* 123 (November 1982): 747–54 (expanded version of [3]); (6) Rifkin, "Bach's 'Choruses': The Record Cleared," *High Fidelity* 32 (December 1982): 58–59 (response to [4]); a "fuller response" by Rifkin entitled "Bach's 'Choruses' The Record Amplified" was available by mail from the Classical Music Editor of *High Fidelity*); (7) Marshall, "Bach's Chorus: A Preliminary Reply to Joshua Rifkin," *Musical Times* 124 (January 1983): 19–22 (reply to [5]); (8) Rifkin, "Bach's Chorus: A Response to Robert Marshall," *Musical Times* 124 (March 1983): 161–62 (reply to [7]).
4. NBR, 145–51; BDOK I, 60–64.
5. Schering 1936.

6. Glöckner 2006, 19–22; Glöckner 2018, 100–104. See also Richter 1907.
7. Michael Maul voices this reservation in Maul 2013, 52–53.
8. The witness was one Johann Christian Trömer (ca. 1697–1756) writing in 1745—admittedly well after the premiere (and only known performance) of the work on May 12, 1727. See NBA I/36, KB (edited byWerner Neumann), 11. On the possible parody relationship between the cantata and the B-Minor Mass, see Häfner 1977; for its implications for the performance forces, see Stauffer 1997, 213; also Stauffer 1993.
9. Michael Maul recently discovered documents that seem to indicate that Bach in Leipzig regularly paid two singers for each part. The strong implication is that at least that many singers normally performed each part during the regular church service. How many (if any) additional—unpaid—singers drawn from among the pupils of the Thomaschule might have regularly participated as well is still not clear. Maul 2013.
10. Toward the conclusion of Lesson [chapter] 3 ("The Composition of Music") of his famous 1939/40 Norton Lectures at Harvard University entitled *Poetics of Music in the Form of Six Lessons*, Stravinsky maintained: "The more constraints one imposes, the more one frees one's self of the chains that shackle the spirit." Stravinsky 1956, 68.

Chapter Seven

1. Johann Adolph Scheibe, *Der Critische Musicus, Sechstes Stück*. Hamburg, May 14, 1737. English translation in NBR, 238. The German original, as transcribed in BDOK II, 286–87, reads: "Dieser grosse Mann würde die Bewunderung gantzer Nationen seyn, wenn er mehr Annehmlichkeit hätte, und wenn er nicht seinen Stücken durch ein schwülstiges und verworrenes Wesen das Natürliche entzöge, und ihre Schönheit durch allzugrosse Kunst verdunkelte ... denn er verlangt die Sänger und Instrumentalisten sollen durch ihre Kehle und Instrumente eben das machen, was er auf dem Claviere spielen kan. ... Alle Manieren, alle kleine Auszierungen ... druckt er mit eigentlichen Noten aus; und das entziehet seinen Stücken nicht nur die Schönheit der Harmonie, sondern macht auch den Gesang durchaus unvernehmlich. Alle Stimmen sollen mit einander, und mit gleicher Schwierigkeit arbeiten, und man erkennet darunter keine Hauptstimme. ... Die Schwülstigkeit hat [ihn] von dem natürlichen auf das künstliche, und von dem erhabenen auf das Dunkle geführt; man bewundert ... die beschwerliche Arbeit und eine ausnehmende Mühe, die doch vergebens angewendet ist, weil sie wider die Natur streitet."
2. Memorandum to the Leipzig Town Council, dated August 15, 1736. NBR, 176; BDOK I, 87–88.
3. The word does not appear in such early important dictionaries as the five-volume *Versuch eines vollständigen Grammatikalisch-kritischen Wörterbuches der hochdeutschen Mundart* by Johann Christoph Adelung (Leipzig, 1774–86) or the comprehensive *Deutsches Wörterbuch* of Jacob and Wilhelm Grimm (Leipzig, 1877), or even in the modern German-English section of *Der neue Muret-Sanders, Langenscheidts Enzyklopädisches Wörterbuch der englischen und deutschen Sprache*, revised edition (Berlin, 1974). It is occasionally listed in modern German dictionaries (where it is spelled "intrikat").
4. Marshall 1989, 3.
5. Both essays are reprinted in Marshall 1989.

6. Marshall 1989, 79.
7. Dürr 1971, 13–14.
8. U. Kirkendale 1980. Although Kirkendale's specific arguments regarding the ordering and symbolic meaning of the individual items of the *Musical Offering* are debatable, her suggestion that the organization of a musical composition in this period bears similarities to the structural divisions of a classical oration as described in Marcus Quintilianus's *Institutio oratoria* is not only entirely plausible but in fact was already put forth by Gallus Dressler in his *Praecepta musicae poeticae* of 1563 and was common into the eighteenth century. See Buelow 2001a.
9. Eggebrecht 1970, esp. 260–72.
10. The term was coined in this century by Arnold Schering. See Buelow 2001a, also Buelow 2001b.
11. The German orthography and punctuation after W. Neumann 1974, 127; the English translation is mine.
12. On the Theology of the Cross and its significance in Bach's church music, see Chafe 1991.
13. See Lowinsky 1989, esp. 74–76.
14. See Poulin 1994, xiii. A comparison of the wording in the 1738 treatise with the pertinent passages from Niedt's *Musicalische Handleitung* (Hamburg, 1700) appears in BDOK II, 334.
15. As translated in Poulin 1994, 10–11, slightly emended. ["Der General Bass ist das vollkommste Fundament der Music welcher mit beyden Händen gespielet wird dergestalt das die lincke Hand die vorgeschriebene Noten spielet die rechte aber Con- und Dissonantien darzu greift damit dieses eine wohlkingende Harmonie gebe zur Ehre Gottes. . . . Wo dieses nicht in acht genommen wird da ists keine eigentliche Music sondern ein Teuflisches Geplerr und Geleyer." BDOK II, 334.]
16. The nature and extent, if any, of Bach's relationship and indebtedness to the Enlightenment have become matters of keen controversy in recent years. See R. Erickson 2011 and Marissen 2018.
17. Manuel 1983, 3.
18. In this connection see chapter 12.
19. Shaw made the comment on the occasion of the centenary of Beethoven's death (n.b., not Mozart's, as often asserted), putting it as follows: "Beethoven had a moral horror of Mozart, who in *Don Giovanni* had thrown a halo of enchantment round an aristocratic blackguard, and then, with the unscrupulous moral versatility of a born dramatist, turned round to cast a halo of divinity round Sarastro, setting his words to the only music yet written that would not sound out of place in the mouth of God" (Shaw 1981, 744).
20. Eggebrecht 1970, 272–84. See also the prologue to this volume.

Chapter Eight

Versions of this essay were presented as lectures at Tufts and Brandeis Universities, at the Baldwin-Wallace College Bach Festival, and, in 2010, at a symposium at the Juilliard School, New York, in honor of Maynard Solomon—to whom the essay is dedicated—on the occasion of his eightieth birthday.

1. See the epigraph to chapter 3.
2. Pfau 2008, Schabalina 2008, Glöckner 2009.
3. Stauffer 2008.
4. NBR, 145. The German original in BDOK I, 60. The controversial performance implications of the document are discussed in chapter 6.
5. NBR, 158 (emended). ["in *Componir*ung der Kirchen *Musique* sowohl als zum *Orchestre* meinen unermüdeten Fleiß." BDOK I, 74.] With his choice of the word "orchestre" Bach may have meant the theater. See Marshall 1989, 59–63.
6. A concise overview appears in Melamed 2018, 130. Rathey 2016 offers a comprehensive interpretation of the work along with a discussion of its origins.
7. In the autograph composing score of BWV 214 the final version is superimposed on the original draft. See the facsimile published in NBA I/36, edited by Werner Neumann (1963), ix; the transcription here is reproduced from NBA I/36, KB (1962), 84–85.
8. In this connection, see Marshall 1991, 181–84.
9. On Bach's performances of the Locatelli concerto, see Stauffer 2008, 139–40. In this connection, see also Rathey 2016, 197–207, esp. 202–4.
10. Marshall 1989, 271–93.
11. See the analysis in Dürr 1971, 255–56.
12. Wollny 2002.
13. Chapter 10 (ex. 10.1) reproduces an example from the same document which reveals Friedemann struggling with, and Sebastian effortlessly completing, an exercise in sixteenth-century style.
14. Transcription from Wollny 2002, 281.
15. A modern edition, edited by Max Schneider, was originally published in 1935 (reprinted 1966).
16. A representative selection of the texts of the polemical exchanges is available in NBR, 337–53; they are presented in their entirety in BDOK II, 286–87, 296–305, 309–10, 322, 340–62, 432–33. Regarding Birnbaum, see also chapter 4.
17. For an extensive overview of numerous recent treatments of the Bach–Scheibe controversy, including the incorporation of new documents, see Jerold 2011.
18. NBR, 176; DOK I, 88. See chapter 7 in this volume.
19. The documents pertaining to the "prefects' dispute" appear in NBR, 172–85; BDOK I, 82–91, BDOK II, 268–76. On Bach's unexplained five-week absence from Leipzig in 1744, see Langusch 2007; on his recruitment of a substitute (one Gottfried Benjamin Fleckeisen) to conduct the services in his stead for a two-year period in the mid-1740s, see Maul 2015.
20. Translation after Gregory Butler 1983a, 295
21. Ibid., esp. 294–95.
22. Ibid., 295.
23. Ibid., 296.
24. See chapter 5.

Chapter Nine

1. "Nicht Bach, Meer sollte er heissen"—if one is to believe one Karl Gottfried Freudenberg, a Breslau organist who visited Beethoven in July 1825 and later set down his reminiscences. See Forbes 1967, 2:956.

2. Adorno 1982, 13–17, 145–61. Translated into English as "Late Style in Beethoven" and "Alienated Masterpiece: The *Missa Solemnis*," in Adorno 2002, 564–68, 569–83.
3. Said 2006, 12, 91.
4. Ibid., 6, 7.
5. See chapter 8.
6. Said 2006, 16, 17.
7. A cogent overview of the known and presumed models for the individual movements of the Mass appears in Melamed 2018, 128.
8. May 2017, 14–19. The Nägeli announcement appears in NBR, 506–7.
9. In a private communication, the broadcaster Christopher Lydon informed me that Smith maintained during an interview in the late 1990s on the Boston-area radio program *The Connection* (WBUR), that the St. Matthew Passion "was the greatest of all human accomplishments, individual or collective—in effect 'greater than the pyramids, greater than *The Brothers Karamazov*, greater than baseball or the US Constitution' and that he invited callers to argue the point. The only close second we seemed to agree on—second on the list of all time human peaks—was the Mass in B minor."
10. Thomas 1974, 45.
11. See Leaver 2013 and 2017, 189–90; Sposato 2017 and 2018.
12. Strauss's late works dominate the discussion in the chapter entitled "Return to the Eighteenth Century," in Said 2006—the author declaring that "the centrality of Strauss to my investigation of late style is especially acute (25)."
13. Leaver 2017, 190.
14. Some have discerned the Gregorian model in the two main themes of the movement, as well. See Stauffer 1997, 132–37.
15. Lowinsky 1961, 39.
16. Joel Lester offers, in addition to a provocative theological interpretation, an extensive and enlightening harmonic analysis of the *Et expecto* passage. See Lester forthcoming.
17. See Rifkin 2002.

Chapter Ten

This chapter is dedicated to Richard Kramer.
1. Kramer 2008, 37.
2. This essay will consider, in turn, Wilhelm Friedemann (1710–84), Carl Philipp Emanuel (1714–88), Johann Gottfried Bernhard (1715–39), Johann Christoph Friedrich (1732–95), and Johann Christian (1735–82). Johann Christoph Friedrich and especially Johann Gottfried Bernhard have often been ignored in discussions of the Bach sons—a practice that had already begun in the eighteenth century.
3. Cramer 1783–89.
4. NBR, 413, modified by the present author. ["Der alte Sebastian hatte drey Söhne. Er war nur mit dem Friedemann, dem großen Orgelspieler, zufrieden. Selbst von Carl Philipp Emanuel sagte er (ungerecht!): 's is Berliner Blau! 's verschießt!—Auf den Londoner *Chrétien Bach* wandte er den Gellertschen Vers immer an: 'Der Jürge kömmt gewiß durch seine Dummheit fort!' Auch hat dieser wirklich unter den drey Bachen die größte

Fortüne gemacht.—Ich habe diese Urtheile aus Friedemanns Munde selbst." Cramer 1792, 159n, cited in BDOK III, 518.] In a private communication Hans-Joachim Schulze has kindly provided the author with additional bibliographical information pertaining to this source.

5. Not in NBR, translated by the present author. ["mit seinem Sohne Friedemann! mit dem die Orgel gewissermaaßen ausgestorben ist, war er vergnügt. 'Das ist mein lieber Sohn,' pflegte er zu sagen, 'an dem ich Wohlgefallen habe.'" Cramer 1793, 755; cited in BDOK III, 519.]

6. Schulenberg 2010, 3, x (emphasis added).

7. Ibid., 3, 5 (emphasis added).

8. For Friedemann's intrigue against Kirnberger, see Falck 1913, 52–53.

9. "Und sein Herr Bruder in Hamburg will auch von ihm nichts wissen." Geck 2003, 25, citing Bitter [1868] 1973, 2:323.

10. According to Peter Wollny, Friedemann sold autograph scores of his father's chorale cantatas to Johann Georg Nacke during the years 1759–62—presumably owing to the hardships of the Seven Years' War. See Wollny 1993, 18–19.

11. The documents are transcribed in BDOK I, 71–74.

12. J. S. Bach's autograph of the work, written on the same paper used for the letters of application he penned in Friedemann's name for the Dresden position, was in Friedemann's possession. See Schulze 1984, 17.

13. The manuscript is preserved as D-B, Mus. ms. Bach P 330. See NBA IV/8, KB, edited by Karl Heller (1979), 23. The manuscript dates from J. S. Bach's later Weimar period, ca. 1714–17. See Dadelsen 1958, 79; and Schulze 1984, 157–61.

14. ". . . lässt man die ganze Angelegenheit besser in jenem Halbdunkel." Geck 2003, 26.

15. Wollny 2002.

16. The details are provided in Richter 1905, 54–55.

17. "Dem Landgrafen zu Hessen-Darmstadt ohnlängst berufener Capell Meister." Falck 1913, 44.

18. Wollny 2003, 176–79.

19. "Der Vater mag seine Augen allzu beharrlich auf ihn gerichtet haben—nicht nur zu Lebzeiten, sondern im Sinne eines Über-Ichs auch über seinen Tod hinaus." Geck 2003, 31.

20. "Für den durch sein großes musikalisches Genie berühmten Herrn (Wilhelm Friedemann) Bach unternahm er . . . in den Jahren 1778 und 1779 die Verfertigung einer ernsthaften Oper (nach Marmontel) Lausus und Lydie . . . doch ist selbige, weil die Komposition kränklicher Umstände des Komponisten wegen unbeendigt verblieben, bis jetzt noch ungedruckt." Plümicke 1781, 338; cited in Falck 1913, 55–56.

21. Falck 1913, appendix, 31.

22. For details on the fiasco with Anna Amalia and Kirnberger, see Falck 1913, 52–53.

23. Schulenberg 2010, 264.

24. Ibid., 263 (emphasis added).

25. Geiringer 1954, 310.

26. Yearsley 2012, 173–74.

27. Ibid., 174. The "Comparison" is published in NBR, 400–408. David Schulenberg harbors doubts about Emanuel's authorship of the essay. See Schulenberg 2014, 267, and

his online discussion: http://4hlxx40786q1osp7b1b814j8co.wpengine.netdna-cdn.com/
david-schulenberg/files/2014/03/cpeb_supplement_2_02.pdf.

28. "Seb. Bach war Original weil er keinem nahe war. Ist diese Bemerkung richtig so mußte
der Sohn, der ihm am nächsten kam, nothwendig weniger Original, d.h. Unoriginal seyn
und so denken wir von Friedemann Bach, ohne ihn damit zu verkleinern." Translation
and transcription in Wollny 1993, 6.

29. See Burney 1773, 1:208. See also Newman 1965, 371, for an alternative translation of
this passage.

30. From a conversation reported by the Hamburg poet Matthias Claudius (1740–1815) in
a letter written in 1768. See Ottenberg 1987, 159.

31. Thus on all surviving title pages of the four parts of the *Klavierübung*. BDOK I, 224,
227–28, 230–32, 235–36, 240.

32. See Werbeck 2003 and Wolff 2004.

33. Geck 2003, 43.

34. Bitter [1868] 1973, 1:182, citing Zelter 1801, 46. However, Mary Oleskiewicz has
argued against the veracity of Zelter's statement and the view that Bach was unappreciated by the king. See Oleskiewicz 2007.

35. For an insightful discussion of the cordial relationship between Emanuel Bach and
Telemann, see Exner 2016.

36. Charles Sanford Terry, for example, wrote in his 1929 biography of Johann Christian
Bach, "To their grave reproach, Bach's eldest sons permitted his widow to suffer the cruel
hardships of her last years." Terry 1967, 4.

37. After Sebastian's death, his widow received stipends from a number of Leipzig institutions, among them the municipal government and the university (Hübner 2004). These
funds alone, however, would hardly have sufficed to provide her with an adequate
income: she was therefore obliged to augment them with other revenues. In addition to
the sale of her late husband's and stepsons' publications she evidently rented furnished
space in her apartment. This, and other commercial activity would have enhanced Anna
Magdalena's income (Spree 2019).

38. One can argue whether Emanuel's Magnificat "acknowledges its patrimony" in the
famous setting of the text by J. S Bach. David Schulenberg considers the influence
of Sebastian's Magnificat, BWV 243, to be quite limited. He emphasizes, rather, that
Emanuel's "stylistic models were not works of J. S. Bach but those of somewhat younger
composers such as Hasse and the Graun brothers" and concludes that on the whole
the work represents "[C. P. E.] Bach's turning away from his father's approach to vocal
music" (Schulenberg 2014, 21, 111–13). On the other hand, Hans-Günter Ottenberg
maintains that "much of the choral writing is unmistakably indebted to J. S. Bach,"
claiming that "the opening motives of 'Fecit potentiam' and 'Deposuit potentes' are borrowed almost literally from the elder Bach's *Magnificat*" (Ottenberg 1987, 54).

39. Letter of September 16, 1778, to J. G. I. Breitkopf. See Bach 1997, 125.

40. For a succinct summary of the current state of knowledge (and conjecture) on this most
neglected of the Bach sons, see Kulukundis 2016.

41. Bach had served as organist of the Blasiuskirche in Mühlhausen from June 1707 to June
or July 1708. In 1702, as a seventeen-year-old, he had successfully auditioned for the
organist position at the Jacobikirche in Sangerhausen. The reigning duke overruled the
selection committee, however, and decreed that the appointment must go to a native

son. The incident is known only from Sebastian Bach's own testimony contained in a letter dated November 18, 1736, to Johann Friedrich Klemm, in which he recommended his son Johann Gottfried Bernhard for that same post (NBR, 187).

42. NBR, 200. ["Mit was Schmerzen und Wehmuth aber diese Antwort abfaße. . . . Meinen (leider mißrathenen) Sohn habe seit vorm Jahre . . . nicht mit einem Auge wieder gesehen . . . daß damahln vor selbigen nicht alleine den Tisch, sondern auch den Mühlhäuser Wechsel (so seinen Auszug vermuthlich damahlen *causirete*) richtig bezahlet, sondern auch noch einige *Ducaten* zu Tilgung einiger Schulden zurück ließ, in Meynung nunmehro ein ander *genus vitae* zu ergreiffen. Ich muß aber mit äußerster Bestürtzung abermahligst vernehmen, daß er wieder hie und da aufgeborget, seine LebensArth nicht im geringsten geändert, sondern sich gar *absentir*et und mir nicht den geringsten *part* seines Aufenthalts biß *dato* wißend gemacht. Waß soll ich mehr sagen oder thun? Da keine Vermahnung, ja gar keine liebreiche Vorsorge und *assistence* mehr zureichen will, so muß mein Creütz in Gedult tragen, meinen ungerathenen Sohn aber lediglich Göttlicher Barmhertzigkeit überlaßen . . . habe das zuversichtliche Vertrauen, Dieselben [i.e. Klemm] werden die üble Aufführung meines Kindes nicht mir *imputiren*. . . . [Als] ersuche Eu: HochEdlen gantz dienstlich, daß Dieselben die Gütigkeit haben u. genaue Erkundigung seines Aufenthalts einziehen u. mir so dann sichere Nachricht zu ertheilen belieben mögen, um so dann die letzte Hand anzulegen, u. zu versuchen, ob unter Göttlichem Beystand das verstockte Hertz gewonnen u. zur Erkändniß gebracht werden könne." BDOK I, 107–8.]

43. Cramer 1793, 753; BDOK III, 519.

44. Forkel 1802, 44; NBR, 458.

45. The letter, in the original, is dated "den 27ten. 10br." (As transcribed in BDOK I, 123, the month meant is December, not October, as rendered in NBR, 241.)

46. See J. S. Bach's famous letter of October 28, 1730, to his childhood friend, Georg Erdmann: "There I had a gracious Prince, who both loved and knew music, and in his service I intended to spend the rest of my life." NBR, 151. ["Daselbst hatte einen gnädigen und *Music* so wohl liebenden als kennenden Fürsten; bey welchem auch vermeinte meine Lebenszeit zu beschließen." BDOK I, 67.]

47. Geck 2003, 87.

48. Geiringer 1954, 384.

49. Before leaving the parental home Friedrich served his father during the second half of the 1740s as a copyist. His handwriting appears in the original autograph score of the B-Minor Mass, the performance materials of the St. John Passion and a number of additional compositions by J. S. Bach and other composers. See Wollny 2016.

50. Terry 1967, 142.

51. Manfred Bukofzer developed the concept of "luxuriant [or "harmonically saturated"] counterpoint" in his classic monograph. See Bukofzer 1947, 221.

52. "Mezendore" was published as no. 12 in Marpurg 1756. Regarding Christian's use of the theme from BWV 1029, Ernest Warburton, in his entry for the song in his thematic catalog of the works of Johann Christan Bach (Wb, 1999), writes: "The parody of the opening of JSB's Sonata in G Minor for viola da gamba and obbligato keyboard BWV 1029 (with the mode changed from minor to major) suggests the irreverence more often found in the youngest members of a large family rather than in their older siblings" (Wb, 385). Since it is likely that Christian composed the song (published by 1755) sometime

soon after his father's death in 1750, such "irreverence" toward the recently departed father—if that was in fact Christian's intention—began early indeed.

53. "... als in ihm die Bekanntschaften verschiedener ital. Sängerinnen, die Lust erweckten, Italien zu sehen." Gerber [1790] 1977, 1:83.

54. Quantz 1754 [1951], 318. Emanuel's roles at court, including a discussion of musical venues in which he performed, are discussed in Oleskiewicz 2017, 26–49.

55. In his extensive discussion of accompaniment in the second part of the *Versuch*—where one would most expect to find at some point advice specifically on playing continuo in the context of opera—the closest Philip Emanuel comes to mentioning the topic appears in the section on recitative (paragraph 6). He offers some suggestions there about playing "in intermezzos and comic operas with much noisy action and other works for the theater where the action often occurs backstage" (Bach 1762, 316; English version, 422).

56. Oleskiewicz 2011, 98–100.

57. "Hinter ... meines Bruders itziger Komposition ist nichts. ... Sie fällt hinein und füllt es [das Ohr] aus, läßt aber das Herz leer, das ist mein Urteil von der neuen Musik, der neuen komischen Musik, die auch in Italien, wie mir Galuppi gesagt hat, Mode ist." Cited by Geck 2003, 55.

58. BDOK I, 19; NBR, 57. See the discussion of this ambiguous phrase in chapter 3.

59. Two early songs date from Christian's Berlin years: "Der Weise auf dem Lande," Wb H2, dated April 16, 1755, and "Mezendore," Wb H1, published in 1756 by Marpurg in Berlin.

60. BR 1966, 211; also NBR, 293–94; BDOK I, 267.

61. BR, 203; also NBR, 283. ["hat im 16ten *Seculo* der *lutheri*schen *Religion* halben aus Ungern entweichen müßen." BDOK I, 255.]

62. Burney [1789] 1957, 2:866.

63. The impact of J. S. Bach's music on Mozart is the subject of chapter 14.

Chapter Eleven

1. NBR, 293, BDOK I, 267.

2. Gerber [1790] 1977, 1: col. 84. According to Hans-Joachim Schulze, Gerber, while giving the same date, may have had it from an independent source.

3. Johann Nikolaus Forkel, *Musikalischer Almanach fur Deutschland auf das Jahr 1782* (Leipzig, 1782), 150, as cited in Terry 1967, 11.

4. Gerber [1790] 1977, 1: col. 83.

5. Terry's landmark biography was first published in 1929. The references here are to the posthumously published second edition (Terry 1967).

6. Ibid., 11, citing Elise Polko, "Der englische Bach," *Die deutsche Musikzeitung* (1860).

7. Ibid., 11, again citing Forkel 1782, 150.

8. Terry's scholarly integrity, however, compels him to report in a footnote (p. 11): "In the *Imperial Dictionary of Universal Biography*, G. A. Macfarren did not scruple to speak of the 'sensuality' of Christian's disposition." (*The Imperial Dictionary* was originally published from 1857 to 1863. The composer and musicologist George Alexander Macfarren (1813–87) contributed the entry on J. C. Bach.) In the same footnote Terry reports that

Hermann Mendel's [*Musikalisches*]*Conversations-Lexikon* (Berlin, 1870–79) "declares him a drunkard as well."
9. Terry 1967, 13.
10. Schulze 2015, 51–53.
11. Geiringer 1954, 406.
12. Ibid., 407. The letter, dated August 3, 1757, is housed in the Museo internazionale e biblioteca della musica, formerly known as the Civico Museo Bibliografico Musicale Bologna. See Schnoebelen 1979, item 334. Terry erroneously gives the date as August 13 (Terry 1967, 24). Karl Geiringer and, later, Heinz Gärtner, retain the error (Geiringer 1954, 406 and Gärtner 1994, 125).
13. Geiringer 1954, 407.
14. Terry 1967, 14. The original reads: "il speziale favore del Sig: Cavagliere Litta mi ha aggiunto un altro mese di dimora qui." Schnoebelen 1979, item 303.
15. Geiringer, 1954, 408–9.
16. Gärtner 1994, 155, citing Benedetto Croce, *I Teatri di Napoli* (Naples, 1891), 496–97.
17. Gärtner 1994, 138.
18. Ibid., 156.
19. See chapter 10.
20. Gärtner 1994, 148–49.
21. Ibid., 149. One resists the temptation to wonder whether the art-loving count Firmian shared his friend Winckelmann's well-known homosexual orientation. On Firmian, see Schmid 1955, 28.
22. Terry informs us on the first page of his J. C. Bach biography (1967, 1) that "in Italy he was known as Giovannni Cristiano, in France as Jean-Crétien, and in England as John Christian." He shall be so dubbed henceforth in this essay.
23. Geiringer 1954, 413.
24. Burney [1789] 1957, 2:1018. See Gerber [1812] 1966, 1: col. 4. See also Fritzsch 2016, 119–33, at 119.
25. Terry provides the details. Their first residence was in Meard's Street; then (i.e., "in or before 1765" and until Michaelmas 1771) in King's Square Court—now called Soho Square; finally (from Michaelmas 1771 until sometime in 1773), in Queen's Street, Golden Square. See Terry 1967, 75, 92, 110.
26. Knape, Charters, and McVeigh 2001, 15.
27. Roe 2016, 144.
28. Geiringer 1954, 414. Elisabeth Augusta Wendling (1752–94), herself a successful singer—who also, in the words of Mozart "plays the piano very charmingly" [spiellt recht hübsch Clavier] (letter of November 8, 1777; *Letters*, 362; MBA 2:110)—was in fact seventeen years younger than Christian.
29. A well-placed contemporary witness to the events of 1772, namely, the Staatskanzler Prince Karl August von Hardenberg, made the same claim. See Corneilson 2015, 476.
30. *Letters*, 379. ["sie haben eine einzige tochter die sehr schön ist, und die der Bach in England hat wollen heurathen." MBA 2:136.]
31. Geiringer 1954, 414.
32. Roe 2016, 135, 137.
33. Terry 1967, 103; Roe 2016, 138.
34. The information in this paragraph is based on Roe 2016, 144–50.

35. Obviously not the flat he was sharing in Soho at the time with John Christian.
36. Terry 1967, 103–4, citing *Reminiscences of Henry Angelo, with memoirs of his late father and friends*, 2 vols. (London, 1828–30).
37. See the discussion in Terry 1967, 104–5, from which all the quotations in this paragraph are taken. "Mrs. Papendiek" is Charlotte Papendiek (1765–1840), whose not always accurate memoirs were published posthumously by her granddaughter.
38. Roe 2016, 144.
39. Burney [1789] 1957, 2:873.
40. Roe 2016, 138.
41. Terry 1967, 138.
42. *Letters*, 606; MBA 2: 458.
43. Terry 1967, 161n9.
44. Concerning Tenducci, see Fiske and Monson 1992.
45. *Letters*, 606; MBA 2:458.
46. Roe 2016, 146.
47. Ibid., 147.
48. Knape, Charters, and McVeigh 2001 16, on which page the quotations cited later in this paragraph appear.
49. Ibid., 15.
50. Ibid., 16.
51. Terry 1967, 104.
52. Ibid., 104.
53. Knape, Charters, and McVeigh 2001, 15.
54. Ellen T. Harris reports that at the time "sodomy was punishable by death." She specifies particularly, "in 1707–1709 and again in 1726–1727, suspected homosexuals were rounded up in London in significant numbers and sentenced to the pillory, to hang, or both in succession." (Harris 2001, 230–31.) The volume's Prologue: "The Ways of the World" (1–24) provides a cogent, highly informative survey of the societal mores and taboos affecting the various forms of sexual expression in England—and Italy, as well— in the seventeenth and eighteenth centuries.
55. Roe 2016, 134.
56. Ibid., 148
57. Ibid., 149.
58. Ibid., 154.
59. See the quote from G. A. Macfarren, cited in Terry 1967, 11n5.

Chapter Twelve

1. It is no longer fashionable to divide the eighteenth century neatly into two equal parts and apportion the first half to Bach and Handel and the second to Mozart and Haydn. The recent trend in musical historiography, as in the writing of history generally, is to try to understand the history of music more in terms of its institutions rather than its "great men." Moreover, one now tends to define the eighteenth century as a largely continuous period. Rather than focus on the so-called style shift apparently bisecting the century at

its midpoint into, roughly speaking, a "Baroque" and a "Classical" part, the current preference is to conceive of the century largely in terms of what, at least from the social perspective, was undeniably its dominant institution: Italian opera—especially opera seria. Such a conception, needless to say, is particularly unkind to J. S. Bach. Indeed, the revisionist version of music history, as postulated, for example, by Carl Dahlhaus (Dahlhaus 1985), dismisses Bach altogether as a historically irrelevant "outsider," an "esoteric who knowingly withdrew from the world and drew the compositional consequences from that." See the discussion in the Prologue.

2. Friedrich Rochlitz, "Verbürgte Anekdoten aus Wolfgang Gottlieb Mozarts Leben," *Allgemeine Musikalische Zeitung* (November 21, 1798), cols. 116–17. Quoted and translated in NBR, 488. The original in BDOK III, 558–59. Another excerpt from the passage is cited in chapter 14. See also Solomon 1991, 28–29.

3. Bach's teaching method is discussed in Marshall 2019.

4. Paris, July 31, 1778 (*Letters*, 587). Mozart apparently uses "genius" here and elsewhere as a synonym for "talent." ["denn lection geben ist hier kein spass . . . sie därfen nicht glauben daß es faulheit ist—Nein!—sondern weil es ganz wieder mein genie, wieder meine lebensart ist." MBA 2:427.]

5. Mozart's first exposure to Bach's music took place at least as early as 1770. See chapter 14.

6. *Letters*, 800. ["ich gehe alle Sonntage um 12 uhr zum Baron von Suiten—und da wird nichts gespiellt als Händl und Bach.—ich mach mir eben eine Collection von den Bachischen fugen.—so wohl sebastian als Emanuel und friedeman Bach." MBA 3:201.]

7. Mozart's transcriptions of these works are discussed in chapter 14.

8. For further discussion of this point, see Marshall 1989, 70.

9. Letter of November 8, 1777 (*Letters*, 363). ["Ich kann nicht Poetisch schreiben; ich bin kein dichter. ich kann die redensarten nicht so künstlich eintheilen, daß sie schatten und licht geben; ich bin kein mahler. ich kann sogar durchs deüten und durch Pantomime meine gesinnungen und gedancken nicht ausdrücken; ich bin kein tanzer. ich kan es aber durch töne; ich bin ein Musikus." MBA 2:110–11.]

10. Letter of September 26, 1781 (*Letters*, 769). ["die Musick . . . das Ohr niemalen beleidigen, sondern doch dabey vergnügen muß, folglich allzeit Musick bleiben Muß . . . der Janitscharen Chor ist . . . alles was man verlangen kann—kurz und lustig;—und ganz für die Wiener geschrieben." MBA 3:162–63.]

11. Letter of July 27, 1782 (*Letters*, 810). ["ich habe sie ex D gemacht weil es ihnen lieber ist." MBA 3:215.]

12. Mozart describes the fugue's origin in a letter of April 20, 1782, to his sister Nannerl. The letter and the composition itself are discussed in chapter 14.

13. Letter of December 28, 1782, to Leopold Mozart (*Letters*, 833). ["hie und da—können auch *kenner allein* [emphasis in the original] satisfaction erhalten—doch so—daß die nicht-kenner damit zufrieden seyn müssen, ohne zu wissen warum." MBA 3:245–46.]

14. Letter to Leopold Mozart, dated Vienna, July 31, 1782 (*Letters*, 811). ["ich mag nichts hinschmiren." MBA 3:216.]

15. The text of the 1785 dedication appears in *Letters*, 891–92. The Italian original reads: "una lunga, e laboriosa fatica" (MDL, 220).

16. Letter to Leopold Mozart, dated Mannheim, December 3, 1778 (*Letters*, 638). ["ach, wenn wir nur auch clarinetti hätten!—sie glauben nicht was eine sinfonie mit flauten, oboen und clarinetten einen herrlichen Effect macht." MBA 2:517.]

17. Letter to Leopold Mozart, February 15, 1783 (*Letters*, 840). ["die Neue Hafner Sinfonie hat mich ganz surprenirt—dann ich wusste kein Wort mehr davon;—die muß gewis guten Effect machen." MBA 3:257.]

18. The losses might be considerable. Bach most likely composed a substantial number of instrumental ensemble works—duo and trio sonatas, concertos, and so on—during his Köthen years and again during the years of his association with the Collegium musicum in Leipzig, all of which have largely disappeared. See chapter 8.

19. Marshall, 1989, 67–69. The assertion there that "almost every one of Bach's cantata manuscripts closes with the inscription: *SDG!*" (68) is an overstatement. In a close evaluation of the original sources, Michael Marissen has detected considerable inconsistency and variation over time (and from genre to genre) in Bach's use of the formula—as well as in his use of the notation *J. J.* (*Jesu juva*) at the beginning of his compositions. He reports that "about 60" of the approximately 140 surviving autograph scores to Bach's church cantatas, "actually do not read 'S. D. G.' at the end." See Marissen forthcoming.

20. "Ich sei nicht schlechthin sicher, ob die Engel, wenn sie im Lobe Gottes begriffen sind, gerade Bach spielen—ich sei aber sicher, daß sie, wenn sie unter sich sind, Mozart spielen und daß ihnen dann doch auch der liebe Gott besonders gerne zuhört." Barth 1956, 12.

21. Storr 1985, 76–77.

22. Davies 1989, 145–60.

23. *Letters*, 756. ["ich habe ihr was fertig ist hören lassen.—sie sagte mir auf die lezt, daß, . . . das, was ich bis dato geschrieben, gewiß gefallen wird.—ich gehe in diesen Punckt auf *keines Menschen lob oder tadel*—bevor so leute nicht alles *im ganzen*—gehört und gesehen haben." (Emphasis in the original). MBA 3:145.]

24. Letter of April 12, 1783 (*Letters*, 846). ["Ich bitte sie auch wenn es möglich ist mir die *Nachricht* wegen meiner academie zu kommen zu lassen." MBA 3:265.]

25. *Letters*, 730. ["alles was mir der Erzbischof in den drey audienzen erbauliches sagte . . . und was mir izt wieder dieser herrliche Mann gottes Neues erzehlte, machte eine so trefliche Wirkung auf meinen körper daß ich abends in der opera mitten im Ersten Ackte nach hause gehen musste, um mich zu legen.—dann ich war ganz erhitzt—zitterte am ganzen leibe—und taumelte wie ein besoffener auf der gasse—blieb auch den folgenden tag als gestern; zu hause—den ganzen vormittag aber im Bett." MBA 3:113.]

26. *Letters*, 917. ["und kämen mir nicht so oft so schwarze Gedanken (die ich nur mit Gewalt ausschlagen muß), würde es mir noch besser von Statten gehen." MBA 4:69.]

27. *Letters*, 963–64. ["ich kann Dir meine Empfindung nicht erklären, es ist eine gewisse Leere—die mir halt wehe thut—ein gewisses Sehnen, welches nie befriediget wird, folglich . . . immer fortdauert, ja von Tag zu Tag wächst . . . es freuet mich auch meine Arbeit nicht." MBA 4:150.]

28. The "Bäsle" letters, as well as Mozart's erotic letters to his wife, are discussed further in chapter 13.

29. This observation is elaborated from other points of view in chapters 1 and 2.

30. Freyse 1955.

31. Storr 1985, 70.

32. See Bach's comment on the nature of the thorough bass, discussed in chapter 7.

33. See Marshall 1989, 71–73.
34. From a letter to Karl Friedrich Zelter from June 1827. See NBR, 499. The original reads: "Ich sprach mir's aus: als wenn die ewige Harmonie sich mit sich selbst unterhielte, wie sich's etwa in Gottes Busen, kurz vor der Weltschöpfung, möchte zugetragen haben." *Goethes Briefwechsel mit Zelter* (Goethe n.d., 221).

Chapter Thirteen

1. Other films considered by the panel were: *Farinelli, Immortal Beloved,* and *Impromptu.* The four presentations—by Ellen T. Harris, Lewis Lockwood, and Jeffrey Kallberg, respectively—were published in MQ 1997. The original form of the present essay, with the title, "Film as Musicology: *Amadeus,*" appears there, pp. 173–79.
2. "Film Forum *Amadeus.*"
3. Perry-Camp 1984, 117.
4. Some examples of the historical inaccuracies registered by Perry-Camp: Salieri and Mozart did not use modern conducting techniques; Mozart never misbehaved at the courts of Colloredo or Joseph II; Leopold did not meet his daughter-in-law for the first time in Vienna (they first met in Salzburg); Salieri did not commission the Requiem from Mozart, nor was he present at Mozart's death; Mozart did not drink himself to death, nor was there a rainstorm on the day of his funeral; and so forth.
5. Perry-Camp 1984, 119.
6. Ibid., 118.
7. Ringer 1984.
8. Michiko Kakutani, in a *New York Times* article, quotes Peter Shaffer as follows: The movie "has become much more a celebration of the music. . . . In the film . . . music almost becomes a character, the most important character" (Kakutani 1984). In a *Times* article of his own, Shaffer wrote: "In the picture, the music naturally became more prominent than in the play. . . . The cinema positively *welcomes* music in floods—and, of course, acoustical inundation is very much the fate of drowning Salieri. Music, sublime and unstaunchable, pouring in a stream over a gasping man's head, is of course the central subject of the film" (emphasis in original). Shaffer 1984.
9. Cited here as MDB.
10. The standard English translation remains Emily Anderson, *The Letters of Mozart and his Family,* cited throughout this volume as: *Letters.*
11. Chapter 15 identifies the most significant contributions in recent years to our knowledge of Mozart's sketches and compositional process.
12. Possibly many sketches and other preliminary drafts for K. 482—as for numerous other compositions—are lost. No drafts or fragments for the work are extant. The catalog of Mozart's sketches published in Konrad 1992 lists exactly one surviving sketch for the concerto. It contains the music for two measures that were inadvertently omitted from the autograph score. They therefore shed no light at all on the genesis of the work. Konrad 1992, 167, 314.
13. The definitive critical edition of letters of the Mozart family (MBA) includes one letter (in Italian) supposedly from Mozart to Da Ponte, written in September 1791, and one

supposedly from Schikaneder to Mozart, dated September 5, 1790, but remarks that both are almost certainly spurious. See the transcriptions in MBA 4:156, 532 and the commentary in MBA 6:423, 676.

14. On December 16, 1774, Mozart added a postscript to one of his father's letters. While Leopold's letter was addressed to his wife, Wolfgang's note was addressed to his sister, Nannerl. It reads: "I have a toothache. [*Ich habe zahnwehe.*] johannes chrisostomus Wolfgangus Amadeus Sigismundus Mozartus Mariae annae Mozartae matri et sorori, ac amicis omnibus, praesertimque pulchris virginibus, ac freillibus, gratiosisque freillibus | S. P. D." (*Letters*, 251–52, MBA 1:507. The orthography here as in MBA.) Anderson translates the Latin (following the series of his names): ". . . sends many greetings to Maria Anna Mozart, his mother and his sister, and to all his friends, and especially to pretty girls and Fräuleins. Salutem plurimam dicit." On May 10, 1779, in a letter to his cousin "Bäsle" Mozart writes: "Whether I, [Ob ich] Johannes Chrysostomus Sigismundus Amadeus Wolfgangus Mozartus . . ." (*Letters*, 651–52; MBA 2:547).

15. MDB, 415; MDL, 363.

16. See Solomon 1995, 491. The final chapter of Davies 1989 is devoted to a consideration of the numerous suggestions that have been proposed as to the cause of Mozart's death. In the end the author proposes that the composer died of Schönlein-Henoch syndrome, another manifestation of a streptococcal infection.

17. Niemetschek [1808] 1978, 67. The German equivalent for the phrase "the ungainliness of his appearance," which appears before the words "his small build" in Helen Mautner's English translation (Niemetschek 1956, 53), does not appear in the German original (at least not in the 1808 edition).

18. MDB, 537. ["spielte immer mit Etwas, z.B. mit seinem Chapeau, Taschen, Uhrband, Tischen, Stühlen gleichsam Clavier." MDL, 460.]

19. Ibid., 542. ["fand ich . . . jemand, den ich, seines eleganten Äußern wegen für einen kaiserlichen Kammerherrn hielt." MDL, 464.]

20. Ibid., 533.

21. *Letters*, 823. ["wegen dem schönen rothen frok welcher mich ganz grausam im herzen kitzelt . . . denn so einen frok muß ich haben, damt es der Mühe werthe ist die knöpfe darauf zu setzen, mit welchen ich schon lange in meinen gedanken schwanger gehe . . . diese sind Perlmutter. . . . Ich möche alles haben was gut, ächt und schön ist." MBA 3:232–33.]

22. Or murdered—perhaps by Franz Hofdehmel, whose wife, Magdalena (b. 1766), reportedly a keyboard student of Mozart's, he suspected of having had an affair with him. The long-standing speculation is developed in Carr 1983 (esp. chap. 7, entitled, "Magdalena").

23. MDB, 524.

24. See Leopold's letter to his daughter, dated April 28, 1786: "*Le Nozze di Figaro* is being performed . . . for the first time. . . . Salieri and all his supporters will again try to move heaven and earth [to down his opera]" (*Letters*, 897). ["Heute . . . gehet *Le Nozze di Figaro*, das erste mahl in Scena. Es wird viel seyn, wenn er reußiert, denn ich weis, daß er erstaunliche starke Cabalen wider sich hat. Salieri mit seinem ganzen Anhang wird wieder Himmel und Erden in Bewegung zu bringen sich alle Mühe geben." MBA 3:536.] In his monumental Mozart biography, Hermann Abert quotes Sophie Haibel as having reported that Mozart's friendliness extended even to "Salieri, der ihn nicht leiden

mochte," but gives no source for the quotation (Abert 1956, 1:731; English translation, 628). Alexander Thayer, the venerable Beethoven biographer—and also the author of the first English-language biography of Salieri (first published serially in 1863–64)—makes the same claim: again without citing a specific source: "Mozart, in his intercourse with his compeers in art, was friendly, good-humored and mild in judgment, 'also in respect to Salieri, who did not like him,' as Frau Sophia Haibl [*sic*], his wife's sister records." Thayer 1989, 92.

25. *Letters*, 970. ["Du kannst nicht glauben, wie artig beide waren,—wie sehr ihnen nicht nur meine Musick, sondern das Buch und alles zusammen gefiel.—Sie sagten beide ein *operone*—würdig bey der größten festivität vor dem größten Monarchen aufzuführen,— und Sie würden sie gewis sehr oft sehen, den sie haben noch kein schöneres und angenehmeres Spectacel gesehen.—Er hörte und sah mit aller Aufmerksamkeit und von der Sinfonie bis zum letzten Chor, war kein Stück, welches ihm nicht ein bravo oder bello entlockte." MBA 4:161–62.]

26. See chapter 12. The letters first appeared in unexpurgated form in the first edition of Emily Anderson's English translation in 1938. They were not published in the original German until the 1960s, when they appeared in the MBA.

27. The social context and use of off-color language in the Mozart family correspondence is discussed extensively in Eibl and Senn 1978.

28. Mozart's letter of January 31, 1778 (*Letters*, 456–57). ["Madame Mutter! | Ich esse gerne Butter. | Wir sind Gottlob und Dank | Gesund und gar nicht krank. | . . . Ich bin bei Leuten auch | die tragen den Dreck im Bauch, | doch lassen sie ihn auch hinaus | So wohl vor, als nach dem Schmaus. | Gefurzt wird allzeit auf die Nacht | Und immer so, daß es brav kracht. | Doch gestern war der fürze König, | deßen Fürze riechen wie Hönig. . . . Nun will ich mich nit mehr erhitzen | Mit meiner Poesie; nur will ich Ihnen sagen | Daß ich Montag die Ehre hab, ohne viel zu fragen, | Sie zu embrassiren und dero Hand zu küssen, | Doch werd' ich schon vorhero haben in die Hosen geschißen. | à dieu Mamma | Dero getreues Kind | ich hab' den Grind | Trazom." MBA 2:245–47.]

29. *Letters*, 278. ["adio ben mio leb gesund, Reck den arsch zum mund. ich winsch ein guete nacht, scheiss ins beth das Kracht." MBA 2:14.]

30. *Letters*, 783. ["die Natur spricht in mir so laut, wie in Jedem andern, und vieleicht läuter als in Manchem grossen, starken limmel. Ich kann ohnmöglich so leben wie die Meisten dermaligen Jungen leute.—Erstens habe ich zu viel Religion, zweytens zu viel liebe des Nächstens und zu Ehrliche gesinnungen als daß ich ein unschuldiges Mädchen anführen könnte, und drittens zu viel Grauen und Ecke, scheu und forcht vor die krankheiten, und zu viel liebe zu meiner gesundheit als daß ich mich mit hurren herum balgen könnte; dahero kann ich auch schwören daß ich noch mit keiner frauens=Person auf diese art etwas zu thun gehabt habe." MBA 3:180.]

31. *Letters*, 919–20. ["Wie geht es Dir? Denkst Du wohl so oft auf mich, wie ich auf Dich?—alle Augenblicke betrachte ich Dein Portrait—und weine—halb aus Freude, halb aus Leide!—erhalt mir Deine mir so werthe Gesundheit und lebe wohl, Liebe! . . . Adieu—ich küsse Dich Milionen mal auf das zärtlichste und bin ewig Dein bis an Tod getreuester." MBA 4:79.]

32. *Letters*, 922. ["Wenn ich dir alles erzehlen wollte, was ich mit deinem lieben *Porträt* anfange, würdest du wohl oft lachen.—zum beySpiell; wenn ich es aus seinem Arrest herausnemme, so sage ich: grüss dich gott Stanzerl!—grüss dich gott, grüss dich

gott;—Spizbub;—knallerballer;—Spizignas—bagatellerl—schluck und druck!—und
wenn ich es wieder hinein tue; so lasse ich es so nach und nach hinein rutschen, und
sage immer, Stu!—Stu!—Stu!—aber mit dem *gewissen Nachdruck*, den dieses so viel
bedeutende Wort, erfordert; und bey dem lezten schneller, gute Nacht: Mauserl, schlaf
gesund;—Nun glaube ich so ziemlich was dummes | für die Welt wenigstens |hinge-
schrieben zu haben—für uns aber, die wir uns so innig lieben, ist es gewis nicht dumm."
MBA 4:81.]

33. *Letters*, 924–25. ["Liebes Weibchen, ich habe eine menge bitten an dich; . . . bitte ich
Dich nicht allein auf *Deine* und *Meine Ehre* in deinen Betragen Rücksicht zu nehmen,
sondern auch auf den *Schein*.—seye nicht böse auf diese Bitte.—Du mußt mich eben
dießfalls noch mehr lieben, weil ich auf Ehre halte." MBA 4:84.]

34. *Letters*, 927. ["ich bin so froh wenn ich einmal wieder bey Dir bin, meine Liebe!—Das
erste aber ist, daß ich Dich beym Schopf nehme; wie kannst Du denn glauben, ja nur
vermuthen, daß ich Dich vergessen hätte? . . . für diese Vermuthung sollst du gleich
die erste Nacht einen derben Schilling auf Deinen liebens-küßenswürdigen Aerschgen
haben, zähle nur darauf. Adjeu— | ewig Dein | Einziger Freund und Dich von | Herzen
liebender Mann | W. A. Mozart." MBA 4:88.]

35. *Letters*, 929. ["den 1:t Juny werde ich in Prag schlafen, und den 4:—den 4:t?—*bey mei-
nem liebsten weiberl*;—richte dein liebes schönstes nest recht sauber her, denn mein büb-
derl verdient es in der That, er hat sich recht gut aufgeführt und wünscht sich nichts
als dein schönstes . . . zu besitzen. Stelle dir den Spitzbuben vor, dieweil ich so schreibe
schleicht er sich auf den Tisch und [zeigt] mir mit [fragen] ich aber nicht faul [geb]
ihm einen derben Nasenstüber—der [bursch] ist aber nur . . . jetzt brennt [auch] der
Schlingel noch mehr und läßt sich fast nicht bändigen." MBA 4:90.]

36. In the chapter entitled "Mozarts Persönlichkeit," Abert writes: "Er war und blieb auch
in dieser Hinsicht Künstler, d.h. sinnlicher Mensch, dessen Welt die der Anschauungen
und Gefühle, aber nicht die Begriffe war." (Abert 1956, 2:3.) In the English translation
the phrase "sinnlicher Mensch" is misleadingly translated as "sentient being" rather than
as a "sensual" person or individual. See the English version 2007, 731.

37. Mozart's opinions on a variety of topics are systematically presented in Marshall 1991.
(His comments on literature, the arts, and current events are cited there, pp. 95–109; his
philosophical outlook, pp. 160–70.)

38. MDB, 250; the Italian original in MDL, 220.

39. Solomon 1995, 315–16.

Chapter Fourteen

1. As quoted in Zenck 1986, 83 (emphasis added). The original reads: "Durch diese seine
besonders die letzteren zehn Jahre in Wienn geschriebenen Kunstwerke schwang sich
Mozart so in die Höhe, daß er sowohl in Wienn als ganz Deutschland, in ganz Europa
als der größte Meister anerkannt wurde, welcher Sebastian Bachs Kunst, Händels Stärke,
Haydns launigste Klarheit und Anmuth in sich verband."

2. Nissen [1828] 1972, *Anhang*, 25–26. The original reads: "Nachdem man allmählig mehr
auf das Leichte, Populäre, Sentimentale hinarbeitend, mit Ausnahme weniger Meister,
sich immer weiter von der alten Seb. Bach'schen Gründlichkeit entfernt hatte, trat

Mozart auf, der, mit tiefer Verehrung für Bach erfüllt, in seinen eigenen Compositionen, italienische Anmuth mit deutscher Kraft, und merklich mit Bach'scher Kunst (in Reichthume der Harmonie und in den melodischen figurirten Bässen, in contrapunctischer Behandlung überhaupt) verknüpfte, und nebst Jos. Haydn eine neue Epoche der Tonkunst begründete, mit welcher derjenige moderne Styl began."

3. Chapter 37. English version: Abert 2007; German reprint edition: Abert 1956.

4. Einstein 1945, 151, 153.

5. Rosen 1997, 20n1.

6. Finscher 1985, 274. The original reads: "Der entscheidende Durchbruch Mozarts zum klassischen Stil, sein Beitrag zur Ausbildung dieses Stils als einer Synthese, die man mit einigem Recht als Universalstil bezeichnen kann und in der die historisch ältere Idee einer Synthese der Nationalstile aufgehoben wurde, gelang nicht in der Symphonie, überhaupt nicht eigentlich in einer Gattung, sondern primär durch eine biographische Situation, in der sich die lebenslang eingeübte Auseinandersetzung mit Mustern zur praktisch gleichzeitigen Konfrontation mit zwei künstlerisch überwältigenden Eindrücken zuspitzte: der Begegnung mit Bach und Händel im Hause des Barons van Swieten und der Begegnung mit Haydns Streichquartetten opus 33."

7. Finscher 1982. The original reads: "Das Jahr 1782 wird so zum Epochenjahr, zum eigentlichen Geburtsjahr des klassischen Stils, und die Geburtshelfer sind Bach und Händel." Finscher's original German is obviously both more cogent and more vivid, thanks mainly to the untranslatable "Geburtshelfer"—unless one is prepared to accept "midwives" with reference to Bach and Handel.

8. A revised version of the essay appears as chapter 12 in this volume. The original version was published in JRBI 22 (1991): 16–32.

9. Sadie 1964, 23–24.

10. Ibid., 24.

11. Zaslaw 1989, 9–10.

12. Konrad 1992, 470. The original reads: "Wenigstens die Meinung sei geäußert, daß die ständige Betonung sowohl von Constanze Mozarts angeblicher Fugenleidenschaft, die den Gatten stimuliert habe, als auch von der besonders im deutschsprachigen Schrifttum beinahe zum Mythos stilisierten Begegnung des Komponisten mit der Musik Johann Sebastian Bachs die sachliche Beurteilung der historischen und vor allem musikalischen Implikationen von Mozarts kontrapunktischem Denken nicht wesentlich fördern."

13. See chapter 12.

14. "Nachricht von dem gegenwärtigen Zustande der Musik Sr. Hochfürstl, Gnaden des Erzbischoffs zu Salzburg im Jahr 1757" (title cited after Zaslaw 1989, 2n1). A complete English translation of Leopold's "Report" appears in Zaslaw's volume as Appendix C.

15. BDOK II, 46–47; BDOK III, 649–50.

16. Hammerstein 1956, 13; also Schmid 1948, 90.

17. Maul 2018.

18. See Abert 1956, 1:5 (English version, 5); also Buelow 2001c.

19. Niemetschek 1956, 21. ["In Paris und London legte man ihm Sachen vom Händel und Bach vor, die er mit Akkuratesse und dem angemessenen Vortrage zur Verwunderung jedes Kenners vom Blatt wegspielte." Niemetschek [1808] 1978, 16.]

20. Only the last eight measures of the 103-measure composition are not by Mozart. The work was completed by Abbé Stadler.

21. See Dennerlein 1951, 165–67.

22. Plath 1976/77, 161. The watermark studies of Alan Tyson corroborate a pre-Viennese dating of the paper of this autograph. See NMA X/33/2, *Textband*, 52.
23. BDOK II, 467, 469.
24. BDOK III, 117.
25. W. Kirkendale 1966.
26. *Letters*, 801. ["Baron van suiten . . . hat mir alle Werke des händls und Sebastian Bach |: nachdem ich sie ihm durchgespiellt | nach hause gegeben" MBA 3:202].
27. On van Swieten's career, see Olleson 1980; on his library, see Holschneider 1963.
28. Van Swieten's collection, by the way, also contained Handel's keyboard suites, C. P. E. Bach's sonatas and other keyboard pieces, sonatas and fugues by Domenico Scarlatti, keyboard pieces by Geminiani, and sonatas of Clementi. (Holschneider 1963.) Mozart no doubt got to know quite a few of these works as well.
29. Letter of April 20, 1782 (*Letters*, 801). ["die ursache daß diese fuge auf die Welt gekommen ist wirklich Meine liebe konstanze . . . weil sie mich nun öfters aus dem kopfe fugen spiellen gehört hat, so fragte sie mich ob ich noch keine aufgeschrieben hätte?—und als ich ihr Nein sagte.—so zankte sie mich recht sehr daß ich eben das künstlichste und schönste in der Musick nicht schreiben wollte; und gab mit bitten nicht nach, bis ich ihr eine fuge aufsetzte, und so ward sie." MBA 3:202–3.]
30. Sadie 1964, 24.
31. Lowinsky 1989, 911–12.
32. *Letters*, 833. The German version reads: "[I]ch hätte lust ein Buch—eine kleine Musicalische kritick mit Exemplen zu schreiben" (MBA 3:246).
33. The basic "block" of invertible counterpoint—to use the terminology of Werner Neumann (Neumann 1953)—was first described by Donald Francis Tovey. See Tovey 1935, 197 (from which ex. 14.11 is taken).
34. *Allgemeine Musikalische Zeitung* 1 (1799): 117. Translation in NBR, 488; the original in BDOK III, 558–59.
35. Hammerstein 1956, 15–16.
36. See NBA III/1, KB, edited by Konrad Ameln (1967), 94.
37. The title for the work in Mozart's *Verzeichnüß* reads: *Ein OrgelStücke für eine Uhr.* See the facsimile edition (Mozart 1990), f. 26v.
38. Handel's collection, published by Walsh, as the composer's *Troisième Ouvrage*, appeared around 1735, that is, virtually contemporaneously with Bach's *Klavierübung* II. The individual compositions, however, were evidently composed in the second decade of the eighteenth century: the G-minor is thought to have been composed ca. 1711, the remaining five fugues ca. 1717/18. See Marshall 2019.
39. On this point, see my "On Bach's Universality" (Marshall 1989, 65–79).

Chapter Fifteen

1. Konrad 2002, 223–76. The statistics presented in the following paragraphs are based on Konrad's tabulation.
2. See the three-measure sonata incipit in F, K. 15nn, the twelve-measure fragment for a minuet in C, K. 15rr, and the twenty-three-measure fragment of a fugue for four voices

and continuo, K. 15ss, all in the new complete edition of Mozart's works: NMA IX/27/1, edited by Wolfgang Plath (1982), 163, 166–68.

3. See Plath 1976/77, 170.

4. See Mozart 1990, 43–49; Konrad 2002, 265.

5. Konrad 1992 offers an exhaustive study of Mozart's sketches and fragments.

6. Conceivable examples are: the Adagio for Violin and Orchestra in E, K. 261; the Rondo for Violin and Orchestra in B-flat, K. 269/261a; the Andante for Flute and Orchestra in C, K. 315/285e; the Rondo for Piano in D, K 485; or the Adagio in B Minor for Piano, K. 540. Some of these could be substitution movements or additions to completed works. Of course, they could have been intended as independent items. Mozart, for example, describes K. 540 in his personal catalog as "Ein Adagio für das Klavier allein"— suggesting that he considered it (at least at the time) to be an independent composition.

7. Tyson 1987, 26–28. Tyson specifically mentions five pieces: the Kyrie fragments K. 196a (Anh. 16), K. 258a (Anh. 13), K. 323 (Anh. 15), K. 422a (Anh. 14), and the Gloria fragment K. 323a (Anh. 20). Ulrich Konrad assigns K. 323 to the year 1790, the four others to 1787. Konrad 2002, 257–58, 269.

8. According to Plath 1976/77: 139–40, the canons, K. 73i, 73k, 73r–73x, date from 1772, not 1770; the fugue fragment, K. 401/375e, dates not from 1782 but rather late summer 1772 (p. 161) and the fugue fragment, K. Anh. 41/375g, not from 1782 but rather 1777 (p. 168). According to Tyson, the fugue fragment in G, K. Anh. 45/375d, dates from 1785/86, not 1782 (Tyson 1987, 141.) The discussion of Mozart's engagement with the music of Bach in chapter 14 is inevitably a discussion of his engagement with the fugue.

9. See Mozart's letter of November 12, 1778 (*Letters*, 631; MBA 2:505–7).

10. The autograph is preserved in the Bibliothèque Nationale in Paris (Département de la Musique). A facsimile of the entire fragment appears in Konrad 2002, 30–37. It is transcribed in NMA V/14/2, edited by Christoph-Hellmut Mahling (1975), 136–52.

11. See Levin 1968/70, 304–26.

12. The fragment is in the possession of the Internationale Stiftung Mozarteum, Salzburg. A facsimile appears in Konrad 2002, 44–51; a transcription appears in NMA V/14/2, 153–61.

13. See NMA V/14/5, edited by Franz Giegling (1987), xv.

14. Mozart 1997 reproduces in facsimile all the surviving sources for both movements of the concerto, with informative introductory essays by Christoph Wolff and Robert D. Levin. A facsimile appears as well in Konrad 2002, 52–59, 60–69.

15. In contrast to the obviously dismembered state of the surviving autograph of K. 370b, Mozart's manuscript of the Rondo, K. 371, was generally considered to be complete. In fact it was missing a complete bifolio—four pages—containing a total of sixty measures. The bifolio reappeared in 1988. Its discovery was reported on the same occasion that the original version of the present essay was delivered, namely, at the 1991 bicentennial Mozart Congress in Salzburg. See Rolf 1991.

16. Tyson 1987, 35.

17. The autograph is in the possession of the Rychenberg-Stiftung, Winterthur. A complete facsimile is published in NMA V/14/4, edited by Franz Giegling (1977), 165–76.

18. Beginning with measure 180, the notation of the bass line in the autograph is in A major, not G—an indication that from this point on Mozart was already conceiving the work

in its later version for (basset) clarinet in A. As reported in NMA V/14/4, ix, these measures were added in a darker ink and sharper pen point—presumably after a considerable interruption in time.

19. In his commentary for the incipient Horn Concerto, K. 370b, Levin claims that it is the "*only* first-movement concerto fragment by Mozart whose opening orchestral ritornello is not fully scored" (original italics; facsimile edition, Mozart 1997, 16). He evidently overlooked K. 621b.

20. In this connection, it is necessary to note the existence of drafts for an Oboe Concerto in F, K. 293/416f—dating, like the double concerto, K. 315f, from the autumn of 1778—and for a Horn Concerto in E Major, K. 494a—dating from 1785 or 1786. (Facsimiles in Konrad 2002, 37–40 and 124–27, respectively.) Finally, an unfinished quintet movement in sonata form, scored for clarinet, basset horn, and strings in F, K. Anh. 90/580b—and dating, like the Basset Horn Concerto fragment, from 1787—contains the music for the complete exposition to the double bar. Significantly, the opening section through the arrival on the V/V is completely scored, while the remainder alternates between principal-part notation and full scoring—a combination, then, of "block" and "horizontal" composition. It is transcribed in NMA VIII/19/2, edited by Ernst Fritz Schmid (1958), 45–49.

21. Ulrich Konrad's three landmark publications—Konrad 1992, 1998, 2002—are, to date, the most valuable contributions to the topic.

22. *Letters*, 587. ["daß ich gern speculire—studiere—überlege." MBA 2:427.]

23. *Letters*, 855. ["da ich aber gerne langsam und mit überlegung arbeite." MBA 3:278.]

24. See Marshall 1991, esp. 23–35, for additional documentation bearing on Mozart's compositional process.

25. *Letters*, 166. ["Ich kan nicht viell schreiben dann die finger thuen sehr weh von so viel Recitativ schreiben." MBA 1:397.]

26. Novello [1829] 1955, 78. ["Wenn irgendeine große Konzeption in seinem Geiste entstand, war er völlig wie abwesend, ging in der Wohnung auf und nieder und wußte nicht, was um ihn her vorging." Novello 1959, 73.]

27. See the facsimile edition of the autograph scores for *The Six "Haydn" String Quartets*. Mozart 1985.

28. See Schafer 1987.

29. Constanze Mozart 1799.

Epilogue

1. For recent studies of the Mozart fragments, see Tyson 1987, Konrad 1992 and 2002, and chapter 15 in this volume.

2. The most recent revised edition, Köchel 6, appeared in 1964.

3. For the correct amount of the fee, see Wolff 1994, 2.

4. The unsigned obituary, "Memoir of Johann Peter Salomon" (by one P. Ayrton), appeared, fifteen years after Salomon's death in 1815, in the *Harmonicon* (1830), 45. See Unverricht 1980. The passage above is quoted in Landon 1988, 19.

5. Letter from Vienna, dated October 19, 1782, to Leopold Mozart, in reference to recent successful British military actions against the French. *Letters*, 828; MBA 3:239.

6. Letter from Paris, dated August 7, 1778, to Abbé Joseph Bullinger, recording Mozart's displeasure at the French rejoicing about a recent victory over the English in the American colonies. *Letters*, 596. See also Marshall 1991, 108.

7. Landon 1976, 153.

8. On the political and military developments (including the executions of Louis XVI and Marie Antoinette) that led Haydn to postpone his planned 1793 visit to England, see Landon 1976, 214–22.

9. MDB, 406–7; also Solomon 1995, 478.

10. See Constanze Mozart's petition of December 11, 1791, to Emperor Leopold II. MDB, 421–22.

11. Emanuel Schikaneder claimed to have given the work its hundredth performance by November 1792 and its two hundredth by October 1795. Abert 1956, 2:622; English edition, 1248. These claims, however, were exaggerated. Branscombe 1991, 161.

12. The libretto draft is published in Goethe 1993, 221–49. Johann Peter Eckermann (1792–1854) reported of his conversation with Goethe on April 13, 1823: "Wir sprachen sodann über den Text der Zauberflöte, wovon Goethe die Fortsetzung gemacht, aber noch keinen Komponisten gefunden hat, um den Gegenstand gehörig zu behandeln." See Eckermann 1999, 515.

13. Conversation with Eckermann, February 12, 1829: "Es ist ganz unmöglich. . . . Die Musik müßte im Charakter des Don Juan sein; Mozart hätte den Faust komponieren müssen." Eckermann 1999, 306.

14. See his letters of November 29, 1780, and November 10, 1781 (*Letters*, 674, 777–78; also Marshall 1991, 96, 98).

15. Constanze Mozart's reminiscences are reported in Novello [1829] 1955, 94–95. ["Mozart las gerne und kannte Shakespeare in der deutschen Übersetzung." Novello 1959, 88.]

16. The information in this paragraph is taken from Loewenberg 1978, cols. 352–53, 438, 545–46.

17. "Auf den gebt Acht, der wird einmal in der Welt von sich reden machen." First quoted by Otto Jahn; discussed further in Abert 1956, 2:306: English edition, 984.

18. Johannes Hummel on his son, Johann Nepomuk (published in 1873), quoted in MDB, 570. ["Er soll alles frei haben, Lehre, Logis, Kost." MDL, 482.] On Hummel's experiences while living in Mozart's residence, see Kroll 2007, 11–18.

19. On Beethoven's lessons with Haydn, see Landon 1976, 202–5.

20. Carter 2001.

21. Ibid.

22. The first two, again, being *Gli equivoci* (after *The Comedy of Errors*) and *La scuola de' maritati* (after *The Taming of the Shrew*).

23. Letter of May 31, 1827, to Abbé Maximilian Stadler (MBA 4:491).

24. Tyson 1987, 26–28. See also chapter 15.

25. See the letters of May 1790 to Archduke Franz and ca. April 25, 1791, to the municipal court of Vienna, respectively (*Letters*, 938–39, 949–50).

26. See Mozart's letter of June 2, 1781, to his father: "It is perfectly true that the Viennese are apt to change their affections. . . . And, even granted that they do get tired of me, they will not do so for a few years, certainly not before then." *Letters*, 739. ["die Wiener

sind wohl leute die gerne abschiessen . . . und dann, lassen wir es zu, so wäre der fall erst in etwelchen Jahren, eher gewis nicht." MBA 3:124–25.]

27. Tyson 1987, 46, 93, 139, and 335, n. 3, regarding the string quartet fragments in F Major, K. 589b; E Minor, K. 417d; and G Minor, K. 587a, respectively.

28. Ibid., 342n35, regarding the G-minor piano sonata fragment, K. 312 (590d).

29. Eibl 1965, 90–91.

30. Letter from Paris, dated September 11, 1778, to Leopold Mozart. *Letters*, 612. ["ein Mensch von mittelmässigen Talent bleibt immer mittelmässig, er mag reisen oder nicht—aber ein Mensch von superieuren Talent | welches ich mir selbst, ohne gottlos zu seyn, nicht absprechen kann wird—schlecht, wenn er immer in den nemlichen ort bleibt." MBA 2:473.]

Works Cited

Abert, Hermann. 1956. *W. A. Mozart.* 2 vols. 7th printing. Leipzig: VEB Breitkopf & Härtel. (Orig. pub. 1923.) Translated by Stewart Spencer; edited by Cliff Eisen (New Haven, CT: Yale University Press, 2007).

Adlung, Jacob. [1758] 1953. *Anleitung zur musikalischen Gelahrtheit.* Facsimile edition by Hans-Joachim Moser. Kassel: Bärenreiter Verlag.

Adlung, Jacob. [1768] 1961. *Musica mechanica organoedi.* Facsimile edition by Christhard Mahrenholz. Kassel: Bärenreiter Verlag.

Adorno, Theodor W. 1982. *Gesammelte Schriften, 17: Musikalische Schriften 4: Moments musicaux. Neugedruckte Aufsätze 1928–1962.* Frankfurt am Main: Suhrkamp Verlag.

Adorno, Theodor W. 2002. *Essays on Music.* Selected, with Introduction, Commentary, and Notes by Richard Leppert, New Translations by Susan H. Gillespie. Berkeley: University of California Press.

Bach, Carl Philipp Emanuel. 1762. *Versuch über die wahre Art das Clavier zu spielen.* Vol. 2. Berlin: Winter. Translated by William J. Mitchell as *Essay on the True Art of Playing Keyboard Instruments* (New York: W. W. Norton, 1949).

Bach, Carl Philipp Emanuel. 1997. *The Letters of C. P. E. Bach.* Translated by Stephen L. Clark. Oxford: Clarendon Press.

Bach, Johann Sebastian. 1931. *Quodlibet. Ein Fragment für vier Singstimmen.* Edited by Max Schneider, *Veröffentlichungen der Neuen Bachgesellschaft* 32, 2. Leipzig: Breitkopf & Härtel.

Bach, Johann Sebastian. 1935. *Notenbüchlein für Anna Magdalena Bach* (1725). Edited by Arnold Schering. Frankfurt am Main: Friedrich Hofmeister.

Bach, Johann Sebastian. 1959. *Clavier-Büchlein vor Wilhelm Friedemann Bach.* Facsimile edition with a preface by Ralph Kirkpatrick, New Haven: Yale University Press.

Bach, Johann Sebastian. 1960? *Brief an den Jugendfreund Georg Erdmann vom 28. Oktober 1730.* Facsimile edition with a commentary by Nathan Notowicz, *Faksimile-Reihe Bachscher Werke und Schriftstücke,* 3. Leipzig: Deutscher Verlag für Musik.

Bach, Johann Sebastian. 1973. *Hochzeitsquodlibet 1707: Ein Fragment, BWV 524.* Facsimile edition with commentary by Werner Neumann and Günther Kraft. Leipzig: VEB Verlag für Musik.

Bach, Johann Sebastian. 1977–83. *Das wohltemperierte Klavier.* 2 vols. Edited by Walter Dehnhard. Vienna: Wiener Urtext Ausgabe.

Bach, Johann Sebastian. 1980. *Das Wohltemperierte Klavier II.* Facsimile of the autograph manuscript in the British Library. Add. MS. 35021, with an introduction by Don Franklin and Stephen Daw. London: The British Library.

Bach, Johann Sebastian. 1988. *Klavierbüchlein für Anna Magdalena Bach 1725.* Edited by Georg von Dadelsen. Kassel: Bärenreiter.

Badura-Skoda, Eva. 1991. "Komponierte J. S. Bach 'Hammerklavier-Konzerte'?" BJ 77: 159–71.

Badura-Skoda, Eva. 2017. *The Eighteenth-Century Fortepiano Grand and its Patrons from Scarlatti to Beethoven.* Bloomington: Indiana University Press.

Badura-Skoda, Paul. 1993. *Interpreting Bach at the Keyboard.* Oxford: Oxford University Press.

Bail, Ulrike, ed. 2006. *Die Bibel in gerechter Sprache.* Gütersloh: Güterslohe Verlagshaus.

Barbour, J. Murray. 1947. "Bach and *The Art of Temperament.*" MQ 33: 64–89.

Barth, Karl. 1956. *Wolfgang Amadeus Mozart.* Zurich: Theologischer Verlag.

Beißwenger, Kirsten. 1992. *Johann Sebastian Bachs Notenbibliothek.* Kassel: Bärenreiter.

Besseler, Heinrich. 1955. "Bach als Wegbereiter." *Archiv für Musikwissenschaft* 12: 1–39.

Bitter, Carl Hermann. [1868] 1973. *Carl Philipp Emanuel und Wilhelm Friedemann Bach und deren Brüder.* 2 vols. Leipzig: Zentralantiquariat der Deutschen Demokratischen Republik.

Bloom, Harold. 1973. *The Anxiety of Influence: A Theory of Poetry.* New York: Oxford University Press.

Blume, Friedrich. 1962, "Umrisse eines neuen Bach-Bildes." *Musica* 16: 169–76.

Blume, Friedrich. 1963. "Outlines of a New Picture of Bach." *Music and Letters* 44: 214–27.

Blume, Friedrich. 1970. *Classic and Romantic Music.* New York: W. W. Norton.

Botwinick, Sara. 2004. "From Ohrdruf to Mühlhausen: A Subversvie Reading of Bach's Relationship to Authority." JRBI 35, no. 2: 1–59.

Branscombe, Peter. 1991. *W. A. Mozart*, Die Zauberflöte. Cambridge: Cambridge University Press.

Brokaw, James A. 1985. "Recent Research on the Sources and Genesis of Bach's *Well-Tempered Clavier*, Book II." JRBI 16, no. 3: 17–35.

Brokaw, James A. 1986. "Techniques of Expansion in the Preludes and Fugues of J. S. Bach." PhD diss., University of Chicago.

Buelow, George. 2001a. "Rhetoric and Music: Baroque, Musical Figures." NGD2 21: 262–63.

Buelow, George. 2001b. "Figures, Theory of Musical." NGD2 8: 792–93.

Buelow, George. 2001c. "Mizler, Lorenz." NGD2 16: 770–71.

Bukofzer, Manfred. 1947. *Music* in *the Baroque Era.* New York: W. W. Norton.

Burney, Charles. 1773. *Carl Burney's . . . Tagebuch seiner Musikalischen Reisen.* Hamburg: Bode.

Burney, Charles. [1789] 1957. *A General History of Music From the Earliest Ages to the Present Period.* 2 vols. Edited by Frank Mercer. New York: Dover.

Büsing, Otfried. 2015. "Hatte Nottebohm recht?—Überlegungen zur Fuga a 3 Soggetti aus Bachs Kunst der Fuge." BJ 101: 193–203.

Büsing, Otfried. 2016. "Kurze Duplik auf Thomas Daniels Replik zu 'Hatte Nottebohm recht?'" BJ 102: 57–62.

Butler, Gregory. 1983a. *"Der vollkommene Capellmeister* as a Stimulus to J. S. Bach's Late Fugal Writing." In *New Mattheson Studies*, edited by George J. Buelow and Hans Joachim Marx, 293–305. Cambridge: Cambridge University Press.

Butler, Gregory. 1983b, "Ordering Problems in J. S. Bach's *Art of Fugue* Resolved." MQ 69: 44–61.

Butt, John. 1990. *Bach Interpretation: Articulation Marks in Primary Sources of J. S. Bach.* Cambridge: Cambridge University Press.

Calov, Abraham. 2017. *Bach's Bible: The Calov Bible, Die Heilige Bibel 1681–92. Facsimile of the Original Preserved in Concordia Seminary Library, St. Louis*. Franeker, NL: Uitgeverij van Wijnen.

Carr, Francis. 1983. *Mozart & Constanze*. New York: Avon Books.

Carter, Tim. 2001. "Da Ponte, Lorenzo." NGD2 7: 8–11.

Chafe, Eric. 1991. *Tonal Allegory in the Vocal Music of J. S. Bach*. Berkeley: University of California Press.

Chafe, Eric. 2014. *J. S. Bach's Johannine Theology: The* St. John Passion *and the Cantatas for Spring 1725*. New York: Oxford University Press.

Claus, Rolf Dietrich. 1998. *Zur Echtheit von Toccata und Fuge d-moll BWV 565*. 2nd ed. Köln: Verlag Dohr.

Cone, Edward T. 1974. "Bach's Unfinished Fugue in C Minor." In *Studies in Renaissance and Baroque Music in Honor of Arthur Mendel*, edited by Robert L. Marshall, 149–55. Kassel: Bärenreiter.

Constantini, Franz Peter. 1969. "Zur Typusgeschichte von J. S. Bachs Wohltemperiertem Klavier." BJ 55: 31–45.

Corneilson, Paul. 2015. "The Case of J. C. Bach's *Lucio Silla*." In *J. C. Bach*, edited by Paul Corneilson, 473–85. Burlington, VT: Ashgate, 2015. (Orig. pub. *Journal of Musicology* 12 [1994].)

Cornell, Robert. 1991. "The Development of String Sound in the Thuringian Organ of the Eighteenth Century." *Early Keyboard Studies Newsletter* 5, no. 4 (July): 6–7.

Cox, Howard H., ed. 1985. *The Calov Bible of J. S. Bach*. Studies in Musicology 92. Ann Arbor: UMI Research Press.

Cramer, Carl Friedrich. 1783–89. *Magazin der Musik*. Hamburg: Musicalische Niederlage.

Cramer, Carl Friedrich. 1792–93. *Menschliches Leben: Gerechtigkeit und Gleichheit*, no. 8 (Achtes Stück); no. 13 (dreizehntes Stück). Altona and Leipzig: Kavensche Buchhandlung.

Cron, Matthew. 1997. "Bibliographical Check-List of the Minimalist Argument and Contrary Evidence with Regard to the Original Performing Resources for Music by J. S. Bach" (appended to Don L. Smithers, "The Emperor's New Clothes Reappraised: Or Bach's Musical Resources Revealed"). JRBI 28, no. 1–2: 77–81.

Dadelsen, Georg von. 1957. *Bemerkungen zur Handschrift Johann Sebastian Bachs, seiner Familie und seines Kreises*. Trossingen: Hohner-Verlag.

Dadelsen, Georg von. 1958. *Beiträge zur Chronologie der Werke Johann Sebastian Bachs*. Tübinger Bach-Studien 4/5. Trossingen: Hohner-Verlag.

Dahlhaus, Carl. 1985. "Das 18. Jahrhundert als musikgeschichtliche Epoche." In *Die Musik des 18. Jahrhunderts*, edited by Carl Dahlhaus, 1–8. Neues Handbuch der Musikwissenschaft 5. Laaber: Laaber Verlag.

Dahlhaus, Carl. 1986. "The Eighteenth Century as a Music-Historical Epoch." Translated by Ernest Harriss. *College Music Symposium* 26: 1–6.

Daniel, Thomas. 2016. "Hatte Nottebohm Unrecht? Zur unvollendeten Fuge a 3 Soggetti aus Bachs Kunst der Fuge." BJ 102: 45–55.

Davies, Peter J. 1989. *Mozart in Person: His Character and Health*. New York: Greenwood Press.

Dennerlein, Hans. 1951. *Der unbekannte Mozart: Die Welt seiner Klavierwerke*. Leipzig: Breitkopf & Härtel.

Downes, Edward O. D. 1961. "The Neapolitan Tradition in Opera." In *Report of the Eighth Congress of the International Musicological Society, New York 1961*, edited by Jan LaRue, 277–84. Kassel: Bärenreiter.

Dreyfus, Laurence. 1987a. *Bach's Continuo Group*. Cambridge, MA: Harvard University Press.

Dreyfus, Laurence. 1987b. "The Kapellmeister and His Audience: Observations on 'Enlightened' Receptions of Bach." In *Alte Musik als ästhetische Gegenwart: Kongressbericht Stuttgart 1985*, edited by Dietrich Berke and Dorothee Hanemann, 180–89. Kassel: Bärenreiter.

Dreyfus, Laurence. 1996. *Bach and the Patterns of Invention*. Cambridge, MA: Harvard University Press.

Dürr, Alfred. 1971. *Die Kantaten von Johann Sebastian Bach*. 2 vols. Kassel: Bärenreiter.

Dürr, Alfred. 1976. *Zur Chronologie der Leipziger Vokalwerke J. S. Bachs*. 2nd ed. Kassel: Bärenreiter. (Orig. pub. 1957.)

Dürr, Alfred. 1977. *Studien über die frühen Kantaten Joh. Seb. Bachs*. 2nd ed. Wiesbaden: Breitkopf & Härtel. (Orig, pub. 1951.)

Dürr, Alfred. 1984. *Zur Frühgeschichte des Wolhtemperierten Klaviers I von Johann Sebastian Bach*. Göttingen: Vandenhoeck & Ruprecht.

Dürr, Alfred. 1988. "Tastenumfang und Chronologie in Bachs Klavierwerken." In *Im Mittelpunkt Bach: Ausgewählte Aufsätze und Vorträge*. Kassel: Bärenreiter, 220–31. (Orig pub. 1978.)

Eckermann, Johann Peter. 1999. *Gespräche mit Goethe in den letzten Jahren seines Lebens*, ed. Christoph Michel, ser. 2, vol. 12 (vol. 39) in Johann Wolfgang Goethe: Sämtliche Werke, Briefe, Tagebücher und Gespräche, Bibliothek deutscher Klassiker, 167. Frankfurt am Main: Deutscher Klassiker Verlag.

Eggebrecht, Hans Heinrich. 1970. "Über Bachs geschichtlichen Ort." In *Johann Sebastian Bach*, edited by Walter Blankenburg, 247–89. Wege der Forschung 170. Darmstadt: Wissenschaftliche Buchgesellschaft. (Orig. pub. 1957.)

Eibl, Joseph Heinz. 1965. *Wolfgang Amadeus Mozart: Chronik eines Lebens*. Kassel: Bärenreiter.

Eibl, Joseph Heinz, and Walter Senn, eds. 1978. *Mozarts Bäsle Briefe*. Kassel: Bärenreiter.

Einstein, Alfred. 1945. *Mozart: His Character, His Work*. Translated by Arthur Mendel and Nathan Broder. New York: Oxford University Press.

Eppstein, Hans. 1976. "Chronologieprobleme in Johann Sebastian Bachs Suiten für Soloinstrument." BJ 62: 35–57.

Erickson, Raymond. 2009. "Introduction: The Legacies of J. S. Bach." In *The Worlds of Johann Sebastian Bach*, edited by Raymond Erickson, 1–64. New York: Amadeus Press.

Erickson, Raymond. 2011. "The Early Enlightenment, Jews, and Bach." *MQ* 97: 518–47.

Erikson, Erik H. 1962. *Young Man Luther*. New York: W. W. Norton.

Erikson, Erik H. 1969. *Gandhi's Truth*. New York: W. W. Norton.

Exner, Ellen. 2016. "The Godfather: Georg Philipp Telemann, Carl Philipp Emanuel Bach, and the Family Business." JRBI 47/1: 1–20.

Falck, Martin. 1913. *Wilhelm Friedemann Bach: Sein Leben und Seine Werke, mit thematischem Verzeichnis seiner Kompositionen*. Leipzig: C. F. Kahnt Nachfolger.

Faulkner, Quentin. 1984. *J. S. Bach's Keyboard Technique: A Historical Introduction*. St. Louis: Concordia Publishing House.

Faulkner, Quentin. 1991. "Some Characteristics of Eighteenth-Century Thuringian Organs." *Early Keyboard Studies Newsletter* 5, no. 4 (July): 3–5.

Feder, Stuart. 1992. *Charles Ives: "My Father's Song": A Psychoanalytic Biography*. New Haven: Yale University Press.

"Film Forum: *Amadeus*." 1984. *Eighteenth-Century Life* 9: 116–22.

Finscher, Ludwig. 1982. "Bach—Mozart." In *Sommerakademie Johann Sebastian Bach 1982: Almanach*, 18–29. Stuttgart: Sommerakademie.

Finscher, Ludwig. 1985. "Mozart und die Idee eines musikalischen Universalstils." In *Die Musik des 18. Jahrhunderts*, edited by Carl Dahlhaus, 267–78. Neues Handbuch der Musikwissenschaft 5. Laaber: Laaber Verlag.

Fischer, Johann Kaspar Ferdinand. 1965. *Sämtliche Werke für Klavier und Orgel*. Edited by Ernst von Werra. New York: Broude Brothers. (Orig. pub. 1901.)

Fiske, Roger and Dale E. Monson. 1992. "Tenducci, Giusto Ferdinando." In *The New Grove Dictionary of Opera*, edited by Stanley Sadie, 4: 689. London: Macmillan.

Forbes, Elliot, ed. 1967. *Thayer's Life of Beethoven*. 2 vols. Princeton: Princeton University Press.

Forkel, Johann Nikolaus. 1802. *Ueber Johann Sebastian Bachs Leben, Kunst und Kunstwerke*. Leipzig: Hoffmeister und Kühnel. Translated by Hans T. David and Arthur Mendel as *On Johann Sebastian Bach's Life, Genius and Works*. In NBR, 419–82.

Franklin, Don O. 1989. "Reconstructing the Urpartitur for WTC II: a Study of the 'London Autograph' (BL Add. MS 35021)." In *Bach Studies*, edited by Don O. Franklin, 240–78. Cambridge: Cambridge University Press.

Freud, Sigmund. 1939. *Moses and Monotheism*. Translated by Katherine Jones. New York: Random House.

Freud, Sigmund. 1989. *Freud-Studienausgabe*, 10: *Bildende Kunst und Literatur*. Frankfurt/Main: S. Fischer Verlag.

Freyse, Conrad. 1955. "Wieviele Geschwister hatte J. S. Bach?" BJ 42: 103–7.

Freyse, Conrad. 1956. "Johann Christoph Bach (1642–1703)." BJ 43: 36–51.

Fritzsch, Thomas. 2016. "Johann Christian Bachs Kompositionen für die Viola da gamba— Eine Spurensuche." In *The Sons of Bach: Essays for Elias N. Kulukundis*, edited by Peter Wollny and Stephen Roe, 119–33. Ann Arbor: Steglein Publishing.

Gardiner, John Eliot. 2013. *Bach: Music in the Castle of Heaven*. New York: Knopf.

Gärtner, Heinz. 1994. *John Christian Bach: Mozart's Friend and Mentor*. Translated by Reinhard G. Pauly. Portland, OR: Amadeus Press.

Geck, Martin. 2003. *Die Bach-Söhne*. Hamburg: Rowohlt Taschenbuch Verlag.

Geiringer, Karl. 1954. *The Bach Family: Seven Generations of Genius*. London: Allen & Unwin.

Geiringer, Karl. 1966. *The Johann Sebastian Bach: The Culmination of an Era*. New York: Oxford University Press.

Gerber, Ernst Ludwig. [1790/92] 1977. *Historisch-Biographisches Lexicon der Tonkünstler*. 2 vols. Graz: Akademische Druck- u. Verlagsanstalt.

Gerber, Ernst Ludwig. [1812/14] 1966. *Neues historisch-biographisches Lexikon der Tonkünstler*. 2 vols. Graz: Akademische Druck u. Verlagsanstalt.

Glöckner, Andreas. 2006. "Alumnen und Externe in den Kantoreien der Thomasschule zur Zeit Bachs." BJ 92: 9–36.

Glöckner, Andreas. 2008. *Kalendarium zur Lebensgeschichte Johann Sebastian Bachs*. Expanded new edition. Leipzig: Evangelische Verlagsanstalt.

Glöckner, Andreas. 2009. "Ein weiterer Kantatenjahrgang Gottfried Heinrich Stölzels in Bachs Aufführungsrepertoire?" BJ 95: 95–115.

Glöckner, Andreas. 2018. *Dokumente zur Geschichte des Leipziger Thomaskantorats. Vol. 2: Vom Amtsantritt Johann Sebastian Bachs bis zum Beginn des 19. Jahrhunderts.* Leipzig: Evangelische Verlagsanstalt.

Goethe, Johann Wolfgang. 1993. *Dramen 1791–1832,* ed. Dieter Borchmeyer and Peter Huber, ser. 1, vol. 6. In Johann Wolfgang Goethe: *Sämtliche Werke, Briefe, Tagebücher und Gespräche.* Bibliothek deutscher Klassiker 97. Frankfurt am Main: Deutscher Klassiker Verlag.

Goethe, Johann Wolfgang. n.d. *Goethes Briefwechsel mit Zelter,* ed. Will Vesper. Berlin: Deutsche Bibliothek.

Goethe, Johann Wolfgang. 2017. *Goethes Gespräche,* ed. Woldemar Freiherr von Biedermann. 10 vols. Norderstedt: Hansabook. (Orig. pub. 1889–96.)

Grimm, Jacob, and Wilhelm Grimm. 1984. *Deutsches Wörterbuch.* Munich: Deutscher Taschenbuch Verlag (Orig. pub. 1854–1971.)

Häfner, Klaus. 1977. "Über die Herkunft von zwei Sätzen der h-moll Messe." BJ 63: 55–74.

Hammerstein, Reinhold. 1956. "Der Gesang der geharnischten Manner: Eine Studie zu Mozarts Bachbild." *Archiv für Musikwissenschaft* 13: 1–24.

Harris, Ellen T. 2001. *Handel as Orpheus: Voice and Desire in the Chamber Cantatas.* Cambridge, MA: Harvard University Press.

Haynes, Bruce. 1985. "Johann Sebastian Bach's Pitch Standards: The Woodwind Perspective." *Journal of the American Musical Instrument Society* 9: 55–114.

Haynes, Bruce. 2002. *A History of Performing Pitch: The Story of "A."* Lanham, MD: Scarecrow Press.

Hill, Robert. 1987. "The Möller Manuscript and the Andreas Bach Book: Two Keyboard Anthologies from the Circle of the Young Johann Sebastian Bach." PhD diss., Harvard University.

Hill, Robert, ed. 1991. *Keyboard Music from the Andreas Bach Book and the Möller Manuscript.* Harvard Publications in Music, 15. Cambridge, MA: Department of Music, Harvard University.

Hlawicka, Karol. 1961. "Zur Polonaise g-Moll (BWV Anh. 119) aus dem 2. Notenbüchlein für Anna Magdalena Bach." BJ 48: 58–60.

Hofmann Klaus. 1988. "'Fünf Präludien und fünf Fugen': Über ein unbeachtetes Sammelwerk Johann Sebastian Bachs." In *Bericht über die Wissenschaftliche Konferenz zum V. Internationalen Bachfest der DDR . . . 1985,* edited by Winfried Hoffmann and Armin Schneiderheinze, 227–35. Leipzig: VEB Deutscher Verlag für Musik.

Holschneider, Andreas. 1963. "Die musikalische Bibliothek Gottfried van Swietens." In *Bericht über den internationalen musikwissenschaftlichen Kongress Kassel* 1962, edited by Georg Reichert and Martin Just, 174–78. Kassel: Bärenreiter.

Hübner, Maria. 2004. *Anna Magdalena Bach: Ein Leben in Dokumenten und Bildern. Mit einem biographischen Essay von Hans-Joachim Schulze.* Leipzig: Evangelische Verlagsanstalt.

Jauernig, Reinhold. 1950. "Johann Sebastian Bach in Weimar." In *Johann Sebastian Bach in Thüringen,* edited by Heinrich Besseler and Günther Kraft, 49–105. Weimar: Thüringer Volksverlag.

Jerold, Beverly. 2011. "The Bach-Scheibe Controversy: New Documentation," JRBI 42, no. 1: 1–45.

Kakutani, Michiko. 1984. "How 'Amadeus' Was Translated from Play to Film." *New York Times,* September 16.

Keller, Hermann. 1950. *Die Klavierwerke Bachs*. Leipzig: C. F. Peters.

Kirkendale, Ursula. 1980. "The Source for Bach's *Musical Offering:* the *Institutio oratoria* of Quintilian." JAMS 33: 88–141.

Kirkendale, Warren. 1966. *Fuge und Fugato in der Kammermusik des Rokoko und der Klassik*. Tutzing: Hans Schneider.

Knape, Walter, Murray R. Charters, Simon McVeigh. 2001. "Abel family." NGD2 1: 14–18.

Kobayashi, Yoshitake. 1988. "Zur Chronologie der Spätwerke Johann Sebastian Bachs: Kompositions- und Aufführungstätigkeit von 1736 bis 1750." BJ 74: 7–72.

Konrad, Ulrich. 1992. *Mozarts Schaffensweise*. Göttingen: Vandenhoeck & Ruprecht.

Konrad, Ulrich, ed. 1998. *Skizzen*. NMA X/30/3. *Supplement*. Kassel: Bärenreiter,

Konrad, Ulrich, ed. 2002. *Fragmente*. NMA X/30/4. *Supplement*. Kassel: Bärenreiter.

Kraft, Günther. 1956. "Zur Entstehungsgeschichte des 'Hochzeitsquodlibets,'" BJ 43: 140–54.

Kramer, Richard. 2008. "Carl Philipp Emanuel Bach and the Aesthetics of Patricide." In *Unfinished Music*, 25–46. New York: Oxford University Press. (Orig. pub. 2004.)

Kroll, Mark. 2007. *Johann Nepomuk Hummel: A Musician's Life and World*. Lanham, MD: The Scarecrow Press.

Kübler-Ross, Elisabeth. 1969. *On Death and Dying*. New York: Macmillan.

Kulukundis, Elias N. 2016. "Johann Gottfried Bernhard Bach: Fact and Fiction—A Remembrance and Birthday Tribute." In *The Sons of Bach: Essays for Elias N. Kulukundis*, edited by Peter Wollny and Stephen Roe, 260–69. Ann Arbor: Steglein Publishing.

Landon, H. C. Robbins. 1976. *Haydn in England, 1791–1795*. Vol. 3, *Haydn: Chronicle and Works*. Bloomington: Indiana University Press.

Landon, H. C. Robbins. 1988. *1791: Mozart's Last Year*. New York: Schirmer Books.

Langusch, Steffen. 2007. "'. . . auf des Herrn Capellmeisters Bach recommendation . . .'— Bachs Mitwirken an der Besetzung des Kantorats der Altstadt Salzwedel 1743/44." BJ 93: 9–43.

Leaver, Robin A. 1978. "Bach and Luther." JRBI 9/3: 9–12.

Leaver, Robin A. 1983. *Bachs theologische Bibliothek, eine kritische Bibliographie / Bach's Theological Library: A Critical Bibliography*. Beiträge zur theologischen Bachforschung 1. Neuhausen-Stuttgart: Hänssler-Verlag.

Leaver, Robin A. 1985. *J. S. Bach and Scripture: Glosses from the Calov Bible Commentary*. Introduction, Annotations, and Editing by Robert A. Leaver. St. Louis: Concordia Publishing House.

Leaver, Robin A. 2013. "Bach's Mass: 'Catholic or Lutheran?'" In *Exploring Bach's B-minor Mass*, edited by Yo Tomita, Robin A. Leaver, and Jan Smaczny, 21–38. Cambridge: Cambridge University Press.

Leaver, Robin A., ed. 2017. *The Routledge Research Companion to Johann Sebastian Bach*. London: Routledge.

Ledbetter, David. 2002. *Bach's Well-tempered Clavier: The 48 Preludes and Fugues*. New Haven: Yale University Press.

Lester, Joel. Forthcoming. "Tone-painting the Mysterious: The 'Et expecto' from Bach's B-minor Mass." JRBI 51, no. 1.

Levin, Robert D. 1968/1970. "Das Konzert for Klavier und Violine D-Dur KV Anh. 56/315f und das Klarinettenquintett B-Dur, KV Anh. 91/5l6c: ein Ergänzungsversuch." MJb: 304–326.

Lindley, Mark. 1980a. "Temperaments." NGD 18: 660–74.

Lindley, Mark. 1980b. "Well-tempered Clavier." NGD 20: 337–38.

Little, Meredith, and Natalie Jenne. 2001. *Dance and the Music of J. S. Bach. Expanded Edition*. Bloomington, IN: Indiana University Press.

Loewenberg, Alfred. 1978. *Annals of Opera, 1597–1940*, 3rd ed. Totowa, NJ: Rowman and Littlefield.

Lowinsky, Edward E. 1961. *Tonality and Atonality in Sixteenth-Century Music*. Berkeley: University of California Press.

Lowinsky, Edward E. 1989. *Music in the Culture of the Renaissance & Other Essays*. Edited and with an Introduction by Bonnie J. Blackburn. Chicago: University of Chicago Press.

Luther, Martin. [1566] 1912. *Tischreden*. Vol. 1, *D. Martin Luthers Werke Kritische Gesamtausgabe*. Weimar: Böhlau.

Luther, Martin. [1538] 1914. Preface to *Symphoniae Iucvndae* . . . (Wittenberg: Rhau). Vol. 50, *D. Martin Luthers Werke. Kritische Gesamtausgabe*. Weimar: Böhlau, 372–73. Translated by Ulrich S. Leupold in *Luther's Works. Vol. 53: Liturgy and Hymns*, 321–24. (Philadelphia: Fortress Press, 1965).

Manuel, Frank E. 1983. *The Changing of the Gods*. Lebanon, NH: University Press of New England.

Marissen, Michael. 1995. *The Social and Religious Designs of J. S. Bach's Brandenburg Concertos*. Princeton: Princeton University Press.

Marissen, Michael. 1998. *Lutheranism, Anti-Judaism and Bach's St. John Passion*. New York: Oxford University Press.

Marissen, Michael. 2016a. *Bach & God*. New York: Oxford University Press.

Marissen, Michael. 2016b. "The Theological Character of J. S. Bach's Musical Offering." In *Bach & God*, 191–225. New York: Oxford University Press. (Orig. pub. 1995.)

Marissen, Michael. 2018. "J. S. Bach Merits Serious Bible Study." *New York Times*, April 1.

Marissen, Michael. Forthcoming. "Bach against Modernity." In *Rethinking Bach*, edited by Bettina Varwig. New York: Oxford University Press.

Marpurg, Friedrich Wilhelm. 1756. *Neue Lieder zum Singen beym Clavier*. Berlin: Gottlieb August Lange.

Marshall, Robert L. 1972. *The Compositional Process of J. S. Bach: A Study of the Autograph Scores of the Vocal Works*. Princeton Studies in Music, 4. Princeton: Princeton University Press.

Marshall, Robert L. 1989. *The Music of Johann Sebastian Bach: The Sources, the Style, the Significance*. New York: Schirmer Books.

Marshall, Robert L. 1991. *Mozart Speaks: Views on Music, Musicians, and the World*. New York: Schirmer Books.

Marshall, Robert L. 2000. Review of Wolff 2000. *New York Review of Books*. June 15, 47–51.

Marshall, Robert L. 2008. "Bach's *tempo ordinario*: A Plaine and Easie Introduction to the System." *Performance Practice Review Online*. (Orig. pub. 1996.)

Marshall, Robert L. 2014. Review of Gardiner 2013. JRBI 45, no. 1: 90–100.

Marshall, Robert L. 2019. "Bach, Handel, and the Harpsichord." In *The Cambridge Companion to the Harpsichord*, edited by Mark Kroll, 263–98. Cambridge: Cambridge University Press.

Maul, Michael. 2011. "'von Cristofori'—Zum Maler des verschollenen Porträts Anna Magdalena Bachs." BJ 97: 251–54.

Maul, Michael. 2013. "'welche ieder Zeit aus den 8 besten Subjectis bestehen muß': Die erste 'Cantorey' der Thomasschule—Organisation, Aufgaben, Fragen." BJ 99: 11–77.

Maul, Michael. 2015. "'zwey ganzer Jahr die Music an Statt des Capellmeisters aufführen, und dirigiren müssen.' Überlegungen zu Bachs Amtsverständnis in den 1740er Jahren." BJ 101: 75–97.

Maul, Michael. 2018. "'Den Tag gewiß 6 Stund zur Information': Der Bach-Schüler Philipp David Kräuter." *Bach-Magazin* 31: 13–15.

May, Ernest. 2017. "Bach's Mass in B minor in the Age of Globalization." In *UMass Amherst Bach Festival & Symposium April* (program book), 14–19.

McClary, Susan. 1987. "The Blasphemy of Talking Politics during the Bach Year." In *Music and Society: The Politics of Composition, Performance, and Reception*, edited by Richard Leppert and Susan McClary, 20–41. Cambridge: Cambridge University Press.

Melamed, Daniel R. 2002. "Die alte Chorbibliothek der Kirche Divi Blasii zu Mühlhausen." BJ 88: 209–16.

Melamed, Daniel R. 2018. *Listening to Bach: The* Mass in B Minor *and the* Christmas Oratorio. New York: Oxford University Press.

Milka, Anatoly. 2014. "Warum endet die *Fuga a 3 Soggetti* BWV 1080/19 in Takt 239?" BJ 100: 11–26.

Mozart, Constanze. 1799. "Anekdoten. Noch einige Kleinigkeiten aus Mozarts Leben, von seinerWittwe mitgetheilt." *Allgemeine Musikalische Zeitung*, 1: col. 855.

Mozart, Wolfgang Amadé. 1985. *The Six "Haydn" String Quartets. Facsimile of the Autograph Manuscripts in the British Library. Add. MS. 37763*. Introduction by Alan Tyson. London: British Library.

Mozart, Wolfgang Amadé. 1990. *Mozart's Thematic Catalogue: A Facsimile. British Library Stefan Zweig MS 63*. Introduction and transcription by Albi Rosenthal & Alan Tyson. Ithaca, NY: Cornell University Press.

Mozart, Wolfgang Amadé. 1997. *Concerto for Horn and Orchestra in E-flat major, K. 370b + 371. A Facsimile Reconstruction of the Autograph Sources*. Foreword by John Brooks Howard and Introductory Essays by Christoph Wolff and Robert D. Levin. Cambridge, MA: Harvard College Library.

Neumann, Frederick. 1978. *Ornamentation in Baroque and Post-Baroque Music, With Special Emphasis on J. S. Bach*. Princeton: Princeton University Press.

Neumann, Frederick. 1985. "Bach: Progressive or Conservative and the Authorship of the Goldberg Aria." MQ 71: 281–94.

Neumann, Werner. 1953. *J. S. Bachs Chorfuge*. Leipzig: VEB Breitkopf & Härtel.

Neumann, Werner. 1974. *Sämtliche von Johann Sebastian Bach vertonte Texte*. Leipzig: VEB Deutscher Verlag für Musik.

Newman, William S. 1965. "Emanuel Bach's Autobiography," MQ 51: 363–72.

Niemetschek, Franz Xaver. [1808] 1978. *Lebensbeschreibung des k.k. Kapellmeisters Wolfgang Amadeus Mozart*. 2nd enlarged edition (Prague). Facsimile edition edited by Peter Krause. Leipzig: VEB Deutscher Verlag für Musik. Translated by Helen Mautner as *Life of Mozart*, with an introduction by A. Hyatt King (London: Leonard Hyman, 1956).

Nissen, Georg Nikolaus. [1828] 1972. *Biographie W. A. Mozarts*. Reprint with a foreword by Rudolph Angermüller. Hildesheim: Georg Olms.

Novello, Vincent and Mary. [1829] 1955. *A Mozart Pilgrimage: Being the Travel Diaries of Vincent & May Novello in the Year 1829*. Edited by Nerina Medici di Marignano and Rosemary Hughes. London: Ernst Eulenburg. Translated into German by Ernst Roth as *Eine Wallfahrt zu Mozart: Die Reisetagebücher von Vincent und Mary Novello aus dem Jahre 1829*. (Bonn: Boosey & Hawkes, 1959.)

Oleskiewicz, Mary. 2007. "Like Father, Like Son? Emanuel Bach and the Writing of Biography." In *Music and Its Questions: Essays in Honor of Peter Williams*, edited by Thomas Donahue, 253–79. Richmond, VA: Organ Historical Society Press.

Oleskiewicz, Mary. 2011. "The Court of Brandenburg-Prussia." In *Music at German Courts, 1715–1760: Changing Artistic Priorities*, edited by Samantha Owens, Barbara M. Reul, and Janice B. Stockigt, 79–130. Woodbridge: The Boydell Press.

Oleskiewicz, Mary. 2017. "Keyboards, Music Rooms, and the Bach Family at the Court of Frederick the Great." *Bach Perspectives 11: J. S. Bach and His Sons*, edited by Mary Oleskiewicz, 24–82. Urbana: University of Illinois Press.

Olleson, Edward. 1980. "Swieten, Gottfried van." NGD 18: 414–15.

Ostwald, Peter. 1985. *Schumann: The Inner Voices of a Musical Genius*. Boston: Northeastern University Press.

Ottenberg, Hans-Günter. 1987. *Carl Philipp Emanuel Bach*. Translated by Philip J. Whitmore. Oxford: Oxford University Press.

Paczkowski, Szymon. 2017. *Polish Style in the Music of Johann Sebastian Bach*. Lanham: Rowman & Littlefield.

Perry-Camp, Jane. 1984. "*Amadeus* and Authenticity." *Eighteenth-Century Life* 9: 117–19.

Pfau, Marc-Roderich. 2008. "Ein unbekanntes Leipziger Kantatenheft aus dem Jahr 1735." BJ 94: 99–122.

Plath, Wolfgang. 1976/77. "Beiträge zur Mozart-Autographie II. Schriftchronologie 1770–1780." MJb: 131–73.

Poulin, Pamela L. 1994. *J. S. Bach's Precepts and Principles for Playing the Thorough-Bass or Accompanying in Four Parts, Leipzig, 1738*. Oxford: Clarendon Press.

Plümicke, Carl Martin. 1781. *Entwurf einer Theatergeschichte von Berlin*. Berlin and Stettin: Friedrich Nicolai.

Prinz, Ulrich. 2005. *Johann Sebastian Bachs Instrumentarium: Originalquellen, Besetzung, Verwendung*. Kassel: Bärenreiter.

Quantz, Johann Joachim. [1754] 1951. "The Life of Herr Johann Joachim Quantz, as Sketched by Himself." Translated by Paul Nettl. In Nettl. *Forgotten Musicians*. New York: Philosophical Library, 280–319.

Rampe, Siegbert. 2016. "Cembalo (Spinett und Virginal)." In *Das Neue Bach-Lexikon*, 171–74. Das Bach-Handbuch 6, edited by Siegbert Rampe. Laaber: Laaber-Verlag.

Rathey, Markus. 2016. *Johann Sebastian Bach's* Christmas Oratorio: *Music, Theology, Culture*. New York: Oxford University Press.

Richards, Annette, ed. 2012. *Portrait Collection*. Carl Philipp Emanuel Bach: The Complete Works, VIII/4. Appendices edited by Paul Corneilson. 2 vols. Los Altos: The Packard Humanities Institute.

Richter, Bernhard Friedrich. 1905. "Die Wahl Joh. Seb. Bachs zum Kantor der Thomasschule i[m] J[ahr] 1723." BJ [2]: 48–67.

Richter, Bernhard Friedrich. 1907. "Stadtpfeifer und Alumnen der Thomasschule in Leipzig zu Bachs Zeit." BJ 4: 32–78.

Riedel, Herbot. 1969. "Recognition and Re-cognition: Bach and the Well-Tempered Clavier." PhD diss., University of California, Berkeley.

Rifkin, Joshua. 2002. "Eine schwierige Stelle in der h-Moll-Messe." In *Bach in Leipzig-Bach und Leipzig: Konferenzbericht Leipzig 2000*, edited by Ulrich Leisinger, 321–31. Leipziger Beiträge zur Bach-Forschung. Hildesheim: Olms-Verlag.

Ringer, Mark. 1984. "*Amadeus*: From Play to Film." Film Forum: *Amadeus*. *Eighteenth-Century Life* 9: 120.

Roe, Stephen. 2016. "Johann Christian Bach and Cecilia Grassi: Portrait of a Marriage" In *The Sons of Bach: Essays for Elias N. Kulukundis*, edited by Peter Wollny and Stephen Roe, 134–57. Ann Arbor: Steglein Publishing.

Rolf, Marie. 1991. "A New Manuscript Source for Mozart's Rondo in E-flat for Horn, K. 371." MJb: 938–45.

Rosen, Charles. 1997. *The Classical Style: Haydn, Mozart, Beethoven*. Expanded edition. New York: W. W. Norton. (Orig. pub. 1971.)

Sadie, Stanley. 1964. "Mozart, Bach and Counterpoint." *Musical Times* 105: 23–24.

Said, Edward W. 2006. *On Late Style: Music and Literature Against the Grain*. New York: Random House.

Schabalina, Tatjana. 2008. "'Texte zur Music' in Sankt Petersburg. Neue Quellen zur Leipziger Musikgeschichte sowie zur Kompositions- und Aufführungstätigkeit Johann Sebastian Bachs." BJ 94: 33–98.

Schafer, Hollace A. 1987. "'A Wisely Ordered Phantasie': Joseph Haydn's Creative Process from the Sketches and Drafts for Instrumental Music." PhD diss., Brandeis University.

Schalk, Carl F. 1988. *Luther on Music: Paradigms of Praise*. St. Louis: Concordia House.

Schering, Arnold. 1936. *Johann Sebastian Bachs Leipziger Kirchenmusik: Studien und Wege zu ihrer Erkenntnis*. Leipzig: Breitkopf & Härtel.

Schmid, Ernst Fritz. 1948. *Ein schwäbisches Mozartbuch* Stuttgart: Alfons-Bürger.

Schmid, Ernst Fritz. 1955. "Auf Mozarts Spuren in Italien." MJb: 17–48.

Schneider, Max, ed. 1966. *Altbachisches Archiv*. In *Das Erbe deutscher Musik*, 2 vols. Wiesbaden: Breitkopf & Härtel. (Orig. pub. 1935.)

Schnoebelen, Anne. 1979. *Padre Martini's Collection of Letters in the Civico Museo Bibliografico Musicale in Bologna: An Annotated Index*. New York: Pendragon Press.

Schott, Howard. 2007. "Bach, Johann Sebastian." In *The Harpsichord and Clavichord: An Encyclopedia*, edited by Igor Kipnis, 22–23. New York: Routledge.

Schubart, Christoph. 1953. "Anna Magdalena Bach. Neue Beiträge zu ihrer Herkunft und ihren Jugendjahren." BJ 40: 29–50.

Schulenberg, David. 2006. *The Keyboard Music of J. S. Bach*. 2nd ed. New York: Routledge.

Schulenberg, David. 2010. *The Music of Wilhelm Friedemann Bach*. Rochester: University of Rochester Press.

Schulenberg, David. 2014. *The Music of Carl Philipp Emanuel Bach*. Rochester: University of Rochester Press.

Schulze, Hans-Joachim. 1963/64. "Frühe Schriftzeugnisse der beiden jüngsten Bach-Söhne." BJ 50: 61–69.

Schulze, Hans-Joachim. 1979. "Ein 'Dresdner Menuett''im zweiten Klavierbüchlein der Anna Magdalena Bach. Nebst Hinweisen zur Überlieferung einiger Kammermusikwerke Bachs." BJ 65: 45–64.

Schulze, Hans-Joachim. 1981. "Johann Sebastian Bachs Konzerte—Fragen der Überlieferung und Chronologie." In *Beiträge zum Konzertschaffen Johann Sebastian Bachs (Bach-Studien 6)*, edited by Peter Ansehl, Karl Heller and Hans-Joachim Schulze, 9–26. Leipzig: VEB Breitkopf & Härtel, 1981.

Schulze, Hans-Joachim. 1984. *Studien zur Bach-Überlieferung im 18. Jahrhundert.* Leipzig: Edition Peters.

Schulze, Hans-Joachim. 2010. "Rätselhafte Auftragswerke Johann Sebastian Bachs: Anmerkungen zu einigen Kantatentexten." BJ 96: 69–93.

Schulze, Hans-Joachim. 2013. "Anna Magdalena Wilcke—Gesangsschülerin der Paulina?" BJ 99: 279–96.

Schulze, Hans-Joachim. 2015. "When Did the Youngest Bach Son Begin His 'Italian Journey'?" and "Once Again: When Did the Youngest Bach Begin his 'Italian Journey'?" Translated by Stephanie Wollny in *J. C. Bach*, edited by Paul Corneilson, 51–56. Burlington, VT: Ashgate. (Orig. pub. in BJ 69 (1983) and BJ 74 (1988), respectively.)

Schweitzer, Albert. 1964. *J. S. Bach.* Translated by Ernest Newman. New York: Macmillan (Orig. pub. 1911.)

Shaffer, Peter. 1984. "Paying Homage to Mozart." *New York Times*, September 2.

Shaw, George Bernard. 1981. "Beethoven's Centenary." In *Shaw's Music: The Complete Musical Criticism of Bernard Shaw*, vol. 3, *1893–1950*, edited by Dan H. Laurence, 742–48. 2nd rev. ed. London: The Bodley Head.

Siegele, Ulrich. 1978. "Bachs Endzweck einer regulierten und Entwurf einer wohlbestallten Kirchenmusik." In *Festschrift Georg von Dadelsen zum 60. Geburtstag*, edited by Thomas Kohlhase and Volker Scherliess, 313–51. Stuttgart: Hänssler-Verlag.

Siegele, Ulrich. 1983, 1984, 1986, "Bachs Stellung in der Leipziger Kulturpolitik seiner Zeit." BJ 69: 7–50; BJ 70: 7–43; BJ 72: 33–67.

Siegele, Ulrich. 1997. "Bach and the domestic Politics of Electoral Sazony." In *The Cambridge Companion to Bach*, edited by John Butt, 17–34. Cambridge: Cambridge University Press.

Siegele, Ulrich. 1999. "Bachs politisches Profil, oder Wo bleibt die Musik?," In *Bach-Handbuch*, edited by Konrad Küster, 5–30. Kassel: Bärenreiter.

Smither, Howard E. 1977. *A History of the Oratorio, Volume 2: The Oratorio in the Baroque Era: Protestant Germany and England.* Chapel Hill: University of North Carolina Press.

Snyder, Kerala J. 1980. "Dietrich Buxtehude's Studies in Learned Counterpoint." JAMS 33: 544–64.

Solomon, Maynard. 1989. "Franz Schubert and the Peacocks of Benvenuto Cellini." *Nineteenth-Century Music* 12: 193–206.

Solomon, Maynard. 1991. "The Rochlitz Anecdotes: Issues of Authenticity in Early Mozart Biography." In *Mozart Studies*, edited by Cliff Eisen, 1–59. Oxford: Clarendon Press.

Solomon, Maynard. 1995. *Mozart: A Life.* New York: Harper Collins.

Solomon, Maynard. 1998. *Beethoven.* 2nd rev. ed. New York: Schirmer Books. (Orig. pub. 1977.)

Speerstra, Joel. 2004. *Bach and the Pedal Clavichord: An Organist's Guide.* Rochester: University of Rochester Press.

Spitta, Philipp. 1962. *Johann Sebastian Bach.* 2 vols. Wiesbaden: Breitkopf & Härtel. (Orig. pub. 1873–80.) Translated by Clara Bell and J. A. Fuller-Maitland as *Johann Sebastian Bach.* 2 vols. New York: Dover Publications, 1951. (Orig. pub. 1884–85.)

Sposato, Jeffrey S. 2017. "Bach, die Messe und der Lutherische Gottesdienst in Leipzig." In *Geistliche Musik und* Chortradition im *18. und 19. Jahrhundert. Institutionen, Klangideale und Repertoires im Umbruch.* Beiträge zur Geschichte der Bach-Rezeption 6, edited by Anselm Hartinger, Peter Wollny, and Christoph Wolff, 99–119. Wiesbaden: Breitkopf & Hartel.

Sposato, Jeffrey S. 2018. *Leipzig After Bach: Church and Concert Life in a German City, 1743–1847.* Oxford: Oxford University Press.

Spree, Eberhard. 2019. *Die verwitwete Frau Capellmeisterin Bach: Studie über die Verteilung des Nachlasses von Johann Sebastian Bach.* Altenburg: Verlag Klaus-Jürgen Kamprad.

Stauffer, George B. 1980. *The Organ Preludes of Johann Sebastian Bach.* Studies in Musicology 27. Ann Arbor, MI: UMI Research Press.

Stauffer, George B. 1983. "Johann Mattheson and J. S. Bach: The Hamburg Connection." In *New Mattheson Studies,* edited by George J. Buelow and Hans Joachim Marx, 353–68. Cambridge: Cambridge University Press.

Stauffer, George B. 1989. "'This fantasia . . . never had its like.' On the Enigma and Chronology of Bach's Chromatic Fantasia and Fugue in D minor, BWV 903." In *Bach Studies,* edited by Don O. Franklin, 160–82. Cambridge: Cambridge University Press.

Stauffer, George B. 1993. Review of John Butt, *Mass in B Minor. Journal of Musicological Research* 13: 257–72.

Stauffer, George B. 1995. "J. S. Bach's Harpsichords." In *Festa Musicologica: Essays in Honor of George J Buelow.* Festschrift Series, 1, edited by Thomas J. Mathiesen and Benito V. Rivera, 289–318. Stuyvesant, NY: Pendragon Press.

Stauffer, George B. 1997. *Bach: the Mass in B Minor.* New York: Schirmer Books.

Stauffer, George B. 2008. "Music for 'Cavaliers et Dames': Bach and the Repertoire of His Collegium Musicum." In *About Bach,* edited by Gregory G. Butler, George B. Stauffer, and Mary Dalton Greer, 135–56. Urbana: University of Illinois Press.

Steblin, Rita. 2002. *A History of Key Characteristics in the Eighteenth and Early Nineteenth Centuries.* 2nd ed. Rochester, NY: University of Rochester Press.

Stinson, Russell. 1989a. *The Bach Manuscripts of Johann Peter Kellner and his Circle: A Case Study in Reception History.* Durham, NC: Duke University Press.

Stinson, Russell. 1989b. "Toward a Chronology of Bach's Instrumental Music: Observations on Three Keyboard Works." *Journal of Musicology* 7: 440–70.

Stinson, Russell. 1996. *Bach: The Orgelbüchein.* New York: Schirmer Books.

Stinson, Russell. 2001. *J. S. Bach's Great Eighteen Organ Chorales.* New York: Oxford University Press.

Stevens, Jane R. 2001. *The Bach Family and the Keyboard Concerto: The Evolution of a Genre.* Warren, MI: Harmonie Park Press.

Storr, Anthony. 1985. *The Dynamics of Creation.* New York: Atheneum. (Orig. pub. 1972.)

Stravinsky, Igor. 1956. *Poetics of Music in the Form of Six Lessons.* Translated by Arthur Knodel & Ingolf Dahl. Preface by Darius Milhaud. New York: Vintage Books.

Subotnik, Rose Rosengard. 1991. "Adorno's Diagnosis of Beethoven's Late Style: Early Symptom of a Fatal Condition." In *Developing Variations: Style and Ideology in Western Music,* 15–41. Minneapolis: University of Minnesota Press.

Talle, Andrew. 2003. "J. S. Bach's Keyboard Partitas and Their Early Audience." PhD diss., Harvard University.

Taruskin, Richard. 1995. *Text & Act: Essays on Music and Performance.* New York: Oxford University Press, 1995.

Terry, Charles Sanford. 1967. *John Christian Bach.* 2nd ed., with a foreword by H. C. Robbins Landon. London: Oxford University Press.

Thayer, Alexander. 1989. *Salieri: Rival of Mozart.* Edited by Theodore Albrecht. Kansas City, MO: The Philharmonia of Greater Kansas City.

Theile, Johann. 1965. *Musikalisches Kunstbuch.* Edited by Carl Dahlhaus, Kassel.

Thomas, Lewis. 1974. *The Lives of a Cell.* New York: Viking.

Tovey, Donald Francis. 1935. *Essays in Musical Analysis. Volume 1: Symphonies.* London: Oxford University Press.

Treitler, Leo, ed. 1998. *Strunk's Source Readings in Music History.* Rev. ed. New York: W. W. Norton.

Tyson, Alan. 1987. *Mozart: Studies of the Autograph Scores.* Cambridge, MA: Harvard University Press.

Unverricht, Hubert. 1980. "Salomon, Peter." NG 16: 428–29.

Webster, James. 2003. "The Eighteenth Century as a Music-Historical Period?" *Eighteenth-Century Music* 1: 47–60.

Werbeck, Walter. 2003. "Bach und der Kontrapunkt: Neue Manuskript-Funde." BJ 89: 67–95.

White, Andrew. 1992. "The Prelude and Fugue in C major from Bach's *Well-Tempered Clavier* [Book I]: Notes on the Compositional Process." JRBI 23, no. 2: 47–60.

Williams, Peter. 1981. "BWV 565: A Toccata in D minor for Organ by J. S. Bach?" *Early Music* 9: 330–37.

Williams, Peter. 2003. *The Organ Music of J. S. Bach.* 2nd ed. Cambridge: Cambridge University Press.

Wolff, Christoph, ed. 1985. *The Neumeister Collection of Chorale Preludes from the Bach Circle. Facsimile Edition of the Yale Manuscript LM 4708.* New Haven: Yale University Press. ("Introduction." in Wolff 1991a.)

Wolff, Christoph. 1991. *Johann Sebastian Bach: Essays on His Life and Music.* Cambridge, MA: Harvard University Press.

Wolff, Christoph. 1992. "The Identity of the 'Fratro Dilettisimo' in the Capriccio B-Flat Major and Other Problems of Bach's Early Harpsichord Works." In *The Harpsichord and its Repertoire: Proceedings of the International Symposium. Utrecht 1990,* edited by Pieter Dirksen, 145–56. Utrecht.

Wolff, Christoph. 1994. *Mozart's Requiem: Historical and Analytical Studies, Documents, Score.* Translated by Mary Whittall with revisions and additions by the author. Berkeley and Los Angeles: University of California Press.

Wolff, Christoph. 2000. *Johann Sebastian Bach: The Learned Musician.* New York: W. W. Norton.

Wolff, Christoph. 2004. "Johann Sebastian Bachs Regeln für den fünfstimmigen Satz," BJ 90: 87–99.

Wolff, Christoph, ed. 2011. *Johann Sebastian Bach Messe in H-Moll, BWV 232. Autograph.* Kassel: Barenreiter.

Wollny, Peter. 1993. "Studies in the Music of Wilhelm Friedemann Bach: Sources and Style." PhD diss., Harvard University.

Wollny, Peter. 2002. "Ein Quellenfund in Kiew: Unbekannte Kontrapunktstudien von Johann Sebastian und Wilhelm Friedemann Bach." In *Bach in Leipzig–Bach und Leipzig: Konferenzbericht Leipzig 2000*, edited by Ulrich Leisinger, 275–87. Hildesheim: Georg Olms Verlag.

Wollny, Peter. 2003. "'. . . welche dem größten Concerte gleichen': The Polonaises of Wilhelm Friedemann Bach." In *The Keyboard in Baroque Europe*, edited Christopher Hogwood, 169–83. Cambridge: Cambridge University Press.

Wollny, Peter. 2016. "Observations on the Autograph of the b-Minor Mass." Translated by James Brokaw. JRBI 47, no. 2: 27–46. (Orig. pub. 2009.)

Yearsley, David. 2012. *Bach's Feet: The Organ Pedals in European Culture*. Cambridge: Cambridge University Press.

Yearsley, David. 2019. *Sex, Death and Minuets: Anna Magdalena Bach and Her Musical Notebooks*. New Material Histories of Music. Chicago: University of Chicago Press.

Zaslaw, Neal. 1989. *Mozart's Symphonies: Context, Performance Practice, Reception*. Oxford: Clarendon Press.

Zelter, Karl Friedrich. 1801. *Karl Friedrich Christian Fasch*. Berlin: J. F. Unger.

Zenck, Martin. 1986. *Die Bach-Rezeption des späten Beethoven*. Stuttgart: Franz Steiner.

Zietz, Hermann. 1969. *Quellenkritische Untersuchungen an den Bach-Handschriften P 801, P 802 und P 803*. Hamburger Beiträge zur Musikwissenschaft 1. Hamburg: Verlag der Musikalienhandlung Karl Dieter Wagner.

Index

An italicized page number indicates a musical example, figure, or table. References for living scholars (without biographical dates) are included only for discussions of their work in the text, i.e., not for simple bibliographical citations.

This page constitutes a continuation of the copyright page.

Eastman Studies in Music

Ralph P. Locke, Senior Editor
Eastman School of Music

Additional Titles of Interest

Anton Heiller: Organist, Composer, Conductor
Peter Planyavsky
Translated by Christa Rumsey

The Art of Musical Phrasing in the Eighteenth Century:
Punctuating the Classical "Period"
Stephanie D. Vital

Aspects of Unity in J. S. Bach's Partitas and Suites: An Analytical Study
David W. Beach

Bach and the Pedal Clavichord: An Organist's Guide
Joel Speersta

Bach's Changing World: Voices in the Community
Edited by Carol K. Baron

Coming to Terms with Our Musical Past:
An Essay on Mozart and Modernist Aesthetics
Edmund J. Goehring

Marianna Martines: A Woman Composer in the Vienna of Mozart and Haydn
Irving Godt

The Music of Carl Philipp Emanuel Bach
David Schulenberg

The Music of Wilhelm Friedemann Bach
David Schulenberg

Musical Theater in Eighteenth-Century Parma: Entertainment, Sovereignty, Reform
Margaret R. Butler

A complete list of titles in the Eastman Studies in Music series may be found
on the University of Rochester Press website, www.urpress.com.